THE HOLINESS-PENTECOSTAL
TRADITION

The Holiness-Pentecostal Tradition

Charismatic Movements in the Twentieth Century

Vinson Synan

William B. Eerdmans Publishing Company
Grand Rapids, Michigan / Cambridge, U.K.

© 1971, 1997 Wm. B. Eerdmans Publishing Co.
255 Jefferson Ave. S.E., Grand Rapids, Michigan 49503 /
P.O. Box 163, Cambridge CB3 9PU U.K.

First edition 1971
Second edition 1997

Printed in the United States of America

10 09 08 07 06 05 04   10 9 8 7 6 5 4

Library of Congress Cataloging-in-Publication Data

Synan, Vinson.
The Holiness-Pentecostal tradition: Charismatic movements in the twentieth century /
Vinson Synan. — 2nd ed.
p.   cm.
Rev. ed. of: Holiness-Pentecostal movement in the United States. 1971.
Includes bibliographical references and index.
ISBN 0-8028-4103-1 (pbk.: alk. paper)
1. Pentecostalism — United States — History — 20th century.
2. Holiness churches — United States — History.
3. Pentecostalism — History — 20th century.
I. Synan, Vinson. Holiness-Pentecostal movement in the United States.
II. Title.
BR1644.5.U6S86   1997
277.3′082 — dc21   97-10579
                                                         CIP

To

Bill Menzies and Horace Ward,
gentlemen scholars and colleagues,
who joined with me in founding
the Society for Pentecostal Studies
at the Pentecostal World Conference
in Dallas, Texas, in 1970

Contents

Contents

Preface

It has been more than a quarter of a century since this book first appeared under the title *The Holiness-Pentecostal Movement in the United States.* For more than twenty-four years, after first being published in 1971, it remained in print without revision. At long last I have revised, enlarged, and renamed the book in an attempt to account for the incredible changes that have occurred in the worldwide church since the book first appeared. The new title, *The Holiness-Pentecostal Tradition: Charismatic Movements in the Twentieth Century,* was chosen with much care. Instead of the word "movement" I have chosen to substitute the word "tradition." This is because I believe that Pentecostalism has grown beyond a mere passing movement to become a major tradition of Christianity. This word is being used despite the fact that most Pentecostals have disdained the word "tradition" as belonging to the older and colder "established" churches, which did not understand the moving power of the Holy Spirit.

In fact, when I did my first research on Pentecostalism around 1965, there were barely 50,000,000 Pentecostals in the world. Now, as this revision appears, that number has grown to encompass some 217,000,000 "denominational Pentecostals" around the globe. Added to this are the millions of "Charismatics" and "Third Wavers" in the mainline churches who were inspired by the Pentecostals. All together, the aggregate number of Pentecostals/charismatic in the world numbered some 463,000,000 in 1995. As the second largest family of Christians in the world after the

Roman Catholic Church, the Pentecostal churches can now justifiably be called a major Christian "tradition."

In my earlier book title, I included the phrase "in the United States" since the purpose and scope of the study was to tell the story of the origins of the movement in the nation that gave it birth. The revised edition attempts to cover the story of the spread of Pentecostalism around the world after the heady days of the Azusa Street awakening. Of course, a book of this kind could not possibly cover the origins of the movement in every nation of the world. I have therefore attempted only to describe the beginnings of the movement in several of the nations where it became a major religious force.

The subtitle, *Charismatic Movements in the Twentieth Century*, points to the various charismatic movements in the mainline churches that had their roots in Pentecostalism. At this point they seem to continue as "movements" in their respective denominations. Whether they become major and lasting traditions remains to be seen.

I also use the word "tradition" for another and possibly more important reason. To me it is clear that the basic premise of Pentecostalism, that one may receive later effusions of the Spirit after initiation/conversion, can be clearly traced in Christian history to the beginnings of the rite of confirmation in the Western churches. This began as an attempt to make practicing, committed, adult Christians out of children who had been baptized as infants several years earlier. It was a very practical and sacramental "second blessing" that conferred the Holy Spirit when the bishop laid hands on the one being confirmed. In ensuing centuries, great doctors and saints of the church created monastic orders for the "religious" who wished to live out a more committed form of Christian life. Many of these spiritual giants, such as St. Benedict, St. Teresa, and St. Francis, laid down "rules" for their followers with "spiritual exercises" that resemble the "blessings" and "deeper experiences" later claimed by the Pentecostals.

In the development of this "second blessing" tradition, one may trace a clear line from the Catholic and Anglican mystical traditions, through John Wesley's second blessing sanctification experience, through the holiness and Keswick movements, to the appearance of modern Pentecostalism. All of these stressed a "deeper" or sometimes "higher" Christian life that went far beyond the level of nominalism that characterized the majority of Christians for most of the history of the church. Although theologians of these various historic streams would profoundly disagree with each other over the timing and content of the "second blessing," they all held tenaciously to the conviction that not all of Christian experience was received at the moment of conversion/initiation.

What made the Pentecostals different from their predecessors was the teaching that the charismata, especially the gift of tongues, was the sign of receiving the subsequent "second blessing." As Kilian McDonnell and George Montague have shown in their landmark book *The Rites of Initiation and Baptism in the Holy Spirit: Evidence from the First Eight Centuries,* the essentials of what Pentecostals call the "baptism in the Holy Spirit" was part of the public liturgy of the churches for at least eight centuries after the day of Pentecost. If this is true, then the Pentecostals may well have rediscovered for the modern church what the New Testament church experienced in the power and gifts of the Holy Spirit.

One of the more controversial aspects of my thesis as stated in *The Holiness-Pentecostal Movement* (1971) was that Pentecostalism was basically a modified "second blessing" Methodist spirituality that was pioneered by John Wesley and passed down to his followers in the holiness movement, out of which came the modern Pentecostal movement. I believe that the passage of time and the research of many scholars have basically supported this position. In the years since 1971, however, I have gained a deeper understanding of the role of the Keswick "Higher Life" contributions to the development of the Pentecostal tradition.

This book, then, is the story of the rise and development of the Pentecostal tradition from the early days of rejection when they were, in the words of David Barrett, members of the most "harassed, persecuted, suffering, and martyred Christian tradition in recent history," to the days of acceptance and stunning growth at the end of the century. This could well be the major story of Christianity in the twentieth century. If what Peter Wagner says is true, that "in all of human history, no other non-political, non-militaristic, voluntary human movement has grown as rapidly as the Pentecostal-charismatic movement in the last twenty-five years," then Pentecostalism indeed deserves to be seen as a major Christian tradition alongside the Roman Catholic, Orthodox, and Reformation Protestant traditions.

I would like to thank many very special friends and colleagues whose advice and counsel have helped me immeasurably over the years. These include Charles Jones, Bill Faupel, Donald Dayton, and Jim Zeigler, historians and researchers who have opened many doors of understanding in my ongoing attempts to understand and record the history of the holiness-Pentecostal tradition.

Vinson Synan
Regent University
Virginia Beach, Virginia
Pentecost Sunday, May 18, 1997

CHAPTER ONE

The Double Cure

1766-1866

Be of sin the double cure,
Save from wrath and make me pure.

Augustus Toplady

John Wesley, the indomitable founder of Methodism, was also the spiritual and intellectual father of the modern holiness and Pentecostal movements, which arose from Methodism in the last century. Contained in his *Journal,* written between 1735 and 1790, and in his published letters and sermons, is Wesley's theology, which has had and continues to have a profound influence on Protestantism. In a lifetime (1703-1791) that spanned most of the eighteenth century, Wesley had time to develop and refine his ideas on theology, society, and ecclesiology. Partly because of the sheer volume of his writings, there have emerged several John Wesleys to whom different people refer for different reasons. Yet the basic premises Methodism rests on, along with all the religious movements originating in Methodism, were meticulously set down by Wesley during his amazing career.[1]

1. The best collection of Wesley's works is Albert Outler, ed., *The Works of John Wesley* (Nashville, 1984-93). Older collections include E. A. Sugden, ed.,

1

In arriving at his mature theological convictions, Wesley borrowed from many sources. His doctrines were distilled primarily from the Anglo-Catholic tradition of his personal background, rather than from the continental Reformed Protestant tradition. Methodism, with its strong Arminian base, was in essence a reaction against the extreme Calvinism which had dominated English social, religious, and political life during much of the seventeenth century. If the Calvinist taught that only the elect could be saved, the Methodist taught that salvation could be found by anyone. If Calvinists could never be sure they were among the elect, Methodists could know from a crisis experience of conversion that they were saved. From the beginning, Methodist theology placed great emphasis on this conscious religious experience. This empirical evidence of salvation is what Wesley and his followers have since offered to the world; and it has been the divergent interpretations of this basic premise that have caused periodic fragmentation within the Methodist fold.

Perhaps the best example of the Methodist quest for evidence of salvation based on conscious religious experience is the case of Wesley himself. The son of an Anglican clergyman, he was educated at Oxford, as were his father and grandfather. After receiving the A.B. and A.M. degrees at Oxford, young Wesley took Anglican orders in 1728 at the insistence of his father. As a twenty-five-year-old youth, he then began an intensive program of religious reading in order to define his own convictions.[2]

Wesley and the Mystical Tradition

In Wesley's devotional reading at this time were several books from the Catholic and Anglican mystical traditions that profoundly influenced his religious views. Among these were Jeremy Taylor's *Rule and Exercises of*

Wesley's Standard Sermons (Nashville, 1920), and Thomas Jackson, ed., *The Works of John Wesley* (Grand Rapids, MI, 1959), a fourteen-volume photocopy of the authorized edition published by the Wesleyan Conference Office in London, England, in 1872. Subsequent references to *The Works of John Wesley* are to this edition.

2. Robert Southey, *The Life of John Wesley* (London, 1820), vol. 1, p. 75. A more recent and excellent study of Wesley is *John Wesley*, ed. Albert Outler (New York, 1964).

Holy Living and Dying, and Thomas à Kempis's *Imitation of Christ*, which he read in 1725. The most influential works, however, were William Law's *Treatise on Christian Perfection* and *Serious Call to a Devout and Holy Life*. Reading *Serious Call* in 1726, Wesley adopted much of Law's thought as his own. In this book Law called for a holiness of life in the laity which the church for centuries had reserved only for the monastics and clergy. "For there is no reason," wrote Law, "why you should think the highest holiness, the most heavenly tempers, to be the duties and happiness of a bishop, but what is as good a reason why you should think the same tempers to be the duty and happiness of all Christians."[3]

The remainder of Wesley's life was spent in pursuit of the holiness of heart and life that Taylor, Kempis, and Law upheld in their works. In seeking further light on the subject of holiness and how it could be attained, Wesley sought to clarify his own thinking. Reading late at night and early in the morning, he devoured the writings of Clement of Alexandria, Plotinus, Augustine, the Cambridge Platonists, Molinos, Madame Guyon, François de Sales, Fénelon, and Pascal. At one point Wesley confessed that he almost became a mystic himself, reluctantly stopping short of what he called a possible "shipwreck of faith". Nevertheless, "out of such insights," asserts one writer, "not yet fully comprehended, grew the doctrines of Methodism, and in particular the Wesleyan doctrine of Christian perfection."[4]

It was this pursuit of holiness that led Wesley to leave England for Georgia in 1735 as a missionary to the Indians. In a letter to a friend written before embarking for America, Wesley declared, "My chief motive, to which all the rest are subordinate, is the hope of saving my own soul." When asked of whether his soul could have been saved in England as well as in Georgia, Wesley replied, "I answer, no; neither can I hope to attain the same degree of holiness here which I may there."[5]

Like many travelers to Georgia both before and since 1735, Wesley found little of either salvation or holiness. The Georgia Indians were not the gentle, innocent people, hungry for the gospel, he had been told

3. William Law, *A Serious Call to a Devout and Holy Life* (New York, 1955 reprint), p. 115. See also John Leland Peters, *Christian Perfection and American Methodism* (New York, 1956), p. 19. Robert Tuttle, *Mysticism in the Wesleyan Tradition* (Grand Rapids, MI, 1989), pp. 17, 91-111.

4. Peters, *Christian Perfection and American Methodism*, p. 20.

5. Wesley, *Letters of John Wesley*, vol. 1, pp. 188-90.

of; indeed they were savage warriors who engaged in constant warfare during his stay. Most of Wesley's Georgia labors were therefore among the whites in and near Savannah. The Indians he found generally degraded and were uninterested in his theology. Even the whites disliked him, accusing him of being too strict, cold, and formal. On one occasion, in the town of Frederica, he was falsely accused and insulted. Eventually he was hauled into court in Savannah for refusal to serve the sacraments to a young lady, and was disgraced before the very people he had come to help. In spite of aid from General James Edward Oglethorpe, the founder of the Georgia colony, and the support of Dr. Thomas Bray's London-based "Society for the Propagation of the Gospel in Foreign Parts," Wesley was in general a failure as a missionary to Georgia. Returning to England in February of 1738, he lamented, "I went to America to convert the Indians; but O! who shall convert me?"[6]

It was on Wesley's return journey from America that he made contact with the German Moravian Pietists who later greatly influenced his thought. On the stormy sea, Wesley was impressed with their calm. Sensing that he did not share their assurance of salvation, he sought to learn more about their perfectionist beliefs. Back in England, he met both the Moravian Bishop Augustus Gottlieb Spangenberg and Peter Bohler, a Moravian missionary en route to Carolina. Bohler told Wesley that "saving faith brought with it both dominion over sin and true peace of mind — both holiness and happiness." Without having yet gone through this experience of conversion and perfect holiness, Wesley began to preach and to seek it.[7]

Wesley's Conversion

Wesley's slow and painful conversion from sacramental Anglicanism to evangelical Methodism came to a climax on May 24, 1738, while attending a reading of Martin Luther's Preface to Romans at a religious society meeting on Aldersgate Street in London. Entering the service with a "strange indifference, dullness, and coldness" after experiencing months of "unusually frequent lapses into sin," Wesley felt his "heart strangely warmed." This was his famous conversion experience — simultaneously

6. Wesley, *The Works of John Wesley,* vol. 1, p. 74.
7. Peters, *Christian Perfection,* p. 23; Wesley, *Journal of John Wesley,* vol. 1, p. 455.

conscious, emotional, and empirical. Yet he did not feel that he had attained his goal of holiness or Christian perfection in this Aldersgate experience, preferring to believe that for him perfect holiness lay in the future.[8]

Later in 1738, Wesley journeyed to the Moravian settlement at Herrenhut, near Dresden. It was here that he met Count Zinzendorf, the German utopian-evangelical who headed the community. Wesley was impressed by the members of the settlement, for they seemed to be "saved from inward as well as outward sin." Later, while conversing with Zinzendorf, Wesley found that the Count did not share his view of a second, perfecting experience of divine grace. In the century that followed, the views of these two men were to be sharply debated theories in evangelical circles, the followers of Wesley believing in a second crisis experience of sanctification and the followers of Zinzendorf teaching that one was perfected at conversion.[9]

Much controversy has surrounded Wesley's own testimony on his experience of sanctification. Some writers within the present holiness movement regard his experience of January 1, 1739, as the time of his sanctification:

> Mr. Hall, Kinchin, Ingham, Whitefield, Hutchins, and my brother Charles, were present at our love-feast in Fetter-Lane, with about sixty of our brethren. About three in the morning, as we were continuing instant in prayer, the power of God came mightily upon us, inasmuch that many cried out for exceeding joy, and many fell to the ground. As soon as we recovered a little from that awe and amazement at the presence of His Majesty, we broke out with one voice, "We praise thee, O God; we acknowledge thee to be the Lord."[10]

8. Peters, *Christian Perfection*, p. 27; Wesley, *The Works of John Wesley*, vol. 1, p. 103. For most advocates of the "second blessing" theory of sanctification, this experience of Wesley's was his conversion and not in any sense his experience of sanctification.

9. M. E. Redford, *The Rise of the Church of the Nazarene* (Kansas City, 1951), p. 34; Wesley, *The Works of John Wesley*, vol. 1, pp. 110-58. For most modern holiness people the Zinzendorfian theory of sanctification is still anathema.

10. Redford, *The Rise of the Church of the Nazarene*, p. 34; Wesley, *The Works of John Wesley*, vol. 1, p. 170. Twentieth-century scholarship has confirmed that Wesley taught sanctification to be a second, definite, instantaneous work of grace. See such works as Harold Lindstrom, *Wesley and Sanctification* (London, 1946), pp. 121-24; M. E. Gaddis, "Christian Perfectionism in America" (Doctoral dissertation, Univer-

From 1739 until 1777, Wesley issued and repeatedly revised a tract entitled "A Plain Account of Christian Perfection as Believed and Taught by the Reverend Mr. John Wesley." This eighty-one-page document has served as a veritable manifesto for all the holiness and perfectionist groups that have separated from Methodism during the past two centuries. In the meticulous, logical style that Wesley mastered as a Lincoln Fellow at Oxford, the founder of Methodism built in this pamphlet the edifice of his doctrine.[11]

Wesley and Christian Perfection

By 1740, Wesley's ideas on theology were fairly well cast in the permanent mold that would shape the Methodist movement. Briefly stated, they involved two separate phases of experience for the believer: the first, conversion, or justification; the second, Christian perfection, or sanctification. In the first experience the penitent was forgiven for actual sins of commission, becoming a Christian but retaining a "residue of sin within."[12] This remaining "inbred sin" was the result of Adam's fall and had to be dealt with by a "second blessing, properly so-called." This experience purified the believer of inward sin and gave a person "perfect love" toward God and humanity.

Wesley never taught "sinless perfection" as some have charged. Since, according to Wesley, sin was defined as "a willful transgression of a known law of God," it was possible for the sanctified believer to live a life of daily victory over conscious willful sin. "Imperfect judgment," however, "and the physical and mental passions common to men, temptation, and the freedom by which, through willful disobedience, he

---

sity of Chicago, 1929); Peters, *Christian Perfection and American Methodism*; and Timothy L. Smith, *Revivalism and Social Reform* (New York, 1957). All maintain that the present holiness denominations are closer to Wesley's actual views than the present Methodist Church. Emory Stevens Bucke et al., *History of American Methodism*, vol. 3, pp. 608-9, agree that Wesley definitely taught a "second blessing, properly so-called," although never leaving a "completely clear" record of his own attainment of it. See also Newton Flew, *The Idea of Perfection in Christian Theology* (London, 1934), pp. 329-41.

11. Wesley, *The Works of John Wesley*, vol. 9, pp. 366-488. Wesley once referred to his doctrine of entire sanctification as "the grand depositum of Methodism."

12. Wesley, *The Works of John Wesley*, vol. 9, p. 400.

might fall again into sin, would remain real." The perfection Wesley taught was a perfection of motives and desires. Total "sinless perfection" would come only after death. In the meantime the sanctified soul, through careful self-examination, godly discipline, and methodical devotion and avoidance of worldly pleasures, could live a life of victory over sin. This perfection, Wesley taught, could be attained instantly as a "second work of grace" although it was usually preceded and followed by a gradual "growth in grace."[13]

Wesley did not always find it easy to keep this doctrine paramount within Methodism. The Calvinist branch of the Methodist societies, led by George Whitefield, roundly rejected the "second blessing" theory. In May of 1768, Wesley wrote his brother Charles in distress that, "I am at my wits' end with regard to two things — the church and Christian perfection. Unless both you and I stand in the gap *in good earnest*, the Methodists will drop them both."[14] Wesley also saw his most trusted advisor, John Fletcher, argue that the second blessing was in reality a "baptism in the Holy Spirit" as well as a cleansing experience. Although he disagreed with Fletcher on this point, Wesley nevertheless appointed Fletcher to be his designated successor as head of the Methodist societies. In his last year of life, Wesley wrote to his friend Adam Clarke, "If we can prove that any of our local preachers . . . speak against it, let him be a local preacher or leader no longer . . . [he] cannot be an honest man."[15] In spite of such infidelity from within and great opposition from without, perfectionism became the distinguishing doctrine of Methodism. It thus became the first great holiness church.

When Methodism was transplanted to America, the doctrine of entire sanctification came along with it. The first Methodist preacher to come to British North America was Captain Thomas Webb, a barracks-master in New York City. In the first recorded Methodist sermon in America in 1766 Webb declared:

13. Bucke et al., *History of American Methodism*, vol. 3, pp. 608-9; George Allen Turner, *The More Excellent Way: The Scriptural Basis of the Wesleyan Message* (Winona Lake, IN, 1951), passim; Peters, *Christian Perfection*, pp. 27-31, 39-43, 54-78; Gaddis, "Christian Perfectionism in America," pp. 162-64; H. C. Sheldon, *History of Christian Doctrine* (New York, 1895), vol. 2, pp. 376-77.

14. Wesley, *The Letters of Wesley*, vol. 5, p. 88.

15. Wesley, *The Letters of Wesley*, vol. 8, p. 249. Fletcher's *Checks to Antinomianism* later became a standard source for Pentecostally-inclined holiness teachers. Unfortunately, Fletcher died before Wesley and never assumed Wesley's position.

The words of the text were written by the Apostles after the act of justification had passed on them. But you see, my friends, this was not enough for them. They must receive the Holy Ghost after this. So must you. You must be sanctified. But you are not. You are only Christians in part. You have not received the Holy Ghost. I know it. I can feel your spirits hanging about me like so much dead flesh.[16]

When the American Methodist Church was formally organized at the famous Christmas Conference in Baltimore in 1784, the leaders sent by Wesley to effect the organization were Francis Asbury and Richard Wright. These men led the conference to adopt the commission Wesley had given them before they left England, "We believe that God's design in raising up the preachers called Methodists in America is to reform the continent and spread scriptural holiness over these lands." The first *Discipline* of the Methodist Church (1788) was so thoroughly perfectionistic that it carried a complete printing of Wesley's "Plain Account of Christian Perfection."[17]

To supervise the American branch of Methodism, Wesley appointed Francis Asbury, an indefatigable preacher and traveler. As firmly committed to the doctrine of holiness as Wesley himself, Asbury claimed to have been "saved" at the age of fifteen and "sanctified" the following year.[18] In 1782 he wrote in his *Journal* that the only preaching that did good was the kind which "presses the use of the means, and urges holiness of heart." Once while ill he wrote, "I have found by secret search that I have not preached sanctification as I should have done. If I am restored, this shall be my theme more pointedly than ever."[19]

---

16. J. F. Hurst, *The History of Methodism* (New York, 1902), vol. 3, p. 1252.

17. Peters, *Christian Perfection*, p. 88; John J. Tigert, *The Doctrines of the Methodist Episcopal Church in America* (Cincinnati, 1902), vol. 2, pp. 3-150. The *Disciplines* carried the "Plain Account" from 1788 to 1808, after which it was not included. For the next century a short statement of Methodist history and holiness doctrine was placed in the prefaces of the *Disciplines*.

18. Peters, *Christian Perfection*, p. 85.

19. Francis Asbury, *The Journal of the Reverend Francis Asbury* (New York, 1821), vol. 1, pp. 235-339.

The Spread of American Methodism

The earliest stronghold for Methodism in colonial America was in Brunswick County, Virginia, centering around the Bath Parish of the Reverend Devereaux Jarratt. Although an Anglican rector, Jarratt cooperated fully with the Methodist pastor Robert Williams and the Methodist societies within his parish. Williams and Jarratt cooperated in revivalistic services that seem quite similar to later Pentecostal worship. The ideal of sanctification was preached in all of these meetings. In the *Brief Narrative of the Revival of Religion* that Jarratt wrote describing the Virginia services of 1775, holiness religion was much in evidence. Many were "panting and groaning for pardon" while others were "entreating God, with strong cries and tears to save them from the remains of inbred sin, to sanctify them throughout. . . ." Numbers of them testified to having been sanctified, "instantaneously, and by simple faith."[20]

At times the emotions of the sanctified Methodists would exceed the limits of control. "Some would be seized with a trembling, and in a few moments drop on the floor as if they were dead; while others were embracing each other with streaming eyes, and all were lost in wonder, love and praise," wrote one observer. Another noted that some wept for grief while others shouted for joy "so that it was hard to distinguish one from the other." At times the congregations would "raise a great shout" that could be heard for miles around. All this the placid Anglican Jarratt observed with some awe, later observing that as the emotional element abated "the work of conviction and conversion abated too."[21]

Despite sharp criticism from the Anglican establishment and the colonial newspapers, the Methodists grew faster in Virginia than anywhere else in America. By 1776 Virginia held half of all the Methodists in America. Much of the drunkenness, cursing, swearing, and fighting that had characterized the colony before the 1773-76 revival gave way for a time to "prayer, praise, and conversing about God. . . ." This revivalistic outbreak was one of the first instances of a Pentecostal-like

---

20. Devereaux Jarratt, *A Brief Narrative of the Revival of Religion in Virginia, in a Letter to a Friend* . . . (4th ed., London, 1779), pp. 7-12; W. W. Sweet, *Religion in Colonial America* (New York, 1965), pp. 306-11; Peters, *Christian Perfection*, pp. 84, 85; Wesley M. Gewehr, *The Great Awakening in Virginia* (Durham, 1930), pp. 143-48.

21. Gewehr, *The Great Awakening in Virginia*, pp. 153-55.

religious revival in the nation, and was a direct antecedent of the frontier Kentucky revivals of 1800.[22]

From this stronghold in Virginia, Methodists began a successful growth that would eventually spread over the entire continent. Eighteenth-century Methodism was essentially a reaction against the prevailing creedal rigidity, liturgical strictness, and "ironclad institutionalism" that had largely depersonalized religion and rendered it incapable of serving the needs of individuals. Methodist perfectionism in America was "a swing toward warmth, feeling, experience, and morality" and away from the mechanical, permissive, de-ethicalized, and formal worship of the times. The growth of this "heart religion," as Wesley termed it, became a phenomenon not only of colonial frontier life but of urban life as well. The appeal to the poor and disinherited was almost irresistible. The optimistic idea that one could find perfection seemed to match the general optimism that prevailed throughout American society. In rejecting the political and social norms of England and Europe, the rising Americans rejected simultaneously the religious norms of the old world.[23]

Virginians were largely responsible for carrying the Methodist-holiness flame to the other colonies. Jesse Lee, an enthusiast, brought the message "against great opposition" to the stern Calvinists of New England. One Congregational minister is reported to have commented on the Methodist ways that were gaining converts daily:

> They are constantly mingling with the people, and enter into all their feelings, wishes and wants; and their discourses are on the level with the capacity of their hearers, and addressed to their understanding and feelings, and produce a thrilling effect, while our discourses shoot over their heads and they remain unaffected. . . . They reach a large class of people that we do not. The ignorant, the drunken, the profane, listen to their homespun, but zealous . . . discourses. . . .[24]

While Americans were fighting their Revolutionary War and establishing their independence from England, their churches were fight-

---

22. Gewehr, *The Great Awakening in Virginia,* p. 155; Peters, *Christian Perfection,* p. 84; see also the Williamsburg *Virginia Gazettes* for unfavorable public reactions to the Methodists (24 AG 39:12, 18 JL 51:22, P. D. 22 JA 67:23, 30 JI 72:23).

23. Gaddis, "Christian Perfectionism in America," p. 162.

24. Gaddis, "Christian Perfectionism in America," p. 237.

ing for and obtaining their own independence of forms and worship. Leading the way were the fiery Methodists. As the frontier reached further and further into the interior of the continent, it was found that the volatile and emotional worship of the Methodists best fitted the temper of the rude frontiersmen. Circuit riders penetrated every corner of the frontier, preaching a religion of the fire-and-brimstone variety that is found today mostly in backwoods camp meetings. In most cases, the Methodist circuit riders urged their newly won converts to "go on to perfection." As soon as penitents had recovered from the ordeal of conversion, they were plunged into the agonizing search for sanctification. In Ohio, the holiness flame was carried by Edward Dromgoole, Benjamin Lakin, and James Gilruth. In Maryland, John Hagerty "cried mightily" upon feeling the sanctifying "power" and afterwards promoted the doctrine in his area. In 1805, Edward Dromgoole went to Georgia and found that the "greater part" of the 1,500 to 2,000 Methodists to whom he preached had experienced the second blessing. "There," he reported, "the work of sanctification goes on sweetly and powerfully in the hearts of many." In Illinois, the formidable Peter Cartwright led tough frontiersmen into the experience of holiness through his rough-and-tumble style.[25]

Camp Meeting at Cane Ridge

Perhaps the most famous outbreak of enthusiastic, Pentecostal-like religion in American history occurred in the great Cane Ridge camp meeting in Kentucky, in 1801. The Cane Ridge camp meeting was preceded by three summers of revival in Logan County conducted by Methodist circuit riders who led many seekers into the sanctification experience. But the highlight of the Kentucky revivals came in Cane Ridge in Bourbon County. Begun in June 1800 by James McGready, William Hodges, and John Rankin — all of them Presbyterian ministers — this revival continued for over a year and exhibited most of the emotional phenomena that have characterized certain branches of American Protestantism ever since. A Methodist minister, John McGee, succeeded in sparking the movement when, while preaching, he was over-

25. W. W. Sweet, *Religion on the American Frontier* (Chicago, 1946), vol. 4, pp. 91, 96, 121, 127, 156-57, 249, 440-43; Smith, *Revivalism and Social Reform*, p. 118.

come by his feelings and "shouted and exhorted with all possible energy." Soon the floor of the Red River Presbyterian Church was "covered with the slain" while "their screams for mercy pierced the heavens." The excitement and curiosity engendered by this service soon mushroomed into a full-scale camp meeting in 1801 at Cane Ridge in Bourbon County under the leadership of another Presbyterian minister, Barton Stone. It was here that the American camp meeting was born.[26]

Those who attended such camp meetings as Cane Ridge generally expected their religious experiences to be as vivid as the frontier life around them. Accustomed to "braining bears and battling Indians," they received their religion with great color and excitement. Their "godly hysteria" included such phenomena as falling, jerking, barking like dogs, falling into trances, the "holy laugh," and "such wild dances as David performed before the Ark of the Lord."[27]

In August 1801 the Cane Ridge revival reached a climax when crowds variously estimated at from 10,000 to 25,000 gathered. In the light of the blazing campfires hundreds of sinners would fall "like dead men in mighty battle." Others would get the "jerks" and shake helplessly in every joint. Peter Cartwright reported that in one service he saw five hundred jerking at once. The unconverted were as subject to the "jerks" as were the saints. One minister reported that "the wicked are much more afraid of it than of small pox or yellow fever." After "praying through" some would crawl on all fours and bark like dogs, thus "treeing the devil." Others would fall into trances for hours, awakening to claim salvation or sanctification. In some services entire congregations would be seized by the "holy laugh," an ecstasy that could hardly be controlled. According to Stone, the most amazing phenomenon was the "singing exersize" whereby the saints "in a very happy state of mind would sing

26. W. W. Sweet, *The Story of Religion in America* (New York, 1950), pp. 228-29; Bernard Weisberger, *They Gathered at the River* (New York, 1958), pp. 20-25; Frederick Morgan Davenport, *Primitive Traits in Religious Revivals: A Study in Mental and Social Evolution* (New York, 1905), pp. 61-78; Archie Robertson, *That Old-Time Religion* (Boston, 1950), pp. 56-57. See also Paul Conkin's *Cane Ridge: America's Pentecost* (Madison, WI, 1989) and *Christian History*, issue 45, vol. 14, no. 1, devoted to "Camp Meetings and Circuit Riders"; especially see Mark Galli's "Revival at Cane Ridge," pp. 9-13 in that issue.

27. Weisberger, *They Gathered at the River*, pp. 20-21. The best scholarly account of Cane Ridge is Paul Conkin's *Cane Ridge*. On pp. 55-63 are accounts of Methodist "sanctifications" that preceded the Cane Ridge excitement of 1801.

most melodiously, not from the mouth or nose, but entirely in the breast."
To him this sound was "most heavenly . . . none could ever be tired of
hearing it." A responsible student of these phenomena has estimated that
by 1805 over half of all the Christians of Kentucky had exhibited these
"motor phenomena."[28]

From Kentucky the revivalistic flame spread over the entire South,
reaching into Tennessee, North and South Carolina, West Virginia, and
Georgia. In most places the same phenomena were repeated. In some
areas another manifestation was reported in addition to those already
described. In the revival that hit the University of Georgia in 1800-1801,
students visited nearby campgrounds and were themselves smitten with
the "jerks" or slain in the spirit.

> They swooned away and lay for hours in the straw prepared for those
> "smitten of the Lord," or they started suddenly to flee away and fell
> prostrate as if shot down by a sniper, or they took suddenly to jerking
> with apparently every muscle in their body until it seemed they would
> be torn to pieces or converted into marble, or they shouted and talked
> in unknown tongues.[29]

28. Davenport, *Primitive Traits in Religious Revivals,* pp. 78-82. Some called these
traits "Methodist fits"; see Robertson, *That Old-Time Religion,* p. 56; Barton Stone,
The Biography of Eld. Barton Stone: Written by Himself with Additions and Reflections
(Cincinnati, 1847), pp. 34-43. Many of these phenomena have been repeated peri-
odically throughout Christian history. They seem confined to no particular time or
place and are not unique to the American South or to "holy rollers." Scenes similar
to Cane Ridge were seen in England while Wesley and Whitefield preached, in
Massachusetts under Jonathan Edwards, and in New York City and Richmond. They
have been especially prominent in the various American "awakenings." In general
they are more often associated with the poorer classes, and they take a similar form
in countries as culturally different as Canada and Chile. For a more official resto-
rationist view of Cane Ridge from the Disciples of Christ perspective, see Anthony L.
Dunnavant, ed., *Perspectives on Barton W. Stone and the Revival* (Nashville, 1992). An
excellent depiction of the "exercises" is given in Galli, "Revival at Cane Ridge," pp.
9-15.

29. E. Merton Coulter, *College Life in the Old South* (New York, 1928), pp. 194-95;
also see Guion Griffis, "Camp Meetings in Ante-Bellum North Carolina," *The North
Carolina Historical Review* (Apr. 1933), for a description of speaking in tongues in early
North Carolina camp meetings. Throughout the nineteenth century, speaking in
unknown tongues occurred occasionally in the revivals and camp meetings that
dotted the countryside. Perhaps the phenomenon was considered just another of the
many evidences that one had been saved or sanctified.

From 1800 until the present day such phenomena have accompanied in some degree most major revivals, regardless of denomination or doctrine. Even the Mormon Church experienced much the same motor phenomena that characterized the early Methodists and later Pentecostals. Shouting, jerking, and dancing were common in their services, and Brigham Young not only spoke in unknown tongues, but interpreted his own messages to his hearers. Mormon choirs were even known to sing songs in unknown tongues in unison.[30]

Within a decade the Western revival that began at Cane Ridge in 1800 became more institutionalized, as the camp meeting became a regular part of American religious life. By 1830 the more frenzied aspects of the revival had become little more than a memory, while primary concern switched from religious experience to doctrine. The emotional type of religion, however, continued to exist, especially on the frontier and in the South, and there was always the possibility of fresh revival outbreaks. Indeed, the nineteenth and twentieth centuries would exhibit periodic awakenings and recessions of revivalistic religion that tended to resemble the ups and downs of the business cycle.[31]

Charles G. Finney and Oberlin Perfectionism

The area in the United States that was most subject to the revival cycle was the well-known "burned-over district" of western New York, so named because of the numerous revivals that had swept over the area. The man most responsible for reinstituting and refining the revival was Charles G. Finney, born in Connecticut but raised in the western part of New York state. While a young man Finney joined the Presbyterian Church, but soon rebelled against its strict Calvinism. In 1821 he experienced a dramatic conversion and shortly thereafter reported a vivid "baptism in the Holy Spirit" accompanied by "unutterable gushings" of praise. Following his license to preach in 1824, he made a study of Christian doctrine and by 1836 became convinced that entire Sanctification was possible in this life. His spellbinding revival sermons were

---

30. Joseph Smith, *History of the Church of Jesus Christ of Latter-Day Saints* (Salt Lake City, 1902), pp. 296-97, 409, 422.

31. Weisberger, *They Gathered at the River,* p. 21; Smith, *Revivalism and Social Reform,* pp. 16-34.

soon filled with perfectionist thought. During the 1820's he led revivals of spectacular proportions, using what he termed the "new measures" of evangelization. In 1837 he went to Oberlin College where, with President Asa Mahan, he added an element of academic respectability to his evangelistic labors. From 1843 until his death in 1875 people flocked to barns, schoolhouses, and open-air meetings to hear him expound his doctrines. According to Finney, after a true experience of conversion a person could achieve the coveted state of Christian perfection or sanctification by simply exercising free will and cultivating "right intentions." Sin and holiness, he explained, could not exist in the same person. While Finney's "Oberlin theology" differed somewhat from the traditional holiness views of the Wesleyans, such differences as there were came mainly from his reformed background.[32]

One of Finney's theological innovations was his increasing tendency to identify the "baptism of the Holy Spirit" as the means of entering into entire sanctification. By 1840, he spoke of "permanent sanctification" through such a baptism. He also proposed the possibility of receiving subsequent "fresh" receptions of the Holy Spirit for believers. The use of this type of "Pentecostal" language served only to widen the wedge between Finney and his former Calvinist colleagues.[33]

John Humphrey Noyes at Oneida

An illustration of the radical possibilities inherent in perfectionism is seen in the life and projects of one of Finney's converts, John Humphrey Noyes. A graduate of Dartmouth College, Noyes later studied for the

32. Smith, *Revivalism and Social Reform*, pp. 104, 140; for a firsthand account of Finney's views see *Memoirs of Reverend Charles G. Finney* (New York, 1876), passim; other excellent sources are found in Robert S. Fletcher's *A History of Oberlin College from Its Foundation Through the Civil War* (Oberlin, 1943), vol. 1, pp. 223-29, and Benjamin B. Warfield, *Perfectionism* (New York, 1931), vol. 1, pp. 166-218. The social and historical setting is well treated in Whitney R. Cross, *The Burned-Over District: The Social and Intellectual History of Enthusiastic Religion in Western New York, 1800-1850* (New York, 1965), pp. 158-250.

33. John Leroy Gresham, *Charles G. Finney's Doctrine of the Baptism of the Holy Spirit* (Peabody, MA, 1987), pp. 8-17, 40-63, 78. Gresham goes so far as to dub Finney "the grandfather of Pentecostalism." Also see Keith Hardman's *Charles Grandison Finney 1792-1875: Revivalist and Reformer* (Syracuse, NY, 1987, 1990).

ministry at Andover and Yale. At Yale he professed to be sanctified and completely perfected. In his new state Noyes felt that it was impossible to commit sin. In time his ideas became so peculiar that he was asked to leave Yale, losing at the same time his license to preach. Noyes's perfectionism finally led him to teach that direct divine revelation was superior to the Scriptures, he himself, of course, being the arbiter of the divine will. Eventually he taught that Christ had returned in A.D. 70 with the destruction of Jerusalem and that heaven and the perfect society was now on the earth.[34]

From 1836 to 1879, Noyes attempted to create communities of "Bible Communists" in Putney, Vermont, and Oneida, New York. The Oneida experiment began in 1848 and was one of the few utopian experiments in the United States that proved to be economically successful. Perhaps the most startling innovation at Oneida was Noyes's institution of "complex marriage." Feeling that heaven, where "there is neither marriage nor giving in marriage," had already come and that the sanctified could not commit sin, Noyes began a program of "reconciliation of the sexes" to parallel man's "reconciliation with God." His system was a type of sanctified promiscuity, theoretically under feminine control, and regulated by confession, conditional continence, and mutual criticism.[35]

In spite of its emotional extremes, its theological variations, and its utopian visionaries, the perfectionist impulse grew in America into a great crusade in the two decades preceding the Civil War. The mood of America during those years was one of optimism and confidence concerning the perfectibility of man and his society. Revolts against the gloomier aspects of the Calvinism that had dominated American religious thought for a century began to take place. Transcendentalism and Unitarianism became refuges for a few romanticist intellectuals, while the Methodist and Baptist Churches served the common folk.

In the Methodist General Conferences of 1824 and 1832 urgent calls were given to the faithful to lay greater stress on holiness. "If

---

34. Warfield, *Perfectionism*, pp. 308-36.

35. The best recent work on Noyes is Spencer Klaw's *Without Sin: The Life and Death of the Oneida Community* (New York, 1994). See pp. 24-29, 30-45, 46-56. Gaddis, "Christian Perfectionism in America," p. 367; Sweet, *Story of Religion in America*, pp. 281-83; Warfield, *Perfectionism*, vol. 2, pp. 219-336; Cross, *The Burned-Over District*, pp. 322-40. Also see Gilbert Seldes, *The Stammering Century* (New York, 1965), pp. 157-97.

Methodists give up the doctrine of entire sanctification, or suffer it to become a dead letter, we are a fallen people," warned the bishops. The tide of perfectionist thought that swept the nation, both in literature and from the lecture platform, caused Methodists to re-examine their roots and eventually to claim the distinction of being America's first promoters of perfectionism. By 1840 perfectionism was becoming one of the central themes of American social, intellectual, and religious life. And from the ground of perfectionist teaching sprang the many reform movements intended to perfect American social life — women's rights, the abolition of slavery, anti-masonry, and the various temperance campaigns.

Throughout the nation Methodist pastors and theologians reread Wesley's writings and saw that they could join the stream of perfectionism and even become leaders in it without violating their own traditions. This was, after all, the original Methodism as it had once been taught by Wesley. The decade of the 1840's, therefore, witnessed a veritable flood of perfectionistic teaching in the Methodist Church. Leading pastors, bishops, and theologians led the movement, giving it institutional and intellectual respectability.[36]

Phoebe Palmer

Among the leading proponents of the new emphasis in Methodism were Mrs. Phoebe Palmer and her physician husband, Dr. Walter Palmer, members of the Allen Street Methodist Church in New York City. These two had been won to the holiness standard by the sister of Mrs. Palmer, Mrs. Sarah A. Lankford, who had begun holding "Tuesday Meetings for the Promotion of Holiness" in her parlor in 1835. By 1839 Mrs. Palmer had not only experienced sanctification, but had become the leader of the meetings. As the "Tuesday Meetings" grew in popularity, hundreds of preachers and laymen from various denominations flocked to her home to hear of the "shorter way" of achieving the perfection and ecstasy that early Christian saints had taken entire lifetimes to acquire. By placing "all on the altar," she taught, one could be instantly sanctified

36. See W. W. Sweet, *Methodism in American History* (New York, 1933), pp. 47-59, and Merle Curti, *Growth of American Thought* (New York, 1964), pp. 298-305. Also see Smith, *Revivalism and Social Reform*, pp. 114-47, and Carl Degler, *Out of Our Past* (New York, 1959), pp. 154-60.

through the baptism of the Holy Ghost. The seekers were encouraged to testify to receiving the blessing "by faith" even if they failed to experience any emotional feelings at the moment. Among those who came and found holiness under the Palmers were leading Methodist pastors and bishops. She counted among her friends and followers no less than four bishops of the Methodist Church: Bishops Edmund S. Janes, Leonidas L. Hamline, Jesse T. Peck, and Matthew Simpson. For the next thirty years the Palmers were the national leaders of the movement, traversing the United States and Canada numerous times, and addressing camp meetings and leading churches on their theme of holiness and perfect love.[37]

The year 1839 also saw the beginning of the first periodical in America devoted exclusively to holiness doctrine, *The Guide to Christian Perfection,* later known as *The Guide to Holiness.* Founded in Boston by Timothy Merritt, this monthly paper carried the testimonies of Phoebe Palmer and her husband. In 1865 *The Guide* was purchased by Dr. and Mrs. Palmer themselves and became quite influential within American Protestantism, particularly among Methodists. At its peak, it enjoyed a circulation of 30,000.[38]

With Methodists and Oberlin perfectionists leading the way, the holiness crusade approached a climax shortly before the Civil War. Ministers of most denominations joined in the campaign for perfection. In 1858 William E. Boardman, a Presbyterian minister, published *The Higher Christian Life,* an attempt to interpret sanctification to those outside the Methodist tradition. This volume immediately became a best-seller and gained influence in England as well as in America. In 1859 A. B. Earle, the nation's leading Baptist evangelist, professed to be sanctified and published his experience in another best-seller, *The Rest of Faith.* Everywhere men and women were seeking perfection. "The ethical

---

37. See Harold E. Raser, *Phoebe Palmer: Her Life and Thought* (Lewiston, NY, 1987), pp. 21-74, 75-148, 227-88. T. Dewitt Talmadge once called Palmer the "Columbus of the religious life." See also Bucke et al., *The History of American Methodism,* vol. 2, pp. 1, 609-10; Smith, *Revivalism and Social Reform,* pp. 123-24, 144. An excellent source of Palmer's teaching can be found in the Paulist Press volume on American spirituality titled, *Phoebe Palmer: Selected Writings* (New York, 1988). See also Charles Edward White, *The Beauty of Holiness: Phoebe Palmer as Theologian, Revivalist, Feminist, and Humanitarian* (Grand Rapids, MI, 1986).

38. Smith, *Revivalism and Social Reform,* pp. 115-17; Delbert R. Rose, *A Theology of Christian Experience* (Minneapolis, 1965), pp. 32-39.

ideals to which Emerson and Henry David Thoreau aspired on a highly sophisticated level, plain men of the time sought at a Methodist mourners' bench or class meeting." It was a kind of "evangelical transcendentalism" which thrived in the idealism of a young and growing America. By 1856 holiness had become so popular that Jesse T. Peck's book, *The Central Idea of Christianity*, seemed to express the feeling of a large segment of American Protestantism.[39]

Pre–Civil War Revivals and Divisions

This crusade for holiness, however, was not without disruptive and schismatic tendencies. Along with the drive for perfect sanctification, there arose a parallel drive to stamp out the evil of slavery. Sanctified Christians came to believe that slavery was a blot on society and the church and that it should be abolished. Anti-slavery thought was the direct cause of the formation of the Wesleyan Methodist Church in New York and New England in 1843-44. Orange Scott and other leaders of the new sect charged that by compromising with the evil of slavery the Methodist Episcopal Church had renounced its duty to become, like its founder John Wesley, "evangelically anti-slavery."[40] In 1844 the great division finally came within the Methodist Church itself, with the Southern division espousing and defending slavery and the Northern division becoming more openly against it.[41]

In America, the climactic holiness revival came in 1858. This *annus mirabilis* was also the last religious awakening before the Civil War; and unfortunately, the Southern states were largely untouched by it. Beginning in New York City and spreading over most of the Northeast, the 1858 awakening was primarily urban and Northern. In this remarkable

---

39. Bucke et al., *The History of American Methodism*, vol. 2, pp. 610-12; Smith, *Revivalism and Social Reform*, pp. 114-34. See Warfield, *Perfectionism*, vol. 2, pp. 463-558, for an excellent treatment of the "Higher Life Movement" led by William E. Boardman after 1859.

40. For an evaluation of the Wesleyan Methodist stand on slavery see Donald Dayton, *Discovering an Evangelical Heritage* (New York, 1976). Also see Warren Smith, *John Wesley and Slavery* (Nashville, 1986), and Ira Ford McLeister, *History of the Wesleyan Methodist Church of America* (Marion, IN, 1959).

41. Smith, *Revivalism and Social Reform*, pp. 184-85; Peters, *Christian Perfection*, pp. 125-28; Cross, *The Burned-Over District*, pp. 263-67.

movement business workers turned out *en masse* to sing hymns, and stevedores knelt on the docks to pray. Telegraph companies allowed messages to be sent to "sinners" free of cost at certain times of the day. A "thousand mile prayer meeting" was inaugurated that struck one city after another. Even Henry Ward Beecher, that crusty old opponent of "got up" revivals, joined the crusade after his church filled to capacity night after night with no special urging. The revival of 1858 was as deep and intense as Whitefield's revival of 1740, with one major difference — the slave-holding South never felt its impact.[42]

Long before 1858, the southern churches had largely abandoned the quest for holiness, in theory and in practice. From about 1830 until the outbreak of war, theological energies in the South were directed toward supporting and defending the institution of slavery. A study of the southern Methodist Episcopal Church's pre-war literature shows that perfectionism was barely discernible. In a volume representing the best thought of the church in 1858, only one out of eighteen "representative" sermons was Wesleyan in regard to sanctification. In the southern church, holiness had become a dead letter.[43]

In northern Methodist circles, however, holiness continued to be a lively issue, even at times eclipsing slavery as a topic of debate. In 1860 another division occurred in western New York, this time under the leadership of Benjamin T. Roberts. The dispute concerned questions of dress and rented pews in large Buffalo Methodist churches, and led to a defection from the Genessee Conference. Roberts and his followers, who were dubbed "Nazarites," established the Free Methodist church, in which salvation, holiness, pews, and former slaves would forever be free. In its statement of faith, the Free Methodists inserted a section on

---

42. Robertson, *Old-Time Religion,* pp. 68-69; Smith, *Revivalism and Social Reform,* pp. 63-79. The perfectionist aspect of the revival can be seen in J. A. Wood, *Perfect Love, or Plain Things for Those Who Need Them* (Chicago, 1880), pp. 315-30. Much of a Pentecostalist atmosphere surrounded services in the Methodist Church in Binghamton, New York, in 1858 where the pastor "fell out for three hours" and then prayed all night. During one service "some shouted, some laughed, some wept, and a large number lay prostrate from three to five hours, beyond the power of shouting or weeping."

43. See *The Methodist Pulpit, South* (Washington, 1858), passim; also Gaddis, "Christian Perfectionism," pp. 424-25. For pro-slavery sermonizing see Eric McKitrick, *Slavery Defended: The Views of the Old South* (Englewood Cliffs, NJ, 1963), pp. 86-98.

entire sanctification, placing them squarely in the middle of the "second blessing" holiness tradition.[44]

As the nation drifted inexorably into war, the thrust of American thought became almost entirely political and secular. As the verbal dispute over slavery became a military contest, people forgot about theological and denominational differences. When the guns at Fort Sumter opened fire in April 1861, they signalled the end of the early holiness movement in the United States. The perfection sought by so many, through the double cure of conversion and sanctification, had failed to avert the imperfection of war.

44. B. T. Roberts, *Why Another Sect?* (New York, 1984). This is a reprint of Roberts's 1879 book, *The Earnest Christian.* An excellent recent history of the movement is John McKenna's *A Future with a History: The Wesleyan Witness of the Free Methodist Church, 1860-1995* (Indianapolis, 1995).

CHAPTER TWO

Echoes from the Forest Temple —
The National Holiness Association

1867-1894

> *We affectionately invite all . . . to come together and*
> *spend a week in God's great temple of nature.*
>
> Alfred Cookman

The Civil War was the greatest phase of the nineteenth-century drive toward the reform and perfection of American society. With the evil of slavery abolished from American life, reformers could now turn their attention to eliminating other evils. Fiery-eyed reformers would henceforth involve themselves with such causes as prohibition, women's rights, and political reform. Few causes lacked supporters, and zealous reformers were not lacking causes.

The reforming zeal that would later give rise to the populist revolt and the progressive movement also permeated the nation's churches. No denomination was exempt from the ferment of the times. All churches experienced the challenge to established religion thrown down by Darwinism, socialism, higher criticism, and the social gospel. The flow of population to urban areas threatened the very foundations of rural life. The rise of industrial empires, with the attendant evils of monopolies, political corruption, and unequal distribution of wealth, posed a special dilemma to Protestantism. More and more the ethics and morality of big business began to dominate the thinking of the churches. President W. J. Tucker of Dartmouth College wrote somewhat ruefully of the decades that followed the Civil War: "The generation which was beginning to take shape and character when I came of age was to have the peculiar fortune, whether to its disadvantage or to its distinction, of finding its way into what we now call the 'modern world.'"[1] For better or for worse, the churches, along with the rest of America's institutions, had to make the same painful transition.

The years that followed the Civil War were characterized by a moral depression in America. Returning soldiers with "battlefield ethics" entered not only the houses of business, but also the halls of government and the sanctuaries of the churches. Many of the younger recruits to the ministry entered their vocations with less training than their elders and less respect for the traditions and doctrines of the church. No denomination felt the winds of change more than the Methodist Church. Former customs such as the "mourner's bench" for penitent sinners, class meetings for the "perfection of the saints," and camp meetings for the benefit of both had been abandoned during the war. With the return of peace, little effort was made to revive these apparently antiquated forms.[2]

The first region of the United States to experience a religious revival after the war was the South. In the dark days following the war, the impoverished states of the defeated Confederacy turned to religion for solace. During 1865-67 "a sound of revival was heard from one border to the other." The journals of Methodism teemed with news of great evangelistic efforts. The bishops of the Methodist Episcopal Church, South, meeting in General Conference in 1866, called for a return to Wesleyan principles as an answer to the postwar moral crisis.[3]

In spite of this short-lived southern revival, Protestant Christianity suffered a gradual decline in both membership and interest during the last decades of the century. In 1860, 23 percent of the American population were church members, a proportion not matched again until 1890.[4]

1. Degler, *Out of Our Past*, pp. 338-78.

2. William Warren Sweet, *Methodism in American History*, pp. 332-33; Bucke et al., *The History of American Methodism*, vol. 2, pp. 324-26.

3. *Journal of the General Conference of the Methodist Episcopal Church, South, 1866*, pp. 15-21. See also the statement on holiness in the 1866 *Discipline* of the M.E. Church, South, pp. 3, 74-75; Gaddis, "Christian Perfectionism in America," p. 442.

4. Robertson, *That Old-Time Religion*, p. 70.

Within the Methodist ranks, both north and south, there arose a conviction that a holiness revival of the kind that had swept much of the country in 1858 would once again set things right. In 1870, the bishops of the southern church again called for a re-emphasis on sanctification: "Nothing is so much needed at the present time throughout all these lands, as a general and powerful revival of scriptural holiness."[5]

Many churchmen lamented the loss of old Methodist institutions, such as the class meeting, the camp meeting, and the plainness of dress. As young "progressive" ministers joined the ranks, older preachers looked on sadly at such innovations as robed choirs, organs, and seminary-trained ministers. Some warned that if the camp meeting ceased, then the "heroic fire of Methodism" would die out. Many conservative Methodists believed that the general religious inertia of the times could be cured only by a return to the prewar camp-meeting revivalism.[6]

The Vineland Camp Meeting

While southern leaders grappled with the massive problems of reconstruction and called for a revival of holiness, moves were being made in the North that eventually resulted in a renewed camp meeting and a new holiness crusade. In August 1866, J. A. Wood, who had written the best-seller *Perfect Love* in 1860, remarked to a friend, Mrs. Harriet E. Drake of Wilkes-Barre, Pennsylvania, that the doctrine of sanctification was suffering an eclipse within Methodism. Opposition to "the doctrine and distinctive experience of entire sanctification" was often encountered even in some Methodist camp meetings. In an offhand remark, Wood said he believed "that some camp meetings for the special work of holiness ought to be held." Mrs. Drake, an ardent devotee of the experience of sanctification, immediately volunteered to pay one-half of the cost of a holiness camp meeting if one could be arranged. Wood became obsessed with the idea and later shared it with the Reverend William B. Osborn of the New Jersey Methodist Conference. Also enthused by the idea, Osborn traveled to New York City in April 1867 to

5. Alexander Gross, *History of the Methodist Episcopal Church, South* (New York, 1894), p. 94.

6. Bucke et al., *History of American Methodism*, vol. 2, p. 326; George A. Smith, *The History of Georgia Methodism from 1786 to 1866* (Atlanta, 1913), pp. 396-98.

lay the matter before the Reverend John S. Inskip, pastor of the Green Street Methodist Episcopal Church. With great feeling, Osborn told Inskip, "I feel God would have us hold a holiness camp meeting." Osborn's enthusiasm was so contagious that Inskip immediately approved the idea. With the winning of Inskip the holiness movement gained its most prominent figure, a man who would later become its nationally acknowledged leader.[7]

Inskip and Osborn immediately set the wheels moving for the first camp meeting. A call, signed by thirteen Methodist ministers of New York, was issued for a larger meeting to be held in Philadelphia on June 13, 1867. This call, published in several church papers, was for those interested in "holding a camp meeting, the special object of which should be the promotion of the work of entire sanctification." Meeting in Philadelphia on the appointed date, and after conducting all their business sessions on their knees, the men present voted to hold a camp meeting at Vineland, New Jersey, July 17 through 26, 1867, appointing committees to prepare accommodations and publicity for the event. Naming themselves "The National Camp Meeting Association for the Promotion of Christian Holiness," the group issued a call written by a well-known Methodist pastor, the Reverend Alfred Cookman, addressed to all, "irrespective of denominational ties." Especially welcome were those "who feel themselves comparatively isolated in their profession of holiness." It was hoped that all would "realize together a Pentecostal baptism of the Holy Ghost" and return "with a view to increased usefulness in the churches of which we are members." The call ended with a plea for unity and revival:

> Come, brothers and sisters of the various denominations, and let us in this forest-meeting, as in other meetings for the promotion of holiness, furnish an illustration of evangelical union, and make common supplication for the descent of the Spirit upon ourselves, the church, the nation, and the world.[8]

7. J. A. Wood, *Auto-Biography of Rev. J. A. Wood* (Chicago, 1904), p. 73. For an excellent treatment of the National Holiness Association see Delbert R. Rose, *A Theology of Christian Experience*, pp. 23-78.

8. Rose, *A Theology of Christian Experience*, p. 52. See also A. M. McLean and Joel W. Eaton, eds., *Penuel, or Face to Face with God* (New York, 1869), pp. 6-15, for Inskip's version of the beginning of the Association; and George Hughes, *Days of Power in the Forest Temple* ... (Boston, 1874), pp. 39-60.

With the opening of the Vineland, New Jersey, camp meeting on July 17, 1867, the modern holiness crusade began. This may properly be considered the beginning of the modern holiness movement in the United States. Those who attended felt unanimously that this meeting was destined to "exert an influence over all Christendom" as well as "to initiate a new era in Methodism." Little did these men realize that this meeting would eventually result in the formation of over a hundred denominations around the world and indirectly bring to birth a "Third Force" in Christendom, the Pentecostal movement.[9]

The first "National Camp Meeting for the Promotion of Holiness" was an unqualified success. Although clearly interdenominational, the meeting was dominated by Methodists. Even the famous Methodist Bishop Matthew Simpson and his family attended. Near the end of the meeting a committee of twenty-one was elected to continue the organization and to call for a similar meeting the following year. Inskip was elected the first president of the group, and George Hughes the first secretary. The name adopted for the new group was the "National Camp Meeting Association for the Promotion of Holiness." A call was made for another camp meeting to be held the following year.[10]

The National Holiness Association Movement

In the years following 1867 "National Camp Meetings" were held in Mannheim, Pennsylvania, Round Lake, New York, and in many other locations. From 1867 to 1883 a total of fifty-two "national camps" were held, mostly on Methodist campgrounds and in connection with Methodist annual conferences. Perhaps the most notable "National Camp Meeting" was the one held in Round Lake in 1874, where seven bishops from the Northern and Southern Methodist Churches attended, along with 20,000 other worshippers. The high point was reached when President U. S. Grant arrived for one day of services. The closing meeting was a sacramental service presided over by Bishop Matthew Simpson, who exhorted the ministers with great passion: "Brethren, there never

9. Rose, *A Theology of Christian Experience,* pp. 52-53.
10. Rose, *A Theology of Christian Experience,* pp. 52-61. In later years the name of the group was shortened to "the National Holiness Association"; in 1971 it was changed to the "Christian Holiness Association." a name still used in 1970.

26

was a day when we needed more power than now. We are called to meet, in this land, the tide of heathenism rolling in upon our shores. Infidelity is making its fiercest onset. We need and must have apostolic power." On the final Sunday over four hundred persons testified at a "love feast" to having been sanctified in the meeting.[11]

For several years it seemed as if the Methodist Church would once again become the chief holiness sect in America. Of eight new bishops elected in the Northern General Conference of 1872, four were sympathetic to the holiness movement and none was opposed. In 1869, Randolph S. Foster, one of the newly elected bishops, had published a new edition of his most popular book, *Christian Purity, Or the Heritage of Faith* in which he took the view that sanctification could and should be an instantaneous work of grace. In 1878, the bishops of the Southern church went so far as to criticize their preachers for "the infrequency of its (Christian perfection) proclamation from the pulpit and the irregularity of its experimental power in the church." They called for a new emphasis in the denomination, exhorting, "Let us more than ever reassert this grand doctrine."[12]

Early Successes

Throughout the 1870's and 1880's the movement was aided by a flood of literature, issuing from both official Methodist and independent presses. The National Holiness Association began publication in 1870 of two new periodicals in addition to *Guide to Holiness,* now edited by Inskip: *The Christian Standard and Home Journal,* published in Philadelphia, and *The Advocate of Holiness,* printed in Boston. The books and tracts of Phoebe Palmer enjoyed a particularly wide distribution, *The Way of Holiness* appearing in fifty-two editions by 1867. In addition to these independent publications, the denominational *Christian Advocate, Methodist Quarterly Review, Zion's Herald,* and *Northern Christian Advocate* were filled with holiness articles and appeals.[13]

11. McLean and Eaton, *Penuel,* p. 468; cf. pp. 254-68; Gaddis, "Christian Perfectionism in America," p. 443; Bucke et al., *History of American Methodism,* vol. 2, pp. 612-13.

12. *Journal of the General Conference, 1878,* p. 33.

13. Bucke et al., *History of American Methodism,* vol. 2, pp. 613-15; Smith, *Revivalism and Social Reform,* pp. 114-28.

The holiness crusade enjoyed particular success in the Black Methodist churches, which had been founded on the basis of Wesley's second blessing teaching. The African Methodist Episcopal Church (AME), founded in 1787 by Richard Allen in Philadelphia, and the African Methodist Episcopal Church, Zion, founded in 1821 by James Varick in New York City, had always held strongly to the traditional Wesleyan teaching on entire sanctification. By the late 1870's the Black Methodist churches as well as many Black Baptist churches joined in the holiness crusade. A leading light in this movement was the Black evangelist Amanda Berry Smith, a freed slave, who received the second blessing in John Inskip's Green Street Methodist Church in New York City in 1868 after having attended Phoebe Palmer's Tuesday meetings for the promotion of holiness.[14]

By 1877, the holiness crusade spread rapidly in the AME church as a result of a remarkable revival in the Bethel Church in Philadelphia, the mother church of the movement. Under the leadership of Pastor George C. Whitefield, outstanding speakers were invited from Methodist, Presbyterian, and Baptist churches for a "Holiness Conference" in June of 1877. The meetings were bi-racial, interdenominational, and supportive of female spiritual leadership. White leaders present were NHA President John Inskip, E. I. D. Pepper, and William MacDonald. From the Philadelphia meetings, the holiness message spread far and wide in the African American churches. For several years holiness revivals and "all-day meetings for the promotion of holiness" were held in Black churches throughout the nation led by such leaders as Jabez Campbell, Benjamin Tanner, Levi Coppin, Henry Fisher, and William E. Fuller.[15]

The holiness message was also promoted in Great Britain, Europe, Asia, Africa, and India through the international evangelistic travels of Amanda Smith, whose ministry was as eagerly received by whites as by blacks. Her *Autobiography*, which appeared in 1893, helped to spread the holiness movement across many denominational, theological, and national boundaries.[16]

---

14. Amanda Smith, *An Autobiography* (1893; New York, 1988), pp. 73-91.

15. See David Daniels, "Pentecostalism," in Larry Murphy, J. Gordon Melton, and Gary Ward, eds., *Encyclopedia of African American Religions* (New York, 1993), pp. 585-95.

16. Smith, *An Autobiography*, pp. 240-498. Amanda Smith's long life (1837-1915) covered most of the events of the early holiness and Pentecostal movements.

By 1880 the holiness crusade had assumed nationwide proportions and soon found some of its most ardent supporters in the South. Throughout the period from 1870 to 1885 the idea spread rapidly throughout southern Methodism. During this time, Inskip, President of the National Holiness Association and a full-time revivalist, conducted "holiness revivals" in the South. Preaching in Savannah and Augusta, he found such interest that he organized a "Georgia Holiness Association" in connection with the Georgia Conferences of the Methodist Episcopal Church, South. The leading ministers of the North Georgia Conference joined the organization. Georgia leaders were the Reverends A. J. Jarrell, pastor of the First Methodist Church of Athens, Asbury Dodge, W. P. Lovejoy, Lovick Pierce, and R. P. Martin.[17]

During the height of the movement in Georgia Methodism, 200 of the 240 ministers of the North Georgia Conference professed to having received the experience of sanctification as a "second blessing." Most of these joined the Holiness Association of the North Georgia Conference. A similar association was formed for the South Georgia Conference.[18]

The "Holiness Association" movement became the nationwide arm of the National Holiness Association, with state and local associations being formed in many states of the union. Some were regional, such as the "New England Holiness Association" and the "Iowa Holiness Association," while others reached down to city and county levels. In the South, there were associations for every Methodist district conference as well as for the annual conferences. So fundamental was this movement in southern Methodism that one preacher from the Old Dominion declared that his church was "reconstructing Virginia upon the basis of holiness." Some Southerners felt that reconstruction based on holiness would be much more effective than the political reconstruction of the South which was then in process.[19]

17. Smith, *History of Georgia Methodism*, p. 410.
18. Joseph H. King and Blanche L. King, *Yet Speaketh: Memoirs of the Late Bishop Joseph H. King* (Franklin Springs, GA, 1949), p. 85.
19. Bucke et al., *History of American Methodism*, vol. 2, p. 613. Associations similar to those in Georgia were formed in all the southern states during the 1870s, with the largest numbers in Mississippi, Georgia, Texas, and Kentucky.

Methodists and the Holiness Movement

As in other regions of the nation, the holiness movement in the South began as an urban force among the better educated circles. Leading advocates of the movement were often also leading figures in the Methodist Church. The patriarch of Georgia Methodism, Lovick Pierce, who had been a Methodist preacher since the early days of the nineteenth century, pronounced the holiness movement to be nothing more than "old line, pioneer" Methodism.[20] In the early years of the movement, annual meetings were held in the leading churches of the conference. The interest was so great that Asbury Dodge and some of his friends began publication of a weekly newspaper devoted to holiness and established a holiness camp meeting in a refurbished campground at Indian Springs near Jackson, Georgia.[21]

During this period the holiness crusade found unusual acceptance in the Methodist Church, for several reasons. Many conservatives felt that the movement might be a bulwark against the urbane and highly educated "progressive" ministers who were gaining in numbers and influence. In some places these "progressives" had introduced organs into the churches, along with robed choirs. Even more disturbing was the tendency among them to dispense with class meetings and altar services where seekers knelt to pursue holiness of heart. They also began to admit new members without the aid of previous indoctrination. Many older ministers were also shocked at the fashionable modes of dress these ministers allowed their members to wear. Perhaps the new emphasis on holiness would halt or reverse these disturbing developments.[22]

Others supported the movement because of the theological views held by many of the new "progressive" ministers, many of whom had been educated in Germany. Their favorable views toward the current work of the German "higher critics" disturbed the older ministers. If

20. Lovick Pierce, *A Miscellaneous Essay on Entire Sanctification, How It Was Lost to the Church and How It May and Must Be Regained* (Atlanta, 1897), p. 1.

21. Smith, *History of Georgia Methodism*, p. 401; Rose, *A Theology of Christian Experience*, pp. 70-71. Also see John Brasher, *The Sanctified South: John Lakin Brasher and the Holiness Movement* (Urbana, IL, 1994).

22. Smith, *History of Georgia Methodism*, pp. 396-401; Pierce, *A Miscellaneous Essay*, pp. 16-57; Sweet, *Methodism in American History*, pp. 332-39.

certain passages of scripture proved to have been falsely included in the canon, might not all the biblically based arguments for Christian perfection fall? Also disturbing to many were the discussions concerning the theories of Charles Darwin. The more recently educated ministers seemed to know too much about "evolution" for the comfort of the older ministers. Perhaps the holiness movement would prove to be a bulwark against these "heretical teachings."[23]

Many Methodists also saw the holiness revival as a unifying force which, by crossing denominational barriers, could help unify Methodism. The holiness camp meetings were opportunities for Methodists of the North and South to unite on a common platform and to begin healing the breach caused by the Civil War and reconstruction. Perhaps Wesley's "perfect love" could end bitter divisions in the church and also help in reuniting the nation.

Others felt that the National Holiness Movement might save the camp meeting, an institution that seemed on the verge of dying out. Many of the old campgrounds were still in use, but the long rows of tents had begun to be replaced by well-built cottages; and rather than the customary old-time revival services, the services were now interspersed with lectures on semi-religious and even secular subjects. "Old-time" religious fervor with its shouts and hallelujahs was being replaced by gossip and visiting, as the camps were transformed into "respectable middle-class summer resorts with only a tinge of religion."[24]

The Holiness Crusade

The National Holiness Movement was as successful in reviving the camp meeting as it was in reviving the doctrine of sanctification. By 1887 the National Association reported that it had held "sixty-seven national camp meetings and eleven Tabernacle meetings . . . distributed through sixteen states of the Union, extending to both shores of the Continent and to the far off East." At least twenty-eight camps, officially

23. For an example of current theological thought, see Andrew C. Zenos, *The Elements of Higher Criticism* (New York, 1895), pp. 1-15. See also Joseph E. Campbell, *The Pentecostal Holiness Church, 1898-1948* (Franklin Springs, GA, 1951), pp. 102-10.
24. Sweet, *Methodism in American History*, p. 333.

designated "National Camp Meetings," were in operation by the 1880's.[25]

There was no lack of preachers to fill the pulpits of these hundreds of holiness churches and camp meetings. By 1887 the National Holiness Association listed 206 "holiness evangelists" who gave full time to preaching the doctrine. By 1891 the list had grown to 304. Also contributing to the movement were scores of "weekday meetings for the promotion of holiness" patterned after the famous "Tuesday Meeting" of Phoebe Palmer. By 1891 there were no less than 354 of these meetings listed by the National Association, most of them gathering in private homes.[26]

The holiness movement was not confined to the United States alone. The many preaching tours of the Palmers from 1853 to 1859 had brought the message to the Methodists of Canada. When they traveled to England in 1859, the resulting revival of holiness helped revitalize the very homebase of Methodism. In 1875, Inskip returned to Canada and held successful revivals there. But the "grand tour" of the holiness advocates came in 1880, when Inskip, Wood, and William McDonald made an "around-the-world tour" that reached England, Italy, and India with the doctrine of perfect love. The campaign in India attached a strong holiness cast to the Methodist Mission, which would figure significantly in the Pentecostal revival of the early twentieth century.[27]

Also catching the vision for holiness-oriented Methodist world missions was William Taylor of Virginia who went as a missionary in 1847 to the gold fields of California. Later, after tours of England, Australia, India, and South Africa from 1862 to 1866, he began sending "self supporting" missionaries through the backing of friends in the National Holiness Association. Largely supported by sanctified Methodists, Taylor gained such popularity that in 1884 he was elected to the novel post of "Missionary Bishop" of Africa by the General Conference of the Methodist Episcopal

25. Peters, *Christian Perfection and American Methodism,* p. 138; Bucke et al., *American Methodism,* vol. 2, p. 613. Also see William McDonald, *The Life of Rev. John S. Inskip* (Salem, OH, 1986).

26. Peters, *Christian Perfection and American Methodism,* p. 138. For a view of developing eschatology in NHA leadership see Kenneth O. Brown, "Leadership in the National Holiness Association with Special Reference to Eschatology, 1867-1919" (unpublished thesis, Drew University, 1988).

27. Rose, *A Theology of Christian Experience,* p. 44; Timothy L. Smith, *Called Unto Holiness* (Kansas City, 1962), pp. 22-23.

Church. His missionary efforts resulted in the planting of Methodist churches in India, Africa, and South America, all founded with a strong emphasis on second blessing holiness.[28]

The later British campaigns of the Palmers, Inskip, and William E. Boardman awakened an interest in the holiness doctrine comparable to the response in America. Among those joining in the British holiness crusade were William Booth, founder of the Salvation Army, and Canon Harford-Battersby, Vicar of Keswick. In 1875 a series of summer conventions at Keswick called "the Union Meeting for the Promotion of Christian Holiness" with a special emphasis on the "higher life" became the British equivalent of the American National Holiness Association.[29]

During the 1880's the holiness awakening reached its peak in America. Inskip, the acknowledged leader of the movement, had held huge revivalistic campaigns throughout the nation during the decade before his death in 1884. Supported not only by Methodists, but also by Presbyterians, Baptists, and Congregationalists, this fervent preacher carried his message from California to Georgia. A high point of the movement came when Inskip and a supporting team of preachers held a preaching campaign in Salt Lake City, the center of Mormonism. Night after night Brigham Young and his elders attended in an attempt to intimidate the speakers. Undaunted, the intrepid evangelists obliged their visitors with sermon after sermon on holiness and climaxed the campaign by denouncing Young and the Mormons in a sermon called the "Last Judgment."[30]

The success of the holiness movement was nowhere more pronounced in the South than in Georgia. An early advocate of the movement in that state was the Reverend Warren Candler, pastor of the fashionable St. John's Methodist Church in Augusta. In 1883 he stirred the entire city with a sermon on holiness. The Augusta News reported that Christians of all denominations were discussing his question: "Is it possible for one to live without Sin?"[31] In 1884 Candler, who later became the first president of Emory University in Atlanta, hosted the annual convention of the North Georgia Holiness Association at St. John's Church. Although he never embraced fully the "second blessing" theory, Candler approved of fiery sermons and lusty denunciations of sin, especially the sins practiced by

28. William Taylor, *Story of My Life* (New York, 1896).
29. Smith, *Called Unto Holiness*, pp. 23-25.
30. Bucke et al., *History of American Methodism*, vol. 2, p. 613.
31. Alfred M. Pierce, *Giant Against the Sky* (New York, 1958), p. 47.

uptown congregations like his own. Candler himself was unmatched in his "holiness sermons" on the evils of drinking, dancing, theater-going, card playing, swearing, and "even wine on the family tables."[32]

Candler used the holiness movement in the North Georgia Conference to gain the Bishopric of the Southern Methodist Church. Sensing the strength of the movement, he allied himself with it in the 1880's and was elected Bishop largely because of the support he mustered among its advocates. In later years Candler stood with his church in opposition to the movement, but at heart he remained a "holiness preacher."[33]

The holiness movement within Methodism continued with increasing force until the mid-eighties. High recognition of the doctrine was given by the delegates to the Methodist Centennial Conference in 1884. There it was stated that Christian perfection had become so popular among other denominations, "in fact, if not in form," that no longer could Methodists claim it "as their peculiar heritage." Indeed, the newly-imported Salvation Army of General William Booth claimed holiness as its distinguishing doctrine and social work as its public manifestation of the sanctifying grace. The Society of Friends made it clear during this decade that they also were a "holiness church," the doctrines of George Fox being identical with those of John Wesley. The Evangelical United Brethren Church, always closely related to Methodism, inserted a strong holiness section in their Discipline during this period. The Cumberland Presbyterian Church also joined in the cause by inserting a paragraph on sanctification which, if not entirely Wesleyan, gave recognition to the importance of the doctrine.[34]

The Controversy Begins

In spite of the great popularity of the doctrine of holiness after 1867, controversy over it began to be felt in the Methodist Church during the

32. Pierce, *Giant Against the Sky*, pp. 158-59. See Candler's booklet entitled *On with the Revolution: By One of the Revolutionaries* (Atlanta, 1887), pp. 1-12; and Candler's *Christus Auctor, A Manual of Christian Evidence* (Nashville, 1900), which refutes "higher criticism" and defends traditional Methodist social views.

33. Harold W. Mann, *Atticus Greene Haygood* (Athens, GA, 1965), pp. 154-67.

34. Bucke et al., *History of American Methodism*, vol. 2, pp. 616, 618; Redford, *Rise of the Church of the Nazarene*, p. 38; *Discipline of the Evangelical United Brethren Church* (Harrisburg, 1951), pp. 51-56; Smith, *Called Unto Holiness*, pp. 25-26.

1880's. There were many factors that led to controversy and to the rise of opposition to the holiness movement in general, not the least of which was the independent character of the National Holiness Association. From the beginning, this group had been led and supported largely by Methodists, but it remained an interdenominational body. This type of independency was repugnant to the traditionally well-organized and tightly knit polity of the Methodist Church. By 1888 it was reported that there were four publishing houses devoted exclusively to publishing holiness literature. Four years later there were forty-one holiness periodicals being published throughout the country. Most of these enterprises were wholly independent of any church control and were associated with the National Holiness Association.[35]

As early as 1878, searching criticism of the movement had been voiced by Methodist leaders. In that year D. D. Whedon had written in the Methodist Quarterly Review that:

> The holiness association, the holiness periodical, the holiness prayer meeting, the holiness preacher, are all modern novelties. They are not Wesleyan. We believe that a living Wesley would never admit them into the Methodist system.[36]

The Southern Methodist Church early became a defender of the movement through Leonidas Rosser, editor of the Southern Methodist Review. Reminding Methodists that they must avoid "law without liberty," he warned his brethren that "Methodism, itself a great holiness association, was organized in the Church of England." He challenged further, "Let all opposers of these associations . . . show their errors, excesses, and evils, or withdraw their opposition; for in opposing them they oppose Methodism." Such charges and countercharges as these reflected the rift that the holiness movement was erecting among Methodists, and it portended deep trouble for the years ahead.[37]

The most disturbing development to loyal churchmen was the appearance of a "come-outism" movement during the 1880's among the more radical holiness spokesmen. In 1880 Daniel S. Warner had organized the "Church of God," with headquarters in Anderson, Indiana, on

---

35. Peters, *Christian Perfection and American Methodism,* pp. 138-39.

36. Peters, *Christian Perfection and American Methodism,* p. 139.

37. Peters, *Christian Perfection and American Methodism,* p. 140; Sweet, *Methodism in American History,* p. 342; Gaddis, "Christian Perfectionism in America," pp. 436-51.

an anti-denominational platform. Hardin Wallace, from Illinois, began somewhat earlier the holiness "Band" movement in rural east Texas. Also S. B. Shaw of Michigan, one of the most respected leaders of the movement, in the early 1880's organized a short-lived sect known as the Primitive Holiness Mission. Adding fuel to the fire was the publication in 1887 of the "textbook of come-outism," *The Divine Church,* by John P. Brooks. Brooks, from Bloomington, Illinois, had been a loyal Methodist and had edited *The Banner of Holiness* for some years. In 1885 he left the Methodist Church denouncing the "easy, indulgent, accommodating, mammonized" kind of Wesleyanism which tolerated church parties, festivals, and dramatic presentations and "erected gorgeous and costly temples to gratify its pride." Threatened with defiant "come-outism," every Methodist Bishop and minister was forced to stand with or against the holiness movement during the last two decades of the nineteenth century.[38]

The primary battleground in the controversy eventually became the South and Middle West where the holiness movement was making its greatest inroads. By 1885 the most radical section of the holiness ranks was being filled by rural Methodists in these two regions. Traveling evangelists, mostly from Kentucky, Iowa, and Texas, began to tour these areas preaching a much more radical brand of holiness than had been heard in the uptown churches during the earlier phases of the movement. Great emphasis was laid on dress and "worldly amusements" by these preachers, who in addition were not averse to denouncing the "coldness" and "formality" of the Methodist Church itself. These preachers succeeded in capturing the holiness associations in some states, thereby further alienating Methodist loyalists. When the Texas Holiness Association became dominated by "come-outers" under Hardin Wallace, loyal Methodist churchmen organized in 1883 the "Northwest Texas Holiness Association" to counteract the "radicalism" of the older group.[39]

The holiness movement in Texas illustrated another development that was highly disturbing to loyal churchmen and to the older leadership of the National Holiness Association. This was the rise of new doctrines that had never before been emphasized in Methodism. Among the "fanat-

---

38. Bucke et al., *History of American Methodism,* vol. 2, p. 619; Smith, *Called Unto Holiness,* pp. 28-33. "Come-outism" meant leaving the Methodist Church in favor of the independent holiness churches.

39. Smith, *Called Unto Holiness,* pp. 30-33.

icisms" and "heresies" taught in Texas were "sinless perfection," freedom from death, "marital purity," a third work following sanctification called "the fire," abstinence from pork or coffee, and that all "doctors, drugs, and devils" are done with when one is sanctified. To older leaders such as Isaiah Reed, founder of the Iowa Holiness Association, these views were "innovations" and never presented as a part of the holiness movement during almost half a century.[40]

The Beginning of the End

The movement to end the controversy by reading the holiness faction out of Methodism began in the Southern church. The prime mover in this development was Atticus Greene Haygood, a Georgia Methodist minister who later became a leading bishop in his church. In July 1885 he was invited to preach at the Oxford District Conference on the subject of sanctification. Haygood chose the topic "Growth in Grace" and in his sermon denied the need for a "second blessing" of instantaneous holiness, calling instead for a gradual attainment of the sanctified state. To him, holiness teaching was a "do-it-yourself" doctrine of salvation. For the next decade Haygood led the wing of Methodism which opposed the holiness faction and which eventually discredited the movement in the Southern church.[41]

Another factor which led to the downfall of the holiness faction in the Southern Methodist Church was the opposition to the doctrine of sanctification expressed in the seminaries of the church. Before the 1880's the seminaries had been sympathetic to the movement, acting as a theological shelter to its advocates. But the picture began to change in 1884 when Wilbur F. Tillett, a theologian at Vanderbilt University, openly

---

40. References to these teachings may be seen in the *Beulah Christian* (Providence, RI), Nov. 1896, p. 2; Jan. 1897, p. 2; Mar. 1898, p. 4; and *Sent of God* (Tabor, IA), Apr. 15, 1897, p. 7; June 3, 1897, p. 8; June 15, 1899, p. 2. See also S. B. Shaw, *Echoes of the General Holiness Assembly* (Chicago, 1901), pp. 325-26; Rose, *A Theology of Christian Experience*, pp. 73-78.

41. Mann, *Atticus Greene Haygood*, pp. 154-61. Holiness people have felt that Haygood did much to end the movement in Southern Methodism. It is often pointed out by believers that Haygood's subsequent alcoholism and humiliation at presiding over an annual conference while inebriated were retributions for his opposition to the holiness movements.

challenged the concept of sanctification as taught by the holiness partisans. Calling all varieties of holiness teaching "semi-pelagian," Tillett felt that the effect of holiness teaching "was to convince Methodists that they could attain salvation through willing it."[42]

After the opening volleys of Tillett and Haygood, Methodist preachers, writers, and teachers throughout the nation joined the fray. In 1888 J. M. Boland published his highly controversial *The Problem of Methodism*, which questioned the "second blessing" and even Wesley's advocacy of it. The editor of the *Southern Methodist Quarterly Review* warmly applauded the volume and called for an end to all doctrine that "recognized a second change." Following this book came others that only added fuel to the fire. George H. Hayes's *The Problem Solved* and James Mudge's *Growth in Holiness Toward Perfection, or Progressive Sanctification* offered further indictments of holiness teachings.[43]

As more and more of the intellectual and ecclesiastical leaders of Methodism questioned the basic premises of the holiness movement, more defenders of the doctrine arose to speak in its behalf. In 1896, Daniel Steele, who had written a holiness classic, *Love Enthroned*, in 1877, pitched into the fray with a book entitled, *A Defense of Christian Perfection*. The Southern church found a staunch defender of the holiness movement in the Reverend Lovick Pierce, whose career as a Methodist minister went back to 1842. In 1897 he published a volume whose title amply fixed his position in the controversy, *A Miscellaneous Essay on Entire Sanctification: How It Was Lost to the Church and How It May and Must Be Regained*. In this work, Pierce lamented that "Methodism was never so nearly divorced from holiness as it is now." He further asserted that "holiness meetings are absolutely ridiculed by some of our people," causing the church to be "turned over to Satan and the world." Later a bruising attack on the intellectuals who had criticized cherished holiness beliefs was delivered by George W. Wilson in his *Methodist Theology vs. Methodist Theologians*, which appeared in 1904. In this volume Wilson declared that "New England Methodism, where much of this new theology is born, is slowly dying." The reason for it, he felt, was "spiritual compromise in

---

42. Mann, *Atticus Greene Haygood*, pp. 161-62.

43. Bucke et al., *History of American Methodism*, vol. 2; Smith, *Called Unto Holiness*, pp. 42-47. See also J. M. Boland, "A Psychological View of Sin and Holiness," *Quarterly Review of the M.E. Church, South* 12 (1892): 339-54, for an intellectual approach to the anti-holiness argument.

urban congregations" where dancing, card playing, and the theater had detracted members from attending revivals.[44]

An example of the bitterness created by the controversy was the famous Pickett-Smith debate of August 1896 in Terrell, Texas. In fourteen turgid debates, the combatants argued five points of doctrine, Pickett defending and Smith denouncing holiness views. Held under holiness auspices and before a holiness audience, Pickett's arguments seem to have prevailed, but not before much strife and bitterness had been engendered.[45]

The Methodist Rejection

As the controversy deepened, defenders of holiness became less loyal to the church, and defenders of the church became less loyal to the doctrine of holiness. By the mid-nineties Methodist officials in the Southern church were assigning "holiness preachers" to "hard-scrabble" circuits to lessen their influence. If a holiness pastor had been fairly successful in indoctrinating a congregation, his successor would be furnished with an "anti-holiness squad" and instructed to correct his predecessor's folly. In 1885 the North Georgia Conference assigned most of the "holiness" preachers to the Gainesville District, thereby hoping to localize the contagion, but the holiness advocates nearly took over the district. A writer to the *Georgia Wesleyan Advocate* complained that year:

> They have changed the name of our meetings, substituting Holiness for Methodist. They preach a different doctrine . . . , they sing different songs; they patronize and circulate a different literature; they have adopted radically different words of worship. . . .[46]

The great turning point in the struggle came in 1894 at the General Conference of the Methodist Episcopal Church, South. With the

44. Bucke et al., *History of American Methodism*, vol. 2, pp. 623-24; Pierce, *A Miscellaneous Essay*, pp. 4-69; Daniel Steele, *A Defense of Christian Perfection* (New York, 1895); George W. Wilson, *Methodist Theology vs. Methodist Theologians* (Cincinnati, 1904).

45. L. L. Pickett, *The Pickett-Smith Debate on Entire Sanctification* (Terrell, TX, 1896), passim.

46. Mann, *Haygood*, pp. 164-65.

Gainesville experience clearly in mind and with Haygood now occupying a Bishop's chair, it was inevitable that the conference would take some action to stem the tide of controversy that threatened to engulf the church. The resulting statement bore a curious resemblance to the statement previously printed in the *Wesleyan Advocate* and was unquestionably a disavowal of the holiness movement and a declaration of open warfare against its proponents:

> But there has sprung up among us a party with holiness as a watchword; they have holiness associations, holiness meetings, holiness preachers, holiness evangelists, and holiness property. Religious experience is represented as if it consists of only two steps, the first step out of condemnation into peace and the next step into Christian perfection. The effect is to disparage the new birth, and all stages of spiritual growth from the blade to the full corn in the ear. . . . We do not question the sincerity and zeal of these brethren; we desire the church to profit by their earnest preaching and godly example; but we deplore their teaching and methods in so far as they claim a monopoly of the experience, practice, and advocacy of holiness, and separate themselves from the body of ministers and disciples.[47]

With this statement a "war of extermination" began that eventually resulted in the creation of scores of new "holiness" denominations throughout the United States. To holiness partisans, the statement of the Southern church fell like a bomb. It simply meant that there was no longer any hope of re-creating the Methodist Church in a holiness image. The loyalists in the holiness movement were now faced with an agonizing decision, whether to stay with the old church or to join the "come-outers" in the new "Bands," churches, and denominations that were now being formed everywhere. When the Southern church adopted "rule 301" in 1898, giving pastors the power to forbid uninvited evangelists to preach in their circuits, Methodist evangelists were henceforth subject to ecclesiastical litigation for holding meetings without the approval of anti-holiness pastors.[48]

---

47. *Journal, General Conference, M.E. Church, South, 1894*, pp. 25, 26. See also Peters, *Christian Perfection and American Methodism*, p. 148; and Sweet, *Methodism in American History*, p. 343.

48. Bucke et al., *History of American Methodism*, vol. 2, pp. 624-25. Rule 301 was the immediate cause of the founding of the Pentecostal Holiness Church.

Holiness Churches Founded

Many of the most committed holiness advocates determined to stay with the Methodist Church in spite of its new policies. In Georgia such holiness stalwarts as Jarrell, Pierce, and Dodge lived and died in their church. But many others felt that it was impossible to remain in the church. An example of the turmoil some experienced is indicated in the title of a volume describing the problems of B. F. Haynes, one-time editor of the *Tennessee Methodist* and President of Asbury College in Kentucky. In *Tempest-Tossed on Methodist Seas,* Haynes described his life as "simply one of protest" in which his "voice and pen have been kept busy in dissent."[49] As far away as California, other Methodists felt that the time had come to break with their church. In Los Angeles Phineas Bresee and Dr. J. P. Widney organized in 1895 the first congregation of the "Church of the Nazarene," destined in time to become the nation's largest holiness church. In Georgia, a young pastor near Royston, J. H. King, felt he could no longer continue as a Methodist in the light of the church's negative attitude toward holiness. In 1898 he made the decision to leave after being "almost forced to separate from the church I loved better than life." The stories of Hayes, Bresee, Widney, and King were repeated by the hundreds throughout the United States.[50]

It is a matter of interest that the holiness movement fragmented into more than a score of denominations in the period from 1895 to 1905, instead of forming one large, unified group. The machinery was already in operation by which all of these groups could easily have been transformed into a national holiness denomination. The National Holiness Association with its great camp meetings and large convocations, although loosely organized, might have served as the vehicle for such a movement. A simple resolution for a constitutional convention could have produced a new united denomination of possibly one million members, if such a program had been desired. Three "General Holiness Assemblies" were held during the period of controversy over the holiness question, any one of which

49. B. F. Haynes, *Tempest-Tossed on Methodist Seas* (Kansas City, 1914), pp. 98-100. See also Smith, *Called Unto Holiness,* pp. 44-45.

50. King and King, *Yet Speaketh,* pp. 77-78; Carl Bangs, *Phineas Bresee: His Life in Methodism, the Holiness Movement and the Church of the Nazarene* (Kansas City, MO, 1995); E. A. Girvin, *P. F. Bresee: A Prince in Israel* (Kansas City, MO, 1916), pp. 23-151; Smith, *Called Unto Holiness,* pp. 91-121.

could have resolved itself into a new denomination. At the Assemblies which met in Jacksonville, Illinois, in 1880, and in Chicago in 1886 and 1901, many delegates asked for such a step, but leaders steadfastly counseled against "come-outism" and directed the delegates to remain loyal to their denominations. This insistence on loyalty, however, caused the movement to fragment, as groups in different annual conferences left the churches piecemeal in disputes over local conditions.[51]

Placing the break from Methodism in its historical setting produces other interesting possibilities. It is a matter of record that the most radical elements in the holiness movement were in the rural South and Midwest and that most of the holiness denominations began in those regions between 1895 and 1900. It is also a matter of record that the agrarian revolt which culminated in populism and the candidacy of William Jennings Bryan in 1896 also occurred in the same regions at roughly the same time. Both the holiness and the populist movements were protests against the Eastern "establishment." In the same period that Tom Watson and Bryan were fulminating against the "banking interests" of Wall Street and the "monopoly powers" of big business, holiness dissenters were preaching livid sermons against the "autocracy" and "ecclesiastical power" of the Methodist "hierarchy." Whether the populist and holiness revolts were triggered by the exigencies of the 1893 financial panic is something for other writers to explore. Nevertheless, it appears that the rise of holiness denominations after 1894 was a religious revolt paralleling the political and economic revolt of populism.[52]

Of the holiness denominations that sprung up after 1894, most originated in the Midwest and the South. The most radical of these groups was the "Fire-Baptized Holiness Church," which began in Iowa in 1895 and was organized into a denomination in South Carolina in 1898. The eight states where this church began were roughly the same areas where the Northwestern and Southern Farmers' alliances were also

---

51. See Rose, *A Theology of Christian Experience,* pp. 69-77; and Shaw, *Echoes of the General Holiness Assembly,* pp. 274-77. For interesting speculations on what might have happened, see Gaddis, "Christian Perfectionism in America," pp. 455-59.

52. See Smith, *Called Unto Holiness,* pp. 27-53; Bucke et al., *History of American Methodism,* vol. 2, pp. 608-27; Peters, *Christian Perfection and American Methodism,* pp. 133-93; Gaddis, "Christian Perfectionism in America," pp. 462-515; Joseph E. Campbell, *The Pentecostal Holiness Church, 1898-1948* (Franklin Springs, GA, 1951), pp. 192-201.

strong: Iowa, Kansas, Texas, Oklahoma, Florida, Georgia, North Carolina, South Carolina, and Virginia.[53]

As the nineteenth century drew to a close, these holiness groups were well on their way toward development as full-fledged denominations. Never before in the history of the nation had so many churches been founded in so short a time. A measure of the intensity of the conflict over sanctification is the fact that twenty-three holiness denominations began in the relatively short period of seven years between 1893 and 1900. One reason for the magnitude of the problem was the fact that during the last decade of the century, the Methodist Church formed the largest body of Protestants in the nation. Any schism within such a large communion was necessarily of great importance. Of the four million Methodists in the United States during the nineties, probably one-third to one-half were committed to the idea of sanctification as a second work of grace. Those who left Methodist churches to form the holiness denominations numbered no more than 100,000 — an indication that loyalty to the church's organization was greater than loyalty to the church's doctrines.[54]

The men who issued the call for the first gathering of the National Holiness Association in 1867 had no idea they were laying the groundwork, inadvertently, for dozens of new denominations. Yet this week spent "in God's great temple of nature" was destined to echo throughout the religious world. The direct result of the holiness crusade of 1867-94 was the formation of the denominational family known as the holiness movement and the still larger group later known as the Pentecostal movement.

53. King and King, *Yet Speaketh*, pp. 85-87. Interviews with surviving ministers of the 1894-1900 era confirm the loyalty of most holiness people to populism and to William Jennings Bryan (interview with Reverend L. R. Graham, Nov. 10, 1966). The following chapters of this work will further document this hypothesis.

54. Gaddis, "Christian Perfectionism in America," p. 570. George P. Fisher, in his *History of the Christian Church* (New York, 1898), p. 581, estimates that in 1887 Methodists in America numbered 4,532,658, while Catholics counted about 4,000,000 and Baptists 3,727,020.

CHAPTER THREE

The Fire-Baptized Way

Christ is our commander, we know no defeat,
We've sounded the trumpet that ne'er calls retreat,
Then onward, right onward at His blest command,
Clear the way, we are coming, the fire-baptized band.

Thurman A. Carey

The last quarter of the nineteenth century was a period of fundamental change in most phases of American life. In the nation's social
and intellectual life, no institution escaped the searching scrutiny of the
critics. In particular, the religious life of America was subjected to heavy
criticism by many writers. The climate of thought prevailing before 1900
was especially unfavorable toward traditional Protestantism, with its
emphasis on individualism and its seeming neglect of the pressing problems of society. Many American writers from 1870 to 1900 engaged in
a concerted attack on what they considered an "outmoded theology."[1]

Among the writers who most deeply questioned traditional American religious concepts were Edward Eggleston, Harold Frederick, and

---

1. Billy Hawkins Gilley, "Social Trends as Reflected in American Fiction,
1870-1901" (unpublished Ph.D. dissertation, University of Georgia, 1966), p. 124.

John W. De Forest. Eggleston, in particular, was critical of his own Methodist Church. In his 1873 novel, The Circuit Rider, Eggleston questioned primitive Methodism, calling it "no longer adequate." Although admitting that it had served a civilizing purpose on the frontier, he felt that "by 1870 primitive Methodism had outlived its usefulness." Reminding contemporary Methodists that their "stern forbears" had often thrown "weak saints" and "obstinate sinners" alike into contortions of "the jerks," he felt that such practices were now "hypocritical and ostentatious." Although originally the reaction of a "sincere people," these demonstrations were, in his view, "actually alienating the masses."[2]

Other writers saw an end to Protestantism as it had been known before the Civil War. In Harold Frederick's *The Damnation of Theron Ware*, Arlo Bates's *The Philistines,* and John W. De Forest's *The Wetherel Affair,* calls were made for an accommodation with the evolutionary theories of Darwin along with a more "rational thought" which would lead to "social salvation."[3] Other observers saw that the Protestant churches had become centers of middle-class thought and values, while the workingmen were going elsewhere. Samuel Loomis said in 1887 that "the Catholic church is emphatically the workingmen's church. She rears her edifices in the midst of the densest populations, provides them with many seats and has the seats well filled." With Protestantism becoming more divided theologically, socially, and intellectually, and with Catholicism rising both in numbers and self-assurance, it was certain that the religious life of the nation would be greatly altered in the twentieth century.[4]

The Social Gospel

Another theological movement arose during the last years of the century that deeply disturbed conservative religious leaders, and in particular those in the holiness ranks. This movement, known as "the Social

2. Edward Eggleston, *The Circuit Rider: A Tale of the Heroic Age* (New York, 1909), pp. 158-59.

3. Arlo Bates, *The Philistines* (Boston, 1888), p. 324.

4. Carl Degler, *Out of Our Past* (New York, 1959), p. 349; Harold Frederick, *The Damnation of Theron Ware* (1896; Cambridge, MA, 1960), pp. 72-137; John W. De Forest, *The Wetherel Affair* (New York, 1873), pp. 52-53. See also Gilley, "Social Trends," pp. 124-50; and Henry F. May, *Protestant Churches in Industrial America* (New York, 1949), pp. 92-93.

Gospel," was the brainchild of Washington Gladden, a Congregational minister from Massachusetts, and Walter Rauschenbusch, a Baptist minister and teacher at Rochester Theological Seminary. Rejecting capitalism and "capitalistic Christianity," they requested a new system which they called "Christian Socialism." Believing that such "social sins" as poverty, irresponsible use of wealth, social ostracism, and unhealthful and indecent living conditions were as bad as individual sins, they called for a "social conversion" of American life. Gladden's *Workingmen and Their Employers* (1876), *Applied Christianity* (1887), and *Tools and Men* (1893) laid the intellectual foundations for the movement. Rauschenbusch, on the other hand, brought the message to the church in his *Christianity and the Social Crisis* (1907), *Christianizing the Social Order* (1912), and *The Theology of the Social Gospel* (1917). This movement deeply affected all the major churches of America, but none as deeply as the Methodist Church, which by 1908 had adopted the "Social Creed of the Churches" along with other members of the newly created Federal Council of Churches.[5]

The fact that the holiness and Pentecostal movements arose during the same period that such intellectual currents as Darwinism, higher criticism, the social gospel, and the ecumenism of the Federal Council of Churches were gaining ascendancy in much of Protestantism, demands an analysis of relationships. It could well be that the holiness ministers who severed their connections with the various denominations felt that they were protesting against these developments within their churches. Writers within the holiness and Pentecostal movement generally cite these currents of thought as the "false doctrines" against which the movements protested. In this sense, the holiness and Pentecostal churches represented a conservative counterweight among the lower classes to the liberal thinking of the upper and middle classes. In leaving the older churches, the holiness people were protesting against these "modernistic" developments and were attempting to keep alive the "old-time religion" which seemed in danger of dying out in American Protestantism.[6]

5. See Sweet, *The Story of Religion in America*, pp. 356-57, 389-90, and *Methodism in American History*, pp. 355-68; Curti, *The Growth of American Thought*, pp. 610-14; and Rauschenbusch, *Christianity and the Social Crisis* (1907; New York, 1964), pp. viii-xx. For an interpretive view of the movement see Carl Degler's *Out of Our Past*, pp. 338-51.

6. For examples of protest thought within the holiness and Pentecostal movements see Redford, *Rise of the Church of the Nazarene*, pp. 1-40; Campbell, *The Pentecostal Holiness Church*, pp. 27-145; Carl Brumback, *Suddenly from Heaven: A History of the Assemblies of God* (Springfield, MO, 1961), pp. 25-31.

The social gospel movement actually owed a great deal to the perfectionist thought that also produced the holiness movement. Gladden in his *Tools and Men* (1893) wrote: "The end of Christianity is two-fold — a perfect man in a perfect society. These purposes are never separated; they cannot be separated. No man can be redeemed and saved alone. . . ." The impulse toward social reform had originally sprung from the pre–Civil War holiness crusade, and the greater part of Christian social service following the war had been carried out by the perfectionistic Salvation Army and its offspring, The Volunteers of America. In a sense the social gospel movement was a logical outcome of the holiness crusade because both groups shared the assumption that people could be perfected. The two movements parted company, however, on the question of the perfectibility of society; the holiness advocates held that society would be perfected only with the second coming of Christ and the institution of the millennium.[7]

Interestingly enough, the very groups that the social gospel advocates wished to help, that is, the poor, the destitute, and the underprivileged, were the very ones who joined the holiness and Pentecostal churches and most bitterly denounced the Gladdens and the Rauschenbusches. In fact, the holiness people taught a negative "social gospel" of their own. Rather than trying to reform society, they rejected it. In the holiness system of values the greatest "social sins" were not poverty, inequality, or unequal distribution of the wealth, but rather the evil effects of the theater, ball games, dancing, lipstick, cigarettes, and liquor. Perhaps the most serious objection to the social gospel from all religious conservatives was the unsettling suspicion that the leaders of this movement would neglect individual salvation altogether and substitute "social works" for "saving grace."[8]

It was against the background of these theological, intellectual, and social changes that the holiness churches completed their separation from traditional Methodism. It is apparent that theological differences over the subject of entire sanctification as a "second blessing" were not the only factor in the breaks that came after 1894. Indeed, the Methodist churches never entirely discarded the doctrine of the "double cure." As

7. See Smith, *Revivalism and Social Reform,* pp. 225-37; Sweet, *Methodism in American History,* p. 357; Timothy Smith, *Called Unto Holiness* (Kansas City, MO, 1962), pp. 200-204.

8. Liston Pope, *Millhands and Preachers* (New Haven, 1946), pp. 117-40, 162-86.

late as 1919 an apologist for Southern Methodism, Hilary T. Hudson, included a section on "holiness or sanctification" in his book *The Methodist Armor* that might have been acceptable to most holiness people, but by then the holiness churches were already well established.[9]

Post-1894 Holiness Churches

Most of the holiness groups began in the decade after 1894, although a few began earlier and some as late as 1917. The majority of these new churches, however, were organized during the four years following the 1894 General Conference of the Southern Methodist Church. Of the twenty or more major holiness groups that began during this period, only four would later become Pentecostal — all of them in the South. The first of the postwar holiness churches was the "Church of God" with headquarters in Anderson, Indiana. Led by Daniel S. Warner, this group began in 1880 as a secession from the Winebrenner Church of God, a Methodist-like German body. In 1887 the Christian and Missionary Alliance was established in New York by A. B. Simpson, who emphasized foreign missions and divine healing as well as sanctification. These two churches were not fully products of the National Holiness Movement, having had their beginnings in the period before the doctrine of sanctification became controversial.[10]

The two largest holiness denominations that resulted from the National Holiness Movement, the Church of the Nazarene and the Pilgrim Holiness Church, were both the results of a complicated series of mergers of widely separated holiness groups. The Church of the Nazarene emerged in 1914 as a merger of the following groups: the "People's Evangelical Church," which began in New England in 1887;

9. Hilary T. Hudson, *The Methodist Armor or a Popular Exposition of the Doctrines, Peculiar Usages and Ecclesiastical Machinery of the Methodist Episcopal Church, South* (Nashville, 1919), pp. 108-11. On page 109 sanctification is presented as a work commencing *"in* and carried on *after* conversion. It is a *second* blessing, in harmony *with*, yet separate *from*, and subsequent *to*, the work of conversion." For an account of the continuation of the holiness movement within Methodism through the 1940s see Rose, *A Theology of Christian Experience*, pp. 76-270.

10. For accounts of the backgrounds of these groups see Elmer T. Clark's *Small Sects in America* (New York, 1949), pp. 76-81; and F. E. Mayer's *Religious Bodies of America* (St. Louis, 1961), pp. 313, 339.

the "Pentecostal Churches of America," beginning in Brooklyn, New York, in 1894; the "New Testament Church of Christ," founded at Milan, Tennessee, in 1894; the "Church of the Nazarene," started in Los Angeles, California, in 1895; the "Pentecostal Mission," which began in Nashville, Tennessee, in 1898; and the "Independent Holiness Church," organized in 1900 in Texas. In 1908, most of these bodies were merged into one national denomination at Pilot Point, Texas, with the name "The Pentecostal Church of the Nazarene."[11]

The Pilgrim Holiness Church began in 1897 in Cincinnati, Ohio, under the leadership of the Reverend Martin W. Knapp, a Methodist minister. Originally called the "International Apostolic Holiness Union," this church took its name in 1922 after mergers with the "Holiness Christian Church" of Pennsylvania, the "Pentecostal Rescue Mission" of New York, and the "Pilgrim Church" of California. Later accessions made the church somewhat larger after 1922.[12]

In addition to the Church of the Nazarene and the Pilgrim Holiness Church, there were dozens of smaller groups that fragmented from Methodism and other denominations during the 1890's and after, but because of their small size and lack of significant growth they played minor roles in the holiness and later Pentecostal movements. With interesting variations of doctrine, government, and worship, these groups continued their existence under such names as "The Missionary Bands of the World," "The Church of Daniel's Band," the "Burning Bush," the "Hepzibah Faith Missionary Association," and "The Pillar of Fire."[13]

---

11. The most scholarly history of the Church of the Nazarene is Timothy Smith, *Called Unto Holiness*. Other histories are J. B. Chapman, *A History of the Church of the Nazarene* (Kansas City, 1926), and Redford, *The Rise of the Church of the Nazarene* (Kansas City, 1951). In 1919 the "Pentecostal Church of the Nazarene" dropped the word "Pentecostal" to distinguish itself from the tongue-speaking "Pentecostal movement," which began in 1906. Since that time it has been known as the "Church of the Nazarene."

12. Clark, *Small Sects in America*, p. 76; Gaddis, "Christian Perfectionism in America," pp. 509-14.

13. Information about these groups may be found in Clark, *Small Sects in America*; F. E. Mayer, *The Religious Bodies of America* (St. Louis, 1961); and Benson I. Landis, *Yearbook of American Churches* (New York, 1966).

Pentecostal Sanctification

In the decade of the 1890's, a major shift began to appear among many holiness leaders emphasizing the "Pentecostal" aspects of the second blessing. This led to a change in terminology which could be called "Pentecostal sanctification." One of the leaders in this development was Henry C. Morrison of Asbury College, who in 1897 dropped the name "Methodist" from his magazine and renamed it the *Pentecostal Herald*. In the same year, the *Guide to Holiness* added to its name the words *"and Pentecostal Life"* in response to the "signs of the times" which indicated that "the Pentecostal idea" was "pervading Christian thought and aspiration more than ever before."[14]

Another leader in this change was R. C. Horner, a Canadian holiness evangelist who in the early 1890's founded a radical movement that later produced at least three Canadian holiness denominations. In several books, Horner pointed out that second blessing sanctification, as taught by John Wesley, did not include a "baptism in the Holy Spirit" as generally understood by the Methodist-holiness movement at large. In his 1891 book, *Pentecost,* Horner taught that the baptism in the Holy Spirit was in reality a *"third work"* of grace subsequent to salvation and sanctification which empowered the believer for service. This view was elaborated in his two volume work *Bible Doctrines* which appeared in 1909.[15]

Also prominent in Horner's meetings were such "physical manifestations" as "prostration," "ecstasy," and "immediate laughter," which led to his being separated from the Methodist church. The most far-reaching effect of Horner's teaching was to separate in time and purpose the experiences of second-blessing sanctification and the "third blessing" of "baptism in the Holy Spirit," a theological distinction that became crucial to the development of Pentecostalism.

Under the influence of Horner and others, several extremely legalistic and emotionally demonstrative holiness denominations arose during this period that became a part of the later Pentecostal movement. In much the same way that populist politics underwent its most convulsive

14. This shift is documented in Donald Dayton's *Theological Roots of Pentecostalism* (Grand Rapids, MI, 1987), pp. 87-113.
15. See Dayton, *Theological Roots of Pentecostalism,* pp. 91-100, and Charles Jones, *A Guide to the Study of the Holiness Movement* (Metuchen, NJ, 1974), pp. 283-86.

phase in the South and Middle West, the holiness movement had its most turbulent experience in the same areas.

Benjamin Hardin Irwin

One of the most radical of the holiness denominations that issued from the National Holiness Association movement was the "Fire-Baptized Holiness Church," which had its beginnings in Iowa in 1895. It was perhaps inevitable that a new church should come from Iowa, since the state had been a major holiness stronghold for at least two decades. Organized in 1879 by Isaiah Reed, the "Iowa Holiness Association" became the first such organization west of the Mississippi River. By the 1890's it had spread into the neighboring states of Missouri and Nebraska. By the late 1890's the Iowa Association had grown to encompass a larger enrollment of ministers and laymen than had the rest of the National Association. Many of the more radical doctrines that later influenced the rise of Pentecostalism had their beginnings in Iowa.[16]

The founder of the Fire-Baptized Holiness Church was Benjamin Hardin Irwin of Lincoln, Nebraska, a member of the Iowa Holiness Association. Born and reared in Mercer County, Missouri, Irwin was educated for the law profession. After some years of mediocre practice, he was converted in a Baptist church and later forsook law to enter the Baptist ministry. As an ordained minister, Irwin came into contact with holiness teachings by ministers of the Iowa Association, which at that time embraced his home city of Lincoln. Seeking and receiving the experience of sanctification in 1891, Irwin became a devout advocate of holiness doctrine and experience. Being a studious young man, he began to study the Scriptures and the writings of John Wesley and his colleague John Fletcher. In his own words, he soon became a "John Wesley Methodist," and in time joined the Wesleyan Methodist Church.[17]

Out of the vast amount of Methodist and holiness theological literature, Irwin was most influenced by the writings of Fletcher, who seemed to teach an experience following sanctification called a "baptism of burning love." More often the terminology "baptism with the Holy

16. Rose, *A Theology of Christian Experience,* pp. 74, 75; Campbell, *The Pentecostal Holiness Church,* pp. 192-95.
17. Irwin, "The Whole Armour," *Live Coals,* Mar. 9, 1900, p. 5.

Ghost and fire" was used. Fletcher also taught that one could receive several "baptisms," if such were needed. In his *Checks to Antinomianism,* Fletcher called for the sanctified to "enter the full dispensation of the Spirit" until they lived "in the pentecostal glory of the church . . . baptized with the Holy Ghost. . . ." In other passages he spoke of those who were "baptized with fire" and thereby "endued with power from on high." These and other statements led Irwin to conclude that there was a third experience beyond sanctification called "the baptism with the Holy Ghost and fire" or simply "the fire."[18]

Having already been sanctified, Irwin began to seek the "baptism of fire" for himself. In October, 1895 in the city of Enid, Oklahoma, he received an experience in which he felt to be "literally on fire" and where 'the walls of the room seemed to be on fire." In his florid language Irwin described the experience as "a luminous seven-fold light" in which "everything about me seemed to be on fire — actually burning, blazing, glowing." Afterward he began to preach this "third experience" among the holiness people of the Middle West, especially in Wesleyan Methodist and Brethren in Christ circles. His services soon began to draw large crowds, a special attraction being the renewed exhibition of the emotional phenomena that had characterized the Cane Ridge revivals earlier in the century. Those receiving "the fire" would often shout, scream, speak in other tongues, fall into trances, receive the holy dance and holy laugh, and even get the "jerks." Vivid testimonies soon appeared describing the fiery experiences of Irwin's followers. One description indicated the ethos of the movement:

> Some said they felt the fire burning in their souls, but others claimed it as burning in their bodies also. It was felt in the tongue, in the fingers, in the palm of the hand, in the feet, in the side, in the arms, and so on. Then the Bible itself often felt warm to those who had the fire in them. The church would seem to be lighted with fire, the trees of the wood would appear as flames of fire, the landscape would seem to be baptized in the glory of the fire. As one rode from one appointment to another, according to their testimonies, they seemed to be enveloped with the holy fire. The noise of the engine seemed to sound notes of

18. John Fletcher, *The Works of the Reverend John Fletcher* (New York, 1851), vol. 2, pp. 356, 632-69; vol. 4, pp. 230-32; J. H. King, "History of the Fire-Baptized Holiness Church," *The Pentecostal Holiness Advocate,* Mar. 24, 1921, p. 4; Campbell, *The Pentecostal Holiness Church,* pp. 194-95.

praise to God, and the clatter of the wheels beneath the cars seemed to be saying, *Glory to God, hallelujah!* The coaches themselves were fire-lighted, and the wheels beneath seemed to be wheels of fire. Fire! Fire! Holy Fire!!! was the ring of their testimonies.[19]

For several years beginning in the early 1890's Irwin's teaching became the talk of the holiness movement. His doctrine also gained currency in the many holiness periodicals to which he contributed. The people of the South first met his doctrine in the monthly *Way of Faith,* a holiness paper published in Columbia, South Carolina which strongly favored Irwin's movement. A regular contributor to this paper, Irwin often advertised his booklet *Baptism of Fire* for two cents a copy.[20]

Although many thousands attended Irwin's meetings and professed to receive the "baptism of fire," the greater part of the holiness movement rejected his message. The holiness people had always taught that the "second blessing" of sanctification was also the "baptism with the Holy Spirit" and that both were aspects of the same experience. The older "loyalist" wing of the holiness movement, made up of such stalwarts as Isaiah Reed and S. B. Shaw, denounced the doctrine as "the third blessing heresy" and forbade its being preached in their churches and camp meetings. Despite this opposition, the "Fire-Baptized" movement continued to grow, especially in the rural areas of the Middle West and South.[21]

The fire-baptized apostle Irwin continued to preach with such fervor and success that the entire holiness movement became familiar with his doctrine. In time the opposition of Reed and the well-organized Iowa Holiness Association caused him to form his own separate group. Finally in 1895 Irwin formed the "Iowa Fire-Baptized Holiness Associa-

19. G. F. Taylor, *The Pentecostal Holiness Advocate,* May 22, 1930, p. 8. See also Vinson Synan, *The Old-Time Power: A History of the Pentecostal Holiness Church* (Franklin Springs, GA, 1973), pp. 81-102.

20. B. H. Irwin, "The Baptism of Fire," *Way of Faith,* Nov. 13, 1895, p. 2. See also *The Way of Faith,* Apr. 15, 1896, p. 4. This paper was the outstanding holiness periodical in the South, and later played a leading part in reporting the Pentecostal outbreak in California. For a local North Carolina view of these events see Eddie Morris, *The Vine and the Branches* (Franklin Springs, GA, 1981), pp. 5-26.

21. For denunciations of Irwin see Shaw, *Echoes of the General Holiness Assembly,* p. 106, and several articles in the *Beulah Christian* (Providence, RI): "Fanaticism," Nov. 1896, p. 2; "New Theories," Jan. 1897, p. 2; and "Sanctification and Fire," Mar. 1898, p. 4. See also "Fanaticism," *Sent of God* (Tabor, IA), June 15, 1899, p. 2.

tion" at Olmitz, Iowa to propagate the doctrine in holiness ranks. With this Iowa Association as a base, Irwin traveled over the nation preaching his fiery gospel and organizing state associations wherever he went.[22]

Irwin also organized in 1895 "Fire-Baptized Holiness Associations" in Kansas, Oklahoma, and Texas. Everywhere people fell "under the power" and came out claiming the experience of "the fire." The South received the message in a series of revivals that Irwin held from 1896 through 1898. The first Southern city to hear him was Piedmont, South Carolina, where in December 1896 services were held in the Wesleyan Methodist Church. It was reported that he "struck the South in cyclone fashion." Even stalwart holiness advocates felt that his services were "on the wild order," but this was no deterrent. He continued his canvass of the South, organizing Fire-Baptized Associations wherever he went. During 1897 he preached in Royston, Georgia; Williston, Florida; and Abbottsburg, North Carolina. As a result of these efforts, Fire-Baptized Holiness Associations were formed in Florida, Georgia, South Carolina, North Carolina, and Virginia. In addition to these associations, others were formed during the same year in the Canadian provinces of Ontario and Manitoba. Although an unorganized group of loyal followers in Tennessee promoted the fire-baptized doctrines in the state's eastern mountain regions, efforts of other groups to organize associations in Pennsylvania and Ohio were unsuccessful..[23]

The Fire-Baptized Holiness Church

By mid-1898 definite state and provincial organizations had been formed in Iowa, Kansas, Texas, Oklahoma, South Carolina, North Carolina, Georgia, Florida, Virginia, Ontario, and Manitoba. In each association Irwin had appointed an "overseer" to conduct the affairs of the group, while he took for himself the title "General Overseer." With such a rapidly growing organization behind him, Irwin then decided to organize a central governing authority. Consequently, from July 28 to August 28,

22. Campbell, *The Pentecostal Holiness Church*, p. 197.
23. King, "History of the Fire-Baptized Holiness Church," Mar. 31, 1921, pp. 10-11. More recent histories include Synan, *The Old-Time Power*, pp. 81-101; and Douglas Beacham, *A Brief History of the Pentecostal Holiness Church* (Franklin Springs, GA, 1983), pp. 43-49.

1898, a national convention was held in Anderson, South Carolina, where a *Discipline* was adopted along with other general rules for the infant denomination. Irwin was named General Overseer for life and various other offices were created and filled. The fact that Irwin could license and ordain ministers and assign them to churches illustrates the ecclesiastical nature of the union. It was in every respect a new denomination.[24]

Attending the 1898 Anderson organizational meeting was Joseph H. King, a Methodist pastor from Royston, Georgia, who cast his lot with the new church. Also joining the movement at this time was an African-American minister from South Carolina, William E. Fuller from Moundsville, South Carolina, who was elected to the general board of the denomination. Fuller, who had defected from the African Methodist Church (AME) to follow Irwin, became overseer of the black churches that were formed, most of them resulting from his own efforts. The church continued to be interracial until 1908, when the black churches, reflecting the growing trend toward segregation, separated with the blessings of the whites to form their own group under Fuller's leadership.[25]

Soon after the Anderson conference, Irwin was able to raise enough money to purchase a printing plant with which to issue a periodical for the new group. The new press was set up adjacent to his residence in Lincoln, Nebraska, and in October 1899 the first issue of *Live Coals of Fire* appeared. With Irwin as editor, and a Canadian, A. E. Robinson, as printing assistant, the paper was distributed throughout the United States. It was the first publication in America that taught that the baptism of the Holy Ghost and fire was subsequent to the experience of sanctification. As such, it was quite influential in producing the climate of thought and doctrinal interpretation that produced the Pentecostal movement a few years later. Although the Fire-Baptized movement did not teach that speaking with other tongues was the initial evidence of

---

24. King, "History," p. 11; see also King and King, *Yet Speaketh*, pp. 77-87; Campbell, *The Pentecostal Holiness Church*, pp. 198-201; and *Constitution and General Rules of the Fire-Baptized Holiness Church* (Royston, GA, 1905), pp. 2-4.

25. For Fuller's testimony see *Live Coals of Fire*, Jan. 26, 1900, p. 1. By 1900 Fuller had organized fifty black churches and conducted a convention of his black fire-baptized followers. Issues of *Live Coals of Fire* listed several ministers as "colored" during the 1890s. See *Live Coals*, Oct. 6, 1899, p. 1; Nov. 3, 1899, p. 1; and Dec. 1, 1899, p. 2.

receiving the baptism with the Holy Spirit, this phenomenon was not unknown among those who received "the fire."[26]

Also in the year of 1899, Irwin took steps to develop a national headquarters in the town of Beniah, Tennessee, a tiny village on a railroad line about nine miles north of Cleveland, Tennessee. On donated land, Irwin made plans to establish a "school of the prophets" and "missionary training school" from which he planned to spread the fire-baptized movement around the world. With the support of "Ruling Elder," Daniel Awrey, who lived in Beniah, Irwin organized a Tennessee Fire-Baptized Holiness Convention and made plans to move all his operations to Tennessee. Other fire-baptized evangelists, William Martin, Joe Tipton, and Milton McNabb, joined with Awrey in the effort to make Beniah a center of holy fire.[27]

The Fire-Baptized Church might have consolidated a large element of the holiness movement if Irwin had exercised more foresight in his leadership of the new church. Its mushrooming growth indicated a wide acceptance of his views among holiness people, even those within the Methodist Church. *Live Coals of Fire* carried reports of extraordinary meetings and successes, colored with references of the blood and thunder variety. One writer reported in an early issue that "the fire is still spreading. People may oppose us, preachers may preach against the experience, and devils may howl, but we have come to stay to preach blood and fire till Jesus comes."[28] Irwin and his followers had little patience with denominational holiness leaders who criticized his meetings. In 1900 he denounced Georgia Wesleyans who he charged with being "twice dead,

26. An interested observer of Irwin's meetings was Charles Parham, the patriarch of the Pentecostal movement, who was repelled by the noise and emotion of the meetings but was impressed by Irwin's "third blessing" doctrine. See *The Apostolic Faith*, Apr. 25, 1925, pp. 9-14, for Parham's views of Irwin's meetings. Prominent fire-baptized people who spoke in tongues before 1906 were Miss Agnes Ozman in Kansas and Mrs. Sarah A. Smith of Camp Creek, North Carolina. See John Nichols, *Pentecostalism* (New York, 1966), p. 104; Clyde S. Bailey, *Pioneer Marvels of Faith* (Morristown, TN, n.d.), p. 20; and Campbell, *The Pentecostal Holiness Church*, pp. 208-9. For Irwin's influence on Parham, see James Goff, *Fields White Unto Harvest: Charles Fox Parham and the Missionary Origins of Pentecostalism* (Fayetteville, AR, 1988), pp. 54-57, 194.

27. See B. H. Irwin, "The School of the Prophets," *Live Coals of Fire*, Jan. 12, 1900, p. 1. Martin, Tipton, and McNabb were later to gain fame as founding evangelists of the Church of God, which developed in nearby Cleveland, Tennessee.

28. Thurman A. Carey, quoted in *Live Coals of Fire*, Apr. 4, 1906, p. 2.

plucked up by the roots, and utterly without the Spirit." These he called "hog eating, nicotine professors of holiness, chewing, smoking, snuffing, and smelling like a hog on a dung hill, filthy, depraved and nasty. Yet they were in good standing in the church."[29]

Several developments between 1898 and 1900 prevented the Fire-Baptized movement from developing into the national church that it promised to become. One was the inclusion of additional doctrines that frightened even "radical" holiness people away. Taking Fletcher's premise that many "effusions" or "baptisms" might be necessary to perfect the experience of Christian believers, Irwin began to teach that there were additional "baptisms of fire." These he named the baptisms of "dynamite," "lyddite," and "oxidite." By early 1900 the Fire-Baptized faithful were being taught not only a "third blessing" but also a fourth, a fifth, and even a sixth. This "chemical jargon" never took root within the movement and was later rejected by King and other leaders when Irwin left the church. But for a time the movement was pervaded by what some called a "pathetic pursuit of this religious rainbow's end."[30]

Around the nation Holiness journals roundly rejected "Irwinism" with his many "baptisms." The Iowa Holiness Association where Irwin had started was severely divided over the fire-baptized movement, with most pastors, evangelists, and periodicals denouncing the movement. Some holiness periodicals not only rejected Irwin's many baptisms, but lampooned his followers in no uncertain terms. An outspoken critic was A. M. Hills, who wrote to the *Holiness Advocate* about a woman who claimed no less than six experiences:

> August 1st, 1898, I was pardoned of my sins. On the following Sunday at eleven o'clock, *God sanctified me wholly.* A few days later I received the Comforter. Later in October, God gave me the Baptism of fire. The devil and all the hosts of hell cannot make me doubt this. When my sister Mattie was married, I fell into a trance and saw a vision. During services a night or so afterwards, God showed me that I needed more power for service, so I made my wants known, and prayer being

29. This example of Irwin's colorful rhetoric is found in *Live Coals of Fire,* Jan. 26, 1900, p. 1.
30. Charles R. Conn, *Like a Mighty Army, Moves the Church of God* (Cleveland, TN, 1955), p. 43; Campbell, *The Pentecostal Holiness Church,* p. 204. The vast majority of holiness people rejected these "experiences" as Irwin taught them because they were not found to be taught in the scriptures.

offered, my faith took hold of God's promises, and I received the *Dynamite*. A few nights after this I received the *definite experience of lyddite*. This gives the devil trouble, and he wonders what is coming next. Well, I am in for all that God has for me.

In the words of Hill, who described the testimony as "fanaticism," this poor soul should have sought for and received one more blessing, "the baptism of common sense."[31]

The influence of this explosive terminology continued to be felt, however, long after the doctrine was rejected by the body as a whole. In 1904 Fuller wrote to the *Live Coals of Fire* reporting that he was "still on this blood, fire and dynamite line...." He further praised God for "the blood that cleans up, the Holy Ghost that fills up, the fire that burns up, and the dynamite that blows up." Such vivid preaching characterizes the African-American branch of the church to this day.[32]

In addition to the "dynamite heresy," Irwin taught many other doctrines that were later rejected by the movement. Like all other holiness churches, the Fire-Baptized Church opposed extravagance of dress and the wearing of "needless ornamentation" by women members. This emphasis was as old as John Wesley and was generally accepted by the National Holiness Movement. Indeed the puritanical temper of the late Victorian age was nowhere observed more strictly than in holiness circles. Irwin, however, carried this belief to its logical conclusion and placed male members under the same restrictions as women. It thus became a sin for a man to wear a necktie; Irwin and his preachers declared that they would "rather have a rattlesnake around their necks than a tie." Irwin also taught that it was a sin to eat hog meat, catfish, oysters, or anything forbidden by the dietary laws of the Old Testament.[33]

Irwin's Failure

A blow that almost destroyed the young church came in late 1899 when it was discovered that Irwin, the founder of the church, was living a life

31. Synan, *The Old Time Power,* p. 93.
32. *Live Coals of Fire,* Jan. 11, 1904, p. 2.
33. G. F. Taylor, "Our Church History," *The Pentecostal Holiness Advocate,* Feb. 3, 1921, p. 9.

that more resembled an apostate than an apostle. In Omaha, Nebraska in the spring of 1900 he confessed to "open and gross sin" which brought "great reproach" to the church. Loyal members of the movement were shocked and saddened at this development. When his disgrace was known, Irwin resigned as Overseer of the church and his place was taken by King, the thirty-one-year-old Georgian, who, with "a heavy heart," traveled to Olmitz, Iowa, in June 1900 to conduct the second "General Council" of the denomination. On June 5th, King was formally elected to succeed Irwin as "General Overseer" and as editor of *Live Coals of Fire*, and he later moved to Iowa to conduct the affairs of the badly shaken denomination. Irwin's defection caused much havoc within the church he had founded. Since several of the state associations ceased to function, the youthful King faced the task of holding the infant church together in the discouraging years that followed.[34]

The Fire-Baptized Holiness Church served as an important link in the chain that later produced the modern Pentecostal movement. By teaching that the baptism of the Holy Ghost was an experience separate from and subsequent to sanctification, it laid the basic doctrinal premise of the later movement. It is probable that Charles F. Parham, the man who initiated the Pentecostal revival in Topeka, Kansas, in 1901, received from Irwin the basic idea of a separate baptism of the Holy Ghost following sanctification. Indeed, for a time in 1899, Parham promoted the "baptism of fire" in his *Apostolic Faith* magazine. In a social, doctrinal, and intellectual sense, the Fire-Baptized Holiness Church was a direct precursor of the modern Pentecostal movement in North America.[35]

Throughout the 1890's and early 1900's several other holiness groups were formed, with the doctrine of entire sanctification as their major tenet. All of them owed their doctrine to Methodism, although not all of them were Methodists. Almost everywhere new churches were

34. King, "History," p. 10; Campbell, *The Pentecostal Holiness Church*, pp. 200-201; King and King, *Yet Speaketh*, pp. 102-6. See also King's earlier work, which is his first published autobiography, *From Passover to Pentecost* (Memphis, 1914), pp. 163-67. The Fire-Baptized Holiness Church later merged with The Pentecostal Holiness Church in 1911 and took the name of the latter group. Organized as a national church in 1898, it is the oldest denomination that later became part of the Pentecostal movement.

35. For other evaluations of Irwin's fire-baptized movement and its relation to the Pentecostal movement see Kendrick, *The Promise Fulfilled*, p. 33; Brumback, *Suddenly from Heaven*, p. 9; and Campbell, *The Pentecostal Holiness Church*, p. 195.

organized as "holiness" preachers traversed the countryside, preaching in schoolhouses, tents, abandoned churches, and under "brush arbors." Many of these new churches, often numbering no more than fifteen to thirty members, were to become mother congregations of groups that eventually developed into major denominations. Indeed, it would seem that most preachers who "came out" of their denominations during this time inevitably made holiness doctrines the hallmark of their creeds.[36]

Sanctified Presbyterians

The holiness movement of the late 1890's was not entirely rural or Methodist, as many have assumed, but included significant urban groups also. Some of these groups were inaugurated by Presbyterian ministers who adopted the theology of the holiness movement. Two Southern ones were the Brewerton Presbyterian Church of Greenville, South Carolina, and the Pentecostal Mission of Nashville, Tennessee. The former was organized as a result of the preaching of the Reverend N. J. Holmes, pastor of Greenville's Second Presbyterian Church. Holmes had studied law at the University of Edinburgh and had been a prominent lawyer in South Carolina before entering the Presbyterian ministry. After preaching for some years in various Presbyterian Churches, he heard of Dwight L. Moody's emphasis on sanctification and became interested in the doctrine. After a long talk with Moody on a trip to Massachusetts, Holmes sought for and obtained the experience of sanctification in 1896. Because of his new emphasis on entire sanctification, he was tried by his presbytery and forced to withdraw from the church. He later joined the Brewerton Presbyterian Church, founded in 1899 by other holiness-minded Presbyterians, who had amended the "longer" and "shorter" Presbyterian catechisms to include the doctrine of sanctification as a "second blessing."[37]

---

36. The group of churches known as the "Churches of God" will be treated in the next chapter because of their importance to southern Pentecostalism as a whole.

37. N. J. Holmes, *Life Sketches and Sermons* (Franklin Springs, GA, 1920), pp. 7-97. See also Iva Thomas, *The History of Holmes Theological Seminary* (Franklin Springs, GA, n.d.), pp. 2-9; *The Voice of Holmes*, May 1948, pp. 2-3; Campbell, *The Pentecostal Holiness Church*, pp. 263, 423-32.

Having always felt an urge to teach theology to young people planning to enter the ministry, Holmes inaugurated a Bible institute near Greenville in November of 1898. As early as 1893 he had conducted short Bible courses at a cottage on Paris Mountain near Greenville. The first name of the young school was the "Altamont Bible and Missionary Institute," and it was Wesleyan in doctrine. After many changes in name and location, the school was permanently located in Greenville, South Carolina, and was eventually renamed "The Holmes Theological Seminary." From its earliest days, Holmes's school maintained ties with the Fire-Baptized Holiness Church and the later Pentecostal Holiness Church. Although Holmes questioned Irwin's idea of a "baptism of fire," he later joined the Pentecostal movement, bringing his school with him. With a continuous history dating back to 1898, Holmes eventually could claim to be the oldest Pentecostal school in the world.[38]

Another Presbyterian who joined the ranks of the holiness movement was the Reverend J. O. McClurkan of Nashville, Tennessee. Of the Cumberland Presbyterian persuasion, McClurkan started the "Pentecostal Mission" in 1898 in Nashville after hearing revivalist Sam Jones praise the holiness people in a city-wide campaign the previous year, asserting that he had "never seen a holiness man that wasn't a prohibitionist from his hat to his heels."[39]

Also contributing to McClurkan's interest in the doctrine was the appearance in 1897 of Presbyterian evangelist J. Wilbur Chapman's book, *The Surrendered Life.* The "Pentecostal Mission" became the center for several holiness-minded ministers, including John T. Benson, later prominent as a publisher, and B. F. Haynes, former editor of the Tennessee Methodist. Due to McClurkan's Calvinistic background, the theology of the "Pentecostal Mission" was closer to the Oberlin theology of Charles G. Finney than the National Holiness Movement. For many years this group endeavored to unite all the holiness factions in the Southeast and at one time allied itself with A. B. Simpson's Christian and Missionary Alliance. Holmes attended the conventions of this group as an observer until 1907 when his defection to the Pentecostal movement closed the doors of fellowship with most other holiness people.[40]

---

38. Holmes, *Life Sketches and Sermons,* pp. 93-149. According to notes found in his Bible, Holmes received the "baptism of fire" on one occasion but later repudiated it.
39. Smith, *Called Unto Holiness,* p. 181.
40. Holmes, *Life Sketches and Sermons,* p. 152.

McClurkan's "Pentecostal Mission" was in many ways more radical than the National Holiness Movement. From its beginning it taught the doctrine of divine healing "as in the atonement," the "premillennial second coming of Christ," and a view of sanctification which emphasized the indwelling of the Holy Spirit rather than the cleansing aspect of the doctrine. Rejecting the Pentecostal doctrine of speaking with tongues as evidence of receiving the Holy Spirit, the Pentecostal Mission eventually merged with the Church of the Nazarene in 1915 and became the major strength of that denomination in the Southeast. This group is the only major holiness group in the South that did not later enter the Pentecostal movement.[41]

A. B. Crumpler and the Pentecostal Holiness Church

Another holiness church that was destined to play a major role in the Pentecostal movement was the Pentecostal Holiness Church, which began in North Carolina. The founder of this group was a Methodist minister from Sampson County, North Carolina, the Reverend A. B. Crumpler, who in the 1880's had moved to Missouri where he came into contact with holiness teachings. In 1890, at a District Conference of the Methodist Church, he was sanctified under the preaching of Beverly Carradine, a leading preacher in the National Holiness Movement. Returning to North Carolina after 1890, Crumpler began to preach sanctification in the Methodist churches of his native state. By 1897 an outbreak of interest in the doctrine caused by Crumpler's preaching led him to organize the "North Carolina Holiness Association." Becoming quite active in holiness circles, he also contributed articles and reports of his meetings to J. M. Pike's *Way of Faith* magazine in Columbia, South Carolina, and to George Watson's *Living Words,* published in Pittsburgh, Pennsylvania. At the height of the 1896 holiness revival, Crumpler preached to thousands in churches, tents, and arbors all over the state. In only one week of services he reported 80 souls "converted" and 125 "wholly sanctified," with the movement "sweeping this country."[42]

41. Smith, *Called Unto Holiness,* pp. 180-204; Redford, *Rise of the Church of the Nazarene,* pp. 40-60.
42. *The Way of Faith,* Apr. 15, 1896, p. 5; *Living Words,* Apr. 1903, p. 16; June 1903, p. 16.

Since the Southern Methodist Church had declared war on the holiness movement at the 1894 General Conference, Crumpler ran into trouble with his superiors in the church. In October 1899 the North Carolina Annual Conference tried him for insubordination for refusing to stop preaching the doctrine of sanctification after being enjoined from doing so by his ecclesiastical superior, a violation of "Rule 301" which had been adopted by the Methodist Episcopal Church, South in 1898. Crumpler thereupon withdrew from the church "for the sake of peace and harmony," feeling that he had been tried for "preaching the glorious doctrine of Methodism."[43]

Following his separation from the Methodist Church, Crumpler continued to preach throughout the eastern part of North Carolina, bringing great controversies to the Methodist churches of that area. Adding to the conflict was a paper he began to publish in 1900 called *The Holiness Advocate.* Since the large number of people that had been sanctified in his meetings felt unwelcome in their Methodist churches, he also formed a new church for them. Meeting in the spring of 1900 in Fayetteville, North Carolina, Crumpler and a few other former Methodist ministers formed a new denomination which they named "The Pentecostal Holiness Church." The reasons for creating this new church were stated by Crumpler: "That those who had been saved and sanctified, many of whom belonged to no church, and many of whom had been turned out of their churches for professing holiness, might have a congenial church home." Before leaving Fayetteville, Crumpler framed a *Discipline* for the new denomination and made plans to organize new churches as soon as possible. Before the end of 1900 churches had been organized in Antioch, Goldsboro, and Magnolia, with prospects for several more in other communities.[44]

Crumpler's Pentecostal Holiness Church was quite similar to all the other holiness groups that had been founded during the last quarter of the century. Its statement of faith contained all the usual Wesleyan language regarding "entire sanctification as a second definite work of grace." Other holiness doctrines were also spelled out which marked this

43. G. F. Taylor, "Our Church History," Jan. 20, 1921, p. 9; Campbell, *The Pentecostal Holiness Church,* pp. 217-20.

44. G. F. Taylor, "Our Church History," Feb. 17, 1921, pp. 8-10; Campbell, *The Pentecostal Holiness Church,* pp. 221-32; *Discipline of the Pentecostal Holiness Church* (Franklin Springs, GA, 1961), pp. 5-6; *The Holiness Advocate,* July 15, 1904, pp. 4-5.

group as a part of the "radical" wing of the holiness movement. Divine healing and premillennialism also received a prominent place, as did strictures against "worldliness," "oyster stews," "needless ornamentation," and "tobacco."[45]

In 1901 the group changed its name to "The Holiness Church," dropping the name "Pentecostal." This step was taken because many members were using the term "Pentecostal church" to identify themselves, rather than the more "reproachful" term "Holiness Church." This name continued to be used until 1909, after the church had changed its articles of faith in 1908 to make it officially a part of the Pentecostal movement. The adjective "Pentecostal" was then restored to the name.[46]

Free Will Baptists

Also developing in North Carolina was one of the few Baptist groups in the nation to accept the Wesleyan doctrine of holiness. The Free-Will Baptist Church, which had beginnings in New England in the eighteenth century, reached the state in 1855. In that year the Stony Run Free-Will Baptist Church was organized and with it the denomination's Cape Fear Conference. Originally an Arminian reaction to the stern Calvinism of New England Protestantism, the Free-Will Baptists from the beginning accepted the basic premises of Methodism.[47]

It was not until the height of the holiness crusade of the 1880's that this group adopted a strictly Wesleyan perfectionist creed. The 1883 Discipline stated that sanctification "commences at regeneration" and continues with one "constantly growing in grace," a language that seemed influenced by Finney's Oberlin views of holiness. The statement in the Discipline of 1889, however, was given a much more Wesleyan tone, showing the influence of the National Holiness Movement. Sanctification in this issue was described as "an instantaneous work of God's grace in a believer's heart whereby the heart is cleansed from all sin and made

45. See *Discipline of the Pentecostal Holiness Church* (1902), pp. 9-18.
46. Campbell, *The Pentecostal Holiness Church*, pp. 234, 251. The *Discipline* (1961) states that the word "Pentecostal" was dropped because they did not speak with other tongues as on the day of Pentecost (Acts 2:4), but this seems to be a later interpolation. See p. 6.
47. *Discipline of the Pentecostal Free-Will Baptist Church* (Dunn, NC, n.d.), pp. 8-9.

pure by the blood of Christ." With their 1899 statement, the Free-Will Baptists of North Carolina followed the trend of perfectionist thinking that was permeating other denominations outside the Methodist fold. After 1906 the group also followed the trend among southern holiness churches in adopting the Pentecostal view of the baptism of the Holy Spirit. In 1912 a division occurred within the Cape Fear Conference resulting in the formation of the "Pentecostal Free-Will Baptist Church," which immediately dissociated itself from the main body of the denomination.[48]

The United Holy Church

Another North Carolina holiness denomination that began in this period was the "United Holy Church" with origins in the town of Method, North Carolina, not far from Raleigh. During a revival there in 1886 at an African-American Baptist church, the doctrine of sanctification was preached. Church officials saw the doctrine as contrary to Baptist theology and practice, and after the revival closed the holiness faction was asked to leave the church. The small group of dissidents organized a church which became the nucleus of a small holiness denomination. Other groups in other parts of North Carolina joined the small church at various times between 1886 and 1902, when a formal organization was effected.[49]

The leader in the organizational meeting, W. H. Fulford, was an Elder in Irwin's Fire-Baptized Holiness Church. The denomination's first president was Elder C. M. Mason of Wilmington, North Carolina. Because of its doctrinal position, the new denomination adopted the name "The United Holy Church of America." In 1903 Elder Fulford was elected President, and served in this capacity until 1916 when Elder H. L. Fisher was chosen to lead the group. The United Holy Church developed as an independent black holiness denomination that spread widely over the South. Under the influence of related holiness churches

48. *Discipline of the Pentecostal Free-Will Baptist Church*, p. 10.
49. H. L. Fisher, *History of the United Holy Church of America* (n.p., n.d.), pp. 1-7. A scholarly account of the United Holy Church beginnings is found in Chester W. Gregory's *The History of the United Holy Church of America, Inc., 1886-1986* (Baltimore, 1986); see pp. 30-46.

this denomination followed other southern holiness groups into the Pentecostal movement after the turn of the century.[50]

Throughout the South hundreds of local independent holiness congregations formed during this period but never expanded beyond their local areas. Many others were formed in community-shaking revivals and then quietly died due to subsequent indifference or acute persecution. Most of the Southern holiness churches, as pointed out earlier, belonged to the more "radical" wing of the holiness movement, emphasizing such new doctrines as divine healing, the premillennial second coming of Christ, a "third blessing" of "the fire," and puritanical dress codes.

Although some of the holiness churches of the South, such as McClurkan's Tennessee-based "Pentecostal Mission," joined the more conservative groups such as the Church of the Nazarene and the Wesleyan Methodist Church, most of them followed the midwestern and southern trend toward the radicalism of the times. A long-run result of this trend was that the greater part of the southern holiness movement was predisposed to accept the even more radical doctrines of the Pentecostal movement when it began in 1906.

The conservative holiness denominations, which included the Church of the Nazarene, the Pilgrim Holiness Church, the Wesleyan Methodist Church, the Christian and Missionary Alliance, and the Free Methodist Church, ultimately accounted for only a small proportion of the holiness population in the southern states. It was perhaps typical of the times that when Irwin first held meetings in South Carolina and Georgia, the Wesleyan Methodist Churches that invited him soon disbanded and became Fire-Baptized Holiness Churches. Indeed many of the older churches of today's Pentecostal-holiness movement began their existence as Wesleyan Methodist Churches.[51]

One of the most far-reaching manifestations of holiness religion occurred among the people who adopted variations of the name "Church of God." Because of their importance they will be considered in detail in the next chapter, but it should be remembered that they developed

---

50. Fisher, *History of the United Holy Church of America*, p. 8.

51. An interesting example is the Beulah Church near Elberton, Georgia, which was organized in 1896 as a Wesleyan Methodist Church but reorganized as a Pentecostal Holiness Church in 1911. See *The Minutes of the Beulah Pentecostal Holiness Church* (Franklin Springs, GA, 1896-1956), pp. 1-16.

in the same context as the Fire-Baptized Holiness Church, the Pentecostal Holiness Church, and the others discussed in this chapter. These groups, along with all the others, were a result of the holiness crusade of 1867-1900 and were destined to become Pentecostal after 1906.

In the end it was the more radical "Fire-Baptized Way" that prevailed among the holiness people of the South and Midwest, rather than the more conservative Nazarene concept of sanctification. The "third blessing heresy" of Irwin's church was destined to become the orthodox position of the southern holiness/Pentecostal groups, with the single addition of speaking in tongues as the evidence of baptism by the Holy Ghost. By the time this doctrine swept over the holiness movement in 1906, the Southern segment of the movement was psychologically and doctrinally prepared to accept it as an integral part of their beliefs.

CHAPTER FOUR

The Churches of God

Like a mighty army, moves the Church of God;
Brothers, we are treading where the saints have trod.
We are not divided, all one body we,
One in hope and doctrine, one in charity.

Sabine Baring-Gould

As the holiness movement fragmented from the older denominations throughout the United States, new sects sprang into being in every region of the nation. As noted earlier, many of these groups used the term "holiness" in their names, while others preferred the word "Pentecostal." No other name, however, became as popular as "the Church of God." Between 1880 and 1923 no less than two hundred groups adopted some version of this name to designate their churches. Out of this number, perhaps a score could be classed as major groups.[1] The first holiness body to call itself "The Church of God" was D. S. Warner's church, which began

---

1. Frank S. Mead, *Handbook of Denominations in the United States* (New York, 1965), p. 74; Clark, *Small Sects in America*, pp. 102-5; Mayer, *Religious Bodies of America*, pp. 331-38. There are so many independent groups with this name that a full investigation and classification would be impossible. They range from "The (Orig-

68

in 1880 in Anderson, Indiana. The body represented a split from the older "Winebrenner Church of God" which had churches in the Northeast and Midwest. Three years later a man named A. M. Kiergan organized the "Church of God (Holiness)," protesting official Methodist pressure against the holiness associations of the South and Midwest.[2] These and several other less significant groups formed sects using the name "Church of God" before the period of sect formation began in earnest shortly after 1894. In general, groups that formed before 1894 belonged to the holiness persuasion and would not identify with the Pentecostal movement after 1906; those beginning after 1894 became Pentecostal later.

The greatest sect-forming period in the South was 1894-98, following the anti-holiness policy statement of the General Conference of the Southern Methodist Church. In widely scattered places outbreaks of holiness preaching produced new churches calling themselves "Church of God." The only connecting link between them was the doctrine of entire sanctification, a teaching that caused great excitement in communities where it was first preached. The cause of the excitement— some of it took the form of opposition — was the holiness doctrine, implicit or otherwise, that a person could live entirely without sin.

The Church of God–Mountain Assembly

In 1895 the doctrine of sanctification was introduced to McCreary County, Kentucky, with the preaching of J. H. Parks, a United Baptist pastor. This new doctrine, as Parks preached it, claimed the attention of three other Baptist pastors in the area: Steve Bryant, Tom Moses, and William Douglas. All of these ministers were affiliated with the local South Union Baptist Association of the United Baptist Church. From 1895 to 1903 they preached the most un-Calvinistic doctrine of holiness, winning many converts. The rise of this "heresy" among their preachers and churches gave great concern to the leaders of the Baptist Association. Finally, in 1903 the association held

---

inal) Church of God" to the "Runaway Church of God," and endorse a wide variety of doctrines and practices. Most of the earlier groups chose the name without knowledge of the other groups' existence. In most cases it was chosen because it was a "Bible name," being mentioned several times in the New Testament.

2. Mayer, *Religious Bodies,* pp. 331-32; Harold Paul, "The Religious Frontier in Oklahoma" (unpublished Ph.D. dissertation, University of Oklahoma, 1965), pp. 19-20.

a full-session trial and Parks and his followers were expelled from the denomination, their credentials as ministers revoked. The charge against them was that they taught that "men could be lost after regeneration," a serious heresy to these predestinarian Baptists. After the trial five Baptist churches left the denomination in sympathy with the holiness leaders.[3]

By 1906 these five churches met in a "General Assembly" at the "Jellico Creek Church" in Whitley County, Kentucky, and organized a new denomination named "The Church of God." Several years later this small group of holiness people, isolated in the Kentucky mountains, were told that other denominations were using the same name. Accordingly, in 1911 they added the words "Mountain Assembly" to distinguish their group from the others.[4]

The Church of God in Christ

The year 1895 also saw the beginning of another holiness group, which eventually emerged as the largest African-American Pentecostal denomination in the nation, the "Church of God in Christ." The founders of this group were Elders C. H. Mason and C. P. Jones, ministers of missionary Baptist churches in Mississippi. Mason, the dominant personality of the two, had been licensed as a Baptist minister in 1893. Later that year he had entered Arkansas Baptist College to further prepare himself for the ministry, but left after three months because he felt "there was no salvation in schools or colleges."[5]

Two years later Mason and Jones traveled to Lexington, Mississippi, where they came in contact with the holiness doctrine of entire sanctification. The two men accepted the doctrine and began vigorously to preach it in the Baptist churches of the area. They were soon ejected from their Baptist Association for preaching and claiming to have received the experience. These churchless preachers then held a "holiness"

3. Luther Gibson, *History of the Church of God, Mountain Assembly* (n.p., 1954), pp. 4-5.
4. Gibson, *History of the Church of God, Mountain Assembly*, p. 8.
5. The best history of the church is Ithiel Clemmons, *Bishop C. H. Mason and the Roots of the Church of God in Christ* (Bakersfield, CA, 1996); see pp. 1-20. See also C. A. Ashworth, *Yearbook of the Church of God in Christ* (Memphis, 1961), p. 9; Kendrick, *The Promise Fulfilled*, p. 197.

revival in February 1897 in a cotton gin house in Lexington, Mississippi. The revival became the organizational meeting for a new denomination called "The Church of God in Christ," a designation Mason had previously settled on while walking down a street in Little Rock, Arkansas. In late 1897, in Memphis, Tennessee, the new church was incorporated as a chartered denomination.[6]

This church was the first southern holiness denomination to become legally chartered, a source of great advantage to the group. Ordained ministers of Mason's church could now be legally bonded to perform marriages, and could also claim clergy rates on the railroads. As a result, many white ministers of independent holiness congregations received ordination from Mason, making his organization interracial. The church's interracial character became even more pronounced after the Pentecostal revival of 1906, when scores of white ministers joined Mason's church.[7]

Like many of the holiness and Pentecostal bodies, the Church of God in Christ owed its existence to a strong and dominating founder. Mason stamped his personality on his church far more emphatically than any other holiness leader. Called by his followers a "Greater than the Apostle Paul," Mason outlived all the other founders of major holiness sects and during his lifetime saw his group become the largest black Pentecostal church in the world and the largest Pentecostal denomination in the United States.[8]

The Church of God (Cleveland, Tennessee)

The year following the separation of the Church of God in Christ saw the beginnings of another group in the mountains of Tennessee and

6. Clemmons, *Bishop C. H. Mason*, pp. 20-39. See also *The Evangelist Speaks*, Nov. and Dec. 1966, p. 1. *The Whole Truth* is the national paper of the denomination. See also U.S. Bureau of the Census, *Religious Bodies*, 1926, vol. 2, pp. 380-81. An early biography of Mason is Mary Mason's *The History and Life Work of Bishop C. H. Mason, Chief Apostle, and His Co-Laborers* (Memphis, 1934); see pp. 1-12.
7. *The International Outlook* (Los Angeles), Jan.-Mar. 1963, p. 4.
8. Mason died in 1963 at the age of 97 and was buried in his massive (10,000 seats) "Mason's Temple" in Memphis, Tennessee, the first such burial allowed in the history of the city. The street where his temple is located was renamed "Mason Street" in his honor. See the 1966 *Official Convocation Program* (Memphis, 1966), p. 61.

North Carolina, an organization destined to make the term "Church of God" a household word in the South. In 1896 the doctrine of entire sanctification reached the hill folk of western North Carolina when three men from east Tennessee came over the mountains and held a revival in the Schearer Schoolhouse in Cherokee County. These three, William Martin, Joe M. Tipton, and Milton McNabb, were evangelists who had left local Methodist and Baptist Churches in the Coker Creek Community near the North Carolina border to join the fire-baptized movement led by B. H. Irwin. Revival fires were burning throughout the Carolinas in 1896, as Irwin and Carradine preached in South Carolina and Crumpler spread the holiness flame in eastern North Carolina. Tipton and Martin had been in contact with the fire-baptized movement, which had made an abortive attempt at organizing a state association in Tennessee. Centering their efforts in east Tennessee, near the Coker Creek home of Mrs. Sarah A. Smith, the fire-baptized doctrine spread throughout the countryside. The revival that began in the Schearer Schoolhouse in 1896 formed the nucleus of what later became the Church of God of Cleveland, Tennessee.[9]

An unusual feature of this revival was the fact that several of those who received sanctification reportedly spoke in other tongues when they "prayed through." This manifestation, which seemed strange to the mountain folk, caused great excitement in the community. The Baptist and Methodist pastors in the locality soon denounced the new revival. As the tongues-speaking spread, even children experienced the phenomenon. Because of these demonstrations heavy persecution broke out against the people engaged in the meeting. Before the revival ended, several houses were burned as mobs led by "leading Methodist and Baptist members, " including a justice of the peace and the local sheriff, ransacked and pillaged the homes of worshippers. After a provisional meeting house was burned, the band of worshippers moved to the home of one W. F. Bryant, who assumed leadership of the group.[10]

---

9. L. Howard Juillerat, ed., *Book of Minutes, General Assemblies, Churches of God* (Cleveland, TN, 1922), pp. 7-14; Charles W. Conn, *Like a Mighty Army, Moves the Church of God* (Cleveland, TN, 1955), pp. 16-18; S. Clyde Bailey, *Pioneer Marvels of Faith* (Morristown, TN, n.d.), p. 20. W. B. Martin and Joe Tipton were listed by Irwin as "Evangelists" of the fire-baptized movement who had "done faithful work in this region" before 1899. See *Live Coals of Fire*, Oct. 20, 1899, p. 1.

10. Juillerat, *Book of Minutes*, pp. 11-12.

For the next six years the band of people that had gathered in the revival of 1896 worshipped as an unorganized band of holiness believers. From time to time they were visited by an itinerant Baptist preacher from Tennessee, R. G. Spurling, Jr., who in 1892 had been expelled from his church near Turtletown, Tennessee, for teaching the doctrine of sanctification to the folk in the Liberty Baptist Association. Spurling also preached the need of a "new reformation" in Christianity comparable to the Protestant Reformation of the sixteenth century. These ideas had come from his father, R. G. Spurling, Sr., a "Landmark" Baptist preacher who had gone so far as to organize a band of like-minded followers into a "Christian Union" in 1886 in Monroe County, Tennessee. The Junior Spurling had joined this group, although the group later disbanded for lack of interest, and the members returned to their former churches. Spurling, however, kept alive his desire for reformation, and when the holiness revival began in Cherokee County, he became one of the favorite speakers that Bryant invited to address the group.[11]

The doctrines that Bryant and Spurling preached to the small band of believers who met in the Camp Creek community were similar to those taught in the holiness movement at large. The more radical doctrines of divine healing, the baptism of fire, and the second advent of Christ gained easy acceptance. The central doctrine was entire sanctification, along with a complete rejection of society. But all was not well with this small unorganized band. Irwin's idea of the baptisms of "dynamite," "lyddite," and "oxidite" swept the community, exciting its more emotional members and repelling its most thoughtful. In addition, the typical fire-baptized prohibitions were imposed, against medicines, meats, candies, and neckties. Some members engaged in prolonged fasts until they became gaunt and weak. On top of this, in 1900 Irwin chose the town of Beniah, Tennessee as the national headquarters of his Fire-Baptized Holiness movement and opened a "School of the Prophets." The threat of these Irwinite "fanaticisms" led Pastor Bryant to conclude that a form of government was necessary if the group was going to survive.[12]

11. Conn, *Like a Mighty Army*, pp. 7-16; Juillerat, *Book of Minutes*, p. 13; Homer Tomlinson, ed., *The Diary of A. J. Tomlinson* (New York, 1949), vol. 1, pp. 52-53. Baptist influences on Spurling are examined in Wade Phillips's "Richard Spurling and the Baptist Roots of the Church of God" (paper presented to the Society for Pentecostal Studies, Nov. 1993, Guadalajara, Mexico).

12. E. L. Simmons, *History of the Church of God* (Cleveland, TN, 1938), pp. 11-12; Conn, *Like a Mighty Army*, pp. 39-40. See Irwin's "The School of the Prophets,"

In order to curb these perceived evils, Bryant decided to form an organization that would confer the authority to discipline erring members. Accordingly, on May 15, 1902, the first local church was organized, which was to become the nucleus of the Church of God. The name chosen for the new body was "The Holiness Church at Camp Creek." Bryant was ordained into the ministry and the itinerant Spurling chosen as pastor. Thus almost unwittingly the denomination which was to become one of the world's largest Pentecostal churches came into being.[13] In 1903 another itinerant preacher, A. J. Tomlinson, would make another memorable mark in the history of the Camp Creek church. Tomlinson, who by virtue of his organizational talents was destined to dominate the infant church and spread it throughout the nation, was a mystical Quaker from Indiana. A restless wanderer, he had sold Bibles and tracts from Maine to Georgia as a colporteur for the American Bible Society, and had been an interested observer during the 1896 holiness revival at Camp Creek. Later on, he had settled in Culbertson, North Carolina, near the Georgia border. A deeply religious man, he had already received the experience of sanctification before reaching North Carolina. After settling in Culbertson, he began an orphanage on a farm he had bought and began publication of a religious monthly paper he called *Samson's Foxes*.[14]

Live Coals of Fire, Jan. 12, 1900, p. 1. See also Harold Hunter, "Beniah at the Apostolic Crossroads," a paper presented at the Society for Pentecostal Studies, Wycliffe College, Toronto, 1996 (also available at http://members.gnn.com/Archives/pctii.htm). Mickey Crew's *The Church of God: A Social History* (Knoxville, 1993) seems to have missed the fire-baptized influences on the early years of the Church of God movement.

13. Juillerat, *Book of Minutes*, p. 13; *The Church of God Evangel*, Apr. 7, 1945, pp. 3-15; Conn, *Like a Mighty Army*, pp. 44-45. The Camp Creek church seems to have been the first continuous congregation of the several branches of the Church of God with headquarters in Cleveland, Tennessee. Some controversy exists as to whether the modern Pentecostal movement originated with this group, which had antecedents going back to 1886. For various viewpoints see Conn, *Like a Mighty Army*, pp. xix-xxii; Carl Brumback, *Suddenly from Heaven* (Springfield, MO, 1961), p. 57; Vinson Synan, *Emmanuel College — The First Fifty Years* (Washington, DC, 1968), p. 4; Nils Bloch-Hoell, *The Pentecostal Movement* (Oslo, Norway, 1964), p. 18.

14. A. J. Tomlinson, "A Journal of Happenings" (manuscript version of Tomlinson's *Diary* at the Church of God headquarters in Cleveland), pp. 1-10; Lillie Duggar, *A. J. Tomlinson* (Cleveland, TN, 1964), pp. 17-33. Several versions of Tomlinson's *Diary* exist, including the three-volume one published by Homer Tomlinson from 1949 to 1955 (New York, Church of God World Headquarters). References used here are from the manuscript entitled "Journal of Happenings."

Not satisfied with his membership in the Society of Friends, Tomlinson attended religious services wherever he traveled. Although not an ordained minister, he was often called on to preach. In 1901, on a trip to Shiloh, Maine, he had been baptized by a Mr. Frank Sandford in the Androscogin River. The name of the church he joined was called "The Church of the Living God for the Evangelization of the World, Gathering of Israel, New Order of Things at the Close of the Gentile Age," and some of Sandford's teachings were to influence Tomlinson's later views on eschatology.[15] The members of the Camp Creek church had known Tomlinson for seven years when in 1903 they asked him to join the group. Often he had been invited to preach for them, and in time he came to be regarded as more highly educated than Bryant or Spurling. The decision to join was a difficult one for Tomlinson. Before the day he was supposed to join, he went to the top of a nearby hill called Burger Mountain to pray over his decision. Here, on what his followers now call "prayer mountain," Tomlinson "prevailed in prayer" and received a vision of "the Church of God of the last days." According to his revelation:

> Jesus had started the Church of God when He was here on earth, and a record was kept of its progress and activities for several years after the death of its founder. The period of history known as the Dark Ages had come after the Church of God had departed from the faith and the church was lost to view.[16]

Now Tomlinson had discovered the "True Church of God" at Camp Creek, and accordingly joined the small group the next day, June 13, 1903, with the understanding "that it is the Church of God of the Bible." With the accession of this traveling Bible salesman from Indiana, the struggling little group of mountain people gained a gifted preacher and organizer who, more than any other individual, was responsible for the phenomenal growth of the church into a national church today.[17]

The local reputation of Tomlinson as a deep Bible student and

15. A. J. Tomlinson, *Answering the Call of God* (Cleveland, TN, n.d.), pp. 1-15; Tomlinson, "Journal of Happenings," p. 12.

16. *The Evening Light and Church of God Evangel*, Mar. 1, 1910, p. 1; Duggar, *A. J. Tomlinson*, p. 34.

17. Tomlinson, *Answering the Call of God*, p. 17; "Journal of Happenings," p. 17; Duggar, *A. J. Tomlinson*, p. 35.

well-traveled agent for the American Bible Society led the Camp Creek congregation to elect him immediately as pastor of their church. Spurling and Bryant then departed from Camp Creek to evangelize other mountain communities. Within three years the Camp Creek preachers had established congregations in three other communities, two in Tennessee and one in Georgia. In 1904, Tomlinson was chosen as pastor of three of the four congregations — Union Grove and Luskville in Tennessee, and Camp Creek in North Carolina. The other church, at Jones, Georgia, met in a private home and was soon abandoned.[18]

The Hoosier minister traversed the countryside preaching in his three churches and at many other points. As he preached, the ideas that were to shape the Church of God movement and eventually to divide it, came into sharper focus. To Tomlinson the group he was associated with was the only true and valid Christian communion "this side of the Dark Ages." In the early church "the full blaze of light beamed forth from the Pentecostal chamber and shined forth with radiant glory in the early morning of the Gospel day." Then intervened the long period of apostasy known as the "dark ages" when the church was dormant and backslidden. Now that the true church had been rediscovered in the mountains of North Carolina, "the evening light, the true light is now shining, and the sheep are hearing His voice and are coming from every place where they have been scattered during the cloudy and dark day." In order to prepare the world for the second coming of Christ and the end of the age, the Church of God was destined to reap "the precious fruit of the earth" before it was too late. Eventually the faithful Christians of all denominations in every nation of the world would return to the true church and the Lord would set up his kingdom, beginning at Burger Mountain and ending in Jerusalem.[19]

This apocalyptic view of the mission of the church was at once a source of strength and weakness for the movement. To those who accepted the message, there was only one true church, all others being part of the

---

18. Tomlinson, "Journal of Happenings," passim, entries from 1903-6; Juillerat, *Book of Minutes,* pp. 13-14.

19. A. J. Tomlinson, *The Evening Light and Church of God Evangel,* Mar. 1, 1910, p. 1; Homer Tomlinson, *The Shout of a King* (New York, 1965), pp. 14-20. This exclusivist view continued with little modification until 1937 when it began to moderate and eventually disappear in official church documents. See the *Church of God Evangel,* Jan. 17, 1914, pp. 1-3; July 3, 1915, pp. 1-4; Apr. 1, 1916, p. 1; May 13, 1916, p. 1; June 30, 1934, p. 5; Aug. 14, 1937, pp. 3-14.

"dark ages" of apostasy. This idea bred an exclusivism which bound the members to the church with a tenacious loyalty. But it also created a strong urge to bring others into the true "Church of God" fold, thereby producing a competition for the members of other holiness churches.

The preaching of Tomlinson, Spurling, and Bryant also produced the emotional reactions that had been so familiar in frontier American revivalism. In meetings in Tennessee, Georgia, and North Carolina, Tomlinson reported that the Spirit worked in many ways, with many saints "shouting, weeping, clapping their hands, jerking, and hand shaking." He reported that once, at the Union Grove church, people "fell on the floor, and some writhed like serpents," while others "seemed to be off in a trance for four or five hours." In all of this the preacher felt that the "church seemed to be greatly edified." In most services some claimed to be converted and others sanctified. These demonstrations attracted large crowds wherever Tomlinson preached; reports of his early services put the numbers at five to seven hundred.[20]

The First General Assembly

With surprisingly little opposition from the community, the four churches made great progress under Tomlinson's leadership. By the end of 1905, it was felt that a general meeting of the four churches should be held to better organize the work of the groups. Accordingly a "General Assembly" was convened at the Camp Creek church in January of 1906 to organize a new denomination. Rather than meet in the church house, the Assembly decided to meet in the home of a church member, one J. C. Murphy, because of its convenience and size. Delegates from the four churches met there on January 26 and 27 and conducted the short and simple business of the group. As pastor of the home church, Tomlinson acted as "ruling elder" and secretary and gave direction to the Assembly. It debated such subjects as "feet washing," tobacco, family worship, and the Sunday school. It was decided that feet washing was an ordinance on the same level as the sacrament of communion. Like

20. Tomlinson, "A Journal of Happenings," pp. 21-23. In view of later claims that the Church of God was "the world's oldest Pentecostal church," it is interesting that Tomlinson's journal failed to record a single case of speaking in tongues in his meetings until after the Azusa Street revival of 1906-9.

most other holiness groups, the Assembly adopted a strong statement condemning the use of tobacco, and also approved resolutions supporting family worship and the establishment of Sunday schools. As the work of the Assembly concluded, the twenty-one participants engaged in a sacramental foot-washing service.[21]

The delegates to this Assembly disclaimed the idea that they were establishing a new denomination. The first resolution declared that "we do not consider ourselves a legislative or executive body but judicial only." At the end of the meeting, Secretary Tomlinson wrote on the margin of the minutes:

> We hope and trust that no person or body of people will ever use these minutes, or any part of them, as articles of faith upon which to establish a sect or denomination. The subjects were discussed merely to obtain light and understanding. Our articles of faith are inspired and given us by the holy apostles and written in the New Testament which is our only rule of faith and practice.[22]

Despite the denial of any sect-forming motives, the work of the Assembly inevitably led to the development of a separate denomination. Although Tomlinson had traveled widely and was well aware of the existence of other holiness denominations, he made no effort to affiliate his group with any of them. This body of worshippers thus was and continues to remain a *sui generis* religious group.

The Second General Assembly of the new movement convened at the Union Grove church in Bradley County, Tennessee, in 1907, and made some far-reaching decisions. At that time the nascent organization did not have a name; the local congregations called themselves simply "holiness churches." The problem of anonymity was solved when the delegates voted "harmoniously" to designate the new denomination "Church of God," citing New Testament usage as their authority. The action seems to have been taken without any reference to other churches already using the name.[23]

---

21. Juillerat, *Book of Minutes*, pp. 15-19; Duggar, *A. J. Tomlinson*, p. 39; Conn, *Like a Mighty Army*, pp. 61-69. An excellent study of early Church of God piety is Mickey Crew's *The Church of God: A Social History*; see pp. 1-37.

22. Simmons, *History of the Church of God*, p. 16; Conn, *Like a Mighty Army*, p. 303.

23. Juillerat, *Book of Minutes*, p. 22. The scriptures cited were I Corinthians 1:2 and II Corinthians 1:1.

Another problem the Second General Assembly faced was the form of church government to adopt. Some favored the congregational system for the selection of pastors; others called for appointment by a higher church authority, as in the episcopal system. The decision was a compromise which in reality paved the way for a strong episcopal government: "sometimes the church calls, sometimes sent by those having the responsibility and authority." In time the Church of God developed the most centralized government of all the holiness or Pentecostal denominations in America.[24]

With the closing of the Second General Assembly, the Church of God had become a fully developed, if yet small, denomination. It was also very much a product of the National Holiness Movement, though rather isolated from the other groups across the nation. The vitality of the new church was seen in the great growth that followed the 1902 organization of the Camp Creek church. At that time the body had only 20 members in one church, but by 1910 there were 1,005 members in 31 churches scattered throughout the Southeast. In that year also the church began its first official publication, named *The Evening Light and Church of God Evangel.* By 1911 the number of churches had grown to 58; the phenomenal growth had begun. With its numerous subsequent branches, the Church of God would eventually become one of the largest Pentecostal church bodies in the United States.[25]

The choice of Tomlinson as the first "General Overseer" of the denomination was a fateful one. With his Indiana accent and background as a Bible salesman, he seemed the obvious choice to lead the infant church. Ironically, the most southern of all the Pentecostal denominations counted as their organizer and greatest propagator a northerner, a man who had originally viewed the poverty-stricken South as little more than a mission field. Associated with Tomlinson in the early days of the Church of God movement was his eldest son Homer, who was to gain fame as both presidential candidate of the "Theocratic Party" and self-proclaimed "King of the World." Indeed, before the twentieth century had reached the halfway mark the Tomlinson family could claim the

---

24. Juillerat, *Book of Minutes,* p. 23.

25. Juillerat, *Book of Minutes,* pp. 37-41. In 1911 the name of the paper was changed to *The Church of God Evangel,* the oldest continuous publication in the Pentecostal world.

distinction of organizing three denominations, each calling itself the "Church of God."[26]

In later years Homer Tomlinson was to claim that the entire holiness and Pentecostal movements stemmed directly or indirectly from the work of A. J. Tomlinson. This, of course, represented a distortion of the facts, since the Church of God movement developed in relative isolation from the National Holiness Movement. The theological and organizational foundations of the holiness movements were laid much earlier in the National Holiness Association under Inskip and his successors, and the basic premises for Pentecostalism were laid by Irwin's fire-baptized movement well before Tomlinson joined the holiness church at Camp Creek.[27]

Other Churches of God

In addition to these bodies, many other groups adopted the name "Church of God." Among them were: The (Original) Church of God, The Bible Church of God, The Remnant Church of God, The Justified Church of God, The Holstein Church of God, the Glorified Church of God, the Church of God, Inc., and The Church of God (Apostolic). Practically all of them were holiness groups of the more radical type and identified themselves with the Pentecostal movement after 1906.[28]

By 1906 most of the major holiness bodies in the nation had been formed and were in the process of building denominations. Little thought was given to mergers, as most groups were relatively isolated from each

---

26. A. J. Tomlinson organized "The Church of God" (Cleveland, TN) in 1906, and later "The Church of God of Prophecy" in 1932, to which his younger son Milton became heir after the father's death in 1943. Disgruntled, Homer then founded the "Church of God World Headquarters" with offices in Queens, New York.

27. See Homer Tomlinson, ed., *Diary of A. J. Tomlinson*, vol. 1, pp. 5-13, and *The Shout of a King*, pp. 1-20. Unfortunately, Homer Tomlinson's many unfounded claims found their way into such otherwise reputable works as Elmer T. Clark's *Small Sects in America* (New York, 1949), pp. 100-107. More recent and reliable scholarship accords Tomlinson a very important place in the early Pentecostal movement, but finds the doctrinal origins of the movement elsewhere. See Klaud Kendrick, *The Promise Fulfilled* (Springfield, MO, 1961), pp. 32-68.

28. See Mayer, *Religious Bodies*, pp. 336-37.

other. When the Church of God in Kentucky heard of the Tennessee group, an attempt was made at a merger, but the attempt inevitably failed when the Kentucky group refused to submit to Tomlinson's authority.[29]

The Holiness Code

The body of holiness doctrine had become well established in these new movements by the first decade of the century. In general all of the groups were basically Arminian in their theology and Wesleyan in their view of sanctification. In addition to these premises, which might be considered "orthodox" for the National Holiness Movement, the Southern groups had added several more radical views which set them apart. The "Baptism of Fire" was perhaps the most radical departure from the accepted views of the holiness movement. Yet time had added many more rules and doctrines that were to make the Southern holiness bodies unique. At one General Assembly of the Church of God it was decided that Coca Cola, chewing gum, rings, bracelets, and earbobs were sinful and therefore prohibited to members of the church.[30] Furthermore, the Pentecostal Holiness Church held that it was sinful for a member to wear a necktie or attend a county fair. Most of the groups also denounced lodges, political parties, and labor unions as "instruments of Satan." Buying life insurance was frowned upon as an indication of lack of faith in God. Divine healing was taught in such a way that it was almost placed on a level with the new birth. The prevailing view was that physical healing for the body was provided "in the atonement" along with salvation for the soul. Medicines were widely believed to be "poisons" dispensed by doctors to the faithless. Hence persons who took medicines or visited doctors were considered weak or even completely lost.[31]

The movement was not without its apostates and critics. Because of the emotional aspects of most holiness services the epithet "holy rollers" was applied to most of the people who joined them. This term, similar in its origin to "Quaker," "Shaker," and "Methodist," was never

---

29. Gibson, *Church of God, Mountain Assembly,* p. 10.

30. Juillerat, *Book of Minutes,* pp. 125-27.

31. Juillerat, *Book of Minutes,* pp. 25, 125, 176-77; Campbell, *The Pentecostal Holiness Church,* pp. 203-5; Crews, *Church of God: A Social History,* pp. 38-67.

accepted by any branch of the holiness movement.[32] More serious was the criticism leveled by ministers and theologians of other denominations. Perhaps the most damaging broadside was the volume of criticism by H. A. Ironside entitled *Holiness, The False and the True*, which appeared in 1912. The holiness churches were described by Ironside as hotbeds of "pharisaism," "tattling," "selfishness," and even frequent immorality. Speaking as a former member of the Salvation Army, Ironside's book was taken by many critics to discredit the entire movement, becoming a veritable textbook of anti-holiness theology.[33]

Alexander Dowie

Other critics pointed to the antics of Alexander Dowie, the balding Australian who brought his divine healing services to Chicago in the 1890's. He gained his greatest fame at the 1893 Chicago World's Fair, where his healing services vied with Buffalo Bill's show for popular acclaim. In 1895 Dowie organized his followers into the "Christian Catholic Church" with headquarters in Chicago. In 1900, north of Chicago, Dowie founded a community he named Zion City, a place where "doctors, drugs, and devils were not allowed." The centerpiece of the town was a wooden tabernacle with seating for 8,000 persons. In its heyday, thousands of Chicagoans could ride the train to Zion City for the all-day Sunday services. From his Illinois headquarters, Dowie sent missionaries around the globe; many of them founded thriving movements in Africa. At the peak of his career, Dowie filled the largest auditoriums in the nation including Madison Square Garden in New York City, where he addressed audiences of 15,000 or more.[34]

In 1901, Dowie proclaimed himself to be "Elijah the Restorer." Then, in 1904, he announced that he would "restore apostolic Christianity" now

32. Most holiness churches repudiated the term "holy roller" in official statements, although they were the obvious objects of the epithets. A typical repudiation called the term "slanderous," "reproachful," and "malignant." See Juillerat, *Book of Minutes*, p. 200.

33. H. A. Ironside, *Holiness: The False and the True* (Neptune, NJ, 1912), pp. 1-38.

34. For Dowie's eventual influence on Pentecostalism see Walter Hollenweger, *The Pentecostals: The Charismatic Movement in the Churches* (Minneapolis, 1972), pp. 116-25. Also see Edith Blumhofer's "John Alexander Dowie" in Burgess et al., *Dictionary of Pentecostal and Charismatic Movements*, pp. 248-49.

that he was "the first apostle of a renewed end times church." The next year, after suffering a stroke, he began to lose control of the church he had founded. Nevertheless, during his amazing career, wherever Dowie traveled and whatever he said made headline news, some of it ludicrous and damaging to the holiness movement. "Dowieism" became synonymous, to some critics at least, with "holy rollerism," perhaps because both emphasized sanctification and divine healing. The result was much ill-informed criticism of the holiness movement, though little of the movement in America had any connection with Dowie.[35]

Despite the criticism and occasional violence directed against the holiness movement, it continued to make progress throughout the nation. By the turn of the century there were at least a dozen major, well-organized holiness bodies. Most conspicuous among the southern groups were the Church of God, the Pentecostal Holiness Church, the Fire-Baptized Holiness Church, and the Church of God in Christ. These four bodies were to display a remarkable similarity in doctrine and government, and they were to play leading roles in the Pentecostal movement, which began in 1906.

All these denominations were directed by men with powerful and dynamic personalities. The Church of God continued to grow from its mountain headquarters in Cleveland, Tennessee, under the leadership of the colorful Tomlinson, while the Church of God in Christ, with offices at the other end of the state in Memphis, was led by the soft-spoken, but firm, C. H. Mason. The Fire-Baptized Holiness Church spread out from its headquarters in Royston, Georgia, under the leadership of the scholarly and ascetic J. H. King, while the reins of the Pentecostal Holiness Church were held by A. B. Crumpler in Goldsboro, North Carolina. All of these men led small holiness denominations that were practically identical in doctrine and operated in the same general territory.

In the spring of 1906 the news reached all of these leaders about a meeting then in progress in Los Angeles, California, at the Azusa Street Mission — a meeting heralded as rivaling the events that transpired on the Day of Pentecost in Jerusalem. The reactions of these leaders to the startling news would profoundly affect the future course of the holiness movement in America. The southern holiness churches, the only major holiness groups to join the fledgling Pentecostal movement, would be particularly affected.

35. Gordon Lindsay, *The Life of John Alexander Dowie* (Dallas, 1951), pp. 149-60.

CHAPTER FIVE

The American Jerusalem — Azusa Street

Weird Babel of Tongues
New Sect of Fanatics is breaking Loose
Wild Scene Last Night on Azusa Street
Gurgle of Wordless Talk by a Sister.

Los Angeles Times, April 18, 1906

The Pentecostal revolution which occurred in the holiness movement in 1906 came to the attention of the religious world through
reports of a sensational revival meeting in Los Angeles. The City of the
Angels was first told of the new movement in a report to the *Los Angeles
Times* on April 18, 1906. Under a headline proclaiming "Weird Babel of
Tongues," the writer reported that, "breathing strange utterances and
mouthing a creed which it would seem no sane mortal could understand,
the newest sect has started in Los Angeles." The paper further reported
that:

> Meetings are held in a tumble-down shack on Azusa Street, near San
> Pedro Street, and the devotees of the weird doctrine practice the most
> fanatical rites, preach the wildest theories and work themselves into a
> state of mad excitement in their peculiar zeal. Colored people and a

84

sprinkling of whites compose the congregation, and night is made hideous in the neighborhood by the howlings of the worshippers, who spend hours swaying forth and back in a nerve-racking attitude of prayer and supplication. They claim to have the "gift of tongues" and to be able to comprehend the babel.[1]

This new doctrine was extreme even for Los Angeles, which already was the home of "numberless creeds." The "startling" claims of the new group were considered to be "fanatical" and "irreverent" by the reporter to the *Times.* With amazing accuracy, it was said that "a new sect . . . is breaking loose."[2] Little did the *Times* readers realize that this was the first report of one of the most far-reaching religious meetings of the twentieth century.

Los Angeles in 1906

Los Angeles in April of 1906 boasted a population of 228,298, an increase of 30,684 over the past year. Every month 2,789 people were coming to live in this city, each one bringing his or her own ideas of politics, society, and religion.[3] While newspapers were filled with articles reflecting the pride of a dynamic and growing city, stories revealing the racism and religious intolerance of the times were usually given front-page coverage. The antics of Dowie and his struggles in Zion City, Illinois, were followed daily in the press. The *Times* scored him on April 22, 1906, for being a religious "fakir" and a "colossal humbug." Indeed the baldheaded healer was offered a thousand dollars a week to perform on vaudeville by shrewd show business promoters.[4]

The reputation of Los Angeles as a congenial home for new religious ideas was already well founded before 1906. The largest holiness denomination in America began its history in this city when Phineas Bresee founded the "Church of the Nazarene" there in 1895. For a decade Bresee had conducted "mass holiness meetings" in his "Peniel

1. *Los Angeles Times,* Apr. 18, 1906, p. 1.
2. *Los Angeles Times,* Apr. 18, 1906, p. 1.
3. *Los Angeles Times,* Apr. 14, 1906, p. 1.
4. *Los Angeles Times,* Apr. 11, 1906, p. 1; Apr. 22, 1906, p. 3. Other articles appeared daily in April to June 1906 concerning Dowie's struggle with rebellious members for control of Zion City.

85

Tabernacle" on Main Street to the shouts and hallelujahs of his working-class congregation. By 1906 the Nazarenes had spread to about a dozen congregations in the Los Angeles area, some of them among the blacks.[5]

Another religious innovator in Los Angeles was Joseph Smale, a former pastor of the First Baptist Church, who had opened a mission called the "First New Testament Church" at Burbank Hall. Smale advertised his group in the *Los Angeles Times* as "a fellowship for evangelical preaching and teaching and pentecostal life and service." Holiness Methodists ostracized by their own church over the sanctification issue had by 1906 begun to attend services at Smale's and Bresee's churches. These two holiness preachers represented the "radical fringe" of the religious life of the city. Their churches had grown steadily, though, and by 1906 each of them preached to more than a thousand people at their Sunday services.[6]

The Welsh Revival

The religious odyssey that resulted in Smale's entering the holiness ranks had begun in Wales in 1904, where he participated in the famous Welsh revival under Evan Roberts. Returning to Los Angeles, he had conducted a fifteen-week revival meeting at the city's First Baptist Church. When the church's deacons tired of the revival, Smale resigned to start his New Testament Church. The news of the Welsh revival was spread mainly by means of S. B. Shaw's book, which appeared in 1905, entitled *The Great Revival in Wales.* Also widely read was G. Campbell Morgan's pamphlet, "Revival in Wales." The story of how the twenty-six-year-old Roberts had led the sensational revival, which had seen over 30,000 conversions and 20,000 new church members, swept over the holiness movement with a compelling force.[7]

A young man attending Pastor Smale's services was Frank Bar-

5. Smith, *Called Unto Holiness,* pp. 112-21; *Los Angeles Times,* Apr. 14, 1906, II, p. 71. See Cecil M. Robeck, Jr., "The International Significance of Azusa Street," *Pneuma: The Journal of the Society for Pentecostal Studies,* Spring 1986, pp. 1-4.

6. *Los Angeles Times,* May 12, 1906, II, p. 7.

7. See S. B. Shaw, *The Great Revival in Wales* (Toronto, 1905), which includes accounts of the revival by Morgan and other ministers, in addition to numerous excerpts from the *London Times* and several denominational periodicals.

tleman, a holiness minister who also frequented services at Bresee's Peniel Mission. Bartleman, who had worked his way from Pennsylvania to California by serving in urban rescue missions along the way, had for some time been a regular contributor to J. M. Pike's *Way of Faith* in Columbia, South Carolina, and to Martin W. Knapp's *God's Revivalist* in Cincinnati, Ohio. Already well known in holiness circles, he fell under the spell of the Welsh revival and began to work toward a similar revival in Los Angeles. Deeply impressed by Smale's account of the Welsh phenomenon, Bartleman wrote to Roberts in Wales asking him to pray for a "new Pentecost" in Los Angeles. In all, he wrote three letters, Roberts answering each of them. By March 1906, Bartleman became so agitated for such a revival that he wrote a tract entitled "The Last Call" in which he predicted one last "world-wide revival" before the Day of Judgment. Closing the tract, he prophesied, "Some tremendous event is about to transpire."[8]

Speaking in Tongues

A striking feature of nineteenth-century British revivalism which would soon impress Bartleman was the appearance of "glossolalia," or speaking with other tongues. The phenomenon had first been seen in modern times in Edward Irving's services at the Presbyterian Church on Regent's Square, London, in 1831. Although he never spoke in tongues himself, Irving saw many of his parishioners, including a member of Parliament named Henry Drummond, display this evidence of "receiving the Holy Ghost." At the height of public interest in the proceedings at Regent's Square, Thomas Carlyle and his wife attended services to see what was happening. Irving went so far as to speak of tongues as the "Standing sign" of the "baptism with the Holy Ghost" and the "root and stem" from which all the other gifts flow. As more people began to manifest the tongues phenomenon in his services, Irving attempted to calm the

8. Frank Bartleman, *How Pentecost Came to Los Angeles* (Los Angeles, 1925), pp. 5-43. This book, which includes excerpts from Bartleman's diary and articles from his contributions to various holiness periodicals, constitutes the most reliable record of the Los Angeles revival. It was through Bartleman's reports that much of the holiness movement first heard of the Los Angeles meeting. Some writers, notably British, look on the Pentecostal movement as being an outgrowth of the Welsh revival.

worshippers and to maintain order, but his efforts largely failed. After being accused of "losing mental balance," Irving was tried by the London Presbytery in 1832 and deposed from his pulpit. Afterwards he formed his own denomination which he named "The Catholic Apostolic Church."[9]

Another instance of glossolalia in London occurred in 1875 when Dwight L. Moody preached at a Y.M.C.A. meeting at the Victoria Hall. After speaking to a small group of men in an afternoon service, Moody left the group "on fire" with the young men reportedly "speaking with tongues" and "prophesying." In a sense Moody could be classified as a pre-Pentecostal preacher, although tongues could not be said to have characterized his revival services. This instance, however, indicated that glossolalia sometimes accompanied his preaching.[10]

Tongues were also manifested in the Welsh revival of 1904, although its participants had probably not heard of the experiences of Irving or Moody. The *Yorkshire Post* reported that at the height of the revival under Roberts, young men and women who knew nothing of Old Welsh would in their ecstasy speak in that tongue.[11] On one occasion, a Dutch visiting pastor reportedly preached an entire sermon in English, a language unknown to him.[12] It is possible that Bartleman and Smale were aware of this aspect of the Welsh revival when they began efforts to duplicate it in Los Angeles.

9. Edward Irving, *The Day of Pentecost or the Baptism With the Holy Ghost* (Edinburgh, 1831), p. 28. Jean Christie Root, *Edward Irving: Man, Preacher, Prophet* (Boston, 1912), pp. 70-112. For a recent interpretation of Irving's pre-Pentecostal theology see David Dorries's "Edward Irving and the 'Standing Sign,'" in G. B. McGee, ed., *Initial Evidence: Historical and Biblical Perspectives on the Pentecostal Doctrine of Spirit Baptism* (Peabody, MA, 1991), p. 49. Also see Gordan Strachan, *The Pentecostal Theology of Edward Irving* (London, 1973).

10. Walter J. Hollenweger, "Handbuch Der Pfingstbewegung" (unpublished Ph.D. dissertation, University of Zurich, 1965), vol. 2, p. 360. See also John C. Pollock, *Moody* (New York, 1963), pp. 90-91.

11. *The Yorkshire Post,* Dec. 27, 1904, quoted in Lincoln Moore Vivier, "Glossolalia" (unpublished Ph.D. dissertation, University of Witwatersand, Johannesburg, 1960), p. 117; also *West Africa* 9, no. 219 (Feb. 25, 1905): 163.

12. See Jesse Penn Lewis, "The Revival: Revival in Wales Progresses," *The Christian Patriot,* Oct. 7, 1905, pp. 6-7. Some historians credit such reports to "cryptomnesia," defined as the ability to recall languages already heard in childhood but since forgotten.

Charles Fox Parham

America had also experienced an outbreak of the tongues phenomenon during the same period as the Welsh revival. The person responsible for introducing this practice as a formally stated doctrine was the Reverend Charles Fox Parham of Kansas. It was Parham who first singled out "glossolalia" (speaking in tongues) as the only evidence of having received the baptism of the Holy Ghost, and he taught that it should be a part of "normal" Christian worship rather than a curious by-product of religious enthusiasm. Parham's teaching laid the doctrinal and experimental foundations of the modern Pentecostal movement. It was Parham's ideas preached by his followers that produced the Azusa Street revival of 1906 and with it the worldwide Pentecostal movement.[13]

Parham had begun his ministerial career in Linwood, Kansas, as a supply pastor in the Methodist Episcopal Church. From Methodism he received the teaching of entire sanctification as a second work of grace, an experience he had received and preached as a Methodist. During the 1890's Parham had also come in contact with the more radical elements of the holiness movement, and after much study had adopted the doctrine of faith healing as a part of "the atonement." He had also been in services with Irwin's Fire-Baptized people and had rejected the extreme emotion, but not the idea of a "third experience" of a "baptism with the Holy Ghost and fire." After 1895, when "come-outism" became rampant in Methodism, Parham dissociated himself from the Methodist Episcopal Church and adopted an anti-denominational view to which he adhered for the rest of his life.[14]

13. Most Pentecostal writers acknowledge Parham's place as the formulator of the Pentecostal doctrine, but none call him the "father" of the movement. Because of later questions about his personal ethics his place in Pentecostal history has been de-emphasized. Many refer to the Pentecostal movement as "a movement without a man." See Brumback, *Suddenly from Heaven,* pp. 48-63; Bloch-Hoell, *The Pentecostal Movement,* pp. 18-21. The definitive biography of Parham is James R. Goff's *Fields White Unto Harvest: Charles Fox Parham and the Missionary Origins of Pentecostalism.*

14. Sarah E. (Mrs. Charles F.) Parham, *The Life of Charles F. Parham, Founder of the Apostolic Faith Movement* (Joplin, MO, 1930), pp. 6-24. Parham had been active in the prohibition movement in Kansas and after leaving the Methodist Church blamed his "persecutions" on what he termed "the drinking class" (see p. 25). Goff, *Fields White Unto Harvest,* pp. 17-57.

Bethel Bible School

In 1898 Parham felt that he should begin a "divine healing home" in Topeka where he could gather those who were sick and infirm and pray for their healing. Accordingly, the "Bethel Healing Home" was begun that year and also a bimonthly paper entitled *Apostolic Faith*. Two years later he instituted a school near Topeka which he named the "Bethel Bible School." The school began in October 1900 in a large, rambling house that the local people had christened "Stone's Folly" because of the builder's inability to finish it in the grandiose style he had desired. It was here that forty holiness students gathered for the only year that the school was to exist.[15]

Parham's theology by 1900 had come from many sources. Just prior to the opening of the Topeka school, he had traveled to Chicago to hear Alexander Dowie. From there he had gone to Nyack, New York, to hear A. B. Simpson of the Christian and Missionary Alliance, and to Shiloh, Maine, to investigate Frank Sandford's "Holy Ghost and Us" church. In Sandford's school there was a student named Jeannie Glassey who claimed to speak miraculously in an African dialect proving that she was called to be a missionary to Africa. While in Shiloh, Parham heard glossolalia for the first time when several students came down out of a "prayer tower" speaking in tongues after several hours of intercessory prayer. Returning to Topeka, he felt that there was still something beyond the experience of sanctification, perhaps a charismatic baptism in the Holy Spirit, that would be needed "to meet the challenge of the new century."[16]

By December 1900, Parham had led his students through a study of the major tenets of the holiness movement, including sanctification and divine healing. When they arrived at the second chapter of Acts they studied the events that transpired on the day of Pentecost in Jerusalem, including speaking in tongues. At this juncture, Parham had to leave the school for three days on a speaking engagement. Before leaving, he asked his students to study their Bibles in an effort to find the scriptural

15. Parham, *Charles Fox Parham*, pp. 39-50. Goff, *Fields White Unto Harvest*, pp. 32-70.

16. Parham, *Charles Fox Parham*, p. 48; Brumback, *Suddenly from Heaven*, p. 21. Tomlinson was baptized into Sandford's church in 1901, before joining the Holiness Church in Camp Creek, North Carolina. (See above.)

evidence for the reception of the baptism with the Holy Spirit. Upon returning he asked the students to state the conclusion of their study, and to his "astonishment" they all answered unanimously that the evidence was "speaking with other tongues." This they deduced from the four recorded occasions in the Book of Acts when tongues accompanied the baptism with the Holy Spirit.[17]

Apparently convinced that this conclusion was a proper interpretation of the Scriptures, Parham and his students conducted a watch night service on December 31, 1900, which was to continue into the new year. In this service, a student named Agnes N. Ozman requested Parham to lay hands on her head and pray for her to be baptized with the Holy Ghost with the evidence of speaking in tongues. It was after midnight and the first day of the twentieth century when Miss Ozman reportedly began "speaking in the Chinese language" while a "halo seemed to surround her head and face." Following this experience, Ozman was unable to speak in English for three days, and when she tried to communicate by writing, she invariably wrote in Chinese characters. This event is commonly regarded as the beginning of the modern Pentecostal movement in America. After Ozman experienced "tongues" the rest of the students sought and received the same experience. Somewhat later Parham himself received the experience and began to preach it in all his services.[18]

In a short time the news of what was happening at "Stone's Folly" reached the press of Topeka and Kansas City. Reporters, government interpreters, and language experts soon converged on the school to investigate the new phenomenon. A few days later the *Topeka Capitol*

17. Parham, *Charles F. Parham*, pp. 51-53. The scriptural references are Acts 2:4; 10:46; 19:6; I Corinthians 14:1-33. Both John Mapes Anderson and James R. Goff believe that Parham had already settled on the idea of tongues as the evidence of the baptism in the Holy Spirit resulting in "missionary tongues" prior to the Topeka event. They see the "student consensus" theory as Parham's manipulations to establish a doctrine that he had already formulated. See Anderson, *Vision of the Disinherited: The Making of American Pentecostalism* (New York, 1979), pp. 52-57, and Goff, *Fields White Unto Harvest*, pp. 66-72. See also Vinson Synan, "The Role of Tongues as Initial Evidence," in *Spirit and Renewal: Essays in Honor of J. Rodman Williams*, ed. Mark W. Wilson (Sheffield, U.K., 1994), pp. 67-82.

18. Parham, *Charles F. Parham*, pp. 52-53. Agnes N. La Berge (Ozman), *What God Hath Wrought — Life and Work of Mrs. Agnes N. O. La Berge, Nee Miss Agnes Ozman* (Chicago, 1921), pp. 28-29. The next night Ozman went to Topeka and, after speaking in tongues, was told by a Bohemian that he understood her perfectly.

reported in headlines, "A Queer Faith, Strange Acts . . . Believers Speak in Strange Languages." The *Kansas City World* said that "these people have a faith almost incomprehensible at this day." The wire services picked up the story when Parham and his group of students visited Galena, Kansas, late in January. Concerning this meeting, the *Cincinnati Enquirer* reported that it was doubtful if anything in recent years had awakened the interest, excited the comment, or "mystified the people" as the events in Galena.[19]

A remarkable claim made during these meetings was that the students, Americans all, spoke in twenty-one known languages, including French, German, Swedish, Bohemian, Chinese, Japanese, Hungarian, Bulgarian, Russian, Italian, Spanish, and Norwegian. In a conversation with a *Kansas City Times* correspondent, Parham claimed that his students had never studied these languages and that natives of the countries involved had heard them spoken and had verified their authenticity. Taking these events at face value, Parham immediately began to teach that missionaries would no longer be compelled to study foreign languages to preach in the mission fields. From henceforth, he taught, one need only receive the baptism with the Holy Ghost and he could go to the farthest corners of the world and preach to the natives in languages unknown to the speaker.[20]

William Joseph Seymour

After the meetings in Missouri in 1901, Parham closed his school at Topeka and began a whirlwind revival tour that lasted four years. During this period the Pentecostal doctrine was spread through Kansas, as well as Kansas City, Lawrence, Galena, Melrose, Kwelville, and Baxter Springs, Missouri. By the fall of 1905, he moved his headquarters to Houston, Texas, at the request of friends there, and soon opened another Bible school for the propagation of his views. Housed in a large,

19. Parham, *Charles F. Parham*, pp. 70-96. These articles are reprinted in Parham's *Apostolic Faith*, Nov. 1927, pp. 2-5. Charles F. Parham, *Kol Kare Bomidbar: A Voice Crying in the Wilderness* (Joplin, MO, 1944), pp. 29-38.

20. Parham, *Kol Kare Bomidbar*, pp. 31-32. Very few Pentecostal leaders accepted this premise, although Parham held to it until his death.

21. Parham, *Charles F. Parham*, pp. 131-46.

three-story house, the institution was called simply "The Bible Train-ing School," and during the few months of its operation had an enroll-ment of about twenty-five students. It was at this school that William Joseph Seymour, the apostle of Azusa Street, received his theological training.[21]

Seymour, an African-American born in Louisiana, had moved to Texas early in life. Raised a Baptist, he had adopted holiness views after moving to Indianapolis in 1895, where he joined a local Black Methodist Episcopal Church before coming in contact with the holiness movement. According to Douglas Nelson, from 1900 to 1902 Seymour attended classes in Martin Wells Knapp's "God's Bible School" in Cincinnati where he deepened his understanding of holiness theology. In Cincinnati he joined the "reformation" Church of God, also known as "the Evening Light Saints," with headquarters in Anderson, Indiana. This church, which refused to keep church membership rolls and for-bade its ministers to wear neckties, was open to people of all races. Seymour was welcomed with open arms in both the Bible school and the church. In 1903 he returned to Houston in search of lost relatives, and began to preach in a local black holiness church. A short, stocky man, with one eye damaged by smallpox, Seymour in 1905 was a poverty-stricken southern black with an inquiring mind and a hunger to learn more about the Bible and theology. Hearing of Parham's new school, he determined to improve his religious training if possible.[22]

The racial mores of the South dictated that Seymour, a black, could not attend Parham's school. However, his great desire to attend classes and his apparent thirst for knowledge led Parham to allow him to attend the Bible classes during the day. Since blacks could not legally sit in the same classroom with whites, Parham permitted Seymour to sit in the hallway and hear his lectures through the open door. For several months Seymour heard the new Pentecostal theology from his teacher Parham. He was taught that the holiness movement had been wrong in asserting that sanctification was also the baptism with the Holy Spirit; the latter was a "third experience" separate in time and nature from the "second

22. Douglas Nelson, "For Such a Time as This: The Story of Bishop William J. Seymour and the Azusa Street Revival" (unpublished Ph.D. dissertation, University of Birmingham, U.K., 1981), pp. 9-54. R. L. Fidler, "Historical Review of the Pente-costal Outpouring in Los Angeles at the Azusa Street Mission in 1906," *The International Outlook,* Jan.-Mar. 1963, p. 3.

blessing." Sanctification cleansed and purified the believer, while the baptism with the Holy Spirit brought great power for service. The only biblical evidence that one had received the "baptism" was the act of speaking in tongues as the 120 disciples had done on the day of Pentecost. Any other "baptism," whether it was called sanctification or the "baptism of fire," was not the true baptism of the New Testament. No one should be satisfied, therefore, until having spoken with tongues as "proof" that one had received the Holy Ghost.[23]

All of this Seymour accepted from his new teacher and mentor. While studing under Parham in Houston, though, he never experienced speaking with tongues, in spite of the fact that many others seemed to become adept at it. *The Houston Chronicle* sent reporters to the school in August to report on the events taking place there. It was reported that Houstonians were witnessing "miracles" as students "speak in all tongues known to man." Some claimed that twenty Chinese dialects were spoken, while others were able to "command the classics of a Homer or talk the jargon of the lowest savage of the African jungle."[24]

While these events continued in Parham's school, great numbers of Houstonians visited the services and many received the Pentecostal experience as Parham taught it. Among them was an African-American woman named Lucy Farrow, who had worked as a servant in Parham's home in Kansas. She had received the tongues-attested Pentecostal experience there and returned to Houston as an effective "altar worker," helping seekers "pray through" to the baptism in the Holy Spirit. Another woman who came to the school in Houston was Neely Terry, a native of Los Angeles and a visiting friend of Lucy Farrow. After becoming a friend of William Seymour she later returned to her home in Los Angeles, where she found that her family and some close friends had been excommunicated from the black Second Baptist Church for professing the holiness sanctification experience. Subsequently they organized a small black holiness mission under the auspices of the Southern California Holiness Association, a group led by Mrs. Josephine Washburn and J. M. Roberts. The mission then elected a Mrs. Julie Hutchins to act

23. Charles Parham, "A Critical Analysis of the Tongues Question," *The Apostolic Faith*, June 1925, pp. 2-6. Other sources of Parham's teachings are in Parham, *Charles F. Parham*, and Parham, *Kol Kare Bomidbar*, passim.
24. *The Houston Chronicle*, Aug. 13, 1905, quoted in Parham, *Charles F. Parham*, p. 121.

as pastor of the group. When Miss Terry returned to Los Angeles, she recommended that the little congregation invite Seymour to come and assume the duties of pastor. Seymour accepted the invitation, and with a train ticket paid for by Parham and Miss Terry's friends in Los Angeles, he arrived in February 1906 on a mission that would exceed his fondest expectations.[25]

As he traveled to Los Angeles, Seymour stopped at well-known holiness missions on the way. One of his stops was in Denver, Colorado, at the headquarters of Alma White's "Pillar of Fire" movement, a small holiness group that specialized in the "holy dance" as the evidence of sanctification. Stopping at White's Bible school, Seymour introduced himself as a "man of God" and asked for lodging and meals. Seymour's reception was anything but warm in the Pillar of Fire center. Seymour impressed Mrs. White as a "very untidy person . . . wearing no collar." Writing many years later, she recalled, "I had met all kinds of religious fakers and tramps, but I felt he excelled them all." Such was the reception of the Apostle of Pentecost at the Pillar of Fire headquarters.[26]

In his short stay in Houston, Seymour had built a reputation as a humble man, but one extremely interested in holiness religion. Described by some observers as neat and well-groomed and by others as "dirty and collarless," he hardly seemed the man to lead a historic revival that would usher in the Pentecostal movement. Yet his experience in the midwest and his training at Parham's school in Texas had prepared him for greater things.[28]

25. Fidler, "Historical Review," p. 3; Brumback, *Suddenly from Heaven,* pp. 34-36; Kendrick, *The Promise Fulfilled,* p. 64.

26. Alma White, *Demons and Tongues* (Zeraphath, NJ, 1949), pp. 68-69. The best biography of White is Susie Cunningham Stanley's *Feminist Pillar of Fire: The Life of Alma White* (Cleveland, 1993). Mrs. White's bitter criticism of Seymour may have been influenced by racial prejudice and her later rejection of Pentecostalism.

27. For an evaluation of Seymour's career before Azusa Street see Lian Mac-Robert's *The Black Roots and White Racism of Early Pentecostalism in the USA* (London, 1988), pp. 34-59.

28. Michael Harper, *As at the Beginning: The Twentieth Century Pentecostal Revival* (London, 1965), p. 28; Frank Ewart, *The Phenomenon of Pentecost: A History of the Latter Rain* (St. Louis, 1947), pp. 36-37. A description of Seymour was given in the *Los Angeles Times* on Sept. 9, 1956, on the occasion of the fiftieth anniversary of the Azusa Street revival. See Brumback, *Suddenly from Heaven,* pp. 37-38.

Bonnie Brae Street

When Seymour preached his first sermon at the Holiness Church on Santa Fe Street, he took as his text Acts 2:4 and declared that speaking in tongues was the "Bible" evidence of receiving the Holy Spirit, although he as yet had not received the experience. The Pastor, Mrs. Julia Hutchins, after consulting with J. M. Roberts, president of the Southern California Holiness Association, felt that this teaching was contrary to accepted holiness views, and the following night she padlocked the church door to keep Seymour out, even though most of her members had accepted his message. The evangelist, with nowhere to stay in the city and no money for lodging, was invited to stay at the home of one Richard Asbery, a man who at that point refused to accept Seymour's teaching. Nevertheless, the evangelist began to preach in the living room of Asbery's home, located at 214 Bonnie Brae Street.[29]

For several days prayer services continued in the Asbery home until the night of April 9, 1906, when Seymour and seven others fell to the floor in a religious ecstasy, speaking in tongues. When this occurred, Asbery's daughter fled through the kitchen door, terrified by what she had seen. News of the events on Bonnie Brae Street spread quickly through the neighborhood as the newly baptized enthusiasts went to the front porch to conduct their strange services. The curious soon began to gather as one of the worshippers, Seymour's future wife Jennie Moore, began to play the piano and sing in what was thought to be Hebrew. In the services that followed, demonstrations of tongues were so pronounced that huge crowds gathered in the streets to see what was happening. Whites as well as blacks began to mingle in the crowd as Seymour addressed them from a makeshift pulpit on the front porch. As crowds pressed into the house and onto the porch, the pressure became so great that at one point a floor caved in, but no one was hurt.[30]

29. Fidler, "Historical Review," pp. 3-4. For the reactions of the Holiness Association see Josephine M. Washburn, *History and Reminiscences of the Holiness Church Work in Southern California and Arizona* (New York, 1985). This is a reprint of the 1912 original published by the Record Press of South Pasadena.

30. Fidler, "Historical Review," p. 4; "When the Spirit Fell," *Pentecostal Evangel,* Apr. 6, 1946, p. 7.

Azusa Street

With such interest in evidence, Seymour decided to find larger quarters where revival services could be conducted in a more conventional manner. After a search of the city, an old abandoned African Methodist Episcopal Church (AME) building at 312 Azusa Street was secured to continue the meetings. This building, the first black Methodist church building constructed in Los Angeles, was located in a downtown business section and had most recently been used as a combined tenement house and livery stable. By 1906, the old two-story building was a shambles. The windows and doors were broken out and debris littered the floor, but in many ways it was ideal for such a meeting. Far from residential areas, it could be used for the all-night meetings that characterized the early Pentecostals. It also had the rough-hewn atmosphere of the camp meetings that holiness people had grown accustomed to in their annual pilgrimages to the "forest temple." Another advantage of the "Azusa Stable" was that the poorest of the lower classes could come to it and not be intimidated by the stained-glass trappings of a traditional church. In these unpretentious surroundings, Seymour began to preach to the crowds that followed him from Bonnie Brae Street.[31]

No sooner had Seymour begun preaching in the Azusa location than a monumental revival began. Scores of people began to "fall under the power" and arise speaking in other tongues. News of the Azusa meeting reached the *Los Angeles Times* by mid-April and a reporter described what he called the "wild scenes" of this new "sect of fanatics." Describing Seymour as "an old colored exhorter" who acted as "majordomo of the company," the reporter felt that his "stony optic" eye served to hypnotize unbelievers. Old "colored mammys," he said, were seen to "gurgle wordless talk" in a "frenzy of religious zeal."[32] This first news release on the Azusa Street revival ended with a prophecy that had been given in a vision to a man in the service. In his vision, he saw the people of Los Angeles "flocking in a mighty stream to perdition." He then prophesied "awful destruction to this city unless its citizens are brought to a belief in the tenets of the new faith."[33]

---

31. Fidler, "Historical Review," pp. 4-5; Brumback, *Suddenly from Heaven*, pp. 36-37; Stanley H. Frodsham, *With Signs Following: The Story of the Pentecostal Revival in the Twentieth Century* (Springfield, MO, 1946), pp. 32-33.
    32. *Los Angeles Times*, Apr. 18, 1906, p. 1.
    33. *Los Angeles Times*, Apr. 18, 1906, p. 1.

In fact, an "awful destruction" occurred the very next day, but in San Francisco, not Los Angeles. On April 19, the *Times* headlines screamed, "Heart is Torn from Great City," its pages telling of the great devastation. The worshippers at Azusa Street felt the tremors that shook the entire coast of California and in their religious zeal felt there was a divine connection between the two. The natural earthquake in San Francisco was followed by a "spiritual earthquake" on Azusa Street, and in the weeks to come rose to a level of near hysteria.[34]

The Revival Spreads

As the Azusa revival continued, hundreds and later thousands of people began to flock to the mission, both the curious and the serious. Every day trains unloaded visitors from all over the continent. News accounts of the meeting spread across the nation in both the secular and religious press. The most interested observers were members of the holiness movements around the country. Scores of reports in papers such as *The Way of Faith* in South Carolina carried minute accounts of the events in Los Angeles. Also publicizing the revival was a free, four-page paper entitled *The Apostolic Faith,* published from Azusa Street by Seymour and his assistants.[35]

A visitor to Azusa Street during the three and a half years the revival continued would have met scenes that beggared description. Men and women would shout, weep, dance, fall into trances, speak and sing in tongues, and interpret their messages into English. In true Quaker fashion, anyone who felt "moved by the Spirit" would preach or sing. There was no robed choir, no hymnals, no order of services, but there was an abundance of religious enthusiasm. In the middle of it all was "Elder" Seymour, who rarely preached and much of the time kept his head covered in an empty packing crate behind the pulpit. At times he

34. *Los Angeles Times,* Apr. 19, 1906, pp. 1-10. Early Pentecostals made much of the coincidence of the earthquake and the Azusa meeting, one writer asserting that "in all God's great moves, nature sympathizes with Him." See Frank Ewart, *The Phenomenon of Pentecost,* p. 18; Bartleman, *How Pentecost Came to Los Angeles,* pp. 47-53.

35. *The Apostolic Faith* (Azusa Street), Sept. 1906, p. 1; Bartleman, *How Pentecost Came to Los Angeles,* pp. 61-63; Ewart, *The Phenomenon of Pentecost,* p. 43; also see issues of *The Way of Faith* for 1906-8, where continuous reports of the meetings were published by eyewitnesses.

would be seen walking through the crowds with five- and ten-dollar bills sticking out of his hip pockets that people had crammed there unnoticed by him. At other times he would "preach" by hurling challenges at anyone who did not accept his views or by encouraging seekers at the woodplank altars to "let the tongues come forth." To others he would exclaim: "Be emphatic! Ask for salvation, sanctification, the baptism with the Holy Ghost, or divine healing."[36]

Seymour and the workers in the mission lived on the upper floor where there was also a long room they called "the Pentecostal upper room," a place where seekers were sent to receive their own "pentecostal experience." Visitors to the meeting claimed they could feel a "supernatural atmosphere" within several blocks of the mission. Part of this atmosphere was created by a recurrence of the physical manifestations common at Cane Ridge back in 1800. Sounds of shouting and rejoicing echoed over the lumber yards, stables, and tombstone shops that surrounded the mission. As the meetings continued week after week, more and more people began to attend, until by the summer of 1906 people of every race and nationality in the Los Angeles area were mingling in the crowds that pressed into the mission from the street. There was a total absence of racial discrimination. Blacks, whites, Chinese, and even Jews attended side by side to hear Seymour preach. Eventually what began as a local revival in a local black church became of interest to people all over the nation, regardless of race. In a short while the majority of attendants were white, but always there was complete integration of the races in the services, one man exclaiming, "The color line was washed away in the blood."[37]

Throughout 1906 the revival increased in fervor and interest. In August, Bartleman wrote to *The Way of Faith* that "Pentecost has come to Los Angeles, the American Jerusalem."[38] Reports from the *Apostolic Faith* published at the mission indicated that hundreds were speaking with tongues in addition to the numbers saved, sanctified, and healed. "The waves of Pentecostal salvation are still rolling in Azusa Street

---

36. Ewart, *The Phenomenon of Pentecost,* pp. 40-49; *Los Angeles Times,* Apr. 18, 1906, p. 1; Bartleman, *How Pentecost Came to Los Angeles,* p. 58.

37. Bartleman, *How Pentecost Came to Los Angeles,* p. 54. Also see Frodsham, *With Signs Following,* pp. 33-34; and Ewart, *The Phenomenon of Pentecost,* p. 42.

38. *The Way of Faith,* Aug. 1, 1906, quoted in Bartleman, *How Pentecost Came to Los Angeles,* p. 63.

Mission," the paper reported. It was also claimed that a woman named Anna Hall had gone to a Russian church in Los Angeles and preached to its communicants in their own language, although it was unknown to her. It was reported that the hearers were "so glad to hear the truth that they wept and even kissed her hands." By December 1906 the paper reported that "the Lord God is in Los Angeles in different missions and churches in mighty power, in spite of opposition." Indeed, by the end of the year many other missions had been opened in the Los Angeles area and others were beginning to operate in cities all over the United States, as visitors to Azusa Street carried the "fire" to their own homes.[39]

Azusa Critics

As the meetings continued at Azusa Street many attended who were critical of the proceedings. Some felt that the emotionalism and enthusiasm were too extreme, even for holiness people, many of whom were not known for especially decorous services. Some of the more radical holiness churches and missions closed their services and came *en masse* to Azusa Street when the services there became well known. One of these was William Pendleton, pastor of a local Holiness Church, whose congregation came over to join the Asuza worshippers despite warnings from J. M. Roberts and the Southern California Holiness Association. Soon such physical demonstrations as the "jerks," the "holy laugh," the "holy dance" and "singing in the Spirit" (which Seymour called "the heavenly choir), were in evidence in the mission. Before long spiritualists and mediums from the numerous occult societies of Los Angeles began to attend and to contribute their seances and trances to the services. Disturbed by these developments, Seymour wrote Parham for advice on how to handle "the spirits," and begged him to come to Los Angeles and take over supervision of the revival. Others reported to Parham that "all the stunts common in old camp meetings among colored folks" were being performed in the services. Even more disturbing to him was the report Parham heard that "white people [were] imitating [the] unintelligent, crude negroisms of the Southland, and laying it on the Holy

39. *The Apostolic Faith*, Sept. 1906, pp. 1-4; Oct. 1906, pp. 1-4; Dec. 1906, pp. 1-4; Dec. 1907, pp. 1-4.

Ghost." Parham, therefore, advised Seymour to continue the services while he went to Zion City to preach to the followers of "Elijah" Dowie who were in a state of confusion due to the efforts of some members to unseat the now obviously deranged "prophet."[40]

Although Seymour attempted to de-emphasize tongues and the uncontrolled fervor of the Azusa Street crowds, his efforts were futile. Nettie Harwood, a critic and disciple of Alma White, visited the mission late in 1906 and reported that people were singing songs "in a far away tune that sounded very unnatural and repulsive." Harwood also claimed that there was much kissing between sexes and even races. She was incensed at seeing a colored woman with her arms around a white man's neck "praying for him." Mrs. Washburn, head of the Holiness Association, wrote in her diary that "strange phenomena and wild, hysterical demonstrations followed such as rolling on the floor, with strange noises, as in deep agony." This was followed by those who would be "seized with a strange spell and commence a jibberish of sounds" claiming "that they had now received the baptism of the Holy Ghost." To her astonishment "some of the brightest and best" members of the church "fell into the fearful delusion." For many of the holiness people who rejected Seymour's baptism he was an "instrument of Satan." To Mrs. White and her Pillar of Fire followers the "winds of perdition" were blowing in Los Angeles.[41]

If some came to criticize, many more came out of curiosity and went away convinced that a genuinely historical revival was occurring. One foreign-born reporter from a Los Angeles newspaper came on assignment to report on the "circus-like" meeting in the Azusa Street "stable." While there, an ignorant woman rose to her feet, looked straight at him and spoke in his native tongue, telling him secrets that only he could have known. He left convinced of the authenticity of the "tongues" experience. The first white man to receive the experience at Azusa was one A. G. Garr, pastor of a holiness mission in Los Angeles. After his "baptism," Garr and his wife went to India where they expected to preach to the natives in their own languages. However, when this was attempted, it ended in failure. After their fiasco in India the Garrs traveled to Hong Kong where they set up a mission and learned Chinese in the more

40. Parham, *Charles F. Parham,* pp. 160-63.
41. Washburn, *Holiness Church Work in Southern California,* pp. 383-89; White, *Demons and Tongues,* pp. 71-73; Ewart, *The Phenomenon of Pentecost,* p. 45.

conventional manner. This was the outstanding attempt at carrying out Parham's teaching concerning the missionary use of tongues, and it ended in failure.[42]

Parham at Azusa Street

It was in October 1906 that Parham, whom Seymour claimed as his "father in the Gospel of the Kingdom," finally arrived in Los Angeles for his much-heralded "general union revival." His arrival had been delayed for months due to a visit to Zion City, Illinois, where he had recruited many new people to his Pentecostal cause while failing in his attempt to take over Dowie's faltering movement. When he came to Azusa Street, he was shocked by the "holy roller" aspects of the services and made efforts to correct the "extremes and fanaticism," which he felt had gone "beyond the bounds of common sense and reason." After preaching two or three times, the "Apostle of the Apostolic Faith" was told by some of Seymour's followers that he "was not wanted in that place." He was then invited to leave because of his denunciations of the "hypnotists" and "spiritualists" who seemed to have taken over the services. He left "disgusted" because many "came through chattering, jabbering and sputtering, speaking in no language at all." After being barred from the Azusa Mission, which now ironically carried the name "Apostolic Faith Gospel Mission," after Parham's own organization, the rejected prophet opened services in a local W.C.T.U. building on the corner of Broadway and Temple Streets. This meeting, however, was short-lived and failed to alter the course of the Azusa Street revival, which continued unabated, night and day, for three more years. After barring Parham from Azusa Street, Seymour suffered a total break with his teacher that was never healed, Parham later denouncing the Azusa leader as being "possessed with a spirit of leadership." For the rest of his life, Parham continued his denunciation of the Azusa Street meeting

---

42. Ewart, *The Phenomenon of Pentecost*, pp. 47, 106; *The Apostolic Faith*, Oct. 1906, p. 2; Homer A. Tomlinson, in *Twentieth Anniversary of the Garr Auditorium* (Charlotte, NC, 1950), p. 3. Garr was known as the "first foreign missionary of the pentecostal movement." In 1930, Garr settled in Charlotte, North Carolina, founding the famous "Garr Auditorium," one of the early urban Pentecostal churches in the South.

as a case of "spiritual power prostituted" to the "awful fits and spasms" of the "holy rollers and hypnotists."[43]

Azusa Street Pilgrims

During the three and a half years that the Azusa Street revival continued, reports were written by visitors from all parts of the nation, and read avidly by most of the holiness people in the United States. Word also spread to Europe that an unusual outpouring of Pentecost had come to California, and hundreds of preachers from around the continent traveled to Los Angeles to see for themselves what was taking place. Most of them were convinced of the genuineness of the teachings and practices that they saw, receiving their own "pentecost" with the evidence of speaking in tongues before returning to their churches. Many who came were destined to found entire denominations of Pentecostal believers. In later years anyone who was an "Azusa recipient" was looked on with awe and covered with an aura of respect and "glory" by his co-religionists. A list of the "pilgrims to Los Angeles" eventually became a veritable honor roll of early Pentecostal leadership.[44]

Among those who later became prominent in the Pentecostal movement was Florence Crawford, who brought the message to the Northwest in her "Apostolic Faith" movement with headquarters in Portland, Oregon. Mrs. Crawford was an early worker with Seymour at Azusa Street, adopting the name "The Apostolic Faith" from Parham's and Seymour's groups. Her movement, which developed into a small denomination, was never officially connected with Parham's group of the same name with headquarters in Baxter Springs, Kansas. Another,

43. Parham, *Charles F. Parham*, pp. 164-202; Parham, "Sermon by Charles F. Parham," in *The Apostolic Faith* (Baxter Springs), Apr. 1925, pp. 9-14. See also Nelson, "For Such a Time as This," pp. 208-12, and MacRobert, *Black Roots and White Racism*, pp. 60-62. One possible reason why Seymour rejected his authority was the rumor that Parham was a practicing homosexual, a charge often made and repeatedly denied by Parham. See Bloch-Hoell, *The Pentecostal Movement*, p. 19; H. J. Stolee, *Speaking in Tongues* (Minneapolis, 1963), p. 63; *Zion's Herald*, July 26, 1907, p. 1; and *The Burning Bush*, Sept. 19, 1907, pp. 5-7, which quotes court proceedings reported in the *San Antonio Daily Express*, June-Sept., 1907.

44. Brumback, *Suddenly from Heaven*, pp. 64-87; Bartleman, *How Pentecost Came to Los Angeles*, pp. 54-60.

the Reverend William H. Durham of Chicago, traveled to Los Angeles and then returned to his "North Avenue Mission" to found the Pentecostal movement in the Midwest. From Durham's church, leaders of the later Pentecostal Assemblies of Canada received the Pentecostal message. New York City saw its first Pentecostal church organized in December 1906 when a black preacher, "Elder" Sturdevant, arrived from Los Angeles and opened a mission in a room at 351 West Fortieth Street. The New York City press reacted to the West Side group in similar fashion to that of Los Angeles when Azusa Street started a few months earlier. Calling the votaries in the hall "a group of Negroes of the poor and uneducated class," the paper declared that "the heights of frenzy they reach seem in many instances to go beyond the limits of normal physical endurance."[45]

A Worldwide Movement

Others who spread the message from Azusa Street were: Mrs. Rachel Sizelove in Missouri, Samuel Saell in Arizona, Glenn A. Cook in Indiana, D. W. Kerr in Ohio, R. E. McAlister in Ottawa, Ontario, C. H. Mason in Tennessee, and G. B. Cashwell in North Carolina.[46] One of the most important persons influenced by the Azusa Street revival was the Norwegian Methodist pastor T. B. Barratt, who was on a tour of the United States in 1906-07. While in New York, he heard of the Los Angeles meeting and began a correspondence with Seymour about the new Pentecostal doctrine. In November 1906, he received the Pentecostal experience in New York and soon afterwards returned to Oslo. Beginning an Azusa-type meeting in Oslo in December 1906, Barratt soon had Norwegian Methodists and Baptists speaking in other tongues, as well as performing the "holy laugh" and the "holy dance." Spectacular news coverage caused great public interest in the Norwegian capital, and created great crowds of spectators at the meetings that followed. From 1906 till his death in 1940, Barratt served as a veritable prophet of

---

45. *The New York American,* Dec. 3, 1906, quoted in Bloch-Hoell, *The Pentecostal Movement,* pp. 39-51; R. R. Crawford, *A Historical Account of the Apostolic Faith* (Portland, OR, 1965), pp. 44-64.

46. Mason and Cashwell will be treated in detail in the next chapter because of their importance to other movements in the South.

Pentecost in Northern Europe. He is credited with beginning the Pentecostal movements in Sweden, Norway, Denmark, Germany, France, and England.[47]

The Azusa Street revival is commonly regarded as the beginning of the modern Pentecostal movement. Although many persons had spoken in tongues in the United States in the years preceding 1906, this meeting brought the practice to the attention of the world and served as catalyst for the formation of scores of Pentecostal denominations. Directly or indirectly, practically all of the Pentecostal groups in existence can trace their lineage to the Azusa Mission. Even in India an outbreak of tongues was reported in 1908 that had all the characteristics of the Azusa meeting. Under the direction of one Pandita Ramabai, the inmates of a girls' orphanage spoke and prayed in English, Greek, Hebrew, and Sanskrit in the years 1905-08. Indeed, the developments that followed the 1894 break with Methodism reached a climax in Los Angeles in 1906, and from there the holiness-Pentecostal movement spread to the farthest reaches of the world.[48]

Historians have had difficulty in explaining the conditions that produced the Pentecostal movement and in placing it in its proper ecclesiastical perspective. Some have suggested that Pentecostalism arises "during or immediately after great national or cosmic catastrophes," or during periods of "widespread religious apathy." In the case of the California Pentecostal revival centering on Azusa Street, none of these factors seemed to be present. No great wars or catastrophes brought it on, although the San Francisco Earthquake occurred after the meeting began. And the great holiness controversy that had convulsed the religious world since 1867 suggested anything but religious apathy.[49]

The Pentecostal movement arose as a split in the holiness movement and can be viewed as the logical outcome of the holiness crusade that had vexed American Protestantism, the Methodist Church in par-

---

47. T. B. Barratt, *When the Fire Fell* (Oslo, Norway, 1927), pp. 99-126; Bloch-Hoell, *The Pentecostal Movement*, pp. 65-86, 178-79.

48. *The Chicago Daily News,* Jan. 14, 1908, carried reports of the glossolalic outburst in India; quoted in Vivier, "Glossolalia," p. 118. See also Turner, *Pentecost and Tongues,* pp. 134-36; Donald Gee, *All with One Accord* (Springfield, MO, 1961), p. 29; Robeck, "The International Significance of Azusa Street," pp. 1-4.

49. F. E. Mayer, *The Religious Bodies of America,* p. 315. It also may be added that World War I, the depression, and World War II failed to produce any new movements equaling those of the 1894-1906 period.

ticular, for more than forty years. The repeated calls of the holiness leadership after 1894 for a "new Pentecost" inevitably produced the frame of mind and the intellectual foundations for just such a "Pentecost" to occur. In historical perspective the Pentecostal movement was the child of the holiness movement, which in turn was a child of Methodism. Practically all the early Pentecostal leaders were firm advocates of sancti-fication as a "second work of grace" and simply added the "Pentecostal baptism" with the evidence of speaking in tongues as a "third blessing" superimposed on the other two. Both Parham and Seymour fully main-tained the Wesleyan view of sanctification throughout their lives.[50]

The Azusa Street Mission continued to function as an independent African-American city church for several years after the original revival ended in 1909, the white people having left it exclusively to the blacks. Seymour later left the mission and traveled extensively throughout the United States as an evangelist while his wife attended to the church. After Seymour's death in 1922, his wife served as pastor until her death, and in 1931 the building was torn down as a potential fire hazard. After Mrs. Seymour's death, the land where the mission had stood was taken by the city for non-payment of taxes. At one point a prominent Pente-costal denomination refused to buy the Azusa Street property because, in their own words, they were "not interested in relics." Parham returned to his home in Baxter Springs, Kansas, where his annual Apostolic Faith Convocations attracted thousands of followers until his death in 1929. Yet the movement that Parham and Seymour unleashed in Topeka and Los Angeles was destined to begin a new and important chapter in the history of Christianity.[51]

50. Parham, "A Critical Analysis of the Tongues Question," *The Apostolic Faith*, June 1925, pp. 2-6.

51. Parham, *Charles F. Parham*, pp. 389-420; Bloch-Hoell, *The Pentecostal Move-ment*, p. 54. Nelson, "For Such a Time as This," pp. 273-74.

CHAPTER SIX

Pentecost Comes South

---

*I went to the Holiness Church to services here today
and heard Brother G. B. Cashwell preach. He has been
to California and got Pentecost and speaks in an unknown tongue. Some seeking the experience here. (Dunn,
North Carolina, December 30, 1906)*

Thurman Carey

The news of the Azusa Street revival in Los Angeles spread over the entire nation and to many parts of the world before the end of 1906. Members of holiness churches were the ones most affected by the news from California. Seymour's paper, *The Apostolic Faith*, was sent without cost to thousands of ministers and lay people everywhere. Sensational articles about people speaking with tongues "just like the Apostles did on the day of Pentecost" appeared in every issue. Copies of the irregularly issued paper were avidly read and passed from hand to hand. Holiness preachers from coast to coast read with wonder and great interest of the "Pentecostal outpouring" at Azusa Street, where people not only spoke with tongues, but sang hymns and prophesied in foreign languages. Reports of supernatural interpretations of tongues, divine healing of diseases, visions of tongues of fire, and spectacular scenes of religious ecstasy exercised a peculiar attraction to most of those who read them.[1]

The holiness people of the South followed the progress of the meeting through the pages of *The Way of Faith,* the outstanding holiness periodical of the area. For many months during 1906 and 1907, Bartleman sent regular reports to editor J. M. Pike, who published them from his offices in Columbia, South Carolina. In the same building was located the "Oliver Gospel Mission," an urban holiness rescue mission for the poor and destitute. Pike had also allowed the Holmes Bible Institute to conduct classes in the building from 1903 to 1905. The prestige of Pike and his paper among the holiness community added weight to Bartleman's reports concerning Azusa Street. In August 1906 he wrote to *The Way of Faith* that "strong men lie for hours under the mighty power of God, cut down like grass. The revival will be a world-wide one, without doubt." This kind of report on the Azusa Street revival was read by holiness leaders around the nation. To anyone with a strong holiness background, all of this news was of great interest, to put it mildly. To many, it was irresistible.[2]

Tongues in the Holiness Movement

The scenes at Azusa Street as described by Seymour and Bartleman were nothing new to many holiness people. The "Fire-Baptized Way" was already well known, especially in the South and also in the Middle West. Many of the holiness people had felt that some physical evidence would often accompany sanctification to prove that a person had "prayed through." Some thought that the best proof of being baptized with the

1. Bloch-Hoell, *The Pentecostal Movement,* pp. 42, 43, 145-47. For the theologically minded it should be explained that the Greek term for speaking in tongues is *glossolalia.* Also, Pentecostal apologists made a sharp distinction between tongues as the "evidence" that one had received the baptism with the Holy Spirit, and the "gift of tongues" which may be exercised throughout life for devotional purposes. No distinction is usually made between unknown tongues and ecstatic utterances in known languages. For further theological discussion see John Nichols, *Pentecostalism* (New York, 1966), pp. 12-13; Carl Brumback, *What Meaneth This? A Pentecostal Answer to a Pentecostal Question* (Springfield, MO: Assemblies of God Publishing House, 1946), pp. 261-72; Wade H. Horton, ed., *The Glossolalia Phenomenon* (Cleveland, TN, 1966), pp. 21-65 and passim; Joseph H. King, *From Passover to Pentecost* (Memphis, 1914), pp. 113-43; and Gary McGee, ed., *Initial Evidence.*
2. *The Way of Faith,* Aug. 1906. L. R. Graham, personal interview with the author, Memphis, Tennessee, 1966.

Holy Ghost was the ability to perform the "holy dance." Others taught that "hallelujah earthquakes" would be felt by the newly-baptized, while some thought the best evidence was a shouting in drunken ecstasy, like the disciples on the day of Pentecost. Tongues had been experienced by a number of holiness people over the years, but they were considered to be only one of many "evidences" or "proofs" of sanctification. Before 1906 holiness writers felt that tongues should be part of "a normal gospel meeting," although most felt that the words "other tongues" referred to "the new language of new converts." W. B. Godbey, the outstanding Greek scholar in the National Holiness Movement, ignored tongues in his *Commentary on the New Testament,* calling instead for a return of "the old-time, knockdown power" to the church.[3]

A case of tongues speech in a Midwestern holiness camp meeting in 1881 was prophetic of the divisions that would come later with the advent of Pentecostalism:

> One day right in the midst of a great sermon, a woman from Carrol County, a Holiness professor, sprawled out at full length in the aisle. This was in itself not much to be thought of, for to tumble over now and then was expected. But the unexpected happened in this case. It kept some of the sisters busy to keep her with a measurably decent appearance. Directly she began to compose a jargon of words in rhyme and sing them in a weird tune. She persisted until the service was spoiled and the camp was thrown into a hubbub. Strange to say, the camp was divided thereby. Some said it was a wonderful manifestation of divine power, some said it was a repetition of speaking in unknown tongues as at Pentecost. But every preacher on the grounds without exception declared it to be of the devil. But the camp was so divided in opinion that it had to be handled with the greatest of care.[4]

Although most holiness people probably heard of speaking with tongues for the first time in connection with Azusa Street, the practice was well known to scholars of biblical and church history. According to

3. W. B. Godbey, *Commentary on the New Testament* (Cincinnati, 1896), vol. 4, pp. 231-34; Thomas Waugh, *The Power of Pentecost* (Chicago, n.d.), p. 101; A. B. Simpson, *Emblems of the Holy Spirit* (Nyack, NY, 1901), pp. 1-128. None of these mentions tongues as an evidence of the Holy Spirit.

4. A. M. Kiergan, *Historical Sketches of the Revival of True Holiness and Church Polity from 1865-1916* (Fort Scott, KS, 1971), cited in Donald Dayton, *Theological Roots of Pentecostalism,* pp. 177-78.

the records, many periods of Christian history from St. Paul to Charles Parham had been punctuated by occasional outbreaks of glossolalia. Examples of the phenomenon had been known among the Montanists in second-century Italy, the Albigenses in twelfth-century France, and the Waldensians in thirteenth-century Italy. The Mormons and the Shakers had also experienced the phenomenon in eighteenth- and nineteenth-century America. The Irvingites had made tongue-speaking a cardinal doctrine of their "Catholic Apostolic Church" in England during the 1830's, while an outbreak of tongues in Providence, Rhode Island in 1874 led the public to call the followers of R. B. Swan, a local pastor, the "gift people." In later years, the great Welsh revival of 1904-05 had been characterized by striking examples of the practice. The 1906 outbreak of tongues at Azusa Street was clearly a recurrence of a well documented if not well known Christian phenomenon.[5]

The American South was the scene of several instances of tongue-speaking during the nineteenth century. Frontier camp meetings such as the one at Cane Ridge in 1800 saw examples of the practice, mostly in the form of singing in the spirit. A great increase of glossolalia came in the 1890's, however, when the climax of the National Holiness Movement resulted in the formation of new denominations. One of the first faith-healing evangelists in America, Mrs. M. B. Woodworth Etter, reported occurrences of tongues in a mass healing revival in St. Louis in 1890. A young girl was reported to have spoken and written "very intelligently" in a foreign language unknown to her. Beginning her ministry as a member of the United Brethren Church in the eighties, Mrs. Etter claimed that some people had "spoken in tongues all along through my ministry." In addition to tongues, Etter claimed to have the "gifts of healing, casting out devils, miracles, and visions."[6]

---

5. For a scholarly examination of tongues, as both historical fact and psychological phenomenon, see George Barton Cutten, *Speaking with Tongues* (New Haven, 1927), pp. 11-184. Other later works on the subject are Ira J. Martin, *Glossolalia in the Apostolic Church* (Berea, KY, 1960); Vivier, "Glossolalia"; John L. Sherrill, *They Speak with Other Tongues* (New York, 1964); and Nichol, *Pentecostalism*. See also Gaddis, "Christian Perfectionism in America," pp. 37-222; Philip Schaff, *History of the Christian Church* (New York, 1910), vol. 1, pp. 423-62; and Stanley Frodsham, *With Signs Following* (Springfield, MO, 1946), pp. 7-30. An excellent survey of tongues as believed by Pentecostals is given in Gary McGee's *Initial Evidence: Historical and Biblical Perspectives on the Pentecostal Doctrine of Spirit Baptism* (Peabody, MA, 1991).

6. Mrs. M. B. Woodworth Etter, *Marvels and Miracles; Signs and Wonders* (In-

In the same year that Mrs. Etter was preaching in St. Louis, Daniel Awrey, a man who later became prominent in Pentecostal circles, spoke in tongues in a prayer meeting in Delaware, Ohio. Later moving to the town of Beniah, Tennessee, Awrey came in contact with the Fire-Baptized holiness movement. In 1899 in Beniah, Awrey's wife along with a dozen others spoke in tongues when they received the "baptism of fire." Publicizing his experiences in the holiness press, Awrey became well known to holiness people and was a founding member in 1898 at the organizational council of the Fire-Baptized Holiness Church in Anderson, South Carolina.[7]

Perhaps the greatest instance of speaking with other tongues before 1906 occurred in the Camp Creek revival in North Carolina in 1896. In this meeting many people, including "men, women and children . . . spoke in tongues under the mighty spirit of God." Many years later it was estimated by those who had been present that over one hundred persons were thus exercised in the meeting. This event preconditioned the members of the Church of God in nearby Cleveland, Tennessee, to accept the doctrine of tongues as the initial evidence of receiving the Holy Spirit when the news of Azusa Street swept the South.[8]

The experiences of Parham and his Bible school students in Topeka and Houston from 1901 to 1905 were also important harbingers of the historic events in Los Angeles. One historian has estimated that over a thousand Americans had spoken with tongues before the Azusa Street revival, but the probability is that thousands more had done the same in the many camp meetings and revivals that reached high levels of fervor after the Civil War.[9]

The importance of the Azusa Street revival was that it acted as the

---

dianapolis, 1922), pp. 68-70. In two other books entitled *Signs and Wonders God Wrought in the Ministry for Forty Years* and *The Acts of the Holy Ghost,* Etter recorded the most colorful and fantastic ministry in all Pentecostal literature. Much of it, however, is open to serious question as authentic history.

7. Bailey, *Pioneer Marvels,* pp. 19-20; Kendrick, *The Promise Fulfilled,* p. 35; *The Pentecostal Holiness Advocate,* Mar. 31, 1921, p. 11. Awrey later joined the Assemblies of God and died in Liberia as a Pentecostal missionary.

8. Juillerat, *Book of Minutes,* p. 11; Homer Tomlinson, *Diary of A. J. Tomlinson,* vol. 1, p. 37; A. J. Tomlinson, *The Last Great Conflict* (Cleveland, TN, 1913), pp. 200-215. Many in the Church of God bodies point to this event as the beginning of the Pentecostal movement in the United States.

9. Frodsham, *With Signs Following,* pp. 25-29; Parham, *Kol Kare Bomidbar,* pp. 29-38.

catalyst that congealed tongue-speaking into a fully defined doctrine. For years the phenomenon had been recognized but not singled out as a necessary evidence of the baptism with the Holy Ghost. It was Parham's insistence that tongues were necessary as the only "bible evidence" of the Holy Ghost baptism that caused division within the holiness ranks. The adherents of the Pentecostal doctrine had now settled on a single incontrovertible and repeatable kind of evidence, supported by biblical references and uniform for all. In his first sermon on Pentecost in 1901, Parham offered tongues as a solution to the problem of evidences:

> Now all Christians credit the fact that we are to be recipients of the Holy Spirit, but each have their own private interpretations as to his visible manifestations; some claim shouting, leaping, jumping, and falling in trances, while others put stress upon inspiration, unction and divine revelation. . . . How much more reasonable it would be for modern Holy Ghost teachers to first receive a Bible Evidence, such as the Disciples, instead of trying to get the world to take their word for it.[10]

It was precisely this settlement, that tongues were "the" evidence of the reception of the Holy Spirit, that gave Pentecostalism its greatest impetus. It at once solved the problem of proving to one's self and the world that one had received the experience. Pentecostalism thus succeeded in "doing what the Holiness Movement could not do" in that it offered the believer a "repeatable and unmistakable motor expression which, in effect, guaranteed one's possession of the Spirit."[11] In addition to solving the problem of evidence, the attaching of tongues to the Holy Ghost baptism had a strong basis in the New Testament, a fact that easily convinced many holiness people, practically all of whom interpreted the Bible literally.

Gaston Barnabas Cashwell

Most of those who read of the meeting at Azusa Street in holiness papers reacted favorably to the "California Pentecost." In Falcon, North

10. Parham, *Kol Kare Bomidbar*, p. 27.
11. James N. Lapsley and John H. Simpson, "Speaking in Tongues," *The Princeton Seminary Bulletin*, 58 (Feb. 1965): 6-7.

Carolina, at the campground headquarters of Crumpler's Holiness Church, preachers read each issue of *The Way of Faith* with great interest. One of the young preachers, George Floyd Taylor, reported that on reading his first account of the revival, "my heart said amen."[12] Another of Crumpler's preachers, Gaston Barnabas Cashwell, of Dunn, North Carolina, not only said "amen" at the news from Los Angeles, but decided to travel there to see for himself what was happening and, if possible, to receive his own Pentecostal experience.

Cashwell, destined to become the "Apostle of Pentecost" to the South, was a large man of some 250 pounds. Blond-haired and fair-faced, he was in 1906 a middle-aged man who had forsaken the Methodist ministry to join the ranks of the Pentecostal Holiness Church in 1903. When the annual conference of the church met in Lumberton, North Carolina, in November 1906, Cashwell was conspicuously absent. The Chairman of the Conference, Crumpler, read the following letter to the puzzled delegates:

> If I have offended anyone of you, forgive me. I realize that my life has fallen short of the standard of holiness we preach; but I have repented in my home in Dunn, North Carolina, and I have been restored. I am unable to be with you this time, for I am now leaving for Los Angeles, California, where I shall seek for the Baptism of the Holy Ghost.[13]

Those present were greatly interested in Cashwell's journey. Many had felt sympathetic toward the Azusa Street meeting and some had begun to pray for a similar outbreak to occur in the East, but Cashwell was the only one venturesome enough to cross the continent in quest of the Pentecostal experience.

On his arrival in Los Angeles, Cashwell went directly to the Azusa Street Mission. What he saw there was somewhat unsettling to this Southern gentleman. With Seymour preaching and the majority of worshippers black, he at first thought of leaving without participating in the service. After traveling so much distance, though, he felt he must attend, even if he failed to participate. During his first service in the mission, a young black man walked over to him and placed his hands on his head, praying for him to be "baptized with the Holy Ghost." This caused "chills

12. G. F. Taylor, *The Spirit and the Bride* (Dunn, NC, 1907), p. 39.
13. *The Pentecostal Holiness Advocate,* May 29, 1930, p. 1; Bailey, *Pioneer Marvels of Faith,* p. 48.

113

to go down my spine," Cashwell later reported. At first deeply prejudiced against "Negroes," he saw his prejudice fading as interest in speaking with tongues began to overwhelm him. After a few services he "lost his pride" and asked Seymour and several other blacks to lay hands on his head in order for him to be "filled." He soon received the Pentecostal experience and reportedly began to speak in the German language.[14]

Azusa Street East: Dunn, North Carolina

Cashwell did not tarry long in the "American Jerusalem" after his experience at Azusa Street. Returning to his home in Dunn, North Carolina, he rented an old three-story building that had previously been used as a tobacco warehouse. The Pentecostal meeting he planned would be for the Southeast what Azusa Street had been to the West. Beginning on December 31, 1906, the meeting would result in the conversion of most of the southeastern holiness movement to the Pentecostal view.[15]

Prior to the Dunn meeting, Cashwell had invited all the ministers of the Fire-Baptized Holiness Church, the Pentecostal Holiness Church, and the Free-Will Baptist Church to attend. The results far exceeded anything that had ever been seen in the southern holiness movement. Thousands of people jammed the old warehouse to see and hear firsthand about the "tongues movement." Practically the entire ministerium of the Pentecostal Holiness and the Fire-Baptized Holiness Churches attended, most of them going to the altar and receiving the Pentecostal experience that Cashwell preached. G. F. Taylor, one of the youngest ministers in Crumpler's church, was so intensely expecting to be "baptized" that in only five minutes after seeing the preacher who had been to Azusa Street "the Holy Ghost was talking" with the young minister's tongue.[16]

As the Dunn meeting continued, many Baptists, Methodists, and Presbyterians joined the holiness people at the services. For over a month the old warehouse resounded to Cashwell's preaching and the shouts of

14. G. B. Cashwell, "Came 3,000 Miles for His Pentecost," *The Apostolic Faith*, Dec. 1906, p. 3; L. R. Graham, one of Cashwell's early friends, personal interview with the author, 1966; Frodsham, *With Signs Following*, pp. 41-42. Also see Synan, *The Old-Time Power*, pp. 103-22.

15. Campbell, *The Pentecostal Holiness Church*, pp. 240-41; Florence Goff, *Tests and Triumphs* (Falcon, NC, 1923), p. 51.

16. Taylor, *The Spirit and the Bride*, p. 39.

the newly baptized. Scores of holiness preachers "went down to the altar" and came up "speaking in tongues, singing in tongues, laughing the holy laugh, shouting and leaping and dancing and praising God," in scenes reminiscent of the Cane Ridge camp meetings a hundred years earlier. One preacher of the Free-Will Baptist Church, H. H. Goff, attended the meeting and returned without receiving his "baptism." His children met him at the door saying, "Papa, Papa, have you got the tongues?" Replying in the negative, he added, "but I want it worse than anything in all the world." A few nights later he received "the tongues" in the warehouse among "a great multitude."[17]

Although many of the preachers of the Holiness Church and the Fire-Baptized Holiness Church attended the Dunn meeting, their leaders, Crumpler and King, were conspicuous by their absence. Crumpler had discussed the new doctrine of tongues with Taylor sometime before Cashwell's return to Dunn and had stated flatly that if Cashwell preached the Pentecostal doctrine "he was going to oppose" him. For some reason, Crumpler had no confidence in Cashwell and for that reason decided to leave the state for the duration of the Dunn revival. Holding a revival of his own in Florida during January 1907, Crumpler was unaware that most of his ministers were in Dunn in complete support of Cashwell's doctrine. This trip would be fatal to Crumpler's future control of the church.[18]

King spent the first days of January 1907 at his home in Toccoa, Georgia, not cognizant of the historic meeting in Dunn, although he already knew of the Azusa Street meeting. While preaching in a camp meeting at Thombury, Ontario, in September of 1906, he had met an old friend, A. H. Argue from Winnipeg, Manitoba, who told him about the Azusa Street revival. As the conversation ended, Argue handed him a copy of Seymour's *Apostolic Faith* magazine describing the new Pentecostal experience. Placing it in his pocket, King forgot it until some days later while riding the train through Buffalo on his way back to Georgia. Reading the paper with great interest, he found that he agreed with all of it. Seymour's teaching about receiving the baptism with the Holy Spirit subsequent to sanctification was what he had "believed and taught

17. Goff, *Tests and Triumphs*, p. 51; Campbell, *The Pentecostal Holiness Church*, p. 241; Thurman A. Carey, *Memoirs of Thurman A. Carey* (Columbia, SC, 1907), p. 21.

18. Campbell, *The Pentecostal Holiness Church*, p. 241. No evidence has been preserved describing the reasons for Crumpler's mistrust of Cashwell.

for a number of years." The claim of speaking with other tongues seemed to him a reasonable position since the paper did not claim it as the only evidence of the baptism. Arriving in Toccoa, he heard more reports from California and was "pleased to learn of this mighty work." At the time of the Dunn meeting, King was in his home in Toccoa engaged in ten days of "prayer and fasting for an outpouring of the Holy Spirit."[19]

The Dunn meeting came to a close at the end of January 1907, but services continued in the Dunn Pentecostal Holiness Church where Cashwell had preached before the revival was moved to the warehouse. The Dunn meeting generated great excitement all over the Southeast. Accounts of it were carried in the *Way of Faith* and spread far and wide. Holiness people from Danville, Virginia, to Birmingham, Alabama, bombarded the evangelist with requests for similar revivals in their communities. As he traveled through the South from 1906 to 1909, Cashwell established himself firmly as the "pentecostal apostle to the South."[20]

From Dunn, Cashwell toured the South holding revivals in Memphis, Tennessee; West Union, Clinton, and Lake City, South Carolina; High Point, North Carolina; Danville, Virginia; Toccoa and Valdosta, Georgia; and Birmingham, Alabama. Wherever he went huge crowds gathered to hear him preach the new gospel of Pentecost and tongues. Everywhere, holiness preachers either joined his cause or openly opposed him. His opening volley in every meeting would be, "Come on, preachers, bring your Bibles out." To those who came he taught that speaking with other tongues was the only biblical evidence of receiving the Holy Ghost. To the seekers at the mourner's bench he would say, "Keep on praying, He [the Holy Spirit] will testify when He comes in." In every meeting, scores testified to receiving the experience of speaking with other tongues. Of these meetings Taylor wrote excitedly in September 1907, "So a great revival is now upon us, and it is sweeping the world. This is the latter rain." With such interest in his work, Cashwell began publishing a paper before the end of the year called *The Bride-*

---

19. King and King, *Yet Speaketh*, pp. 111-13.

20. The best accounts of the Dunn revival are found in Taylor, *The Spirit and the Bride*, pp. 44-95; F. M. Britton, *Pentecostal Truth, or Sermons on Regeneration, Sanctification, the Baptism of the Holy Spirit, Divine Healing, the Second Coming of Jesus, etc.* (Royston, GA, 1919), pp. 235-43; King and King, *Yet Speaketh*, pp. 111-14; Goff, *Tests and Triumphs*, pp. 49-53; and Campbell, *The Pentecostal Holiness Church*, pp. 240-44.

groom's Messenger, a periodical intended by its editor "to take care of the pentecostal work of the South." Through the pages of this publication countless more learned of the Pentecostal message.[21]

Cashwell and King

Convincing the masses and the pastors of the holiness churches was a relatively easy task for Cashwell, but converting the denominational leaders was a more difficult matter. His first confrontation with a church leader came in February 1907, when the Fire-Baptized Holiness congregation in Toccoa, Georgia, invited him to hold some special services. Attending this revival was J. H. King, the General Overseer of the Fire-Baptized Holiness Church and pastor of the Toccoa congregation. Although he had spent much of January praying and fasting for an "outpouring" of the Holy Spirit, King was not at all prepared to accept Cashwell's teaching as the fulfillment of the revival he was seeking. When Cashwell arrived in Toccoa, King, an astute student of the Greek New Testament, prepared to join him in a theological battle over tongues, a doctrine he still questioned. Taking Dean Alford's *Critical Notes on the New Testament* in Greek, Wesley's *Notes,* and a New Testament, he spent several hours examining the biblical texts dealing with speaking with tongues. To his astonishment, all that he read confirmed in his mind the correctness of Cashwell's views. After a great intellectual struggle, he arrived at the first service "with an open mind." He soon found himself not only in agreement with the new Pentecostal view, but at the altar seeking the experience. The next night, February 15, 1907, he received the experience, and thereafter became one of the nation's leading exponents of Pentecostal theology. Putting the new theology into practice, King immediately renounced Irwin's teaching on the baptism of fire, changed the name of *Live Coals of Fire* to *The Apostolic Evangel,* and promised henceforth to print the testimonies only of those who accepted tongues as evidence.[22]

The next holiness leader to accept the Pentecostal view from Cash-

---

21. *The Pentecostal Holiness Advocate,* Nov. 8, 1917, p. 8. L. R. Graham, personal interview with the author, Nov. 1966; Taylor, *The Spirit and the Bride,* pp. 39-59.

22. King and King, *Yet Speaketh,* pp. 116-21; King, *From Passover to Pentecost,* pp. 167-82. See *The Apostolic Faith* (Los Angeles), Feb.-Mar. 1907, p. 5.

well was N. J. Holmes, whose "Altamont Bible School" in 1906-07 was located on Paris Mountain outside Greenville, South Carolina. On first hearing of the Dunn meeting, Holmes was doubtful about the "tongues baptism." In 1905 a student in the school had spoken with tongues in a prayer meeting, causing great wonder and excitement among the student body. The Azusa Street meeting and the Dunn revival had been reported in *The Way of Faith* and had been followed closely by faculty and students alike. In the spring of 1907, a student by the name of Lida Purkie attended one of Cashwell's services at West Union, South Carolina, and returned to the school a confirmed Pentecostal. Completely stirred by this event, the student body voted to send Holmes to West Union to investigate the phenomenon. Holmes returned convinced that "God was in it," although he disagreed with Cashwell's theology. In the weeks that followed, many of the students received the experience and began to speak with other tongues. The outbreak became so intense that "neither Holmes nor the teachers knew what to do" about it. Eventually a study of the scriptures convinced Holmes and his wife, as well as L. R. Graham, Holmes's assistant, that the Pentecostal doctrine was correct. By April 1907, Holmes and practically the entire faculty and student body had spoken with tongues. From that time forward Holmes's school became a bastion of Pentecostal theology.[23]

The Pentecostal Holiness Church

In his efforts to convert the leader of his own church, A. B. Crumpler, to the Pentecostal view, Cashwell met with failure. On his return from Florida in February 1907, Crumpler wasted no time in opposing the new doctrine that seemed to be sweeping his church. In several articles in the *Holiness Advocate,* he had vigorously denounced Cashwell and his "jabbering" followers. But by that time the majority of his readers were

---

23. Holmes, *Life Sketches and Sermons,* pp. 36-58; Thomas, *History of Holmes Theological Seminary,* pp. 13-14; L. R. Graham, personal interview with the author, Nov. 1966. Dr. Paul F. Beacham and Mrs. Nina Holmes, in a personal interview with the author, Jan. 11, 1967, stated that Holmes first opposed Irwin's "baptism with fire" in 1898. His conversion to Pentecostalism came as a result of his study of tongues in the Scriptures. Holmes College of the Bible (the present name) was the first institution of higher learning to embrace the Pentecostal view.

Pentecostal in sentiment if not in fact. By the end of 1907 the subscription list had fallen so low, because of protest to his articles, that publication had to be suspended. For several months Cashwell's "pentecostal party" vied with Crumpler's "anti-pentecostal party" for control of the church. By 1908 it was apparent that a showdown would come in the church's convention, scheduled to meet that year in Dunn, North Carolina.[24]

The climactic events in the controversy occurred in November 1908, in the denomination's Dunn Convention. Both the Pentecostal and the anti-Pentecostal factions arrived in strength for the meeting. Crumpler's views were by then well known from both his articles in the *Holiness Advocate* and his scathing sermons in various churches. The Pentecostal faction was led by Cashwell, who by 1908 considered himself the natural leader of the Southern Pentecostals, and by G. F. Taylor, whose book *The Spirit and the Bride* had appeared in September 1907, in ringing defense of the new doctrine. Although the Pentecostals were clearly in the majority, they voted to retain Crumpler as president on the first day of the convention.[25]

Before the first day of the convention ended, Crumpler realized he had no hope of overcoming the Pentecostal majority, and he withdrew from the church he had created. Leaving with him was one pastor and his church at LaGrange, North Carolina. The other fourteen churches and most of the other preachers remained with the Pentecostals. With the defection of Crumpler, a member of the Pentecostal party, A. H. Butler, was elected to the vacant president's chair. The work of the convention that followed was devoted to reforming the movement in the Pentecostal image. Cashwell's paper, *The Bridegroom's Messenger,* was adopted as "the organ of this church until further arrangements" to take the place of Crumpler's now defunct *Holiness Advocate.* Cashwell was designated chairman of the committee to revise the *Discipline* of the church.[26]

The *Discipline* was duly revised by the committee, which added a paragraph stating "that on receiving the baptism with the Holy Ghost

24. Campbell, *The Pentecostal Holiness Church,* pp. 241-44.
25. *Proceedings of the Ninth Annual Convention of the Holiness Church of North Carolina* (Dunn, NC, 1908), pp. 3-4; Taylor, "Our Church History," *The Pentecostal Holiness Advocate,* Mar. 17, 1921, pp. 8-9. Taylor's *The Spirit and the Bride* was the first post–Azusa Street book-length defense of the new Pentecostal theology.
26. *Proceedings of the Holiness Church,* p. 4.

we have the same evidence which followed in Acts 2nd, 10th, and 19th chapters, to wit: the speaking with other tongues as the Spirit gave utterance." To further insure the future Pentecostal character of the church, the convention adopted a resolution offered by Cashwell and two of his friends:

> Resolved, that this convention request all pastors and officers of the churches to admit no preacher or teacher into any of our churches who preach or teach against the baptism of the Holy Ghost as taught in our revised *Discipline*.[27]

Thus the little denomination, which in 1908 included fifteen churches, all within the state of North Carolina, became officially a Pentecostal church. The following year the same group, which had been called "The Holiness Church of North Carolina" since 1901, voted to restore the prefix "Pentecostal" to its name since it was now definitely a part of the fast-growing Pentecostal movement.[28]

In the long run, the church's identification with the Pentecostal movement and the loss of Crumpler, its founder, caused little harm to the young church. When the final reckoning was made of gains and losses, it was found that only two churches refused to accept the new doctrine, while only "five or six preachers and a few scattered members" left with Crumpler. Soon afterwards Crumpler returned to the Methodist Church, and remained there for the rest of his life.[29]

In the same area of North Carolina that saw the Pentecostal Holiness Church undergo its doctrinal revolution, the Free-Will Baptist Church also felt the winds of change. As has already been noted, a part of the Free-Will Baptist membership had accepted the holiness teaching before Crumpler's 1896 revivals, and many more during the height of his preaching campaigns in the state. When Cashwell returned to Dunn from Los Angeles in 1906, many Free-Will Baptist ministers also accepted the Pentecostal message. In time a controversy erupted between the Pentecostal and non-Pentecostal elements of the church, resulting eventually in the organization of the "Pentecostal Free-Will Baptist

27. *Proceedings of the Holiness Church*, pp. 6-7.
28. *Proceedings of the Tenth Annual Convention of the Pentecostal Holiness Church*, 1909, p. 6.
29. *The Advocate*, May 29, 1930, p. 1; Dec. 27, 1917, p. 14; Campbell, *The Pentecostal Holiness Church*, p. 249.

Church" with headquarters in Dunn, North Carolina. Many Southern Baptist members also became converts to Pentecostalism through the efforts of traveling evangelists who made converts in private homes, brush arbors, and tent meetings throughout the area.[30]

One of the more ecumenical results of the Dunn Pentecostal revival was the merger of the Pentecostal Holiness Church with the Fire-Baptized Holiness Church in 1911. Since the two denominations operated in practically the same territory and shared the same doctrines after 1906, a merger seemed desirable. Accordingly, the Pentecostal Holiness Church adopted a motion offered by G. F. Taylor at its 1909 convention, inviting the Fire-Baptized Holiness Church and the Pentecostal element of the Free-Will Baptist Church to join them. In the following months the Fire-Baptized Holiness Church accepted the proposal and appointed a commission to negotiate with representatives of the Pentecostal Holiness Church. The Free-Will Baptists, however, voted not to participate in the merger proceedings.[31]

The convention that effected this merger took place in Falcon, North Carolina, during January 1911. Meeting in the octagonal tabernacle on the grounds of the historic Falcon Campgrounds, the two groups worked out the intricate problems of merger in only a few days. The consolidation was ratified on January 30, with only two dissenting votes out of a total of thirty-eight cast. The new organization voted to adopt the name of the younger and smaller group, the Pentecostal Holiness Church. Since J. H. King, General Overseer of the Fire-Baptized Holiness Church, was absent from the convention, being at the time on a world tour of the mission fields, another member of his church, S. D. Page, was elected to fill the newly created office of "General Superintendent." Elected as his assistants were King, who was given responsibility for foreign missions, and A. H. Butler, former head of the Pentecostal Holiness Church, as head of the "home missions" division. At the

30. *Discipline of the Pentecostal Free-Will Baptist Church, Inc.,* pp. 8-16; Stewart, *History of the Free-Will Baptists,* pp. 411-16; Goff, *Tests and Triumphs,* pp. 49-65. H. T. Spence, in an interview with the author on Nov. 11, 1966, described how a traveling "tongues" preacher brought the Pentecostal message to his Baptist Church in Raleigh in 1908. After getting this new "funny religion," the entire Spence family joined the local Pentecostal Holiness Church.

31. Campbell, *The Pentecostal Holiness Church,* pp. 251-55; *Proceedings of the Pentecostal Holiness Church, 1909,* p. 7. The most complete account of the merger is in Synan, *Old-Time Power,* pp. 126-32.

time of the consolidation, the new church had congregations in the states of North Carolina, South Carolina, Georgia, Florida, Virginia, Oklahoma, and Tennessee. The year following, a Negro convention was added to the denomination, but it was to be extremely short-lived, being dropped from the roll in 1913.[32]

In 1915 another merger was enacted, combining the Pentecostal Holiness Church with the Tabernacle Pentecostal Church of South Carolina. The latter church had been formed by N. J. Holmes in connection with his Bible College in Greenville, South Carolina, in 1910. First called the Brewerton Presbyterian Church, it later changed its name to the Tabernacle Pentecostal Church to designate its doctrinal position. Although Holmes and his college church in Greenville did not participate in the merger, several former Presbyterian Churches in South Carolina joined the Pentecostal Holiness Church at a meeting in Canon, Georgia, in 1915.[33] These mergers, which produced the present Pentecostal Holiness Church, illustrated that both the Pentecostal and holiness movements contained strong ecumenical tendencies.

After bringing the Pentecostal message to the eastern seaboard through the 1906-7 Dunn revival, Cashwell received invitations to preach throughout the South. Word of his revival campaigns was spread through the pages of his *Bridegroom's Messenger, The Apostolic Evangel* and the *Way of Faith.* From 1906 to 1909 his services were in great demand; invitations came by the score for him to preach the Pentecostal message in many states. Following the Dunn and Toccoa meetings, Cashwell was invited to Memphis and Birmingham to preach to interested groups who had read of his services in the East. In May 1907, he traveled to Memphis, where a tent meeting caused a minor sensation, with much glossolalia in evidence. As a result of this meeting the first Pentecostal church of Memphis was organized. Following the Memphis meeting, Cashwell journeyed to Birmingham, where another important Pentecostal outbreak occurred. Two men who received the Pentecostal experience in

32. *Discipline of the Pentecostal Holiness Church, 1965,* pp. 6-7; *Minutes of the First General Convention of the Pentecostal Holiness Church, 1911,* pp. 1-4; Campbell, *The Pentecostal Holiness Church,* pp. 255-59; King and King, *Yet Speaketh,* pp. 142-294. On his world tour King traveled to Japan, China, India, the Near East, and northern Europe. During the tour he met the earliest Pentecostal leaders in these lands and helped to shape the world Pentecostal movement by his sermons and lectures.

33. *Manual of the Pentecostal Holiness Church,* 1965, p. 7; Campbell, *The Pentecostal Holiness Church,* pp. 263-66.

Birmingham were H. G. Rodgers and M. M. Pinson, both former Methodist ministers. They later formed a Pentecostal Association in the Mississippi Valley, which eventually became a part of the Assemblies of God denomination. Cashwell's preaching tour through Western Tennessee and Alabama was the first instance of the Pentecostal doctrine being taught in the mid-southern region.[34]

Cashwell in Cleveland, Tennessee

News of the Pentecostal revival sweeping the South came to the leaders of the Church of God in Cleveland, Tennessee, through the preaching of Cashwell in Birmingham. Although many had spoken with tongues in the Fire-Baptized revival at Camp Creek, North Carolina, in 1896, the Church of God had not embraced it as a formal doctrine. The first direct contact its General Overseer , A. J. Tomlinson, had with the new doctrine was in a meeting with M. M. Pinson in Birmingham, Alabama, in June 1907. While preaching there, Tomlinson was amazed to hear Pinson and others speaking in foreign languages. After a week of services with Pinson, he wrote in his *Diary* that "glorious results" came from the revival, adding the terse statement "speaking in tongues by the Holy Ghost." On his return to Cleveland, he found that many of his preachers had already received the experience. He then determined to invite Cashwell to Cleveland so that his churchmen could hear the doctrine from the lips of the southern "Apostle of Pentecost" himself.[35]

Tomlinson and other Church of God leaders had been much interested in the spreading Pentecostal revival throughout the year 1907. In January of that year Tomlinson had preached on "The Baptism with the Holy Spirit" to the denomination's General Assembly and had seen several of his subordinates receive this experience with the accompaniment of tongues, although he himself had not, even though he had sought it on several occasions.[36] Finally, at the close of the General Assembly at

34. B. F. Lawrence, *The Apostolic Faith Restored* (Springfield, MO, 1916), pp. 90-95; Bailey, *Pioneer Marvels,* pp. 33-34. Pinson and Rodgers were two of the leading founders of the Assemblies of God, a church destined to become the largest Pentecostal denomination in the United States.

35. Tomlinson, "Journal of Happenings," June 14, 1907; *Church of God Evangel,* Mar. 8, 1916, p. 2.

36. Tomlinson, *Answering the Call of God,* p. 9.

Cleveland in January 1908, Cashwell was preaching in a revival at the local Church of God. On Sunday, January 12, after the close of the General Assembly, Cashwell began to preach on the subject of Pentecost. Tomlinson listened intently. While Cashwell continued to preach, the General Overseer slipped out of his chair "in a heap on the rostrum at . . . Cashwell's feet." While lying there Tomlinson received the Pentecostal experience and according to his own testimony, spoke in ten different languages. From that point on, the Church of God and all its subsequent branches became full-fledged members of the Pentecostal movement.[37]

Following Tomlinson's baptism under Cashwell's preaching, the Church of God experienced one of its greatest advances under the impetus of the new Pentecostal message. Congregations sprang up in both Chattanooga and Cleveland. A tent meeting held in September 1908 caused the Cleveland newspaper to report that "the Holiness people have practically captured all east and northeast Cleveland, and their strength is materially increasing."[38] The next month a local preacher wrote in panic that "our town and country is flooded with false Pentecostal doctrine — satanic power and influence is taking its sway." It was evident from these meetings that the Pentecostal doctrine struck a responsive chord in southern Protestants. The Church of God was beginning to move "like a mighty army" across the land.[39]

Following the lead of the larger group in Cleveland with the same name, the Church of God (Mountain Assembly) in Kentucky also received the Pentecostal doctrine. Hearing of the Azusa Street meeting through various holiness periodicals in 1906, the group's leaders, notably J. H. Bryant and J. H. Parks, introduced the doctrine to their church. Much persecution followed during the years 1906 and 1907, with bands of rowdies interrupting services and trying to discourage the spread of the "holy rollers," but the little church survived the challenge. In the years following 1906 church growth was slow and tedious, mainly because of its isolation.[40]

---

37. Tomlinson, "Journal of Happenings," Jan. 13, 1908; *Answering the Call of God*, pp. 9-10; Homer Tomlinson, *Diary of A. J. Tomlinson*, vol. 1, pp. 27-36; Conn, *Like a Mighty Army*, pp. 84-85. Tomlinson's baptism is one of the most graphic and detailed in all Pentecostal literature. See Tomlinson, *Diary of A. J. Tomlinson*, vol. 1, pp. 27-29.

38. *The (Cleveland) Journal and Banner*, Sept. 17, 1908, p. 3; quoted in Conn, *Like a Mighty Army*, p. 87.

39. *The (Cleveland) Journal and Banner*, Oct. 29, 1908, p. 1.

40. Gibson, *History of the Church of God, Mountain Assembly*, pp. 51-53.

The Church of God in Christ

Early in 1907 news of the Pentecostal revival in Los Angeles came to the attention of the leaders of the Church of God in Christ in Memphis. The two dominant personalities in this infant holiness church, C. H. Mason and C. P. Jones, reacted differently to the accounts from California. Mason, convinced from an early age that "God endowed him with supernatural characteristics, which were manifested in dreams and visions," felt strangely drawn to investigate the Pentecostal services at Azusa Street. Jones, on the other hand, was cool to the idea of speaking with other tongues. In March 1907, Mason persuaded two of his fellow ministers, J. A. Jeter and D. J. Young, to travel with him to Los Angeles to investigate the Azusa Street revival. Arriving in California, the three went directly to Azusa Street where they were delighted to see Seymour, a fellow black, in charge of the services — which by then were largely attended by whites. During their five-week stay, all three men received the Pentecostal experience and returned to Memphis as convinced Pentecostals. From Los Angeles, Mason went to Norfolk, Virginia to attend the 300th anniversary of the founding of the Jamestown colony in Virginia. Fired by his Los Angeles experience, he preached Pentecost to his fellow blacks in Norfolk and Portsmouth, and made several thousand converts.[41]

Division in Jackson

Upon his return to Memphis, Mason found that another Azusa Street veteran, Glenn A. Cook, a native of Los Angeles, had preceded him with the Pentecostal message. Cook, a white man, had already made many Pentecostal converts. But the intrusion of Pentecostal doctrine under Cook's and Mason's leadership alienated Jones, then "General Overseer" and "Presiding Elder." Soon the Pentecostal faction, under Mason, and the non-Pentecostal faction, under Jones, became locked in a leadership struggle. One of the two men who accompanied Mason to Azusa Street, J. A. Jeter, sided with Jones, while D. J. Young followed Mason and the Pentecostal faction. At the church's General Assembly that met in Jack-

41. Clemmons, *Bishop C. H. Mason,* pp. 26, 45-48; Mason, *Bishop C. H. Mason,* pp. 18-22; Fidler, "Historical Review of the Pentecostal Outpouring in Los Angeles," p. 14; Kendrick, *The Promise Fulfilled,* pp. 197-98.

son, Mississippi, in August 1907, the Pentecostal controversy dominated the proceedings. After a "very lengthy discussion," the Assembly "withdrew from C. H. Mason and all who promulgated the doctrine of speaking with tongues the right hand of fellowship." In response, Mason and fourteen churches in Tennessee, Arkansas, Mississippi, and Oklahoma withdrew from the Assembly. Jones, remaining in control of the non-Pentecostal faction, later changed the name of his group to "The Church of Christ (Holiness) U.S.A." in 1911.[42]

Later that same year Mason convened another Assembly in Memphis, this one representing the Pentecostal group that had been expelled in Jackson. In this first "General Assembly" of the new Pentecostal church, the old name, "Church of God in Christ," was retained and a Pentecostal paragraph added to the articles of faith. The doctrine of entire sanctification as a second work of grace was retained, thereby keeping the church in the holiness tradition. Mason and his chief aide, D. J. Young, immediately began publication of a new periodical, *The Whole Truth,* to promote Pentecost in the church. From its reorganization in 1907, the Church of God in Christ grew rapidly to become the largest black Pentecostal group in the world. So great was Mason's prestige that many white Pentecostal ministers accepted ordination at his hands. From 1907 to 1914 the church was interracial, and many whites joined it; as an incorporated denomination, the Church of God in Christ could obtain clergy passes for the railways, and aid them in being bonded for weddings. Many of the men who founded the white "Assemblies of God" church in 1914 were thus ordained in the Church of God in Christ by Bishop Mason.[43]

With the conversion of Mason to the Pentecostal position, the Pentecostal invasion of the South was complete. In only a few months much of the holiness movement in the South had been converted to Pentecostalism. Some holiness bodies, such as J. O. McClurkan's Pentecostal mission in Nashville and the Wesleyan Methodist Church, refused to countenance the "new light" on Pentecost. The thousands of holiness

42. Charles E. Jones, "Church of God in Christ," in Burgess, et al., *Dictionary of Pentecostal and Charismatic Movements,* pp. 204-5; *Yearbook of the Church of God in Christ, 1960-1961,* p. 9; Kendrick, *The Promise Fulfilled,* p. 198; Mason, *Bishop C. H. Mason,* p. 22; Landis, *Yearbook of American Churches* (New York, 1965), p. 33; Clemmons, *Bishop C. H. Mason,* pp. 61-71.

43. *Yearbook of the Church of God in Christ, 1960-1961,* p. 9; Fidler, "Historical Review of the Pentecostal Outpouring in Los Angeles," p. 14; Kendrick, *The Promise Fulfilled,* p. 80. *The Yearbook of American Churches, 1965,* pp. 33-37, credits Jones's

devotees remaining in the Methodist Episcopal Church, South, remained largely untouched by the movement. Other leaders, such as A. B. Simpson, head of the Christian and Missionary Alliance, rejected the Pentecostal view only after much investigation and even seeking for the experience. The surviving members of the older, more conservative wing of the holiness movement sternly denounced the new movement. W. B. Godbey, L. L. Pickett, George D. Watson, and many others rejected "tongues" as unscriptural and even "demon-inspired." But by 1908 the die was cast, especially in the South. With the major southern holiness bodies — the Church of God, the Pentecostal Holiness Church, the Fire-Baptized Holiness Church, and the Church of God in Christ — all now firmly in the Pentecostal camp, future major growth in the South was to be on the side of the Pentecostals. In many areas the term "holiness church" would become synonymous in the public mind with Pentecostalism.[44]

B. H. Irwin at Azusa Street

An interesting breakthrough for the infant Pentecostal movement was the winning of B. H. Irwin to the new Pentecostal experience. By 1906 Irwin, who had left his Fire-Baptized movement in disgrace in 1900, was living in California and had come into contact with the Azusa Street meetings. He soon received a new tongues-attested "third blessing" and spoke in tongues. Discarding his previous "baptisms" of fire, dynamite, lyddite, and oxidite, he now proclaimed that the "tongues" baptism was the correct one that he had been seeking all along. By

---

Church of Christ (Holiness) with having 7,621 members in 146 churches, while Mason's Church of God in Christ claimed 413,000 members in 4,100 churches. By 1996, the Church of God in Christ claimed over 6,000,000 members in the United States, while the Church of Christ (Holiness), numbered some 15,000. See Vinson Synan, "The Role of Tongues as Initial Evidence," pp. 67-83.

44. See Holmes, *Life Sketches and Sermons,* pp. 152-70; Taylor, *The Spirit and the Bride,* p. 52. For the views of the Church of the Nazarene, see Smith, *Called Unto Holiness,* pp. 319-20. The classical holiness view also found strong expression in *The Pentecostal Herald,* edited from Asbury College by Henry Clay Morrison from 1888 to 1942 and thereafter by J. C. McPheeters. Throughout this period, this influential voice of the holiness movement expressed a staunch anti-tongues position.

1907, a restored Irwin was leading Pentecostal services from California to Oregon.[45]

The key to the amazing spread of the Pentecostal movement into the South was the receptive attitude of the various holiness leaders in the months from 1906 through 1908. The winning of King, Tomlinson, and Mason was crucial to the Pentecostal advance. All three were deeply committed to the holiness movement and adhered to the second work theory of sanctification. When the Pentecostal revival came, they merely added a "third experience" to the first two. When doctrinal difficulties later brought the experience of sanctification into question, the Southern churches held firmly to the perfectionism they had inherited from Methodism. By accepting the "radical" doctrine of speaking with other tongues, they displayed their willingness to change. By retaining and staunchly defending the conservative doctrine of sanctification, they illustrated their uncompromising orthodoxy.

Among the casualties of the new movement was the "pentecostal prophet to the South" himself. After 1908, Cashwell found that he could not control the movement he had been so responsible for beginning. A temperamental and egotistical man, he succeeded in making enemies as well as friends for the movement. In 1909, he defected from the Pentecostal Holiness Church and returned to the Methodist Church, as Crumpler had done before him. But try as he might, he could not undo his own brief preaching tour of 1906 through 1908. Nor could he erase its results — the bringing of three holiness denominations into the Pentecostal movement, a seismic shift that would profoundly affect the religious future, not just of the South, but of the entire country.[46]

45. See *The Apostolic Faith* (Los Angeles), Nov. 6, 1907, p. 4; Feb.-Mar. 1907, p. 1; Apr. 1907, p. 4. For a vivid description of his tongues baptism see his letter to Thomas B. Barratt in David Bundy's "Spiritual Advice to a Seeker . . ." in *Pneuma*, Fall 1992, pp. 167-68.

46. Cashwell's name was dropped from the roll of the Pentecostal Holiness Church in 1910; see the *Proceedings of the Pentecostal Holiness Church in 1910*, p. 4. See also Bailey, *Pioneer Marvels of Faith*, pp. 48-49. Campbell states in his *The Pentecostal Holiness Church*, p. 241, that Cashwell "did grievously fail God and bring reproach on the cause of the full gospel," although he does not include the nature of his failure. Other contemporaries claimed that he ministered faithfully until his death in 1916. Part of this information is based on H. T. Spence's interview with the author, Nov. 11, 1966.

CHAPTER SEVEN

Missionaries of the One Way Ticket

*Folk from all denominations are rushing to the meetings.
A number have received their pentecost and are speaking in tongues. . . . Many are seeking salvation and
souls are being gloriously saved. Hundreds are seeking
a clean heart, and the fire is falling on the purified
sacrifice. People who have attended the meetings are
taking the fire with them to the towns round about.*

T. B. Barratt (Oslo, 1907)

Because of the work of Cashwell and Mason from 1906 to 1909, the American South became the first region in the world where Pentecostalism put down deep roots and significantly changed the spiritual landscape. As a religion of the poor and disinherited, Pentecostalism found fertile soil in the impoverished South, where both blacks and whites struggled to eke out an existence on the economic and social margins of society. The first Pentecostal denominations in the world, including the Church of God in Christ, the Pentecostal Holiness Church, the Church of God (Tennessee) and the Assemblies of God, took root in the states of the old confederacy. Indeed, in the decades to come, the southern Pentecostal groups would play major roles in developing the ethos and character of the movement. But the dynamic forces unleashed at Azusa Street soon transcended all boundaries of culture, nationality, and theological tradition.

During the three "glory years" at Azusa Street (1906-09), the center of the movement was clearly Los Angeles, under the direction of Seymour and his staff. Within weeks of the opening services there, speaking in tongues and other gifts of the Spirit were being reported in many other parts of the world. For example, by January 1907, headlines in *The Apostolic Faith* spoke prophetically of the "Beginning of a Worldwide Revival." Under a headline proclaiming "Pentecost Both Sides the Ocean [*sic*]," the February-March 1907 issue reported outbreaks of tongues in London, Stockholm, Oslo, and Calcutta. Later issues told of Pentecostal beginnings in Africa, Canada, Hawaii, China, Denmark, Australia, and even in Jerusalem. As Bartleman predicted, the Pentecostal revival was "a worldwide one without doubt."[1]

Europe

In addition to the ministers who received their Pentecostal experience directly at Azusa Street, thousands of others were influenced indirectly. Among these was Thomas Ball Barratt of Norway, a sanctified Methodist minister who, at the turn of the century, was serving as a leading Methodist pastor in Norway. In 1906, he came to the United States with the aim of raising funds for a city mission in Oslo (then known as Christiana), the capital city of the nation.

While in New York, Barratt heard of the Azusa Street revival and instinctively recognized it as the long-prayed-for latter day outpouring of the Holy Spirit. Like many others at the time he thought it would be necessary to travel to Los Angeles to receive his baptism. Before he completed his plans for the trip, however, he received the Pentecostal experience in his New York hotel room on October 7, 1906, after praying for up to twelve hours a day. A man who had studied voice under Edvard Grieg, Barratt not only shouted and spoke in "seven or eight languages,"

---

1. See *The Apostolic Faith,* Jan. 1906, p. 1; Feb.-Mar. 1907, p. 1; May 1908, p. 1. See also Bartleman's *How "Pentecost" Came to Los Angeles,* pp. 43-66, and Vinson Synan, "Frank Bartleman and Azusa Street," in Frank Bartleman, *Azusa Street* (Plainfield, NJ, 1980), pp. ix-xxv.

but also burst into "a beautiful baritone solo, using one of the most pure and delightful languages I had ever heard."[2]

In December of 1906, Barratt returned to Oslo where he rented a gymnasium seating 2,000 persons for the first modern Pentecostal meeting held in Europe. Here, he reported, many were seeking "a clean heart" so that the Spirit could fall on "the purified sacrifice."[3] In a short time, Barratt was established as the apostle of Pentecostalism in northern and western Europe. Pastors from all over the continent came to visit, and under Barratt's exhortation received their own baptisms in the Holy Spirit. One of his most notable converts was Alexander Boddy, the Anglican Vicar of All Saints' Parish in Sunderland, England. By 1907, Boddy was not only leading interested visitors into the tongues baptism, but was also challenging the Keswick conference to consider the possibility of a "new Pentecost" for England, a suggestion that was roundly rejected by the Keswick leaders. Despite this setback, Boddy in 1908 began publication of a Pentecostal magazine called *Confidence* and, until the outbreak of World War I, conducted annual Whitsuntide Pentecostal conferences in Sunderland.[4]

Another Barratt convert was Jonathan Paul, a leader in the German holiness movement. After a trip to visit Barratt in Oslo in 1907, Paul returned to conduct Pentecostal meetings in the city of Kassel. These meetings resulted in the formation of a new German Pentecostal denomination known as the "Muhlheim Association." In a short time the "tumultuous" meetings in Kassel became so controversial that a group of German evangelicals issued a highly critical "Berlin Declaration" in 1909 that condemned Pentecostalism as being "not from above but from below." They furthermore stated, "We do not expect a new pentecost — we wait for the returning of the Lord."[5] Because of this severe opposition, the Pentecostal movement grew more slowly in Germany than in other European countries.[6]

---

2. Thomas Ball Barratt, *In the Days of the Latter Rain* (Oslo, Norway, 1909). Also see his *When the Fire Fell: An Outline of My Life* (Oslo, Norway, 1927), pp. 99-126.

3. Stanley Frodsham, *With Signs Following*, pp. 71-72.

4. See Edith Blumhofer's "Alexander Boddy and the Rise of Pentecostalism in Britain," *Pneuma* 8 (1986): 31-40; and "John Alexander Dowie," in Burgess et al., *Dictionary of Pentecostal and Charismatic Movements*, pp. 248-49.

5. Ernst Giese, *Und Flicken Die Netze* (Marburg, Germany, 1976), pp. 124-33.

6. Walter Hollenweger, *The Pentecostals: The Charismatic Movement in the Churches* (Minneapolis, 1972), pp. 218-43. Also see David Bundy, "Jonathan Paul," in Burgess et al., *Dictionary of Pentecostal and Charismatic Movements*, p. 664.

One of the most important of Barratt's converts was Lewi Pethrus, a Baptist pastor from Stockholm who visited Barratt in Oslo in 1907 to learn more about the baptism in the Holy Spirit. Under Barratt's prayers, Pethrus spoke in tongues and dedicated himself to propagating the movement in Sweden. On his return from Oslo, he led a monumental revival in his local Baptist church. The Baptist association soon conducted a trial and expelled Pethrus for departing from Baptist doctrine and practice. His congregation, renamed the "Filadelfia" church, eventually grew to became the largest free church in Europe.[7]

The Chicago Connection

While Pentecostalism was spreading rapidly outside the United States, changes were taking place in the nation of its birth that would radically change the movement in a few years. By 1910, the strategic center for the worldwide spread of the movement had shifted from Los Angeles to Chicago. At least three reasons could be cited for this shift. One was the loss of *The Apostolic Faith* mailing list in 1908, when Florence Crawford took it with her to Portland, Oregon. Without this list, Seymour was cut off from his supporters, and, although she continued publication of the paper from Portland, Crawford was unable to achieve the stature needed to succeed Seymour or Parham as the major leader of the movement. A second reason was the apparent rejection and excommunication of the Azusa Street mission by Parham and his followers. A third reason was Parham's loss of influence due to accusations concerning his character. For a short time, the leadership vacuum was filled by the Chicago pastor William H. Durham, a disciple of Seymour who had been baptized in the Holy Spirit at Asusa Street in 1907. At that point Seymour prophesied that Durham would be come an "apostle" of the new movement.[8]

In a short time, Durham's paper, *The Pentecostal Testimony,* became a fountain of information for the movement in both the United States and Canada. Durham's North Avenue Mission in downtown Chicago soon became the new mecca for those seeking the Pentecostal experience. In fact, for the next decade, Chicago served as the de facto worldwide

7. For more on Pethrus, see his *Memoirs* (5 vols. 1953-56), and B. Andstrom's *Lewis Pethrus* (1966).
8. Douglas Nelson, "For Such a Time as This," pp. 62-64, 216-19.

missions and theological center for the fast-growing movement. Durham's later "finished work" theology of gradual progressive sanctification eventually led to the formation of the Assemblies of God in 1914, a denomination destined to become the largest Pentecostal church in the world — claiming by 1995 over 32 million adherents in over 150 nations of the world.

Those attracted to Durham and his mission included not only Aimee Semple McPherson, who later founded the International Church of the Foursquare Gospel, but the founders of many other Pentecostal movements around the world. Some of these were destined to grow into huge "havens of the masses" numbering many millions of members. These early Pentecostals were "missionaries of the one way ticket," since most of them went out with only enough money to get to the mission field and with little or no promise of support for a return ticket.[9]

From Chicago, either directly or indirectly following the influence of William Durham, the movement spread to Canada, Italy, and South America. The seeds of Canadian Pentecostalism were sown when A. H. Argue of Winnipeg visited Durham in 1906 and received his Pentecostal experience. Argue's later ministry throughout Canada led to the founding in 1919 of the country's largest Pentecostal denomination, The Pentecostal Assemblies of Canada.[10]

Italy

Thriving Italian Pentecostal movements were also founded out of Durham's ministry in Chicago. After 1908 fast growing Italian Pentecostal movements were started in the United States, Brazil, Argentina, and Italy by two Italian immigrants to Chicago, Luigi Francescon and Giacomo Lombardy. Francescon, who was born in 1866 in Udine, Italy, had emigrated to the United States at the age of twenty-three and found work in Chicago as a mosaic tile-setter. A year later, in 1890, Francescon was

9. For more on these missionaries, see Vinson Synan, *The Spirit Said "Grow"* (Monrovia, CA, 1992), pp. 39-48.

10. B. M. Stout, "The Pentecostal Assemblies of Canada," *Dictionary of Pentecostal and Charismatic Movements*, pp. 695-99. Also see Thomas William Miller's *Canadian Pentecostals: A History of the Pentecostal Assemblies of Canada* (Mississauga, Ontario, 1994), pp. 21-70.

converted from his native Catholicism in an Italian Waldensian service, and eventually became a member of Chicago's First Italian Presbyterian Church. In 1907, at Durham's North Avenue Mission, he became a Pentecostal. After Francescon received the baptism in the Holy Spirit, Durham prophesied that he was called of God to bring the gospel to the Italian people of the world. That same year, Francescon and a friend, Pietro Ottolini, established the first Italian-American Pentecostal congregation in America, which he called the "Assemblea Cristiana." Soon afterwards he traveled around the United States and Canada, founding other similar congregations. Many of these churches became the nucleus of the present-day Christian Church of North America.[11]

In 1909 Francescon visited Argentina, establishing the "Iglesia Cristiana Pentecostal de Argentina" (100,000 members in 1980). The following year he traveled to Brazil, where he founded the Italian Pentecostal movement known as Congregationi Christiani (3,600 churches with one million members in 1980). In 1908 an associate of Francescon, Giacomo Lombardi, conducted the first Pentecostal services in Italy. On subsequent journeys to their native land, Francescon together with Lombardi founded congregations among family and friends in southern Italy, and in 1928 they organized a national Italian Pentecostal church — which eventually grew to be twice as large as all other Italian Protestants put together.[12]

Brazil

Pentecostalism in Brazil began through the ministry of two young Swedish immigrants to the United States, Daniel Berg and Gunnar Vingren. Immigrants from Sweden who had settled in South Bend, Indiana (near Chicago) in 1902, they had already converted to the Baptist faith in Sweden and had come to America because of economic depression in their native land. In 1909 in South Bend they both received the Pentecostal experience. [13]

---

11. See Giovanni Traettino, "Il Movimento Pentecostali in Italia (1908-1959)" (unpublished Ph.D. dissertation, University of Naples, 1971); Luigi Francescon, *Resumo de uma Ramificao da Obra de Deus* . . . (3rd ed., Chicago, 1958), p. 30. See also Walter Hollenweger, *The Pentecostals,* pp. 85-93.

12. Hollenweger, *The Pentecostals,* pp. 251-66.

13. These stories appear in Berg's *Enviado Por Deus, Memorias de Daniel Berg* (Sao Paulo, 1957).

In 1910 Vingren accepted the pastorate of a Swedish Baptist Church in South Bend, and it was there that the two men heard a prophetic utterance that repeated the word "Para." An interpretation of the word was given which directed both Berg and Vingren to go somewhere in the world called "Para." Since no one in the group had any idea where such a place might be, Berg and Vingren visited the Chicago Public Library, where a search of a World Almanac revealed that there was indeed a province in northeastern Brazil called "Para" on the Para River.

Berg and Vingren immediately made plans to go to Brazil. Friends collected enough offerings to buy two one-way tickets to Belem, capital of the province of Para. On their way to New York, though, they stopped at a Pentecostal mission in Pittsburgh, and in response to a financial appeal gave all their money to another missionary. The next day, as they walked the streets praying about their dilemma, a totally unknown woman came to them and gave them the exact amount to get to New York and to purchase one-way tickets to Belem on a tramp steamer. They had never seen the woman before.

The two arrived in Brazil in November 1910 and began preparations for a missionary ministry. Berg worked at odd jobs while Vingren studied Portuguese. Together, while learning the language, they attended a Baptist church. In a short time many Baptists received the Pentecostal experience through their ministry; and tongues, interpretations, prophecies, and healings began to occur in the services.

The Baptist pastor forbade these manifestations in the sanctuary, but allowed the Swedes to have their Pentecostal meetings in the church basement. Before long almost everyone was in the basement. Thus began the first Pentecostal congregation in Brazil, organized in 1911 with only 18 members. They called their new denomination the "Assembléias de Deus" (Assemblies of God) of Brazil, and began to plant churches all over the country. Their missionary trip in 1910 produced a movement that developed into the largest national Pentecostal movement in the world, claiming twenty million members by 1997.[14]

14. See Vinson Synan, *In the Latter Days* (Ann Arbor, MI, 1984), pp. 62-64. The Brazilians chose the name before the American Assemblies of God were organized and developed separately as an indigenous Brazilian church. Although the American and Brazilian churches share fraternal ties, they have never been organically connected.

Chile

The father of Chilean Pentecostalism was Dr. Willis C. Hoover, a physician from Chicago turned Methodist missionary. In 1889 at the age of 33 Hoover went to Chile as a missionary teacher under William Taylor, the pioneering Methodist holiness missionary bishop. He chose Chile only after receiving an inner call that said, "South America, South America, South America." Although lacking in theological training, Hoover rose rapidly in the Methodist hierarchy, becoming a district superintendent. He also served as pastor of the First Methodist Church in Valparaiso, which at the time was the largest Methodist church in the nation.[15]

Using the techniques of Wesley's early Methodist societies, Hoover organized class meetings, branch chapels, house-to-house visitation and street preaching to gain converts. Most of his members came from the poorest working classes. In 1902, as he began his Valparaiso pastorate, a revival of second-work sanctification swept through the Chilean Methodist churches, similar to the earlier holiness revivals in the United States.

In 1907 Hoover received a book entitled *The Baptism of the Holy Ghost and Fire*, written by Minnie Abrams, a Pentecostal missionary to India. It told of tongues, trances, visions, dreams, and other phenomena occurring among widows and orphans in a girls' school in Puna, India, run by Pandita Ramabai. At about the same time, a poor night watchman told Hoover of a vision in which Jesus appeared to him saying, "Go to your pastor and tell him to gather the most spiritual people in the congregation. They are to pray together every day. I intend to baptize them with tongues of fire." After this, a small group gathered daily at the 5:00 P.M. tea time to pray and wait for revival.

In a short time, incredible things began to happen among the Methodists of Chile. They spoke in tongues, danced in the Spirit, experienced spiritual visions, and prophesied about a mighty awakening that was about to begin. The Methodist churches under Hoover's supervision

15. Hoover told his story in his 1936 book entitled *Historia del Avivamiento Pentecostal de Chile* (Valparaiso, Chile; 1948 reprint). The Methodist Episcopal reactions to Hoover's movement are to be found in J. T. Copplestone's *Twentieth-Century Perspectives: The Methodist Episcopal Church, 1896-1939* (1973); and Wade Barclay, *History of Methodist Missions* (New York, 1949).

suddenly experienced spectacular growth in all parts of the nation as a result of the revival.

The Methodist authorities, however, soon got word of these events, and a delegation sent out by the Board of Foreign Missions in New York held a trial, charging Hoover and his followers for being "unscriptural, irrational, and anti-Methodist." As a result, on September 12, 1909, the Methodist authorities expelled Hoover and 37 of his followers. This small group then organized the "Pentecostal Methodist Church of Chile." Hoover then instructed his followers to preach in the streets every Sunday, and adopted the slogan that "Chile sera para Cristo" ("Chile shall be for Christ") How well they planted churches across the nation is seen in the popular saying that "in every village throughout Chile there is sure to be a post office and a Pentecostal Methodist church"[16]

The results have been astounding. Despite incredible persecutions from both Protestants and Catholics, the Pentecostals have become by far the largest non-Catholic denomination in Chile. The "Catedral Evangelica" in Santiago has been expanded to seat 15,000 persons, with a choir and orchestra of 4,000 members. This church, along with its "annexes," numbered no less than 350,000 adherents in 1990. The total number of Pentecostals in Chile is now approaching the two million mark, 20 percent of the nation's population.[17]

South Africa

South African Pentecostalism owed its origins to the work of John G. Lake (1870-1935) who began his ministry as a Methodist preacher but who later entered the business world as an insurance executive. In 1898 his wife was miraculously healed of tuberculosis under the ministry of Alexander Dowie, of "Zion City" near Chicago. Joining with Dowie,

16. Ignacio Vergara, *El Protestantismo en Chile* (Santiago, 1962), pp. 110-11. See also C. Lalive d'Epinay, *Haven of the Masses* (1969), and Prudencio Damboriena, *Tongues as of Fire: Pentecostalism in Contemporary Christianity* (Washington, DC, 1969).

17. For more information on the recent growth of Chilean Pentecostalism, see David Stoll, *Is Latin America Turning Protestant?* (Los Angeles, 1990), pp. 111-12, 315-16; David Martin, *Tongues of Fire: The Explosion of Protestantism in Latin America* (London, 1990); and Peter Wagner, *Look Out, the Pentecostals Are Coming* (Carol Stream, IL, 1973), pp. 17-18.

Lake became an elder in Dowie's "Zion Catholic Apostolic Church." In 1907, Lake received the Pentecostal experience under the ministry of Charles Parham, who visited Zion while the aging Dowie was losing control of his ministry. From Zion came a host of almost 500 preachers who entered the ranks of the Pentecostal movement, chief of whom was John G. Lake.[18]

In 1908, Lake abandoned the insurance business in order to make a missionary trip to South Africa. From 1908 to 1913, he led a party of five evangelists who spread the Pentecostal message throughout the nation. Before the end of his first year in South Africa his wife died, some believed through malnutrition. Nevertheless, Lake succeeded in founding two large and influential churches. The white branch took the name "Apostolic Faith Mission," the denomination that eventually gave David du Plessis to the world as "Mr. Pentecost." The black branch developed into the "Zion Christian Church," which by 1993 claimed no less than six million members and, despite some doctrinal and cultural variations, was accorded the distinction of being South Africa's largest Christian denomination.

After his African missionary tour, Lake returned to the United States where he founded healing homes and churches in Spokane, Washington and Portland, Oregon before he died in 1935. Throughout the rest of the century, Pentecostal missionaries from many nations spread the movement to all parts of Africa, but of all such endeavors in South Africa, Lake's was the most influential and enduring.

Russia

Soon after Lake returned to the United States, the Pentecostal movement reached the Slavic world through the ministry of a Russian-born Baptist pastor, Ivan Voronaev, who received the Pentecostal experience in New York City in 1919. The "apostle of Pentecost" to Russia and the Slavic nations was a Cossack born in central Russia by the name of Ivan Efimovich Voronaev. Baptized in the Russian Orthodox Church, he was

---

18. John G. Lake, *The Astounding Diary of Dr. John G. Lake* (Dallas, 1987). See also Gordon Lindsay's *John G. Lake: Apostle to Africa* (1981). See also Jim Zeigler's "John Graham Lake," in Burgess et al., *Dictionary of Pentecostal and Charismatic Movements,* pp. 530-31.

converted in 1908 and became a Baptist pastor. Because of severe persecution in Russia, he emigrated to the United States in 1912, founding Russian Baptist churches in San Francisco, Seattle, and New York City.[19]

In 1919, while serving as pastor of the Russian Baptist Church in Manhattan, he came into contact with Pentecostals in Marie Brown's Manhattan church, and after receiving the tongues-attested baptism, he left the Baptists to found the first Russian Pentecostal Church in New York City. This pastorate was short-lived, however, due to an unusual call to return as a missionary to Russia. This happened in a cottage prayer meeting where a prophetic utterance changed the course of his life. The words were: "Voronaev, Voronaev, journey to Russia."

As a result of this prophecy, Voronaev and his family journeyed to Russia in the summer of 1920, where he was instrumental in founding the first Pentecostal churches in Russia. His later ministry in other Slavic lands resulted in the founding of 350 Pentecostal congregations. In 1929, Voronaev was arrested for the first time by the communist authorities and placed in prison. After several more arrests he was finally incarcerated in the Gulag, where he eventually paid the ultimate price — martyrdom — for his faith. In 1943, sensing a chance to escape, he was shot to death in the prison yard and guard dogs tore his body apart. His wife was finally released after serving 24 years in Russian prisons. Somewhere in Siberia his body is buried in an unknown grave. Voronaev was the ultimate missionary of the one-way ticket.[20]

Korea

The classical Pentecostal movement did not reach Korea until 1928, even though various revivals were taking place in Pyongyang and Wonsan during the glory years of Asuza Street, between 1903 and 1907. Occurring among Methodists and Presbyterians and lacking a specific teaching on tongues, in many ways these Korean revivals prepared the way for the later

19. See Steve Durasoff's *Bright Wind of the Spirit: Pentecostalism Today* (Englewood Cliffs, NJ, 1972), pp. 17-22. Hollenweger, *The Pentecostals*, pp. 267-87. Voronaev's son Peter has written his personal account in *The Story of My Life in Soviet Russia* (1969).

20. Personal interview with the author in Moscow, Nov. 1991. Five hundred Russian Pentecostal pastors had direct knowledge of Voronaev's martyrdom.

Pentecostals. One of the direct links with the Azusa Street revival was Mary Rumsey, an American Pentecostal missionary who arrived in Inchon in the spring of 1928.[21] A single woman, Rumsey had received the gift of tongues at Azusa Street in 1907, and had returned to her native New York where she became associated with the Elim Faith Home and Missionary Society in Rochester. Although she was listed by the Elim Fellowship as a Japanese missionary and felt called to Japan, Rumsey at some point received a prophetic word saying "go to Korea." Because of a lack of funds, however, it took over 20 years before she could fulfill her calling.[22]

When Rumsey arrived in Seoul in the spring of 1928, the Japanese occupation of the nation was complete and the authorities allowed little religious freedom. At first she worked in the Methodist hospital headed by R. A. Hardie, who had played a leading role in the revival of 1903. The hospital also served as a temporary home for new missionaries. While ministering at the hospital Rumsey conducted Pentecostal services, introducing tongues and other charismata to her friends, one of which, Hong Huh from the Salvation Army, was to play a leading role in the Pentecostal movement that followed. Together with Huh, Rumsey established the "Subinggo Pentecostal church" in Seoul, and shortly afterwards a new convert named Sung San Park became its pastor. Park, a Korean from Japan, had graduated from a Japanese Bible School before coming to Korea. Ten years later, in October 1938, the Subinggo church ordained three new pastors and renamed their church the "Chosun Pentecostal Church and Mission Center." By then other Pentecostal churches had been established, and by the beginning of World War II there were six Pentecostal congregations and ten ordained ministers.[23]

---

21. Personal interview with Young-Hoon Lee, Seoul, Korea, Dec. 31, 1994. The work of Rumsey is universally recognized as an important link in the development of Pentecostalism in Korea and the founding of the Assemblies of God in particular. See Jae-Bum Lee, "Pentecostal Type Distinctives and Protestant Church Growth" (unpublished Ph.D. dissertation, Fuller Theological Seminary, 1986), pp. 189-90, and Jung-Yul Moon, ed., *Korean Assemblies of God, 30th Anniversary* (Seoul, 1981), pp. 27-39. Information on Rumsey's relationship with the Elim movement can be found in the Archives of the Assemblies of God in Springfield, Missouri. See Mary Rumsey, "Greetings from Japan," *Trust Magazine,* July-Aug. 1929, p. 23.

22. Rumsey's role is also examined in and Boo-Wong Yoo, *Korean Pentecostalism: Its History and Theology* (New York, 1987), and Young Hoon Lee, "The Holy Spirit Movement in Korea," in the *Journal of Soon Shin University* 4 (Dec. 1993): 151-73.

23. Jae Bum Lee, "Pentecostal Type Distinctives," pp. 189-90.

In the same year that Rumsey arrived in Korea an indigenous Pentecostal ministry began under the young Methodist evangelist Yong Do Lee, who brought many to experience the gifts of tongues and healing during his services. Although the relationship between Rumsey and Lee is unclear, both were instrumental in bringing the Pentecostal movement to Korea in 1928. Lee's ministry was sensational and controversial but short-lived; he died in 1932 at the age of 33. One of his lasting contributions to the Korean church was the ministry of the "Prayer Mountain," the first of which he conducted in 1928.

The missionary work of Mary Rumsey was turned over to the American Assemblies of God in 1952, and the first project of the new Korean church was to open a Bible School. In the very first class was a young convert from Buddhism, Paul Yonggi Cho, a man who started a new church in 1958 under a U.S Army tent. After decades of sustained growth, Yonggi Cho's church has become the largest Christian congregation in the world, the Yoido Full Gospel Church in Seoul.[24]

Nigeria

The reverberations of the Azusa Street revival continued to produce major new movements throughout the twentieth century. The largest Christian church in Africa, for example, had indirect roots in Azusa Street. William Kumuyi, who founded the "Deeper Life Bible Church" of Lagos, Nigeria in 1977, was converted in 1964 through the Apostolic Faith Mission, an African missionary project of Florence Crawford's church in Portland, Oregon, which itself had been a direct outgrowth of the Azusa Street mission. In 1977, Kumuyi was expelled by his church for conducting "miracle crusades" that featured "signs and wonders." He then began his own congregation, which by 1995 was drawing over 200,000 worshippers each week to the mother church in Lagos. In addition to this congregation, Kumuyi's Deeper Life movement had grown to over 3,000 churches in Nigeria and hundreds of other churches around the world led by Nigerian missionaries.[25]

24. For the story of Yonggi Cho, see his *The Fourth Dimension* (Plainfield, NJ, 1979), pp. 7-17.

25. See Alan Issacson, *Deeper Life: The Extraordinary Growth of the Deeper Life Bible Church* (London, 1990), pp. 92-144.

Stories like that of Kumuyi could be repeated by the hundreds, as missionaries spread the message globally. By the end of the century these "missionaries of the one-way ticket" had planted Pentecostal churches in nearly every conceivable region of the planet.

CHAPTER EIGHT

Criticism and Controversy

1906-20

Many Pentecostal people have run wild after that which is new and sensational in the last six years, such as "finished work," . . . rejection of the Trinity, antiorganization . . . and many other preposterous, nonsensical sensations. . . .

J. H. King (1917)

It was inevitable that the introduction of religious views as radical and emotionally divisive as the Pentecostals' would cause criticism and controversy both without and within the holiness movement. Coming as a grand division within the older holiness movement, it was not surprising that some of Pentecostalism's earliest and bitterest critics were members of those holiness churches that rejected the tongues doctrine. One of the ironies of church history is that those responsible for new religious movements often become hostile to the results of their own work.

The Pentecostal movement was first and foremost a product of the spiritual milieu of America's holiness movement. Preachers such as S. B. Shaw, George Hughes, and J. A. Wood had for years called for a "new pentecost" that would shake the world. Hughes, a leading member of the National Holiness Association, had in 1901 called for a "world-

143

rocking revival of religion" which would "shake the very foundations of earth." This revival, which was to be "along Pentecostal lines," would be "a fit opening of the 20th Century."[1] As early as 1856 William Arthur, a British Methodist holiness preacher, had called for a Pentecostal effusion that would be followed with "miraculous effects." Among these effects was included a "baptism with purifying flames of fire." His book, prophetically entitled *The Tongue of Fire,* was republished in 1891 by L. L. Pickett and circulated widely among holiness people.[2]

The thinking that produced *The Tongue of Fire* had influenced a new departure in holiness theology by 1875. This development came about as a result of Vicar T. D. Harford-Battersby's holiness conventions at Keswick, England. Begun as the "Union Meeting for the Promotion of Practical Holiness," the Keswick movement was inspired by the 1873 visit of American holiness luminaries W. E. Boardman, Robert Pearsall Smith, and his wife Hannah Whitall Smith. Although the Keswick conventions became the English counterpart of the American National Holiness Association, a difference of emphasis was to result in a different view of sanctification. The English view, heavily influenced by the Keswick conventions, was that entire sanctification was in reality a "baptism with the Holy Spirit" that came as an enduement of power for service. Soon those with Keswick connections spoke of the second blessing as their "baptism" rather than their sanctification. The Keswick teachers also softened the traditional Wesleyan sanctification "eradicationist" language about the "crucifixion of the old man" and began to speak of the "suppression" of the sinful nature. This eventually led to the "suppressionist" school of holiness teachers.[3]

While the English drifted toward a different terminology, the Americans continued to speak of the second work as "sanctification" and continued to stress the Wesleyan doctrines of perfection, purity, and cleansing. Through a monthly paper entitled *The Christian's Pathway to Power,* and numerous books and pamphlets, the Keswick view of "Holy Ghost power" came to be as widely known as Wesley's "Christian perfection." By the 1890's and the early part of the twentieth century, this "Keswick ter-

1. Shaw, *Echoes of the General Holiness Assembly* (1901), p. 54.
2. William Arthur, *The Tongue of Fire, or the True Power of Christianity* (Columbia, SC, 1891), pp. 43-79, 100, 164-67.
3. See David Bundy, "The Keswick Higher Life Movement," in Burgess et al., *Dictionary of Pentecostal and Charismatic Movements,* pp. 518-19.

minology" had permeated much of the American holiness movement and exercised great influence on religious innovators such as Parham and Irwin.[4]

By the time of the Azusa Street revival of 1906 the theological foundations of the Pentecostal movement had been well established. Not surprisingly, many holiness people who had prayed for and predicted a Pentecostal outbreak were ready to accept the events of 1906 in Los Angeles as the answer to their prayers. That many leaders such as King, Cashwell, Tomlinson, and Mason accepted the Pentecostal message, along with hundreds of Methodists, Baptists, and holiness preachers, shows how well the climate of the times favored the new Pentecostal experience and theology.

Holiness Opposition

In spite of the Keswick persuasion within the holiness movement at the turn of the century, many religious leaders not only rejected, but actively opposed, the emanations from Azusa Street. Criticism ranged from mild questioning of the Pentecostals' emotional excesses to positive denunciations and ecclesiastical anathemas. Probably the earliest and bitterest critic was Alma White, leader of the "Pillar of Fire" church, which saw one of its congregations in Los Angeles taken over by Pentecostal enthusiasts in 1906. Calling Seymour and Parham "rulers of spiritual Sodom," White called speaking with other tongues "this satanic gibberish" and Pentecostal services "the climax of demon worship." Her polemic against the movement was published in 1910 in a volume entitled *Demons and Tongues*. The book was representative of early oldschool holiness criticism of the movement.[5]

Another early critic was the famous holiness preacher W. B. Godbey, whose *Commentary on the New Testament* had become a classic in the holiness world. Visiting Los Angeles in 1909, he found the city "on tip toe, all

---

4. Herbert F. Stevenson, *Keswick's Authentic Voice* (Grand Rapids, MI, 1959), pp. 13-22; Smith, *Called Unto Holiness*, pp. 24-25; R. A. Torrey, *The Holy Spirit* (New York, 1927), pp. 1-45. Since Wesley never identified sanctification as the baptism with the Holy Ghost, many Pentecostals still claim to be fully Wesleyan. See Robert A. Mattke, "The Baptism of the Holy Spirit as Related to the Work of Entire Sanctification," *Wesleyan Theological Journal*, Spring 1970, pp. 22-32.

5. Alma White, *Demons and Tongues* (Zeraphath, NJ, 1949), pp. 43, 56, 82-85.

electrified with the movement." On invitation he visited Azusa Street and preached to a "large audience" of Pentecostals. When they asked if he had spoken in tongues, the scholarly Godbey responded with the Latin, "Johannes Baptistes tinxit, Petros tinxet. . . ." Upon hearing this, the Pentecostals exclaimed that he had truly received his "baptism." Repelled by the noise and disorganization of Seymour's service, Godbey departed in complete disenchantment, calling the Azusa people "Satan's preachers, jugglers, necromancers, enchanters, magicians, and all sorts of mendicants." Dismissing the movement as a product of "spiritualism," he used his considerable influence in persuading a large portion of the holiness movement to reject the Pentecostal message. Other leading preachers of the day also added their voices to the rising chorus of criticism. Dr. G. Campbell Morgan, one of the most respected preachers of the twentieth century, called the Pentecostal movement "the last vomit of Satan," while Dr. R. A. Torrey claimed that it was "emphatically not of God, and founded by a Sodomite." Such criticism was accepted at face value by many observers who often knew little or nothing about the new movement.[6]

In his *Holiness, The False and the True*, H. A. Ironside in 1912 denounced both the holiness and the Pentecostal movements as "disgusting . . . delusions and insanities." Characterizing Pentecostal meetings as "pandemoniums where exhibitions worthy of a madhouse or a collection of howling dervishes are held night after night," he charged that such meetings caused a "heavy toll of lunacy and infidelity."[7] Surpassing Ironside in outspoken criticism was H. J. Stolee, who in his *Speaking in Tongues* summarized four decades of criticism. Attributing "mental instability," "mob psychology," "hypnotism," and "demon power" to Pentecostal worship, he conjectured that the "general neurasthenia," or "nerve weariness," of twentieth-century life was responsible for most of the converts to the new religion. Using the language of psychology, he speculated that "tongues" were produced by "hallucinations," "melancholia," "paranoia," "megalomania," "hysteria," and "a cataleptic condition."[8]

6. White, *Demons and Tongues*, pp. 120-27; Taylor, *The Spirit and the Bride*, p. 52; Ewart, *The Phenomenon of Pentecost*, p. 85. See Horace Ward, "The Anti-Pentecostal Argument," in Vinson Synan, ed., *Aspects of Pentecostal-Charismatic Origins* (Plainfield, NJ, 1975), pp. 99-122.

7. Ironside, *Holiness, the False and the True*, pp. 38-39.

8. Stolee, *Speaking in Tongues*, pp. 77, 75-93. "Typical" Pentecostal services are described on pp. 65-84.

Other observers such as Beverly Carradine, well known for many decades in the holiness movement, condemned the new "tongues movement." Writing in 1910, he called the Pentecostals speakers of "gibberish" rather than "the real gift of tongues." Wielding great influence on the other holiness denominations, Carradine helped stem the Pentecostal tide which threatened to engulf the entire holiness movement. Another holiness leader, A. B. Simpson, head of the Christian and Missionary Alliance, rejected the Pentecostal contention that all must speak in tongues as the evidence of their Holy Ghost baptism. After a highly emotional revival in his Missionary Training Institute in Nyack, New York, in May 1907, Simpson faced a doctrinal problem when many of his students and teachers began to speak with other tongues. After much thought, and even seeking for the tongues experience, the president of the institution decided that tongues was only "one of the evidences" of the indwelling of the Holy Spirit. Tongues would be allowed in Christian and Missionary Alliance services, but would not be encouraged. Simpson's position, a compromise unique in the early history of the movement, led ultimately to A. W. Tozer's dictum "seek not — forbid not," a policy formulated in the 1960's, which eventually became known as the "Alliance position." [9]

The ironically named Pentecostal Church of the Nazarene, largest of the holiness denominations, became an early bastion of anti-Pentecostal thought. With the leader of the denomination, Bresee, pastoring the mother church in Los Angeles in 1906, it is not surprising that he and his church opposed the Azusa Street meeting, as it constituted a direct threat to his own congregation. During the years 1906-9 he actively opposed the Azusa people and placed his denomination in direct opposition to the new doctrine. Eventually the name "Pentecostal Church of the Nazarene" became an embarrassment, since many persons confused it with the new Pentecostal or "tongues" movement. To avoid confusion, the denomination voted in the General Assembly of 1919 to

9. See Charles W. Nienkirchen, *A. B. Simpson and the Pentecostal Movement* (Peabody, MA, 1992). See especially pp. 131-40, which show conclusively that the words "seek not, forbid not" was not coined by Simpson but by A. W. Tozer in 1963. See also Beverly Carradine, *A Box of Treasure* (Chicago, 1910), pp. 78-85; Hollenweger, "Handbuch Der Pfingstbewegung," vol. 2, p. 408; Brumback, *Suddenly from Heaven* (Springfield, MO, 1961), pp. 88-97. For a summary of the Christian and Missionary Alliance view see J. T. McCrossan, *Speaking with Other Tongues, Sign or Gift, Which?* (Seattle, 1927), pp. 3-31.

drop the word "Pentecostal" from the name; the church has been known ever since as "The Church of the Nazarene." Following the lead of the Nazarenes, the Wesleyan Methodist Church, The Salvation Army, the Pilgrim Holiness Church, and the Free Methodist Church also dissociated themselves completely from the Pentecostal movement.[10]

Pentecost Defended

The struggling Pentecostals were not without their defenders, however, although few understood the full doctrinal or historical implications of their new movement. Rising to his own defence, Charles Parham in 1907 published his apology for the movement. Entitled *Kol Kare Bomidbar: A Voice Crying in the Wilderness,* the book defended tongues as the "bible evidence" for the baptism in the Holy Spirit.[11] Another book in defense of the movement, *The Spirit and the Bride,* appeared in September 1907, following the Dunn revival. Its author was G. F. Taylor, the young follower of Cashwell and antagonist of Crumpler. With an introduction by J. H. King of the Fire-Baptized Holiness Church, it was issued against "determined and desperate opposition." In the crucial months following the introduction of Pentecostalism to the South, Taylor's book exerted a powerful influence in helping Pentecostals gain control of the southern holiness churches. Another early work that circulated widely in the West and Midwest was David Wesley Myland's *The Latter Rain Covenant and Pentecostal Power,* which appeared in 1910. Both Taylor and Myland held the view that the Pentecostal movement was intended to prepare the church for the second coming of Christ.[12]

In 1914, King, one of the better educated leaders of the movement,

10. M. E. Redford, *The Rise of the Church of the Nazarene* (Kansas City, MO, 1951) pp. 39-42; S. L. Brengle, *When the Holy Ghost Is Come* (New York, 1914), pp. 20-31; Henry E. Brockett, *The Riches of Holiness* (Kansas City, MO, 1951), pp. 108-21; Smith, *Called Unto Holiness,* pp. 319-20. Also see Howard Snyder, *The Divided Flame: Wesleyans and the Charismatic Renewal* (Grand Rapids, MI, 1986).

11. Charles Fox Parham, *Kol Kare Bomidbar: A Voice Crying in the Wilderness* (1944 [1902 reprint]).

12. Taylor, *The Spirit and the Bride,* pp. 8, 122; David Wesley Myland, *The Latter Rain Covenant and Pentecostal Power* (Chicago, 1910), pp. 100-121. Using charts of rainfall in Palestine from 1861-1901, Myland concluded that the second coming of Christ would occur soon after 1906.

published his theological defense of the new Pentecostal doctrine in his *From Passover to Pentecost*, a book that became required reading for thousands of Pentecostal ministers in the years following its appearance. Two years later B. F. Lawrence published another defense, titled *The Apostolic Faith Restored*. This book was followed a decade later by the first serious history of the movement, *With Signs Following*, by Stanley H. Frodsham, an Englishman who had immigrated to the United States. These earlier works were followed by a veritable flood of Pentecostal literature as the denominations developed publishing houses after 1910.[13]

The "Finished Work" Controversy

The budding Pentecostal movement not only faced criticism from without, but also suffered from dissension and controversy within. The years from 1906 to 1914 saw the most fundamental doctrinal cleavage the movement would ever experience: the schism over sanctification as a second work of grace. In the movement's first stages, the Wesleyan view was almost universally accepted. Since most of the early Pentecostal leaders had been prominent or active in the holiness movement, it seemed natural for them to maintain the place of sanctification as a "second blessing" that cleansed the seeker from "inbred sin," thus preparing for the reception of the Holy Spirit. Both Parham and Seymour adhered to this view consistently for the rest of their lives. The southern holiness denominations, led by King, Mason, and Tomlinson, had been founded as a result of the second work controversy in Methodism and the idea of the "double-cure" was deeply ingrained in their doctrine and history. Indeed, entire sanctification had been the very reason for their foundation, making a departure from it virtually unthinkable.

The problem over the second work arose when large numbers of converts began to enter the movement from non-Wesleyan backgrounds, notably from the Baptist Churches. Not schooled in holiness theology, these people thought of Christian experience as involving only two steps — conversion and the baptism with the Holy Ghost. The man who became leader of the group that questioned the necessity of the second blessing was William H. Durham of Chicago. Pastor of the well-known

13. King, *From Passover to Pentecost* (Memphis, 1914); B. F. Lawrence, *The Apostolic Faith Restored* (Springfield, MO, 1916); Frodsham, *With Signs Following*.

North Avenue Mission, Durham had traveled to Azusa Street in 1907, was baptized in the Holy Spirit, and had returned as an enthusiast for the new Pentecostal experience. Although he had previously preached the Wesleyan view of sanctification, Durham determined never to preach it again after his trip to Los Angeles. By the end of 1907, Durham's church had become a mecca for midwestern Pentecostals, his ministry to that region being similar to Cashwell's in the South. From 1906 to 1911 Durham's influence increased among Pentecostals through his monthly periodical *The Pentecostal Testimony* and through his dynamic preaching. Called a "pulpit prodigy," he attracted thousands to his "pentecostal services" in the North Avenue Mission where many of his followers experienced a peculiar shouting experience known as the "Durham jerks."[14]

The controversy began with a sermon Durham preached at a Chicago Pentecostal convention in 1910, in which he sought to "nullify the blessing of sanctification as a second definite work of grace." Calling his new doctrine "The Finished Work," Durham called for a new view which assigned sanctification to the moment of conversion based on "the finished work of Christ on Calvary." Denying Wesley's concept of a "residue of sin" in the believer, he taught that one was perfectly sanctified at conversion and had no need of a later crisis, or "second change." After conversion, a Christian would progressively grow in grace. This position was similar to the "Oberlin theology" developed by Charles G. Finney and Asa Mahan in the years before the Civil War. Durham's teaching cut directly across the accepted view of Pentecostals with a holiness background, and a great controversy ensued which ultimately divided the Pentecostal movement into two theological camps.[15]

The problem was brought to an early crisis when Durham returned to Los Angeles for a preaching mission in February 1911. Coming first to the "Upper Room Mission," by then the largest Pentecostal church

14. For Durham's account of his theological development see his autobiographical "Personal Testimony of Pastor Durham," *Pentecostal Testimony* 2, no. 3 (1912): 1-16. Brumback, *Suddenly from Heaven*, pp. 69-70. J. Rosewell Flower, personal interview with the author on July 13, 1969. Also see Edith Blumhofer, "The Finished Work of Calvary," *A/G Heritage*, Fall 1983, pp. 9-11.

15. Blumhofer, "The Finished Work of Calvary," pp. 98-106; Ewart, *The Phenomenon of Pentecost*, pp. 72-77.

in the city, Durham was invited to leave when his doctrine became known. Not only did Durham's doctrine offend many, but his combative, dogmatic, and denunciatory rhetoric inflamed many others. He then returned to the fabled Azusa Street Mission, which by 1911 was essentially a small local black church, still under Seymour's leadership. Since Seymour was in the East on a preaching tour, Durham was invited to preach in the "Mother Church" of Pentecostalism. With his dynamic personality and new message, Durham soon filled the old mission with crowds from other missions in the city. When Seymour heard of the "finished work heresy" being preached at Azusa Street, he hastily returned and bolted the doors of the mission to Durham, who then moved to another location to continue his revival. News of this event reverberated throughout the Pentecostal movement and brought the crisis into the open.[16]

Those following Durham's teaching referred to sanctification as a "fictitious experience" unsupported by the Scriptures. Opponents of the Chicago pastor charged that he was "attacking the doctrinal foundations of the movement." From 1910 to 1914 the battle raged with much acrimony and "carnality" exhibited on both sides. In Baxter Springs, Missouri, Parham heard of the new view and rejected it, calling it an opening for "animalism" or "spiritualistic counterfeits" into Pentecostal ranks In his opposition to Durham, Parham even "prophesied his destruction within six months." He went on to say, "if this man's doctrine is true, let my life go out to prove it, but if our teaching on a definite grace of sanctification is true, let his life pay the forfeit." Indeed, Durham died suddenly and unexpectedly on a trip to Los Angeles on July 7, 1912, thus seemingly vindicating Parham's position. In response Parham stated, "how signally God has answered." In Portland, Oregon, Mrs. Florence Crawford and her "Apostolic Faith" movement also rejected Durham's doctrine. In the end, the "finished work theory" gained its greatest support among independent and unorganized churches and missions, most of them urban, which by then numbered in the hundreds across the nation. So pervasive was the new view that most of the Pentecostal

---

16. Bartleman, *How Pentecost Came to Los Angeles,* pp. 145-46. While denouncing the doctrine of sanctification at Azusa Street, Durham was attacked by a young holiness girl who had worked as a prostitute before her conversion. She used a hat pin to register her "pointed opposition" to Durham's teachings. See Brumback, *Suddenly from Heaven,* pp. 99-100, 103.

denominations that began after 1911 incorporated it in their statements of faith.[17]

The "finished work" theory failed to move the southern Pentecostal groups, which were already steeped in the holiness movement. In the battle between "finished work" and "second work" the Church of God, the Pentecostal Holiness Church, and the Church of God in Christ stood firmly for the second work of sanctification. For these churches, the belief in entire sanctification as a second work of grace became a test of orthodoxy, and anyone professing to believe in the "finished work" was considered a "false teacher" or a "deluded Yankee." In his *Passover to Pentecost,* King defended the second work as vigorously as he did the first and the third. Surprised and pained "almost beyond degree" that this new idea had penetrated Pentecostal ranks, King described the new doctrine as "Antinomianism . . . dressed up in a Zinzendorfian garb and going through the land with all the intrepidity of a new resurrection."[18] The Church of God and the Church of God in Christ remained largely untouched by the controversy. Like the Pentecostal Holiness Church, their origins as holiness denominations dictated a close adherence to the "second work" view.[19]

17. Parham, "A Critical Analysis of the Tongues Question," *The Apostolic Faith,* June 1925, p. 5; Bartleman, *How Pentecost Came to Los Angeles,* p. 150; Crawford, *A Historical Account of the Apostolic Faith,* pp. 69-70; Ewart, *The Phenomenon of Pentecost,* p. 74. See also Blumhofer, "The Finished Work of Calvary," p. 10, and her *The Assemblies of God: A Chapter in the Story of American Pentecostalism,* vol. 1 (Springfield, MO, 1989), pp. 129, 217-21; and William Menzies, *Anointed to Serve: The Story of the Assemblies of God* (Springfield, MO, 1971), pp. 75-77. Also see Robert Mapes Anderson, *Vision of the Disinherited* (New York, 1979), pp. 153-75.

18. Antinomianism was the belief that a Christian could not commit sin after conversion since the laws of the Old Testament had no force in the New Testament age. Count Zinzendorf, a contemporary of John Wesley, denied that sanctification was a second work of grace.

19. King, *From Passover to Pentecost,* p. 81; Tomlinson, *Diary of A. J. Tomlinson,* pp. 238-39. For comments on the controversy from the periodicals of the various movements, see *The Pentecostal Holiness Advocate,* Sept. 13, 1917, p. 1; June 17, 1926, p. 1; *The Church of God Evangel,* Jan. 10, 1914, pp. 1-3; Mar. 28–June 27, 1914, a series of four major articles entitled "Perilous Times Have Come," Oct. 2, 1915, pp. 1-4; Aug. 24, 1918, p. 1; *The Pentecostal Evangel,* Sept. 4, 1920, p. 5; May 12, 1923, pp. 5-7; *Word and Witness,* Aug. 20, 1912, p. 1; May 20, 1913, p. 1.

The Assemblies of God

As the "finished work" theory spread among the hundreds of independent Pentecostal missions and "assemblies" throughout the nation, calls began to be heard for a unified organization that would provide a denominational home for all those with similar views. Pentecostals in the North and West had been reluctant to join the southern Pentecostal groups in the years following 1906, although they were the only Pentecostal denominations in existence. From 1907 to 1914 many white ministers had been ordained by C. H. Mason, whose Church of God in Christ was chartered by the state of Tennessee. Their affiliation with the Church of God in Christ, however, was purely nominal, extending only to ministerial credentials. As a rule, most of these white ministers preferred to gather informally in "state camp meetings" where their ecclesiastical affairs could be discussed freely without reference to Mason or any other church officials. Rapport was maintained between these ministers and churches by means of various independent periodicals which began circulation after 1906. The most prominent of these was *The Apostolic Faith*, edited by E. N. Bell, formerly a Baptist pastor from Fort Worth, who had become a Pentecostal convert under Durham's preaching in Chicago. This paper had no connection with Parham's or Seymour's publications of the same name. Other influential papers were J. Roswell Flower's *Christian Evangel*, published in Indianapolis, and M. M. Pinson's *Word and Witness*, issued from Arkansas. In these and other periodicals, announcements were made of camp meetings, conventions, and missionary assemblies.[20]

Since the early Pentecostals outside the southern churches felt that denominational organizations were to be avoided, partly because of Parham's anti-denominationalism, interchurch meetings were rare. In various parts of the nation, groups of ministers gathered in local "associations" for fellowship and mutual aid. The earliest of these was the "Apostolic Faith Movement," begun in Orchard, Texas, in April 1906 under Parham's leadership. In 1909 this group broke with Parham and accepted the leadership of two Texas Pentecostal ministers, E. N. Bell and Howard A. Goss. In 1911 the group dropped the name "Apostolic

20. For the Assemblies of God side of the story, see Menzies, *Anointed to Serve*, pp. 80-92. For the Church of God in Christ side, see Clemmons, *Bishop C. H. Mason*, pp. 51-55. See also Kendrick, *The Promise Fulfilled*, p. 79; J. Rosewell Flower, "History of the Assemblies of God" (n.p., n.d.), pp. 17-19.

Faith Movement" and accepted credentials from Mason's "Church of God in Christ." At the same time that Bell's group was emerging in Texas, another group was developing in Alabama under the leadership of Cashwell's convert, H. G. Rodgers. Meeting in Dothan, Alabama, in 1909, this group adopted the name "Church of God" and issued ministerial credentials to its pastors. This name was adopted without knowledge of Tomlinson's church with headquarters in Cleveland, Tennessee. At the second meeting of the infant church in Slocumb, Alabama, in 1911, the group changed its name to "The Church of God in Christ" in deference to Mason's church. Thus by 1911, three groups operated under the name of Mason's church, the one in Texas led by Bell, the one in Alabama led by Rodgers, and Mason's own group in Memphis.[21]

After 1911 a move was initiated by Bell and Rodgers to unite the Texas and Alabama groups, both of which were made up of whites who were becoming increasingly dissatisfied with the existing arrangement with Mason's church. At a meeting in Meridian, Mississippi, in June 1913, a merger was effected which resulted in an all-white church with 352 ministers. Although the group continued to use the name "Church of God in Christ," it began to issue separate ministerial credentials that superseded those issued earlier by Mason. Later that summer, Pinson, editor of *Word and Witness*, and Bell, editor of *Apostolic Faith*, decided to join forces and issue one periodical called *Word and Witness*, with Bell as editor. Before the end of the year the idea of forming a separate white denomination on a national basis gained currency among the leaders of the group, since most of them saw the existing organization as "frail" and "inadequate" and felt an ambiguity in the relationship to Mason's denomination. Accordingly, a call was issued in the December 20th issue of *Word and Witness* for a "General Council" of all "pentecostal saints and Churches of God in Christ" to meet the following April in Hot Springs, Arkansas, for a discussion of their various common problems.[22]

The Hot Springs "General Council" met in the Grand Opera House on Central Avenue during the first week of April 1914. C. H.

---

21. C. C. Burnett, *In the Last Days: An Early History of the Assemblies of God* (Springfield, MO, 1962), pp. 7-9; Brumback, *Suddenly from Heaven*, p. 154; Kendrick, *The Promise Fulfilled*, pp. 79-80; Nichols, *Pentecostalism*, pp. 109-10; Irwin Winehouse, *The Assemblies of God: A Popular Survey* (New York, 1959), pp. 28-30.

22. *Word and Witness*, Dec. 20, 1913, p. 1. Also see Kendrick, *The Promise Fulfilled*, pp. 81-83; and Brumback, *Suddenly from Heaven*, pp. 156-57.

Mason attended as a guest speaker, and preached to the ministers of what he had previously referred to as "the White work" of the Church of God in Christ. Although the three hundred ministers and laymen disclaimed any desire to inaugurate a new "sect" or "denomination," the delegates succeeded in doing just that. Adopting a document entitled "Preamble and Resolution of Constitution," the group created a new denomination named "General Council of the Assemblies of God." Following the keynote address by M. M. Pinson entitled "The Finished Work of Calvary," the new church adopted a statement of faith that included the usual Pentecostal article concerning speaking with tongues, but stated in another article that "entire sanctification" should be "earnestly pursued" as a "progressive" rather than an instantaneous experience. The adoption of this statement placed the new "Assemblies of God" outside the Wesleyan tradition, thus creating the first formal doctrinal division in the Pentecostal movement. The Assemblies of God Constitution became the model of the subsequent "finished work" denominations that coalesced after 1914. The type of government adopted by the new church was essentially congregational, whereas the earlier southern groups had developed strongly episcopal forms. In general the Assemblies of God represented the "Baptistic" type of Pentecostal church while the older ones were of the "Methodistic" type.[23]

The formation of the Assemblies of God was of crucial importance to the future development of the Pentecostal movement, effectively marking the end of a notable experiment in interracial church development. After 1914 the Church of God in Christ became predominately black; the Assemblies of God continued as predominantly white. It also ended the period of doctrinal unity that had existed from 1906. After 1914 the American Pentecostal movement would be about equally divided between "holiness" advocates of the "second work" and "assembly" advocates of the "finished work." Because of this doctrinal cleaving, the dream of uniting all Pentecostals into a single body came to an end. Since the delegates to the Hot Springs Council had come

---

23. *Word and Winess,* Mar. 20, 1914, pp. 2, 3; Apr. 20, 1914, p. 1; May 20, 1914, pp. 1-3; *The Combined Minutes of the General Council of the Assemblies of God,* Apr. 2-12, 1914, pp. 4-8; M. M. Pinson, "The Finished Work of Calvary," *The Pentecostal Evangel,* Apr. 5, 1964, pp. 7, 26-27. Excellent accounts of the formation of the Assemblies of God can be found in Blumhofer, *The Assemblies of God,* vol. 1, pp. 197-216; and William Menzies, *Anointed to Serve,* pp. 97-105.

from all regions of the country, the new church was from the beginning one of the largest Pentecostal denominations in America, and thus destined to wield a large influence on the rest of the movement.

The "Jesus Name" Issue

Despite its auspicious beginnings, the young Assemblies of God Church was soon wracked by a "new issue" that threatened to destroy it in its infancy. This issue became known as the "Jesus only" or "pentecostal unitarian" question and, like the parent movement, had its origins in Los Angeles. The occasion for this new "revelation" was a "world-wide" Pentecostal camp meeting held in the spring of 1913 and attended by hundreds of preachers from across the continent. The first mention of the doctrine, which would shake the Pentecostal movement from coast to coast, came during a baptismal service outside the large camp-meeting tent. The speaker, R. E. McAlister, casually mentioned that "the apostles invariably baptized their converts once in the name of Jesus Christ" and "that the words Father, Son, and Holy Ghost were never used in Christian baptism." Upon hearing these words, "a shudder swept the preachers on the platform," and one preacher even mounted the platform to warn McAlister to refrain from preaching that doctrine or it would "associate the camp with a Dr. Sykes who so baptized." Unknowingly, evangelist McAlister had fired a shot that would resound throughout the movement within a year.[24]

Others hearing McAlister reacted differently. One preacher, John G. Scheppe, "spent the night in prayer" and toward morning "was given a glimpse of the power of the name of Jesus." Awakening the campers, he ran through the camp shouting about his discovery. The following day the campers "searched the Scriptures" concerning the "name of Jesus." Deeply impressed by these happenings was one Frank J. Ewart, who began to discuss the question of baptism "in Jesus' name" with McAlister. Ewart, a native of Australia, had come to Los Angeles by way of Canada and had entered the Baptist ministry. An intense and fearless man, he had defied his church by accepting the Pentecostal doctrine in Portland, Oregon, in 1908. Expelled from the Baptist Church,

---

24. Fred J. Foster, *Think It Not Strange: A History of the Oneness Movement* (St. Louis, 1965), pp. 9, 51, 52; Ewart, *The Phenomenon of Pentecost*, pp. 75-77.

he had come to Los Angeles to become an assistant to William Durham in his last pastorate. Upon Durham's death, Ewart succeeded him as pastor of the Pentecostal church on the corner of Seventh and Los Angeles Streets. By 1913, Ewart was one of the leading figures of the West Coast Pentecostal movement.[25]

Ewart then spent a year formulating his new doctrine before preaching his first "Jesus Name" sermon in Belvedere, just outside Los Angeles, in 1914. According to Ewart's view there was only one personality in the Godhead — Jesus Christ — the terms "Father" and "Holy Spirit" being only "titles" used to designate various aspects of Christ's person. Therefore the idea of a "trinity" was a mistake which had been foisted on the church by the Bishop of Rome at the Council of Nicea in A.D. 325. Consequently, anyone who was baptized in the name of "the Father, the Son, and the Holy Ghost," was not truly baptized at all and was in error. He further taught that to be completely saved, the gift of tongues was essential. For him the new birth, sanctification, and the baptism in the Holy Spirit with tongues constituted one event, received only in the immersion rite and only if administered in the name of Jesus. As for the Trinitarian Pentecostals, the only way to be saved was to submit to re-baptism "in Jesus name." One of Ewart's first converts was Glenn A. Cook, an Azusa Street veteran who had first preached the Pentecostal message to Mason's Church of God in Christ in Memphis in 1907. To correct their historical oversight, Ewart and Cook set up a tank inside a tent and rebaptized themselves "in the name of Jesus" on April 15, 1914. Following their rebaptism they began a determined campaign to reconvert and rebaptize the entire Pentecostal movement into their new "oneness" belief. Ewart soon began spreading the message around the nation through a periodical entitled *Meat in Due Season.* In a short time the story of the "Jesus only" or "oneness" belief had crossed the nation much as the Azusa Street story had done nine years before. Throughout the nation, critics branded the new group as the "Jesus Only" movement, although the leaders preferred the terms "oneness" or "Jesus' Name."[26]

25. Ewart, *The Phenomenon of Pentecost,* pp. 6-7; Foster, *Think It Not Strange,* p. 43.

26. David Reed, "Aspects of the Origins of Oneness Pentecostalism," in Synan, ed., *Aspects of Pentecostal-Charismatic Origins* (Plainfield, NJ, 1975), pp. 143-68. Reed classifies the Oneness Pentecostals as "evangelical unitarian pentecostals"; see p. 162.

The "New Issue" Splits the Assemblies of God

One very important factor in the spread of the "oneness" doctrine was an eastern preaching tour taken by Cook in 1915. Visiting the Assemblies of God Church of Garfield T. Haywood in Indianapolis, he converted this leading black pastor, rebaptizing him along with 465 followers according to the new formula. The news of Haywood's defection caused dismay among the Assemblies of God leaders, since Haywood was its leading black preacher and pastored one of its largest churches. By June 1915, Bell, the head of the church, and other leaders were so alarmed that a special meeting of church officials was called in Little Rock, Arkansas, to combat the new "heresy." For some weeks thereafter Bell published several articles in *Word and Witness*, now the official periodical of the Assemblies of God, denouncing the unitarian concept and defending the Trinity. But Bell's opposition was short-lived. In a camp meeting at Jackson, Tennessee, hosted by H. G. Rodgers, both Bell and Rodgers shocked the denomination by accepting the "Jesus' Name" theory and submitting to rebaptism by a visiting "oneness" preacher named L. V. Roberts. After Bell's and Rodgers' defection the "new issue" became "the issue" in the Assemblies of God Church. For the next year the new doctrine spread, "leaping from church to church and assembly to assembly" until it seemed that the entire denomination would be engulfed by the new view. The rebaptism of H. H. Goss in August by McAlister, whose preaching sparked the movement in Los Angeles in November, seemed ominous to trinitarian partisans.[27]

By the end of 1915 this age-old controversy had proliferated

Ewart, *The Phenomenon of Pentecost*, pp. 50-51; Nichols, *Pentecostalism*, pp. 90, 91; Gordon F. Atter, *The Third Force* (Peterborough, Ontario, 1962), pp. 91-93. The Pentecostal Unitarians accept the term "oneness" but reject the appellation "Jesus Only," the name given by other Pentecostals. Members generally prefer to be known as the "Jesus' Name" movement. For an account of the Oneness movement from a black perspective, see James L. Tyson, *The Early Pentecostal Revival: History of the Twentieth Century Pentecostals and the Pentecostal Assemblies of the World* (Hazelwood, MO, 1992). Also see Anderson, *Vision of the Disinherited*, pp. 176-94.

27. See *Word and Witness*, May 1915, p. 4; *The Weekly Evangel*, June 5, 1915, pp. 1-3; July 3, 1915, p. 1; July 17, 1915, p. 1; Aug. 14, 1915, p. 1; Sept. 15, 1915, pp. 1-2; Foster, *Think It Not Strange*, pp. 54-57; Ewart, *The Phenomenon of Pentecost*, pp. 99-100; Brumback, *Suddenly from Heaven*, pp. 191-210; Winehouse, *The Assemblies of God*, pp. 43-46; Blumhofer, *The Assemblies of God*, vol. 1, pp. 217-43; Menzies, *Anointed to Serve*, pp. 106-21.

through so much of the Pentecostal movement that it threatened to take over completely. The greatest resistance to the doctrine was met in the southeastern states where the Churches of God, the Churches of God in Christ, and the Pentecostal Holiness Churches, with their strong holiness backgrounds, were largely undisturbed by the controversy.[28] From the beginning of the "oneness" movement in 1913, there were leaders in the newly formed Assemblies of God who sternly opposed it. The youthful General Secretary of the denomination, J. Roswell Flower, and John W. Welch, a member of the "Executive Presbytery," organized a resistance movement and rallied the trinitarians for a last-ditch stand. Both unitarians and trinitarians sent large delegations to the Third General Council of the Assemblies of God in St. Louis in October 1915, each hoping to win the church to its side. Although dissension was strong, the council adopted doctrinal statements against the unitarian view. The delegates then adjourned the meeting with great apprehension, knowing that the issue would not be laid to rest until the Fourth General Council in the following year.[29]

This General Council, which met in October 1916 in St. Louis, became the historic meeting that finally settled the place of the unitarians in the Pentecostal movement. In the months preceding the council meeting the controversy sharpened, with every church and preacher forced to take a stand on the "new issue." Charges of "Sabellianism" and "oneism" were countered with accusations of "three-Godism" and "Popish slavery." The trinitarians were able with the help of Flower, Welch, and Pinson to gain the advantage before the council gathered. A decisive stroke was the winning of Bell, still the most powerful man in the church, back to the trinitarian view. By the time the council convened in October it was clear that the trinitarians had the upper hand. Although the young denomination had vowed never to adopt a formal creed, a committee was appointed to prepare a "Statement of Fundamental Truths" to guide the church in the future. Members of both factions listened as the committee read its report

28. *The Church of God Evangel*, May 26, 1923, p. 1; Dec. 14, 1929, p. 1; Dec. 5, 1936, p. 3; Aug. 23, 1947, pp. 3-13. *The Pentecostal Holiness Advocate*, Sept. 6, 1917, p. 10; May 2, 1918, p. 3. Campbell's *Pentecostal Holiness Church* and Conn's *Like a Mighty Army* make no reference to the controversy.

29. *The Weekly Evangel*, July 3, 1915, p. 1; July 17, 1915, p. 1; *Minutes of the General Council of the Assemblies of God*, Oct. 1915, pp. 4-6, 8. See Brumback, *Suddenly from Heaven*, pp. 194-97; and Foster, *Think It Not Strange*, pp. 65-67, for contrasting views of the council.

a few days later, a strongly trinitarian document that declared the propriety of calling the Godhead a "trinity or as one Being of three persons." The unitarians, seeing that they had failed to win the argument, left the meeting in despair and made plans for a later meeting to form their own denomination. In the end, the eighteen-month-old Assemblies of God lost 156 preachers out of 585 and over a hundred congregations, but the "sad new issue" was settled. After this climactic meeting it was clear that the Assemblies of God, and with them the majority of all Pentecostals, would remain trinitarian.[30]

In the years immediately following the controversy, this "new issue" among Pentecostals was largely confined to North America; England, Scandinavia, and the other European nations were largely untouched by the new teaching. Most of the thriving Pentecostal groups in Latin America and Asia also remained untouched, although in later years large "oneness" churches were formed in Russia, Mexico, and Colombia. The Pentecostal unitarian movement was thus mainly an American phenomenon, with its greatest strength in the South and Midwest.[31]

The Pentecostal Assemblies of the World

After failing to capture the older Pentecostal denominations, the oneness Pentecostals decided to establish their own separate denomination. Led by the black minister Haywood of Indianapolis, most of them joined in forming the "Pentecostal Assemblies of the World" in a convention in Indianapolis later in 1916. With roughly equal numbers of white and black ministers and churches, the new group was completely interracial. Its oneness beliefs were written into a statement of faith and published

30. *Minutes of the General Council of the Assemblies of God,* Oct. 1916, pp. 8, 10-13; *The Weekly Evangel,* Mar. 4, 1916, p. 6; Oct. 21, 1916, pp. 4-5, 8; Nov. 25, 1916, p. 8. See also *The Latter Rain Evangel,* May 1915, pp. 2-9; Foster, *Think It Not Strange,* p. 68; Winehouse, *The Assemblies of God,* pp. 202-6; and Carl Brumback, *God in Three Persons* (Cleveland, TN, 1959), pp. 11-19.

31. Gee, *The Pentecostal Movement,* pp. 124, 125. For early Oneness organizational developments see Arthur and Charles Clanton's *United We Stand: Jubilee Edition* (St. Louis, 1995), pp. 1-137; and T. F. Tenney, *The Flame Still Burns: A History of the Pentecostals of Louisiana* (Tioga, LA, 1989), pp. 1-80. More recent doctrinal works include David Bernard's *The Oneness of God* (St. Louis, 1983) and *The Oneness View of Jesus Christ* (St. Louis, 1994).

in the new church *Manual*. A requirement for baptism was that the formula contain the words "in the Name of the Lord Jesus Christ."[32]

The Pentecostal Assemblies of the World continued as an interracial church until 1924 when the white ministers withdrew to form a separate white denomination, explaining that the "mixture of races prevented the effective evangelization of the world." Accordingly, later in the year a largely white group called the "Pentecostal Ministerial Alliance" was formed, an organization exercising authority over its ministerial members but not over churches. In a short time this body developed into a formal denomination known as the "Pentecostal Church, Incorporated."[33]

The United Pentecostal Church

Yet another "oneness" church was organized in 1913 called the "Pentecostal Assemblies of Jesus Christ." This group developed separately from the others and by 1936 had 16,000 members in 245 churches. These congregations were located in twenty-seven states, but concentrated largely in Illinois, Louisiana, and Texas. The "Pentecostal Church, Incorporated" had in that same year 168 churches and 9,681 members in twenty-three states.[34] Since the two groups were identical in doctrine and located in practically the same territory, a move for merger gained strength through the following decade. The result was a union of the two denominations in a special General Conference called for this purpose in St. Louis in 1945. The newly constituted group adopted the name "The United Pentecostal Church," becoming by merger the largest "oneness" denomination in the United States.[35]

32. See the *Minute Book and Ministerial Record of the General Assembly of the Pentecostal Assemblies of the World (1919-1920)* in Tyson, *The Early Pentecostal Revival,* pp. 293-314 and 181-208. Everett Leroy Moore, "Handbook of Pentecostal Denominations in the United States" (unpublished master's thesis, Pasadena College of Religion, 1954), pp. 242-52.

33. Moore, "Handbook of Pentecostal Denominations," p. 254; Kendrick, *The Promise Fulfilled,* pp. 172, 173; Foster, *Think It Not Strange,* pp. 73-78, indicates that the schism was caused by the indignation of northern black ministers at the segregation policies of southern white members.

34. *Religious Bodies: 1936* (Washington, DC, 1941), vol. 2, pp. 1323, 1330.

35. Moore, "Handbook of Pentecostal Denominations"; Elmer T. Clark, *Small Sects in America* (New York, 1956), p. 170; Gordon Melton, *Encyclopedia of American Religions,* 2nd ed. (Detroit, 1987), pp. 39-46, 309-62. Kendrick, *The Promise Fulfilled,*

In addition to the older and larger denominations, several smaller "oneness" groups were formed in the years after 1916, developing separately from the other churches. In 1916, the "Apostolic Overcoming Holy Church of God" was founded by the Reverend W. T. Phillips, a black Methodist. Originating in Mobile, Alabama, this group adopted a unitarian statement of faith, but operated without close ties to other Pentecostal denominations. By 1965 this group claimed a total membership of 75,000 in 300 churches, most of them in Alabama, Illinois, Kentucky, Oklahoma, and Texas.[36]

Another large "oneness" group was the "Church of Our Lord Jesus Christ of the Apostolic Faith," founded by R. C. Lawson in Columbus, Ohio, in 1919. The headquarters of this mostly black group was moved to New York City early in its history. With churches in twenty-seven states, the denomination by 1954 claimed to have 45,000 members in 155 churches. These membership claims, along with those of some of the other black groups, may be excessive, although the numbers may reflect large concentrations of African-Americans in crowded urban ghettos.[37]

Other smaller splinter groups of these churches were founded after 1916, but information and statistics are either lacking or difficult to obtain. Among these are: the Full Salvation Union, founded in 1934 in Lansing, Michigan, by James F. Andrews; the Apostolic Church, founded by the Reverend R. L. Blankenship in Texas in 1945; and the "Jesus Church," founded by Sam Officer in Cleveland, Tennessee, in 1953.[38] In addition to these groups, hundreds of independent congregations holding the "Jesus' name" view sprang up throughout the country, but did not affiliate with any nationally organized denomination. It would be impossible to gather complete and accurate information on these churches, many of which practice such oddities as snake-handling and free love. These fringe groups were generally viewed as heretical by the more orthodox Pentecostals. Pentecostal leaders have estimated that the independent congregations approximated the number of the organized

---

p. 173; Foster, *Think It Not Strange*, pp. 78-81. The "Pentecostal Assemblies of the World" continued to function as the largest black Oneness group in the nation.

36. Landis, *Yearbook of American Churches*, 1965, pp. 14, 15; Moore, "Handbook of Pentecostal Denominations," pp. 269-81.

37. Mead, *Handbook of Denominations, 1965*, p. 86.

38. Moore, "Handbook of Pentecostal Denominations," pp. 290-313. Officer's "Jesus Church" is the only "Oneness" group to issue from the holiness-Pentecostal tradition, all the others having come from the "finished work" wing of Pentecostalism.

ones. A conservative estimate of the number of Pentecostal unitarians in the United States in 1964 was placed at 500,000, over half of them black.[39]

The oneness Pentecostals have generally been considered an integral part of the Pentecostal movement as a whole, although the trinitarian groups tended to view them as simple, innocent, but mistaken. As of 1965, the "Jesus only" denominations were not admitted to membership in the "Pentecostal Fellowship of North America," an ecumenical organization that consisted of sixteen of the "respectable" Pentecostal denominations. However, when Pentecostal leaders cited statistics to show the overall size and growth of the movement, the oneness groups were always included.

By the middle of the twentieth century, observers both within and outside of the Pentecostal movement began to see an openness to dialogue between trinitarian and unitarian Pentecostals. Some observers have even predicted that in time, both groups will be wholly within the fold of traditional trinitarian mainline Protestantism. By the end of the century, however, there were few signs that the oneness churches were about to change their theology. Over the years, non-Pentecostals have tended to see little difference between the trinitarians and unitarians, since both were intensely evangelical and charismatic. Moreover, the Pentecostal "unitarians" also have always made a sharp distinction between themselves and the older Unitarian-Universalist movement which has no connection whatever with the Pentecostal groups.[40]

The advent of the "oneness" unitarian controversy caused other Pentecostal groups to reassess their doctrinal stand concerning the Trinity. In 1917 the Pentecostal Holiness Church added a paragraph to its *Discipline* that strongly supported the traditional trinitarian view. This was significant since previous editions after 1900 had failed to mention the Trinity at all. For several years following 1916 the *Advocate* sternly opposed Pentecostal people who had "run wild after that which was new and sensational." In 1917 the "heresies" which had plagued Pentecostalism were listed by the Pentecostal Holiness Church as "finished work, one name baptism, rejection of the Trinity, anti-organization . . . and many other preposterous nonsensical sensations. . . ." It was obvious by

39. Morton T. Kelsey, *Tongue Speaking* (New York: Doubleday, 1964), pp. 242-43.
40. Kelsey, *Tongue Speaking,* pp. 85, 86; Kendrick, *The Promise Fulfilled,* p. 4; M. J. Wolff, "We Are Not Unitarians," *The Pentecostal Herald,* Mar. 1967, p. 5.

such articles as these that the Pentecostal movement suffered serious convulsions in its early years.[41]

The conflict between the "three God people" and the "Jesus only" Pentecostals continued, especially among the independent congregations. In the late 1940's Archie Robertson found congregations in rural Tennessee that were bitterly divided over the issue. Even among snake-handling partisans in the Appalachian Mountains "cross-ups" persisted into the 1950's over "baptism in one or three names." By this time, however, the major Pentecostal denominations had firmly institutionalized their positions as either trinitarian or unitarian.[42]

The "Initial Evidence" Debate

While the sanctification and oneness controversies took center stage for several years, a serious debate took place within the Assemblies of God over the distinctive Pentecostal doctrine of tongues as the "initial physical evidence" of the baptism in the Holy Spirit. For some years questions about the doctrine simmered beneath the surface of the new church. By September of 1918, the debate boiled over into the General Council, with two former members of the Christian and Missionary Alliance (CMA), Fred F. Bosworth and D. W. Kerr, leading the discussions. Bosworth, who had spoken in tongues under Charles Parham at Zion City, Illinois in 1906, attacked the teaching as a "doctrinal error," charging that Charles Parham was "the first man in the history of the world to publicly teach it." Leading the opposing forces was Kerr who argued that "it is the Word of God, not the experiences of famous men, that is the touchstone for the Pentecostal belief concerning the immediate evidence of the Baptism."[43]

In the end, the vote overwhelmingly favored the initial evidence forces. Bosworth subsequently returned to the CMA where he continued to conduct a mass healing ministry until his death in 1958. After this debate the CMA lost many pastors to the Assemblies of God despite the

---

41. *The Pentecostal Holiness Discipline*, 1917, pp. 5-14, 17-18; *The Pentecostal Holiness Advocate*, Sept. 6, 1917, p. 10; May 2, 1918, p. 3.

42. Archie Robertson, *That Old-Time Religion* (Boston, 1950), p. 173.

43. See Vinson Synan's "The Role of Tongues as Initial Evidence," in Mark Wilson, ed., *Spirit and Renewal: Essays in Honor of J. Rodman Williams*, pp. 67-82.

efforts of A. B. Simpson to keep an openness to the gifts within the church. But for the Assemblies of God, and for most other American Pentecostals, the place of the initial evidence teaching was settled for the time being.[44]

By 1920 the great theological controversies that formed the major cleavages within the movement had been fought out and settled along the general lines that exist today. Although minor questions of church government and interchurch relations caused problems in the ensuing years, the "finished work" and "Jesus' name" questions emerged as the primary divisive issues. The southern Pentecostal groups maintained a surprising solidarity in doctrine and polity throughout these controversies. The three major southern churches — Tomlinson's Church of God, Mason's Church of God in Christ, and King's Pentecostal Holiness Church — rejected both new doctrines, remaining in the Wesleyan "second work" and trinitarian traditions. Their theologies never varied from that taught in the Azusa Street revival. Seymour also rejected the "finished work" and "Jesus only" theories, as did Parham, the doctrinal father of the entire movement.

In the end, the Pentecostal movement split into equal factions over the question of sanctification, with about half the churches siding with the "finished work" partisans and the other half maintaining a traditional Wesleyan "second work" view. About a fifth of all American Pentecostals eventually sided with the unitarians, and the proportions have remained about the same since 1920.[45]

Like all new religious movements, Pentecostalism experienced the twin challenges of external criticism and internal controversy during its formative period. Both challenges resulted in a strengthening and diversifying of the movement. Criticism from outside only succeeded in consolidating it, as Pentecostal converts rose to defend their new-found theology through sermons and publications.

44. Synan, "The Role of Tongues as Initial Evidence," pp. 73-75. Also see McGee, *Initial Evidence*; Ben Aker, "Initial Evidence: A Biblical Perspective," and Klaud Kendrick, "Initial Evidence: A Historical Perspective," in Burgess et al., *Dictionary of Pentecostal and Charismatic Movements*, pp. 455-60.

45. The assertion that only "a few diehards" who are "inconsequential" retained the second work theory of sanctification is obviously not based on fact since 50 percent of all Pentecostals can still be classified thus. See Ewart, *The Phenomenon of Pentecost*, p. 74; and James S. Tinney, "A Wesleyan-Pentecostal Appraisal of the Charismatic Movement," *The Pentecostal Holiness Advocate*, Jan. 7, 1967, pp. 4-10.

Controversy within the movement also succeeded in expanding its scope. Each new doctrinal variation produced new denominations, which in turn spawned new families of denominations through further schisms. The outcome of these controversies was a national movement composed of many submovements. Pentecostalism engendered at least twenty-five separate denominations within fourteen years. In fact, by the middle of the century, some Protestant observers were referring to Pentecostalism as the "Third Force in Christendom" rather than a single denominational cluster arising in the traditional manner.[46]

46. Henry P. Van Dusen, "Third Force in Christendom," *Life,* June 9, 1958, pp. 113-24; Gordon Atter, *The Third Force* (Peterborough, Ontario, 1962), pp. 1-9; McCandlish Phillips, "And There Appeared Unto Them Tongues of Fire," *The Saturday Evening Post,* May 16, 1964, p. 31.

CHAPTER NINE

The African-American Pentecostals

*Glory to God! Makes me feel good to see White and
Colored praisin' God together.*

Archie Robertson, *That Old-Time Religion*

A little known aspect of the modern Pentecostal movement is the
important role of African-Americans in both its inception and development. This striking interracial phenomenon occurred in the very
years of America's most racist period, between 1890 and 1920. In an age
of Social Darwinism, Jim Crowism, and general white supremacy, the
fact that Pentecostal blacks and whites worshipped together in virtual
equality was a significant exception to the prevailing attitudes and practices. Even more significant is the fact that this interracial harmony
occurred among the very groups that have traditionally been most at
odds — the poor whites and the poor blacks.

In the period when most holiness and Pentecostal groups were
forming into recognizable organizations, the racial lines were often in-
distinct, with blacks serving as officials, preachers, and church members.
Only after the various movements began to coalesce into formal denominations did divisions occur along racial lines. The reasons for those later
separations may be found in the existing pattern of race relations in the

167

United States when the Pentecostal movement began in 1906. As a glaring exception to the national norm, particularly in the South, interracial Pentecostal groups were subjected to great social pressure to conform to the segregationist pattern that dominated much of American life in the early twentieth century.[1]

By 1900 the racial lines in American religious life had already been clearly drawn by the harsh realities of the post–Civil War era. The freeing of the slaves had caused a grand division of Protestantism along racial lines. One of the most cherished dreams of Negro slaves was to have their own church where they could worship in a manner congenial to their nature. With the end of the war, black worship services were finally freed from the surveillance of the slaveholders. Although worship services continued to be integrated immediately after 1865, deep problems soon arose that led to all-white and all-black denominations. Increasingly the whites began to resent the presence of large numbers of blacks in their churches, where in many cases blacks outnumbered whites. On their part, the blacks resented white domination of the services, and desired to worship in their own manner under the direction of their own ministers. Consequently, several all-black denominations were formed in the years following the Civil War. In 1870 the Colored Methodist Episcopal Church was founded as a separation from the Methodist Episcopal Church, South. Ten years later the National Baptist Convention was organized from the former black membership of the Southern Baptist Convention. The Primitive and Free-Will Baptists, along with the Cumberland Presbyterians, also experienced similar divisions in this period. The trend towards racial separation continued into the twentieth century. Indeed, by 1929 church membership reports showed that 90 percent of all black Christians belonged to churches restricted to their own race.[2]

---

1. Sources on the black church for this period include C. Eric Lincoln and Lawrence H. Mamiya, *The Black Church in the African American Experience* (Durham, NC, 1990); William C. Turner Jr., "Movements in the Spirit: A Review of African American Holiness/Pentecostal/Apostolics," in *Directory of African American Religious Bodies*, ed. Wardell Payne (Washington, DC, 1991); Sherry DuPree, *Biographical Dictionary of African-American Holiness Pentecostals, 1880-1990* (Washington, DC, 1989); and Charles E. Jones, *Black Holiness: A Guide to the Study of Black Participation in Wesleyan Perfectionist and Glossolalic Pentecostal Movements* (Metuchen, NJ, 1987). See also Richard Hofstadter, *Social Darwinism in American Thought* (Philadelphia, 1945), pp. 86-102, 146-73.

2. Richard Niebuhr, *The Social Sources of Denominationalism* (Hamden, CT,

In terms of time frame, the holiness movement in America paralleled these racial developments. The National Holiness Association was founded in 1867, when the movement for racial separation of the churches was beginning. The decade of the 1890's saw the founding of several holiness denominations in all parts of the nation. Unfortunately, the same decade marked the beginnings of black disfranchisement in the South and of Jim Crow segregation throughout most of the country. Because of the racial climate of the times, the holiness movement divided with few exceptions along racial lines.[3]

Of the numerous holiness denominations that formed during this time, two were African-American groups that would later become Pentecostal. The first was the "United Holy Church," which began in 1886 in Method, North Carolina. Other small bodies joined this church until 1902, when the denomination was formally organized with the help of W. H. Fulford, an elder of the Fire-Baptized Holiness Church. This church generally followed the lead of North Carolina's white holiness churches, adopting after 1906 a statement of faith that placed the group in the Pentecostal family — a move that may have been taken as a result of Cashwell's revival in Dunn in 1906-07. Although identical in doctrine with the Pentecostal Holiness Church and the Church of God, the United Holy Church developed separately, having minimal contact with its white sister denominations.[4]

The church destined to become the largest African-American body of either holiness or Pentecostal origins was the Church of God in Christ. As already noted, this church had its origins in Mississippi, Tennessee, and Arkansas in 1897. Although the founders, Jones and Mason, had been Baptists, they adopted the Wesleyan view of sanctification. After Mason's

---

1929), pp. 239-63; W. D. Weatherford, *The American Churches and the Negro* (Boston, 1957), pp. 25-222; Alexander Gross, *History of the Methodist Episcopal Church, South* (New York, 1894), pp. 133-40.

3. For a perceptive view of black holiness-Pentecostal religion see Cheryl J. Sanders's *Saints in Exile: The Holiness-Pentecostal Experience in American Religion and Culture* (New York, 1996).

4. H. L. Fisher, *History of the United Holy Church of America* (n.p., n.d.), pp. 1-8, and Chester W. Gregory, *The History of the United Holy Church of America, Inc., 1886-1986*, pp. 1-46. In 1949 representatives of this group attended the General Conference of the Pentecostal Holiness Church, but no affiliation was effected. See the *Minutes of the Eleventh General Conference of the Pentecostal Holiness Church, 1949*, p. 27.

trip to the Azusa Street revival in 1907, the church suffered a division over the newly arrived Pentecostal doctrine. With the withdrawal of Jones and the non-Pentecostal faction, Mason became the undisputed leader of the church, which grew rapidly after 1907. At the time of Mason's death in 1961 his denomination numbered over 400,000 members in the United States.[5]

Although the United Holy Church and the Church of God in Christ were functioning denominations in 1906, neither played a direct role in the beginning of the Pentecostal revival at Azusa Street. Seymour, the leading figure at Azusa Street, was a black pastor who had belonged to Parham's Apostolic Faith Movement with its headquarters in Baxter Springs, Kansas. That the central figure of the Los Angeles revival was an African-American is of paramount importance to Pentecostals of all races. Although most Pentecostals acknowledge their debt to Seymour, few are willing to recognize him as the "founder" of the movement. Black Pentecostals refer to him as the movement's "Apostle and Pioneer," and often depict the movement's beginning as an entirely black phenomenon later accepted by whites.[6]

Despite some controversy over the matter, it can be safely said that Parham and Seymour share roughly equal positions as founders of modern Pentecostalism. Parham laid the doctrinal foundations of the movement, while Seymour served as the catalytic agent for its popularization. In this sense, the early Pentecostal movement could be classed as neither "black" nor "white," but as interracial.

There can be no doubt that in its early stages the Pentecostal movement was completely interracial. The Azusa Street meeting was conducted on the basis of complete racial equality. Pentecostals point out that just as the first Pentecost recorded in Acts 2:1-11 included "men out of every nation under heaven," the modern "Pentecost" at Los Angeles included people of every racial background. Participants in the meeting reported that "Negroes, whites, Mexicans, Italians, Chinese, Russians, Indians," and other ethnic groups mingled without apparent prejudice on account of racial origins. The fact that Cashwell was forced to reform his racial prejudices after arriving at the Azusa Street Mission indicates that the trend in early Pentecostal services was toward racial

5. Clemmons, *Bishop C. H. Mason,* pp. 3-59.
6. Fidler, "Historical Review," pp. 3, 4; Bloch-Hoell, *The Pentecostal Movement,* pp. 42-53.

unity in contrast to the segregationist trends of the times. Photographs of the Azusa Street leaders taken in 1907 show whites and blacks united in the operation of the church without any apparent distinctions on account of race.[7]

This interracial period continued during the years from 1906 to 1924, when the last racially based separation occurred. As noted previously, the Church of God in Christ played a unique role from 1907 to 1914 by giving ordination to hundreds of white ministers of independent congregations. During these years the only organized Pentecostal denominations were the Church of God in Christ, the Church of God (Cleveland, Tennessee), The United Holy Church, and the Pentecostal Holiness Church. Of these, only Mason's was legally incorporated, this having been done in Memphis in 1897. Since most white Pentecostal churches outside the South were independent, with no recognized ecclesiastical body to ordain their ministers, they were unable to perform marriages and other ministerial duties requiring official recognition. They were also ineligible for the reduced clergy rates on the railroads. Since the Church of God in Christ was an incorporated religious denomination, scores of white ministers sought ordination at the hands of Mason. Large numbers of white ministers, therefore, obtained ministerial credentials carrying the name of the Church of God in Christ. One group in Alabama and Texas eventually made an agreement with Mason in 1912 to use the name of his church, but to issue ministerial credentials signed by their own leaders. The leaders of this group were H. A. Goss, D. C. O. Opperman, H. G. Rodgers, and A. P. Collins, all of them white. Although technically using the name of the Church of God in Christ, these white ministers were joined to Mason's group by only a "gentleman's agreement," with the understanding that credentials would not be given to anyone "untrustworthy." At times, Mason referred to the white group of ministers in the Church of God in Christ as the "White work of the Church."[8]

By 1914 these white ministers became dissatisfied with this arrange-

---

7. A picture in *The International Outlook,* Jan.-Mar. 1963, p. 4, shows three blacks and eight whites who lived together in the Mission and supervised its activities. See also Nichols, *Pentecostalism,* pp. 61-62; Brumback, *Suddenly from Heaven,* pp. 84-85; Campbell, *The Pentecostal Holiness Church,* pp. 240-42; Bartleman, *How "Pentecost" Came to Los Angeles,* p. 29.

8. Clemmons, *Bishop C. H. Mason,* pp. 48-55. Leonard Lovett, "Black Origins of the Pentecostal Movement," in Vinson Synan, *Aspects of Pentecostal-Charismatic*

ment and called for a convention of Pentecostal leaders to meet in Hot Springs, Arkansas. The purpose of this convention was to form a national Pentecostal denomination that would include all the white ministers and churches. Invitations were sent to King of the Pentecostal Holiness Church and to Tomlinson of the Church of God, but they refused to attend because of the "finished work" doctrine openly espoused by a majority of the Hot Springs delegates. As noted earlier, the Hot Springs Convention resulted in the formation of the Assembly of God, which within ten years became the largest Pentecostal denomination in the United States. Attempts were made to include the Church of God in Christ, and C. H. Mason was invited to give an address. His message, which used the sweet potato as an object lesson, was well received, but Mason himself did not join the new organization.[9]

With the advent of the "oneness" issue in 1914, the young Assemblies of God group was wracked by the most serious controversy of its history. In the end this "new issue" came to have deep racial overtones, resulting in the formation of one of the most fully interracial church bodies in the United States. The father of the "Pentecostal unitarian" movement was a white minister from Los Angeles, Frank J. Ewart, whose movement for rebaptism "in Jesus' name" swept over the Pentecostal movement from 1914 to 1916. Of the hundreds of Pentecostal ministers who accepted rebaptism according to Ewart's formula, none was more important in the long run than the African-American pastor from Indianapolis, Garfield T. Haywood. This man had founded one of the largest congregations in the new Assemblies of God organization. Although a

---

Origins, pp. 123-42. Ethel A. Goss, *Winds of God* (New York, 1958), p. 163; Flower, "History of the Assemblies of God," pp. 16-19. See Cecil Robeck's unpublished paper "The Past Historical Roots of Racial Unity and Division in American Pentecostalism," a paper presented to the founding convention of the Pentecostal and Charismatic Churches of North America, Memphis, October 1994.

9. Clemmons, *Bishop C. H. Mason,* p. 71; Brumback, *Suddenly from Heaven,* pp. 151-61; Kendrick, *The Promise Fulfilled,* pp. 73-93; Nichols, *Pentecostalism,* pp. 108-14. Although race was not mentioned as a basis for forming the Assemblies of God group, it is evident from the record that white ministers using credentials from Mason's Church of God in Christ were dissatisfied with the arrangement. Although the "Call" issued in Bell's *Word and Witness* for the Hot Springs Convention included "all the Churches of God in Christ," none of Mason's group appeared. See Brumback, *Suddenly from Heaven,* p. 157; and *The Pentecostal Evangel,* Apr. 1964, pp. 1-32. See also Menzies, *Anointed to Serve,* pp. 80-105; Blumhofer, *The Assemblies of God,* vol. 1, pp. 197-213; Robeck, "Historical Roots," pp. 30-34.

majority of its members were black, the church was also interracial. A powerful speaker, Haywood exercised a great influence in the councils of the church.

When Cook, one of Ewart's converts, took his fateful eastern tour in 1914, one of his first stops was at Haywood's church in Indianapolis. An Assemblies of God official, J. Roswell Flower, was disturbed at Cook's doctrine and attempted to prevent his progress by warning pastors of his coming. Writing Haywood in alarm after hearing Cook in St. Louis, Flower warned him that the touring evangelist was coming to his city "with an erroneous doctrine." Haywood answered, "Your warning came too late. I have already accepted the message and have been baptized." With the winning of Haywood, many black Pentecostals were destined to become Pentecostal unitarians.[10]

When the issue reached its climax at the 1916 General Council of the Assemblies of God and the trinitarians forced the adoption of a strongly worded trinitarian statement, a large minority of dissenting "Jesus' Name" ministers withdrew from the church to form a new group based on unitarian principles. The leader of these dissenters was Haywood, his large congregation in Indianapolis becoming a focal point for the new movement. In January 1916 the dissenters met in Eureka Springs, Arkansas, to effect a new denomination that could issue ministerial credentials. With America's involvement in World War I looming in the near future, an added urgency was the threat posed to young draft-age ministers by the federal draft law. A hastily formed group took shape, called "The General Assembly of the Apostolic Churches," with former Assemblies of God leaders Opperman and Goss as the top officials.[11]

This new organization soon found that it could not secure government recognition, and with the War threatening, the group searched for an incorporated church they could merge with. Such a group was found on the West Coast, under the name "Pentecostal Assemblies of the World." Founded in 1914 by a "oneness" minister named Frazier, it had already obtained the prized government recognition. In late 1917 the two groups merged and the name "Pentecostal Assemblies of the World" was adopted to designate the entire church. The chairman of the newly

10. Foster, *Think It Not Strange*, p. 54.
11. Foster, *Think It Not Strange*, p. 73.

merged denomination was a white man, C. W. Doak, and the secretary was the African-American Haywood.[12]

For nine years the Pentecostal Assemblies of the World operated as a completely interracial church with roughly equal numbers of blacks and whites serving as both officers and members. One participant, S. C. McLain, a southern white minister, described this interracial period as a "unique fellowship." "Throughout the north and east," he said, "there seemed to be very little, if any, race prejudice. I, being southern born, thought it a miracle that I could sit in a service by a colored saint of God and worship, or eat at a great camp table, and forget I was eating beside a colored saint. But in spirit and truth God was worshipped in love and harmony." A great problem existed, however, in the southern states because "ministers laboring in the South had to conform to law and customs."[13]

In the end it was the southern system of segregation that destroyed the fellowship of the races and split the church along racial lines. Due to southern laws during the time of this fellowship, no racially integrated meetings could be held below the Mason-Dixon Line because of Jim Crow laws governing convention and hotel facilities. Therefore from 1916 to 1924 all church conventions were held in northern cities. Another complication was the fact that most of the northern ministers were blacks while most of the southern ones were whites. With the church conventions held in the North, fewer southerners could attend and were consequently outvoted on vital issues. When the southerners insisted on a convention in a southern city, "a spirit of agitation began to arise" between blacks and whites. A further complication arose in 1921 when the white ministers conducted a "Southern Bible Conference" in Little Rock that was notable by the absence of black participants. This move appeared ominous to Haywood and the other African-American ministers.[14]

The climax of the problem came at the General Conference of the Church in St. Louis in 1924. Meeting early in the week, the whites held a separate conclave which they called "a continuation of the Southern Bible Conference." This was the final wedge that drove the races apart. In an "atmosphere of tension," the white ministers deserted the main

---

12. Foster, *Think It Not Strange*, p. 74; Tyson, *The Early Pentecostal Revival*, pp. 187-208.

13. Foster, *Think It Not Strange*, p. 74.

14. Foster, *Think It Not Strange*, pp. 75-76.

hall as the conference convened and conducted an ad hoc meeting in the church basement. Here it was decided that the white ministers would withdraw from the denomination and leave the church under the direction of Haywood, who would henceforth head a predominantly African-American communion. The white ministers would then organize "another association to meet the needs of the South." Those leaving the church met later and formed the all-white "Pentecostal Ministerial Alliance" in Jackson, Tennessee, in February 1925. Thus ended a striking and unique period of interracial accord.[15]

The two major Southern white Pentecostal denominations, the Church of God and the Pentecostal Holiness Church, also began as interracial communions. From its earliest days the Church of God had African-Americans in its fellowship, as both members and ministers. As the church expanded into several southern states after 1906, the problem of the blacks' status in the church grew proportionately. By 1912 Tomlinson faced the problem of ordaining African-American clergymen and fitting them into the church. Although Tomlinson was an Indiana Quaker by upbringing, he bowed to the southern system to solve his problem. On June 4, 1912, he wrote:

> Had a conference yesterday to consider the question of ordaining Edmund Barr (colored) and setting the colored people off to work among themselves on account of the race prejudice in the South.[16]

As the Church of God continued to develop, the black churches began to demand more self-government and independence from the white-dominated General Assembly. In 1926 a committee of African-American ministers appeared before the General Assembly and requested the privilege of conducting their own separate General Assembly. This right was granted to the black constituency with a provision requiring that the "General Overseer" of the black churches always be a white man. This arrangement continued to be the racial policy of the Church of God until 1966. This church was the only predominantly white Pentecostal denomination that maintained a significant African-American branch as an integral, yet segregated, part of the church.[17]

---

15. Foster, *Think It Not Strange*, p. 76; see Nichols, *Pentecostalism*, pp. 116-19.
16. Tomlinson, "A Journal of Happenings," June 4, 1912.
17. Conn, *Like a Mighty Army*, pp. 132, 182, 201-3; *Church of God Evangel*, Nov. 15, 1919, p. 2.

The Pentecostal Holiness Church also had an African-American branch in its early years. The Fire-Baptized Holiness Church, which later merged with the Pentecostal Holiness Church, had an African-American at its founding convention in Anderson, South Carolina, in 1898. This black minister, W. E. Fuller, was a dynamic preacher who for several years served on the Executive Committee of the denomination. Most of his time was spent in organizing African-American congregations. This he did with great success. In 1904 he claimed five hundred "conversions" while organizing four black congregations in South Carolina and Georgia. After ten years as full members of the Fire-Baptized Holiness Church, the blacks in 1908 held a separate convention in Anderson, South Carolina. In this meeting the black Fire-Baptized Holiness churches voted to separate from the parent body and form their own denomination "because of criticism from the communities of the South against integrated church meetings." In 1926 this group voted to change its name to the "Fire-Baptized Holiness Church of God of the Americas." By 1959 the church had over 6,000 members in 60 congregations and over 300 missions.[18]

Another African-American group separated from the Pentecostal Holiness Church in 1913. The churches forming this group had been a part of the Pentecostal Holiness Church in North Carolina before the 1911 merger with the Fire-Baptized Holiness Church. In the 1913 General Conference, which met in Toccoa, Georgia, the black churches requested through their delegates that they be separated from the main body of the church in order to "carry out a better program" among their own people. They departed with the "good wishes" of the General Conference. The Black Pentecostal Holiness Churches have remained quite small since their separation from the parent body in 1913, their churches being scattered throughout the southeast.[19]

In addition to the African-American bodies already mentioned, several other black Pentecostal denominations sprang up in other parts of the country outside the mainstream of the movement. Probably loosely organized, these churches are not included in the usual histories

---

18. *Discipline of the Fire-Baptized Holiness Church of God of the Americas,* 1962 (Atlanta, GA), pp. 9-12; Bertha Teasley, personal interview with the author, Sept. 12, 1963; Kendrick, *The Promise Fulfilled,* p. 4; W. E. Fuller, *Live Coals,* Jan. 11, 1905, p. 2. See also Synan, *Old-Time Power,* pp. 100-101.

19. *Minutes of the Second General Convention of the Pentecostal Holiness Church,* 1913 (Tocoa, GA), p. 5.

of the Pentecostals. Some were the creations of dominating men who built entire denominations around their personalities. Their statistical reports were often obviously exaggerated, as seen in the "National David Spiritual Temple of Christ Church Union," which claimed 40,000 members in only 47 churches in 1959.[20] Other churches in this category are the "Apostolic Overcoming Holy Church of God," the "Church of Our Lord Jesus Christ of the Apostolic Faith," and "Christ's Sanctified Holy Church, Colored." Some of these groups adopted bewilderingly long names that defied theological classification. One such group presented itself to the world with the fantastic name of "The House of God, The Holy Church of the Living God, The Pillar and Grounds of the Truth, House of Prayer for All People."[21]

Some African-American sects have been classified as Pentecostal because of a seeming similarity in some of their practices. This is especially true of sects that deified their founders, calling them "God," "Christ," "Daddy Grace," or "Father Divine." The most prominent of these are "Daddy Grace's House of Prayer" and "Father Divine's Peace Mission" with churches called "Heavens" in several large Northern cities. Although these groups often demonstrated charismatic or emotional phenomena resembling Pentecostal worship, they have never been recognized as part of the Pentecostal movement as a whole.[22]

Probably the first "black supremacy" religious movement in America was the "Church of the Living God, Christian Workers for Fellowship," which began in Wrightsville, Arkansas in 1889. Founded by William Christian, it continued into the twentieth century under the leadership of Christian's wife and later his son. According to the catechism of this church, Abraham, Isaac, Jacob, David, and Jesus were members of the black race. Quoting Scriptures for support, this document went on to say that "it is as natural to be black as the leopard to be spotted," although it was wrong to "make a difference between people because they are black."[23]

20. Elmer T. Clark, *Small Sects in America* (New York, 1956), p. 119; Landis, *Yearbook of American Churches*, 1965, pp. 76-77.

21. Clark, *Small Sects in America*, pp. 85-132, gives a compendium of these sects and their beliefs. Classification is extremely difficult because of a lack of literature in most groups, and conflicting statements in the literature that exists.

22. Clark, *Small Sects in America*, pp. 122-27.

23. Clark, *Small Sects in America*, pp. 120-21; Landis, *Yearbook of American Churches, 1965*, p. 40. It is possible that the "Black Muslims" and other black supremacist groups received early inspiration from this movement.

Added to all these sects are literally thousands of independent African-American Pentecostal congregations that dot the major cities of America from coast to coast. With the mass migration of blacks to the large cities, storefront versions of their home churches were created. By the 1960's it was impossible to investigate and properly classify these multifarious groups, which often carried names that defied description. Another result of black migration to the North was the fact that in the 1960's the largest congregations of such "southern" denominations as the Church of God in Christ, the United Holy Church, and the Fire-Baptized Holiness Church, were located in New York, Chicago, Detroit, and Philadelphia, rather than in the South.[24]

There are many reasons why African-Americans have adopted the Pentecostal religion in such great numbers. Some of them may be found in the nature of Pentecostal worship, and others in the culture and condition of African-Americans in the United States. In general, the emotional nature of Pentecostal worship has always held a strong appeal to African-American Christians already accustomed to highly-charged modes of worship in the Baptist or Methodist churches of their backgrounds. DuBois' statement that the religious goal of the Negro was "to be mad with supernatural joy" seems to apply to most black Protestant churches, Pentecostal and non-Pentecostal alike.[25] When the traditional churches began to add more form and decorum to their services, the emotionally inclined blacks gravitated to the Pentecostal churches. At least 80 percent of black Pentecostal church members came from other churches, particularly from Baptist and Methodist denominations.[26]

Once in the Pentecostal fold, these members often criticized the "coldness" and "formality" of the older churches. In reality, though, there has been little difference in manner of worship between the black Pentecostals and the rest of black Protestantism, with the exception of speaking in tongues. In recent years, there has been a tendency for emotionalism

24. *1960-61 Yearbook of the Church of God in Christ,* pp. 47-52, 64-68, 78-82, 88-90; *Discipline of the Fire-Baptized Holiness Church of Americas,* pp. 113-21; Fisher, *The United Holy Church,* pp. 25-39.

25. *From Souls of Black Folk,* quoted in Frederick Morgan Davenport, *Primitive Traits in Religious Revivals: A Study in Mental and Social Evolution* (New York, 1905), p. 142.

26. Liston Pope, *Millhands and Preachers* (New Haven, CT, 1942), p. 133.

to decline in traditional African-American churches and a consequent exodus to Pentecostal churches where members feel more "at home."[27]

Because the early Pentecostal movement was essentially a religion of the socially underprivileged, African-Americans naturally gravitated into it, feeling themselves to be truly at home in the Pentecostal environment. For the most part, Pentecostals come from the lower socioeconomic levels, people who in many cases have been neglected by the more traditional denominations. As the older churches became more middle class in both constituency and mentality, groups like the Pentecostals held a strong appeal for the poverty-stricken masses who felt alienated within their own churches. In the early period of its history the Pentecostal movement was almost exclusively working-class. In the South the greatest growth occurred among urban millhands and rural sharecroppers.[28]

Since blacks in the South and elsewhere occupied the bottom rung of the social ladder, it was inevitable that large numbers would be drawn to Pentecostalism, representing as it did the religion of the poor. Also contributing to Pentecostalism's popularity was the fact that educational standards for the ministry were almost non-existent. The African-American "call to preach" continued to come, as Booker T. Washington described it, with the seeker "falling on the floor as if struck by a bullet." This emotional "call" led to an "oversupply" of ministers in most churches. For example, one local church of two hundred members reported having eighteen "regular" preachers.[29] The low educational standards for Pentecostal ministry attracted many blacks who felt they would have a greater opportunity to preach there than in the older denominations.

The opportunity to preach in most black churches was traditionally reserved for men, although there were notable exceptions among the early Methodists. A problem for the black Pentecostal churches was that even though many women seemed to possess powerful ministry gifts, they were usually denied ordination. In most cases women were allowed

27. Ruby F. Johnson, *The Development of Negro Religion* (New York, 1954), pp. 81-132. See also Ruby Johnson, *The Religion of Negro Protestants* (New York, 1956), p. 142.

28. Pope, *Millhands and Preachers,* p. 136.

29. Davenport, *Primitive Traits,* p. 56. See Vinson Synan, "An Equal Opportunity Movement," in *Pentecostals from the Inside Out,* ed. Harold Smith (Wheaton, IL, 1990), pp. 43-50.

to become evangelists or missionaries, but not pastors or bishops. Although the "mothers" of the church were highly honored, few were permitted to preach. An exceptional case was that of Elder Ida Robinson of Philadelphia, a member of the United Holy Church, who received a vision in1924 of people flocking to her from all directions for ministry. In that year she organized the "Mt. Sinai Holy Church" and was consecrated as the first black female bishop in America. Historically, most of her pastors and bishops were women, although men were not barred from high office.[30]

Another attraction to African-Americans was the interracial character of the movement's inception. With one of their own race playing a dominant part in the Azusa Street revival, many blacks thought of the Pentecostal movement as a primarily black phenomenon. To spokesmen of the Church of God in Christ, the movement began as an interracial revival "first received and propagated by a colored man, Elder W. J. Seymour, and by a handful of other colored worshippers" in Los Angeles. This historic fact is a source of great pride to black Pentecostals around the world.[31]

The eventual division of the movement into black and white branches followed a pattern already set by the older Protestant churches before the beginning of the Pentecostal movement. Although some African-Americans accepted these divisions as normal and inevitable with some even requesting them, the majority felt that they were "sinful and embarrassing." In many cases the divisions were blamed on the racial "customs" and "prejudices" of the South, but never on the prejudices of the whites. It is probably safe to assume that black Pentecostals as a whole resent the fact that the movement bowed to the pressures of the times and became divided. To some African-Americans the "Pentecostal problem" is the "cleavage of the races," which must be solved before the movement can "shake the world."[32]

Some black Pentecostals have turned their racial separateness to a distinct advantage in recent years in the conduct of foreign missions programs. The Church of God in Christ experienced a phenomenal growth in mid-century in both Africa and Latin America. Much of this success is perhaps due to the fact that black missionaries do not bear the

30. See Jones, *Black Holiness,* pp. 122-23.
31. Editorial in *The International Outlook,* Oct.-Dec. 1963, p. 14.
32. Editorial, p. 15.

stigma of preaching the "white man's religion." With 400,000 members in the United States, the church claimed a worldwide constituency of over 2,000,000 by 1964. In many cases they were much more successful than white missionaries working in the same areas.[33]

In general, blacks have been an integral part of the Pentecostal movement from its beginning and have contributed much to its distinctive character. With over 1,000,000 members in the United States in 1965, they comprised 5 percent of the total black population. This was more than twice the national percentage of all Pentecostals, which was only 2 percent. These figures reveal that in the United States, black Pentecostals have grown much faster than their white co-religionists.[34] In fact, by the end of the 1990's the Church of God in Christ was the fastest-growing denomination in America. Studies made in 1996 showed that the church was growing at a rate of 200,000 new members a year in 600 new congregations. In that year the U.S. membership stood at 6,750,000 members, making it the fifth largest denomination in the country. As the century draws to a close, the Church of God in Christ gives every indication of becoming the nation's largest black organization by the turn of the century.[35]

In spite of the phenomenal growth of the African-American branches of the American Pentecostal movement, the white churches have given them little acknowledgment. After the interracial period of 1906 to 1924, little or no contact was maintained between the white and black branches. When the "Pentecostal Fellowship of North America" was formed in 1948 at Des Moines, Iowa, to "demonstrate to the world the essential unity of Spirit-baptized believers, fulfilling the prayer of the Lord Jesus 'that they all may be one . . . ,'" not a single African-American denomination was invited to join. Beginning with eight denominations in 1948, the Pentecostal Fellowship of North America added other groups until in 1965 it numbered seventeen denominations — all of them white. No explanation was offered as to why the black churches were excluded. African-Americans, however, have been mem-

---

33. Editorial, pp. 1-15; Nichols, *Pentecostalism,* p. 104; Landis, *Yearbook of American Churches, 1965,* p. 37.

34. Kendrick, *The Promise Fulfilled,* p. 16. Bloch-Hoell, *The Pentecostal Movement,* pp. 56-64, points out that in 1936 blacks constituted 14.5 percent of the Pentecostal movement but only 9.7 percent of the population.

35. Joe Maxwell, "Building the Church (of God in Christ)," *Christianity Today,* Apr. 8, 1996, pp. 22-28; Clemmons, *Bishop C. H. Mason,* pp. 81-139.

bers of the "World Pentecostal Conference" since its organization in Zurich, Switzerland, in 1947.[36]

It is extremely difficult to determine the attitude of the white Pentecostal community toward African-Americans, in both the early and later years of its history. In spite of the interracial character of the movement's early stages, there was still some evidence of prejudice. Parham once criticized the Azusa Street meetings because of their "disgusting" similarity to "Southern darkey camp meetings." Although Seymour was his most famous disciple, Parham spent the later years of his life as an avid supporter of the Ku Klux Klan, praising its members for their "fine work in upholding the American way of life." In 1927, in a speech to the Klan in Saginaw, Michigan, he stated that:

> Only by being "saved" could the Klan "ever be able to realize their high ideals for invisible empire of the Ku Klux Klan . . . to the restoration of the old-time religion."[37]

Most Pentecostals, however, repudiated the Klan, even in the South. In 1946 when the Klan was being revived in Georgia, the *Pentecostal Holiness Advocate* opposed it as being an "anti-American organization — essentially evil and anti-Christian." The southern Pentecostals generally harbored a deep suspicion of the Klan because from the earliest years the Klan persecuted "holiness people" along with Negroes, Catholics, and Jews. A long-remembered part of Church of God history was the fact that Klan "night raiders" had attacked their original congregation at Camp Creek, North Carolina. Although some Pentecostals joined the Klan as individuals and others accepted offerings from the hooded members of the "Empire," their aversion to the Klan remained constant over the years.[38]

Although disclaiming kinship with the Klan, most southern Pentecostals stood firmly with their region in the post–World War II racial controversy. Some church spokesmen referred to "anti-South agitation from the North" as the source of the South's problems. The Church of

---

36. R. O. Corvin, "The Pentecostal Fellowship of North America," *Pentecost,* Dec. 1949, p. 2; Kendrick, *The Promise Fulfilled,* pp. 210-12; Nichols, *Pentecostalism,* pp. 215-18.

37. Charles F. Parham, *The Apostolic Faith,* Mar. 1927, p. 5. For a discussion of Parham's racial views see Goff, *Fields White Unto Harvest,* pp. 128-32.

38. G. H. Montgomery, "Editorial," *The Pentecostal Holiness Advocate,* Sept. 19, 1946, p. 3; Conn, *Like a Mighty Army,* p. 35.

God and the Pentecostal Holiness Church, being the most "southern" of the white Pentecostal churches, expressed the Dixie viewpoint through the early part of the century, but later, as they became national churches, they tended to drop political and racial topics altogether from their periodicals.[39]

Official statements pertaining to race are extremely rare in Pentecostal literature. Since the larger denominations either had African-American branches or had congregations in northern states, their racial policies were generally unstated and unpublished. Throughout the racial turmoil that followed the Supreme Court decision on desegregation in 1954, the voices of the larger Pentecostal churches, both black and white, were conspicuous for their silence. Occasionally a smaller southern denomination would speak out in defense of the Old South. In 1965, the Emmanuel Holiness Church, one of the splinter sects of the old Fire-Baptized Holiness movement, declared ambivalently,

> We welcome all nationalities of people into the Emmanuel Holiness Church in their respective Conference bodies. So be it resolved, that we are opposed to the act of integration of the races.[40]

All denominational statements for or against racial integration failed to obscure one important fact — the practical integration of poor whites and blacks in backwoods Pentecostal revival services. Probably the major instances of complete interracial worship in the South in the twentieth century occurred regularly among the rural devotees of divine healing and snake-handling. Among these radical fringe elements of Pentecostalism, interracial worship was the rule rather than the exception. In a typical snake-handling service near Chattanooga, one observer reported that fully half the congregation under the lamplit tent were Blacks. After the singing of white and Negro spirituals, the white preacher said to his mixed audience:

> Glory to God! Makes me feel good to see whites and colored praisin' God together.[41]

39. G. H. Montgomery, "Christianity, the South, and Race Agitation," *The Pentecostal Holiness Advocate*, Sept. 6, 1946, p. 3; Conn, *The Evangel Reader*, pp. 158-251.
40. *Minutes and Discipline of the Emmanuel Holiness Church Annual State Assemblies of Alabama, Florida, Georgia, North Carolina, and South Carolina, 1965*, p. 6.
41. Robertson, *That Old-Time Religion*, pp. 169-81.

Far from being an isolated case, this interracial service of the "Dolly Pond Church of God" represents a type of race-mixing that has occurred in the South since before the Civil War. Interracial worship in revivals, tent meetings, camp meetings, and pulpit exchanges has been the rule rather than the exception among the Pentecostals of the South. Although much of it disappeared after 1954 when the Civil Rights movement brought social ostracism to the whites who practiced it, interracial worship and even interracial congregations continued into the 1960's among the divine healers in large urban areas. In 1967 one of the largest Pentecostal churches in Washington, D.C. was the white pastor John L. Meares's congregation, which was predominantly black. By the end of the century, it was not uncommon to see large racially integrated churches in cities across the land. An example of this was John Giminez's 8,000-member Rock Church in Virginia Beach, which boasted a racial mix of 50% white and 50% black and Asian.[42]

By 1964 there were signs that the major Pentecostal denominations were officially supporting the African-American's drive for civil rights. In that year the Cleveland Church of God adopted a resolution on "human rights" that declared "Christian love and tolerance are incompatible with race prejudice and hatred." It further declared that "no American should, because of his race, or religion, be deprived of his right to worship, vote, rest, eat, sleep, be educated, live, and work on the same basis as other citizens." This resolution is remarkable in that it was adopted during the political furor created by the passage of the 1964 Civil Rights "public accommodations" act.[43]

In order to implement its "declaration on human rights," the Church of God in 1966 abolished its separate "colored assembly," totally integrating its black churches into the main body of the denomination. All references to "colored" status of churches, ministers, or members were deleted from the official minutes and records of the church. This action was taken and the process completed while the Methodist Church was still debating the fate of its all-black "Central Jurisdiction." In this case, Pentecostals actually surpassed the performance of the more traditional Protestants.[44]

42. J. Floyd Williams and Bishop J. A. Synan, interviews with the author, May 17, 1967. Personal interview with John Giminez, Oct. 20, 1995.

43. *Minutes of the 50th General Assembly, 1964*, pp. 67-68. This church has more members living in the old Confederacy than any other Pentecostal denomination.

44. *Minutes of the 51st General Assembly, 1966*, p. 62.

Although not all Pentecostal groups have taken steps comparable to those of the Church of God, the most recent trend has been towards racial integration. In 1965 the General Conference of the Pentecostal Holiness Church directed its General Executive Board to "seek to establish communication with sincere religious leaders among American Negroes; that an effort be made to form Negro Associate Conferences, and that, in general, sincere action be focused toward constructively assisting our Negro friends with the moral and spiritual problems which are so prevalent and so pressing."[45] Indeed, in 1979, the Pentecostal Holiness Church and the United Holy Church signed an affiliation recognizing each other as "sister Pentecostal churches." By 1967, most Pentecostal colleges had complied with the racial requirements for receiving federal aid, and most of them were actively recruiting African-American students and athletes.

The most prominent institution of higher education in America to recruit blacks was Oral Roberts University in Tulsa, Oklahoma. By 1995, with 25% of its entire student body and 33% of its Graduate School of Theology made up of blacks, ORU had the highest percentage of African-Americans of all major institutions of higher learning in America except the historic black colleges.[46]

In the 1990's there were signs that a modified form of Pentecostalism had begun to sweep through the mainline black denominations. Although all black denominations have been affected, none have felt the impact of Pentecostalism more than the National Baptist Convention. Leading the movement among Baptists was Paul Morton, who in January 1993 formed the "Full Gospel Baptist Fellowship" in New Orleans. Morton, whose spiritual formation was in the Church of God in Christ, was later proclaimed as "bishop" in the new organization headquartered at his St. Stephen's Full Gospel Baptist Church in New Orleans. Similar movements were also gaining strength in the African Methodist Episcopal Church, the Methodist Episcopal, Zion Church, and the Christian Methodist Episcopal Church. The explosive growth of these movements led *Time Magazine* to predict that according to scholars' projections

---

45. *Minutes of the Fifteenth General Conference of the Pentecostal Holiness Church, 1965*, p. 72.

46. See Ken Walker, "An Oral Tradition," *Charisma*, Mar. 1996, pp. 37-42. Interview with Dean Paul Chappell on Feb. 20, 1996, in Fort Mill, South Carolina.

"Pentecostalism could claim half of black churchgoers sometime in the next century."[47]

A major breakthrough in Pentecostal race relations took place in Memphis in 1994 when the old all-white Pentecostal Fellowship of North America was disbanded in favor of a racially inclusive association named the "Pentecostal and Charismatic Churches of North America." In what was dubbed "the Miracle in Memphis," leaders of the mostly white movements repented of their historic racial shortcomings and signed a "Racial Reconciliation Manifesto" pledging to "oppose racism prophetically in all its manifestations." A new Board made up of six whites and six blacks was led by Bishop Ithiel Clemmons of the Church of God in Christ. The high point of the historic gathering was the session where a white Assemblies of God pastor washed the feet of Bishop Clemmons while begging forgiveness for the sins of the past. After this, Bishop Charles Blake of Los Angeles washed the feet of Thomas Trask, General Superintendent of the Assemblies of God. Similar reconciliation moves were initiated by the Southern Baptists, the National Association of Evangelicals, and the Promise Keepers.[48]

With a shorter history and less tradition than the older Protestant denominations, it seemed that the Pentecostal bodies might possibly be more flexible in meeting the racial challenges of the twentieth century. Beginning as the only effective interracial fellowship in American Christianity, they had bowed to the social pressures of the times and divided on racial lines. During the last half of the century, though, there were signs that the Pentecostals might once again lead the way in ecclesiastical race relations.

47. See Richard Ostling, "Strains on the Heart," *Time Magazine,* Nov. 19, 1990, pp. 88-90; and Vinson Synan, "Paul Morton Organizes Full Gospel Baptist Fellowship," *Timelines,* Spring 1993, pp. 1-4.

48. For reactions to the Memphis conference see *The Pentecostal Evangel,* Jan. 1, 1995, pp. 8-9; *Pentecostal Holiness Advocate,* Jan. 1995, pp. 6-7; *Church of God Evangel,* Jan. 1995, p. 23; "Pentecostals Experience a 'Miracle in Memphis,'" *Memphis Commercial Appeal,* Oct. 20, 1994, pp. A1-10; Barbara Reynolds, "Oregon Voters Can Learn from the Memphis Miracle," *USA Today,* Oct. 28, 1994, p. 11A. See also Ithiel Clemmons, "Racial and Spiritual Unity in the Body of Christ," *Advance* (Assemblies of God), Fall 1995, pp. 66-68; and Russell West, "That His People May Be One: An Interpretive Study of the Pentecostal Leadership's Quest for Racial Unity" (unpublished Ph.D. diss., Regent University, Virginia Beach, VA, 1997).

CHAPTER TEN

The Pentecostals in Society

1901-1960

*It is becoming increasingly evident that the pentecostal
movement we are witnessing . . . is an authentic, reformation-revival of historic significance, equal with those
other great movements of centuries past.*

Charles S. Sydnor, Jr., *The Presbyterian Survey* (1964)

The story of the Pentecostals in American society is in many respects
similar to that of the Methodists and Baptists of the eighteenth and
nineteenth centuries. Beginning as total outcasts, they were to gain a
status of suspicious toleration, followed eventually with full acceptance
by the community. The early history of the Pentecostals in society was
in reality a story of mutual rejection. The Pentecostals rejected society
because they believed it to be corrupt, wicked, hostile, and hopelessly
lost, while society rejected the Pentecostals because it believed them to
be insanely fanatical, self-righteous, doctrinally mistaken, and emotionally unstable. In such an atmosphere it was inevitable that much prejudice, hostility, and suspicion would mar the relationship of the early
Pentecostals to society at large.[1]

1. While little has been written on Pentecostals in American society, the

187

In the early days there was a widespread suspicion that Pentecostals practiced and believed everything odd and erroneous; and the suspicion fed the hostility towards them. Whenever a Pentecostal meeting took place in a community, rumors were rife about "magic powders," "trances," "wild emotion," and "sexual promiscuity." Although generally untrue and wildly exaggerated, the rumors eventually entered the nation's folklore and stamped anyone claiming to be "holiness" or "Pentecostal" with the epithet "holy roller." Those who engaged in this "religion of knockdown and dragout" were considered to be uncultured, uneducated blacks or "poor white trash" on the outer fringes of society. A member of a traditional church who joined the Pentecostals was generally considered to have "lost his mind" and to have severed all normal social connections. Within this framework, it is not surprising that the relationship of the Pentecostals to society has been marked with mutual hostility and even violence.[2]

Serpent Handling

Much of the opprobrium directed toward Pentecostals, of course, was brought on by sectarian extremists whose actions added a "grain of truth" to the falsehoods already in circulation. Probably no other religious movement of recent times has attracted so many adherents with unorthodox and "odd" opinions about religion. Probably the most damaging practice has been the rite of "snake-handling," carried out by mountain sects unconnected with the major Pentecostal denominations. Basing

following sources are helpful: Duncan Aikman, "The Holy Rollers," *American Mercury* 15 (Oct. 1928): 180-91; Anton Boisen, "Religion and Hard Times," *Social Action* 5 (March 1939): 8-35; Charles S. Braden, "Sectarianism Run Wild," in *Protestantism: A Symposium* (Nashville, 1944); Nils Bloch-Hoell, *The Pentecostal Movement*, pp. 172-76; Nichols, *Pentecostalism*, pp. 70-93; Stolee, *Speaking in Tongues*, pp. 83-113; and Pope, *Millhands and Preachers*, p. 139. See Martin Marty, "Pentecostalism in the Context of American Piety and Practice," in Vinson Synan, ed., *Aspects of Pentecostal-Charismatic Origins*, pp. 193-233. John Mapes Anderson's *Vision of the Disinherited* is probably the most exhaustive study of the social and economic status of the early Pentecostals in the United States.

2. "The Hypnotic Holy Ghost," *The Roanoke Times*, December 6, 1909, quoted in B. E. Underwood, *Fiftieth Anniversary History of the Virginia Conference of the Pentecostal Holiness Church* (Dublin, VA, 1960), p. 3.

their belief on a literal interpretation of Mark 16, these people have traditionally felt it their religious duty to "take up poisonous serpents" in order to prove their spiritual superiority.[3]

The cult of snake-handlers began in 1909 near the town of Grasshopper, Tennessee, when a Church of God preacher, George Hensley, became convinced that the handling of snakes was a duty of all the "redeemed." Organizing the "Church of God With Signs Following," Hensley soon created havoc in Tomlinson's branch of the Church of God as the practice spread throughout its congregations. For a short time Tomlinson defended the practice in the *Church of God Evangel* as another proof that his was the true church of God, especially after his daughter Iris began to handle snakes. The issue remained unclear within the movement for many years, with some ministers practicing it and others denouncing it. Those who refused to handle snakes were called "backslidden" and "powerless" by the cult's practitioners. The practice became the most widespread in parts of Kentucky, Alabama, and Tennessee. The controversy was finally ended when the Cleveland, Tennessee branch of the Church of God formally denounced it as "fanaticism," and forbade its practice within the church. The Pentecostal Holiness Church also denounced snake-handling, although it never seems to have been practiced in that church.[4]

But if snake-handing was properly denounced, both within and without the Pentecostal churches, other Pentecostal "quirks" that incurred public criticism and misunderstanding were practices intrinsic to the movement: speaking in tongues, interpretation of tongues, the "holy dance," the "holy laugh," and the "laying on of hands" for divine healing.

---

3. Mark 16:17-18 declares, "And these signs shall follow them that believe: in my name shall they cast out devils; they shall speak with new tongues; they shall take up serpents; and if they drink any deadly thing, it shall not hurt them; they shall lay hands on the sick, and they shall recover."

4. Archie Robertson, *That Old-Time Religion*, pp. 169-81, describes a typical snake-handling service. See also Conn, *Like a Mighty Army*, p. 191; *The Pentecostal Holiness Advocate*, August 8, 1918, pp. 8-10; *The Church of God Evangel*, July 1, 1916, p. 1; July 1, 1922, p. 2; February 5, 1949, pp. 8-9; *The Christian Evangel*, August 9, 1919, p. 5. More recent literature on serpent handling includes Burton G. Thomas, *Serpent Handling Believers* (Knoxville, 1993), and David L. Kimbrough, *Taking up Serpents: Snake Handlers of Eastern Kentucky* (Chapel Hill, NC, 1995). The role of Tomlinson and his daughter Iris is told in Mickey Crew's *The Church of God: A Social History* (Knoxville, 1993), p. 84.

To an outsider, the sound of someone speaking in tongues often sent chills of fright rather than conviction of sins. Equally sensational was the practice of "interpreting" the message in "tongues" into English. Taylor, the minister who founded Emmanuel College in Franklin Springs, Georgia, at one time claimed to be able to interpret any message in tongues, whether written or spoken. For several years he received mail from all over the country asking for interpretation. Also a common practice was for some Pentecostals to sing songs in other tongues. Although these practices were considered by Pentecostals to be sure signs of "possession" by the Holy Ghost, the unbelieving public saw them as signs of madness and fanaticism.[5]

Women in Ministry

Another Pentecostal practice that varied from the norm of other churches was that of allowing women to preach. The holiness movement had long allowed women to preach, basing its action on the prophecy in Joel 2:28: "Your sons and your daughters shall prophesy. . . ." Most felt that woman had brought sin into the world through Eve, and should therefore help to take it out again. One writer declared that all great spiritual awakenings featured women preachers who would not "cut off their hair, put on bloomers or rompers, but just prophesy and pray as a woman."[6] Another felt that "when we get our eyes on churches, creedism, and slack up, we elbow the women preachers off." As a result of this thinking, the Pentecostals by the middle of the twentieth century had more women preachers than any other branch of Christianity.

By 1995, for instance, the Assemblies of God in the United States claimed no less than 4,861 ordained women out of 31,752 credentialed ministers (15.3%), with 359 of these serving as senior pastors. In the Pentecostal Holiness Church, which ordained women from the beginning, no less than 17% of all licensed and ordained ministers in 1992 were women. Two churches that continued to deny women's right to

5. L. R. Graham, in a personal interview with the author, November 10, 1966; *The Pentecostal Holiness Advocate*, July 5, 1917, p. 15; Stolee, *Speaking in Tongues*, pp. 65-66; *The Pentecostal Evangel*, June 16, 1920, p. 8.

6. S. D. Page, *The Apostolic Evangel*, June 1, 1918, p. 14; A. J. Tomlinson, "Women Preachers," *Church of God Evangel*, Aug. 28–Sept. 18, 1915 (series).

pastor were the Church of God (Cleveland, Tenn.) and the Church of God in Christ, both of which allowed women to serve as evangelists but not as pastors or church officials. With females comprising some 37% of its ministers, the International Church of the Foursquare Gospel (founded by Aimee Semple McPherson), led all churches except the Salvation army in ordained women ministers. Although some recent studies showed declines in the percentages of ordained women in some churches, the Pentecostals far surpassed mainline Protestant churches in the acceptance of women in ministry.[7]

The first woman preacher to gain fame in the United States was Mary Woodworth Etter, whose divine healing campaigns of the 1890's led her through Florida, South Carolina, Indiana, Iowa, and Missouri. In sensational "campaigns" in churches, tents, and auditoriums, Mrs. Etter claimed to have cured "cancer, dumbness, tumors, deafness, . . . etc." Joining the Pentecostal movement after 1906, she continued her spectacular ministry to the sick. One of Mrs. Etter's "trophies" was a man who reported that, "I had the following diseases: cancer, tumor, heart disease, asthma, catarrh of bronchial tubes, rheumatism, and kidney trouble . . . am now perfectly well." Obviously, Mrs. Etter was a champion, and not even Aimee Semple McPherson a generation later could match her claims as a faith healer. A thorough feminist, Mrs. Etter did much to further the cause of her sex long before the climax of the woman's suffrage movement around 1920.[8]

7. *The Pentecostal Holiness Advocate,* July 11, 1918, p. 6. In 1966 the Pentecostal Holiness Church had 473 women ministers out of a total of 2,638; *Yearbook of the Pentecostal Holiness Church, 1966,* vol. 1, no. 6. See the *Assemblies of God Ministers Report, 1995: Credentials, Marital, and Ministry Status by Gender.* See also Vinson Synan, "Women in Ministry: A History of Women's Roles in the Pentecostal and Charismatic Movement," in *Ministries Today,* Jan./Feb. 1993, pp. 44-50. The Spring 1995 issue of *Pneuma: The Journal of the Society for Pentecostal Studies* was devoted to studies on "Women and Pentecostalism." Of interest were the following: "Women in American Pentecostalism" by Edith Blumhofer (pp. 19-21); "Perfect Liberty to Preach the Gospel: Women Ministers in the Church of God" by David Roebuck (pp. 25-32); and "The Contemporary State of Women in Ministry in the Assemblies of God" by Deborah M. Gill (pp. 33-36).

8. Mrs. M. B. Woodworth Etter, *Marvels and Miracles; Signs and Wonders* (Indianapolis, 1922), pp. 213-23, 303-14. Mary Baker Eddy popularized healing through her "Christian Science" movement during this same period. There is no evidence that Mrs. Eddy was ever influenced by Etter or Dowie, or that the Pentecostals' emphasis on healing was connected with her teaching.

Holiness and Healing

The emphasis on healing that Mrs. Etter and Alexander Dowie of Zion, Illinois, popularized became one of the major attractions of the Pentecostal religion. Pentecostal preachers claimed sensational cures everywhere, ranging from "bad colds" to "raising the dead." Parham, the mentor of Seymour, was a faith healer prior to his "pentecostal" discovery in 1901. Carrying the idea of sanctification and perfection to its ultimate conclusion, he taught that "sanctifying power reached every part of our body, destroying the very root and tendency to disease." Just as John Wesley taught the possibility of entire cleansing from sin, Parham taught an "entire cleansing from disease" in the experience of sanctification. In the early years of the movement, Pentecostals felt it was a sin to take medicine or visit a doctor. One Pentecostal preacher, F. M. Britton, once refused medical aid for one of his sons, and reported proudly that he had "died without drugs." Some years later his wife also died after "refusing medicine." Although threatened with jail for refusing medical attention for his family, Britton never wavered in his views. Another striking case was that of Walter Barney, a Church of God preacher from Wytheville, Virginia, who was tried and convicted for "manslaughter" in 1915 for refusing medical care for a daughter who later died. His conviction, however, was later overturned by a pardon from the Governor of Virginia. Rather than an exception, these cases were the rule for many early Pentecostals, and no revival meeting could be termed a "success" without several cases of healing.[9]

Other Pentecostal beliefs that ran counter to the practices of society brought further criticism and contempt. There was hardly any institution, pleasure, business, vice, or social group that escaped the scorn and opposition of Pentecostal preachers. Included in their catalog of "social sins" were: tobacco in all its forms, secret societies, life insurance, doctors, medicine, liquor, dance halls, theaters, movies, Coca Cola, public swimming, professional sports, beauty parlors, jewelry, church bazaars, and makeup. A Pentecostal who indulged in any of these practices was sure to be branded as a "sinner," and the back door was always open to dismiss anyone suspected of "backsliding." Needless to say, this stringent "holi-

9. Parham, *Voice Crying in the Wilderness,* pp. 39-52; Britton, *Pentecostal Truth,* pp. 244-46; Conn, *Evangel Reader,* p. 97; *Church of God Evangel,* Dec. 1, 1910, pp. 1-2; Jan. 23, 1915, p. 2; Nov. 19, 1949, pp. 12-13; Aug. 19, 1950, pp. 8-9.

ness standard" kept the church rolls small and restricted to only the "sanctified few."[10]

In addition, Pentecostals occasionally claimed "miracles" that strained the credibility of even the most sympathetic observers. Everything from preachers floating free of gravity to balls of supernatural fire were claimed as "proofs" of divine approval. Some testified to having "bloody crosses" appear on their foreheads, while others claimed supernatural "Holy Ghost Oil" on the palms of their hands. While most church officials disavowed these extravagant claims, many critics accepted them as further proof of Pentecostal fanaticism.[11]

Violence

Since the Pentecostals so completely rejected society, it is not surprising that society rejected the Pentecostals. This period of rejection lasted roughly from 1906 to 1923, when Aimee Semple McPherson with her "Foursquare Gospel" movement gave Pentecostalism its first "celebrity" and its first taste of acceptance by the public. It was during this time that the sobriquet "holy roller" was attached to the movement. Unlike the Methodists, Quakers, and Shakers, the Pentecostals refused to accept the nickname. In 1915 Tomlinson's Church of God moved to "disclaim and repudiate the title Holy Rollers in reference to the Church of God." Other Pentecostal denominations have consistently made similar disavowals.[12]

At times public opposition to the budding Pentecostal movement

10. *Live Coals,* July 25, 1906, p. 3; *Living Words,* Apr. 1903, pp. 13-16; Milton Tomlinson, *Basic Bible Beliefs* (Cleveland, TN, 1961), pp. 97-128; *Discipline of the Pentecostal Holiness Church, 1961,* pp. 65-68; Juillerat, *Book of Minutes,* pp. 296-300; C. F. Wimberly, *Are You a Christian?* (Louisville, 1917), pp. 5-32; *The Pentecostal Evangel,* Dec. 23, 1922, p. 5.

11. Gibson, *Church of God, Mountain Assembly,* p. 6, reports that a preacher "rose to the ceiling of the church when a hostile mob entered." On at least two occasions, Church of God ministers reported "balls of fire" over churches and tents that mystified the public. See *The Church of God Evangel,* Nov. 15, 1910, pp. 4-5; Aug. 26, 1916, p. 1.

12. Juillerat, *Book of Minutes,* p. 201; Nichols, *Pentecostalism,* pp. 2, 77; see Allene M. Sumner, "The Holy Rollers on Shin Bone Ridge," *The Nation* 121 (July 29, 1925): 138.

took the form of obstructionism and even physical violence. Nowhere was this violence more extreme and damaging than in the South. One early Pentecostal Holiness preacher reported the following incidents on his southern preaching tours:

> [He] had three tents burned by angry people. Once a group of excited people sought to murder him but were unable to locate his hiding place. At another time he was run out of a certain city; at another he was beaten by an angry man. At another time the police had to give him protection.[13]

Other preachers reported instances of being beaten, gagged, shot with shotguns, thrown in jail, or threatened with death and mutilation. Others reported having churches burned and tents toppled. One Church of God preacher in Mississippi claimed that in 1917 two men "covered him with revolvers, gagged him and dragged him . . . through the woods where they beat him black and blue with a buggy trace, struck him a blow over the eye with a revolver, and broke two of his ribs by kicking him in the side. . . . After they had beaten him, they led him to the railroad and with severe threats compelled him to run."[14] J. W. Buckalew, another Church of God preacher, earned the nickname "Old Rough and Ready" because of his willingness to literally fight for his religion. Because of his many altercations with "anti-holiness" toughs, Buckalew earned a reputation among Pentecostals that rivaled that of Peter Cartwright among the early Methodists.[15]

There are indications that the unpopularity of Pentecostalism seriously hampered its growth in its early years. For every community that accepted a Pentecostal church, there was another that would not. In the western part of Virginia, eight Pentecostal Holiness churches were organized in 1913, all of which died because of opposition and lack of interest. In the course of fifty years only a hundred new churches sur-

---

13. W. H. Turner, "The 'Tongues Movement': A Brief History" (unpublished Master's thesis, The University of Georgia, 1948), p. 45.

14. Conn, *Evangel Reader*, p. 158.

15. For references to violence see Conn, *Evangel Reader*, pp. 144-75; J. W. Buckalew, *Incidents in the Life of J. W. Buckalew* (Cleveland, TN, ca. 1920); Watson Sorrow, *Some of My Experiences* (Franklin Springs, GA, 1954), pp. 60-72; Conn, *Like a Mighty Army*, pp. 29-37, 106-12; Tomlinson, "Journal of Happenings," pp. 1-30; Nichols, *Pentecostalism*, pp. 70-80; and Bailey, *Pioneer Marvels*, pp. 6-15.

vived while sixty others failed.[16] Yet the opposition and persecution served as a consolidating force within the movement, and brought sympathy from a part of the public that abhorred such violence. Although most violent opposition in America had ceased by 1925, instances continued throughout the twentieth century in other parts of the world. This led David Barrett to state in 1988 that "[Pentecostal] members are more harassed, persecuted, suffering, and martyred than perhaps any other Christian tradition in recent history."[17]

Schisms and Realignments

While the Pentecostals and American society were engaged in rejecting each other, the years 1914 to 1925 might accurately be called the period of schism and realignment. The "finished work" and "Jesus Only" schisms of 1914 to 1919 were mainly over doctrinal and theological issues, while the schisms of the 1920's were caused primarily by questions of ecclesiology and by personality clashes. After 1925 the movement had attained the general outlines it would follow to the present time.

A recurring problem for the new Pentecostal bodies was the extent that denominational authority would be allowed in the new organizations. From the time of Charles Parham, there was a fear that too much organization might somehow quench the Spirit. This fear led to the organization of a new body in Chicago in 1919 called "The Pentecostal Assemblies of the U.S.A.," formed in protest against the doctrinal statement adopted by the Assemblies of God in the wake of the oneness controversy. The organizer of the new group was a friend of William H. Durham named John C. Sinclair, who after Durham was the first pastor in Chicago to receive the tongues experience. Although Sinclair was chosen to be an Executive Presbyter at the organization of the Assemblies of God in 1914, he left in church in 1916 to protest the new statement of faith. Sinclair and a group of like-minded ministers later met in Chicago in December, 1919, hoping to create a church where there

16. Underwood, *Fiftieth Anniversary History of the Virginia Conference*, p. 4.

17. David Barrett, "The Twentieth-Century Pentecostal/Charismatic Renewal in the Holy Spirit, with Its Goal of World Evangelization," *International Bulletin of Missionary Research*, July 1988, p. 1.

would be more freedom from ecclesiastical control. In 1921 the church changed its name to "The Pentecostal Church of God."[18]

The Congregational Holiness Church

One of the first schisms caused by personality clashes occurred in the Georgia Conference of the Pentecostal Holiness Church in 1920, resulting in the organization of the "Congregational Holiness Church." The controversy producing this schism began over the doctrine of divine healing. Two ministers, Watson Sorrow and Hugh Bowling, held a view on healing that varied from the generally accepted ideas of the church at that time. The faction led by Sorrow and Bowling held that it was not sinful to use remedies and medicines to aid in the healing of sickness. Another faction led by F. M. Britton and G. F. Taylor held that "the provision in the Atonement for the healing of the body was all-sufficient, and that it was unnecessary to supplement any human means to assist God in effecting a cure." For several months a debate on the issue raged throughout the church and in the pages of *The Advocate.*[19]

The controversy, which began as a doctrinal dispute, also became in time a power struggle between personalities. In 1920, events came to a head in a trial that resulted in the expulsion of Sorrow and Bowling from the church. What the leader of the Pentecostal Holiness Church, J. H. King, described as a "terrible blow" to the denomination, came on January 29, 1921, when the Congregational Holiness Church was organized in High Shoals, Georgia. The adoption of the term "Congregational" displayed the opposition of the new group to the episcopal form of government that was practiced in the mother church. The new Congregational Holiness Church remained a small group confined to the states of Georgia, Alabama, Florida, North Carolina, and

---

18. A good account of the background and founding of the Pentecostal Church of God is found in Larry Martin's *In the Beginning: Readings on the Origins of the Twentieth Century Pentecostal Revival and the Birth of the Pentecostal Church of God* (Duncan, OK, 1994). See also Frank Lindblade's *The Spirit Which Is from God* (Duncan, OK, 1995), a reprint of Lindblade's 1928 book of the same title.

19. Campbell, *The Pentecostal Holiness Church,* p. 277; B. L. Cox, *History and Doctrine of the Congregational Holiness Church* (Greenwood, SC, 1959), p. 7; Sorrow, *Some of My Experiences,* p. 65. See also Synan, *Old-Time Power,* pp. 165-71.

South Carolina. In 1993, it claimed over 8,000 members in 190 churches.[20]

The Tomlinson Church of God

Similar schisms split the Church of God at Cleveland, Tennessee, in 1919 and 1923, resulting in the creation of two new denominations carrying variations of the name "Church of God." The first of these resulted from the strict tithing system that the church had adopted in its General Assembly in 1917. Under this plan, 10 percent of all the income of the local churches would be sent to the headquarters of the denomination to help equalize the salaries of the ministry.[21]

A small group of ministers led by J. L. Scott protested against this policy, feeling that paying tithes should be based on free will rather than coercion, and together they formed the "Original Church of God" with headquarters in Chattanooga, Tennessee. This group too remained small, having in 1965 only 6,000 members in 35 churches, most of them in Tennessee.[22]

A more fundamental and far-reaching cleavage occurred in the Church of God in 1923 as a result of a power struggle between the church's leader and dominant figure, A. J. Tomlinson, and other leaders who constituted the "Supreme Council" of the church. Tomlinson, who had served as General Overseer of the denomination for over a decade, had by 1920 gained almost complete control of the entire operation of the church. Overworked and fatigued by his heavy responsibilities, he began to see himself as holding theocratic authority in the church. This authority was threatened, however, when the church in 1921 adopted a new constitution that curtailed his power.[23]

---

20. King and King, *Yet Speaketh*, p. 316; Cox, *Congregational Holiness Church*, pp. 7-11; Sorrow, *Some of My Experiences*, pp. 65-67; Kenneth B. Bedell, ed., *Yearbook of American Churches, 1995*, p. 266. *The Pentecostal Holiness Advocate* in its 1920-21 issues chronicles the controversy in detail with each side given ample space to air its views. See also B. L. Cox, *My Life's Story* (Greenwood, SC, 1959), pp. 40-42.

21. Juillerat, *Book of Minutes*, pp. 293-96; *Church of God Evangel*, May 4, 1918, p. 1.

22. Landis, *Yearbook of American Churches, 1965*, pp. 34-35; Nichols, *Pentecostalism*, p. 137; Tomlinson, *Diary of A. J. Tomlinson*, vol. 1, pp. 262-63.

23. Simmons, *History of the Church of God*, p. 38; Duggar, *A. J. Tomlinson*, pp. 188-94; *Minutes of the Sixteenth Annual Assembly, 1921*, p. 27.

Dissatisfied with the constitution, Tomlinson called for its abrogation in the Assembly of 1922, but the church was in no mood to accept his suggestions, largely because of charges made during the previous months concerning misappropriation of funds. With Tomlinson "under a cloud" of suspicion, the Assembly voted to create more offices to further decrease his authority. In addition, a commission was appointed to investigate his financial administration of church funds. These restraints were more than the formerly all-powerful Overseer could take, so he tendered his resignation, but on the insistence of friends consented to remain in office another year.[24]

During the following year the "committee on better government" investigated the church's finances and charged Tomlinson with misappropriating some fourteen thousand dollars. In impeachment proceedings that Tomlinson described as "unjust and illegal," the "Council of Elders" in July 1923 relieved the General Overseer of his office for "mishandling church funds." With his connection to the church now completely severed, Tomlinson "walked out on a street corner in Cleveland, Tennessee, under the starry sky with the Church of God banner and started building again." In what he described as "a revolution to save the Church of God from wreck and ruin," he began a new movement that eventually took the name of "The Tomlinson Church of God." In the year that followed, lawsuits were filed in the Chancery Court of Bradley County, Tennessee, to decide which group could claim funds arriving in Cleveland addressed to the "Church of God" headquarters. In a decision later sustained by the Tennessee Supreme Court, the group that had impeached Tomlinson gained rights to the name "Church of God." The loser in the case later adopted the name "Tomlinson Church of God."[25]

All went well with the "Tomlinson Church of God" until the death of its founder in 1943, when a power struggle developed between his two sons, Milton and Homer, for control of the church. In a bewildering

24. Tomlinson, *Answering the Call of God,* p. 38; Conn, *Like a Mighty Army,* p. 174; *The Church of God Evangel,* Dec. 9, 1922, p. 1; *Minutes of the Seventeenth Annual Assembly, 1922,* pp. 17-58.

25. Tomlinson, *Answering the Call of God,* p. 23; Tomlinson, "A Journal of Happenings," entry for Sept. 10, 1923; Conn, *Like a Mighty Army,* pp. 175-90; Kendrick, *The Promise Fulfilled,* pp. 192-93. Tomlinson's side of the controversy is given by his son Homer in the *Diary of A. J. Tomlinson* (New York, 1953), vol. 2, pp. 98-112. See also *The Church of God Evangel,* July 14, 1923, pp. 1-4.

set of moves and countermoves, the younger brother Milton, a printer in the church's "White Wing Messenger" press, was elected as "General Overseer." After Milton's accession to power, Homer was inexplicably expelled from the church. Following this development, Homer went to New York City where he founded a third denomination, "The Church of God, World Headquarters." In March 1953, the former "Tomlinson" Church of God with Milton as Bishop and General Overseer changed its name to "The Church of God of Prophecy," which, it is claimed, designates it as the one true "Church of God."[26]

In recent years, Milton's "prophecy" church has distinguished itself as the developer and custodian of the "Fields of the Woods" shrine in Cherokee County, North Carolina, where over two million dollars have been spent to memorialize the spot where A. J. Tomlinson "prevailed in prayer" in 1903 and thereby founded "the Church of God" of prophecy. Here a vast array of monuments mark the spot on Burger Mountain where all nations of the world, it is claimed, will one day recognize the authority of the Church of God and be brought within the fold. Called the "Biblical Wonder of the Twentieth Century," this shrine is supported by the "Church of God of Prophecy Marker Association."[27] Indicative of the church's progress is the fact that a junior college known as "Tomlinson College" was authorized in 1964 to be located in Cleveland, Tennessee.[28]

The "World Headquarters" Church of God under Homer Tomlinson became known chiefly because of the antics of its leader, who ran for President of the United States several times as the candidate of his own "Theocratic Party." In addition to his other duties, Homer Tomlinson crowned himself "king" of all fifty states and every sovereign nation of the world, including Soviet Russia. By 1965 "Bishop Homer" had also proclaimed himself "King of the World," "the son of God" and "heir to the throne of David." In 1966 he set up his "world headquarters" in Jerusalem and in his 74th year made preparations to "rule the world in righteousness" from his room in that city's Imperial Hotel. His dream

---

26. Homer Tomlinson's version of these events is given in Clark, *Small Sects in America*, pp. 102-4; see also Nichols, *Pentecostalism*, pp. 139-43; *Minutes, 60th Annual Assembly of the Church of God of Prophecy, 1965*, pp. 30, 31; and *Cyclopedic Index of Assembly Minutes, 1906-1949* (Cleveland, TN, 1950), pp. 150-59, 370-75.

27. See *Biblical Wonder of the Twentieth Century* (Cleveland, TN, 1964), pp. 3-37.

28. *Minutes of the 60th Annual Assembly, 1965*, pp. 77-78, 127-31.

came to a sudden end when the self-proclaimed Bishop and King died, in 1969.[29]

Aimee Semple McPherson

In the same year the elder Tomlinson was expelled from the Church of God in Cleveland, Tennessee, a young woman named Aimee Semple McPherson founded yet another Pentecostal body in Los Angeles, known as the "International Church of the Foursquare Gospel." Born on a farm in Ontario, Canada, in 1890, Aimee Kennedy was raised by strict Methodist and Salvation Army parents. As a teenager, Aimee met Robert Semple, a Pentecostal preacher, and was converted to Pentecostalism. Attracted to Semple, she married the young preacher and with him entered the evangelistic ministry. On a missionary trip to China, Semple died and was buried in Hong Kong, leaving Aimee and their young daughter to return to the United States alone.[30]

In 1917, after her marriage to Harold McPherson, Aimee began the evangelistic work that was to make her one of the most celebrated and controversial evangelists of twentieth-century America. Since her early training for the ministry was with Pastor William Durham in Chicago, Mrs. McPherson adopted the "finished work" view of sanctification championed by Durham. For several years she was listed as a minister of the Assemblies of God, but her burgeoning ministry, which caught the public fancy around 1920, made it inevitable that she would become the founder of a separate denomination.[31]

29. An article in Tomlinson's paper *The Church of God,* Oct. 15, 1966, pp. 1-2, proclaimed that Tomlinson had set up the "Throne of God" in Jerusalem whence he had forgiven "one and all" of all their sins.

30. Aimee Semple McPherson, *The Story of My Life* (Los Angeles, 1951), pp. 15-79. Other autobiographical works detailing her life and ministry are *This Is That: Personal Experiences, Sermons and Writings of Aimee Semple McPherson* (Los Angeles, 1923); *In the Service of the King* (New York, 1927); and *The Foursquare Gospel* (Los Angeles, 1946). A critical biography is Lately Thomas's *The Vanishing Evangelist* (New York, 1959). The best sympathetic account is Nancy Barr Mavity, *Sister Aimee* (New York, 1931).

31. Kendrick, *The Promise Fulfilled,* p. 154; *The Pentecostal Evangel,* Nov. 15, 1919, pp. 6-10; May 29, 1920, pp. 8-9; June 10, 1922, p. 9. Several excellent biographies of McPherson have appeared in recent years. These include Daniel Epstein's popularly written *Sister Aimee: The Life of Aimee Semple McPherson* (New York, 1993), and Edith

In 1921, while preaching about the vision in Ezekiel 1:1-28 concerning the beast with the four faces — those of a man, a lion, an ox, and an eagle — Mrs. McPherson conceived the idea of a "Foursquare Gospel." The four corners represented salvation, the Holy Ghost baptism attested by tongues, divine healing, and the second coming of Christ. The center for her activities became the vast "Angelus Temple," built in Los Angeles in 1923 at a cost of one and a half million dollars. With a seating capacity of over 5,000 persons, she kept the "Temple" full for every service. Her sermons were highly dramatic. In one service it was reported that "Sister, in football togs, carried the ball of the Foursquare Gospel for a touchdown, Jesus ran interference." On another occasion the congregation watched in amazement as the evangelist arrived dressed in policemen's clothes, riding a motorcycle:

> She drove recklessly to the front of the auditorium, slammed on the brakes, blew a screech on a police whistle, raised a white gloved hand to the congregation, and shouted: "Stop, you're going to hell!"

With such histrionics, Mrs. McPherson was soon a familiar figure to newspaper readers from coast to coast.[32]

Even more dramatic and controversial was her famous "kidnapping incident" in 1926. In May of that year, the famous leader of "Foursquaredom" disappeared for several weeks after being last seen on a beach in Southern California. After her return she claimed she had been kidnapped and held for ransom in northern Mexico. Her friends staunchly defended her when critics tried to prove that she had in reality gone to a "love nest" with Kenneth G. Ormiston, a radio announcer from her station in Los Angeles. After much controversy in the press and a court trial that attempted unsuccessfully to prove the kidnapping story a hoax, "Sister" Aimee returned to the "Temple" to continue her ministry. In spite of other troubles both public and domestic, on December 28, 1927 Mrs. McPherson incorporated the "International Church of the Foursquare Gospel," with herself as lifetime president.[33]

Blumhofer's more scholarly *Aimee Semple McPherson: Everybody's Sister* (Grand Rapids, MI, 1993).

  32. Bach, *They Have Found a Faith,* pp. 57-87; McPherson, *In the Service of the King,* pp. 239-48; McPherson, *The Foursquare Gospel,* p. 22; *The Pentecostal Evangel,* June 5, 1926, pp. 1-3.

  33. Thomas, *Vanishing Evangelist,* pp. 1-319, traces the story of the kidnapping

Although Mrs. McPherson gained a nationwide following and built a major denomination in her own lifetime, many Pentecostal and non-Pentecostal spokesmen rejected her ministrations. Alma White, the most critical anti-Pentecostal writer of the century, described Mrs. McPherson as a "necromancer, familiar with the black arts," who spoke with the "mutterings of a witch." Others opposed her on more theological grounds. When invited to speak in a Pentecostal Holiness Church in Roanoke, Virginia, in 1926, Mrs. McPherson was refused permission to preach by J. H. King, General Superintendent of the denomination, because of her "finished work" theory of sanctification. Many other ministers and church officials became hostile to her because of the kidnapping incident.[34]

The Open Bible Standard Church

One permanent outcome of the adverse publicity surrounding the alleged kidnapping was the creation of yet another Pentecostal denomination. One of Mrs. McPherson's most successful campaigns was conducted in Des Moines, Iowa, in 1927 and 1928. In a short time three large congregations were formed under the banner of the Foursquare Church. The pastor sent to minister in one of the largest was a Californian with a powerful personality and great organizational ability, Rev. J. R. Richey. Partly due to questions concerning Mrs. McPherson's strict ecclesiastical polity, but mainly because of the kidnapping incident, Richey decided to lead a break with the church in 1932. In the end, the Iowa and Minnesota District of the Foursquare Church voted to separate and form a new group under the name "Open Bible Evangelistic Association," with Richey as leader.[35]

Soon afterwards, the Open Bible group made contact with a similar group in Portland, Oregon known as the "Bible Standard Church," which

---

incident and the subsequent trial. Mrs. McPherson defends herself in *The Story of My Life*, pp. 208-21. A contemporary account is given in Mavity, *Sister Aimee*, pp. 77-320.

34. White, *Tongues and Demons*, pp. 112-15; McPherson, *Story of My Life*, pp. 122-42. The story of Mrs. McPherson's funeral was given wide coverage in *Life* magazine (October 20, 1944, pp. 85-89).

35. Kendrick, *The Promise Fulfilled*, pp. 164-65; Nichols, *Pentecostalism*, pp. 144-45.

had split off from Florence Crawford's Apostolic Faith group in 1919. Led by Fred Hornshuh and A. J. Hegan, this group had objected to the exclusiveness of Mrs. Crawford's group as well as its stern views on divorce and remarriage. In 1935 these two groups merged to form a new Pentecostal denomination which later adopted the name "Open Bible Standard Churches, Incorporated" with headquarters in Des Moines. A striking fact of the merger was that both branches were splinters of denominations founded and controlled by female preachers.[36]

The advent of Aimee Semple McPherson marked a turning point in the history of the Pentecostal movement in the United States. The first Pentecostal well-known to the public at large, McPherson did much to gain tolerance and respect for a religion generally associated with the lowest social strata. Indeed, "Sister Aimee" proved that Pentecostals were capable of producing preachers with as strong a public appeal as the more traditional evangelists. In fact, the twentieth century has seen Pentecostal preachers whose appeal paralleled that of earlier evangelists such as Charles G. Finney and Dwight L. Moody. Just as Billy Sunday shared headlines with Mrs. McPherson during the twenties and thirties, Billy Graham shared top billing with Oral Roberts in the fifties and sixties.

Pentecostals and Social Class

By 1930 there were many indications of trends the Pentecostal movement would follow in the future. It was clear by that time that Pentecostalism would appeal primarily to the lower classes; but as the lower classes became upwardly mobile, the Pentecostals would rise with them. The social transformation of Pentecostal churches into middle-class institutions would come not by converting the middle class, but by entering it *en masse* from below. The major characteristics of Pentecostal worship — emotional fervor, informality, lay clergy, millenarianism, and strict ethical standards — exercised a strong appeal to the working classes. The experience of the Pentecostals closely fulfilled the dictum of Ernst Troeltsch that "the really creative, church-forming religious movements are the work of the lower strata." Some writers have charged that the rise of sects is only a religious guise for a more deep-seated

36. Kendrick, *The Promise Fulfilled,* pp. 166-71.

protest against prevailing social and economic conditions. Others feel that this development is an overt "protest against the failure of religious institutions to come to grips with the needs of marginal groups, existing on the fringes of cultural and social organization." To some extent, all of these generalizations are true of the Pentecostals, and they help explain its great attraction for the lower classes.[37]

There are some weaknesses, however, in explaining the rise of Pentecostalism as primarily an economic and social protest movement. It has been shown that the greatest growth of the Pentecostals (1910-50) occurred when the laboring and farming classes were rapidly declining as a percentage of the total population. Obviously, Pentecostal doctrines and modes of worship were appealing to many who could not be classed as "economically deprived." Although some observers have emphasized psychological and cultural factors as being more important than economic and doctrinal ones, it would appear that to large numbers of people, Pentecostalism represented a continuation of the "old-time religion" as formerly practiced by the more traditional Protestant churches.[38] From their beginnings, Pentecostals have occupied the lowest position on the social scale. In spite of a tremendous growth in wealth, fine church buildings, better educated ministers, and nationally known figures such as Mrs. McPherson and Oral Roberts, Pentecostals remained in the social cellar through the middle of the century. In Gastonia, North Carolina, in 1939, it was reported that in the cotton mills:

> Presbyterian workers feel superior to those belonging to the Methodist and Baptist churches, while members of the latter two denominations regard themselves as definitely higher in the social scale than Wesleyan Methodists. All, in turn, despise the Church of God and deprecate the social status of its members.[39]

37. Richard H. Niebuhr, *The Social Sources of Denominationalism*, pp. 29-30; Liston Pope, *Millhands and Preachers*, p. 140; N. J. Demerath III, *Social Class in American Protestantism* (Chicago, 1965), pp. 40-42.

38. W. S. Salisbury, *Religion in American Culture: A Sociological Interpretation* (Homewood, IL, 1964), p. 455; Demerath, *Social Class in American Protestantism*, p. 42; John B. Holt, "Holiness Religion: Cultural Shock and Social Reorganization," *American Sociological Review* 5 (1940): 740-47; David O. Moberg, *The Church as a Social Institution* (Englewood Cliffs, NJ, 1962), p. 228.

39. Pope, *Millhands and Preachers*, p. 138.

Other studies have indicated that this attitude has continued into the sixties, with the Episcopal Church having the highest social status and the Pentecostal groups the lowest. A 1964 survey of American social attitudes indicated that among traditional Protestants, the churches mentioned as being "least like one's own" were the Pentecostal types and the Catholic Church.[40] Another survey published in the same year revealed that only the Jehovah's Witnesses were ranked lower than the Pentecostal and holiness churches.[41]

After World War II, the Pentecostals began to rise in the social and economic scale along with the rest of American society, partaking of the general postwar prosperity. In the words of John Mapes Anderson, "the Pentecostal movement fits the classic pattern of sects that rise primarily among the socially deprived and later develop "churchly" characteristics as the deprivation of its membership ameliorated."[42]

Pentecostal Growth

Despite their lowly social position and lack of economic power, the Pentecostals have experienced fantastic growth during the twentieth century. Liston Pope, in his survey of Gaston County, North Carolina, found that between 1910 and 1939 there were thirty-six Pentecostal-type churches, compared to eighteen for all other denominations combined, three of which were closed. This example is typical of the mushrooming growth of Pentecostal congregations throughout the nation. Symbolizing things to come, by 1965 the Church of God (Cleveland, Tennessee) with three hundred churches had passed the Presbyterian Church as the third largest denomination in Georgia in the number of congregations. In many states the combined number of Pentecostal churches easily ranked them closely behind the Baptist and Methodist Churches.[43]

40. W. Widick Schroeder and Victor Obenhaus, *Religion in American Culture* (London, 1964), pp. 71-74.

41. Salisbury, *Religion in American Culture*, p. 454. For interesting attitudes toward Pentecostals in the South see William W. Wood, *Culture and Personality Aspects of the Pentecostal Holiness Religion* (The Hague, 1965), pp. 11-67.

42. Anderson, *Vision of the Disinherited*, pp. 223-40.

43. Pope, *Millhands and Preachers*, p. 97; Charles S. Sydnor, Jr., "The Pentecostals," *Presbyterian Survey*, May 1964, p. 31. Sydnor states that the Pentecostals number almost a million in the South, or "approximately the size of our Presbyterian Church, U.S."

The statistics indicate that the Pentecostal churches have experienced phenomenal growth since the twenties. The following table, although not complete, is representative of this growth in the United States during the past ninety years:

	Churches 1926	Members 1926	Churches 1970	Members 1970	Churches 1995	Members 1995
Assemblies of God	671	47,950	8,570	626,660	11,762	2,271,718
Church of God in Christ	733	30,263	4,500	425,000	18,300	6,750,875
Church of God (Cleveland, Tenn.)	644	23,247	3,834	243,532	5,899	700,517
Pentecostal Assemblies of the World	126	7,850	550	45,000	1005	500,000
Pentecostal Holiness Church	252	8,096	1,355	66,790	1645	150,133[44]

One of the major reasons for this growth was the fact that the Pentecostals followed the migration of population to the cities. As shown earlier, the Pentecostal movement began as a city phenomenon, with seminal events in Los Angeles, Chicago, Topeka, St. Louis, Dunn, North Carolina, Portland, and Indianapolis. Aimee Semple McPherson's settling in Los Angeles foreshadowed dozens of "Temples" and "revival centers" that came to dot the nation's largest cities. An outstanding city church in the South was the famous "Garr Auditorium," built in 1931 in Charlotte, North Carolina. Beginning as a tent revival in 1930, Garr's group a year later was able to rebuild the old Charlotte city auditorium into a vast church edifice seating over 2,000. By the time of Garr's death in 1944, he had inaugurated a school of theology, a periodical known as *The Morning Thought*, and an ambitious missionary enterprise in Brazil.[45]

Another example of a "storefront" church that succeeded was Ralph Byrd's "Faith Memorial" Assembly of God Congregation in Atlanta. Beginning in 1935 as an itinerant evangelist in a tent meeting, within ten years Byrd had built a congregation of over 1,000. Moving from the tent, he constructed a wooden tabernacle which was soon too small. He eventually bought a large church building on fashionable

44. These figures were compiled from the U.S. Bureau of the Census, *Religious Bodies: 1926* (Washington, DC, 1929), vol. 1, pp. 60-1091; and *Yearbook of American Churches* (New York for 1990 and 1995).

45. *Twentieth Anniversary of the Garr Auditorium* (Charlotte, NC, 1950), pp. 3-16.

Ponce de Leon Avenue, where he continued to serve a large urban congregation.[46]

The Pentecostals were particularly active in serving the millions of poorer migrants to the larger cities. By the 1960's, northern urban ghettos were experiencing a startling growth of Pentecostal storefront churches. Southern blacks who went north generally carried their religion with them, reestablishing worship centers in any space available, including store buildings and church edifices formerly owned by white congregations who had themselves migrated to the suburbs. Another interesting development was the rise of a large number of Spanish-speaking Pentecostal churches among the Puerto Rican population in New York City. With only 25 of these churches in 1937, New York City had no fewer than 250 by 1967, a thousand percent increase.[47]

Pentecostals and Fundamentalists

Another key to the growth of Pentecostalism was its relative youth and resultant flexibility on some of the issues that convulsed the rest of American Christianity during the twentieth century. While the rest of Protestantism wrestled with the great fundamentalist controversy over Darwin's evolutionary theory during the twenties, the Pentecostals observed the fray from the outside. Although "fundamentalist to a man," the Pentecostals did not play an active part in the controversy. The leading fundamentalist spokesmen were such Baptists, Presbyterians, and Methodists as William Jennings Bryan, Gerald Winrod, and Bob Jones. Since most of these fundamentalist leaders were strict Calvinists, the Pentecostals with their equally strict Arminian theology were unwilling to ally themselves too closely with the movement. Because they were never an integral part of the fundamentalist camp, the Pentecostals emerged without the deep anti-intellectual bias that distinguished much of conservative Protestantism after 1925.[48]

46. Ralph M. Riggs, "Those Store-Front Churches," *United Evangelical Action* (Cincinnati) 4 (Aug. 1, 1945): 4-5. See also William G. McLoughlin, *Modern Revivalism* (New York, 1959), pp. 468-69.

47. Robert D. Cross, ed., *The Church and the City, 1865-1910* (New York, 1967), pp. 262-66; Nichols, *Pentecostalism*, pp. 133-36.

48. *The Pentecostal Evangel*, October 24, 1925, p. 5; Nov. 7, 1925, pp. 4-5. Although much has been made of the "holy roller" aspects of fundamentalism, the

The relationship between the Pentecostals and the fundamentalists has been of some interest since both movements rose to prominence during the same period. A popular misconception has persisted that the Pentecostals were the "ultrafundamentalists" of American religious life.[49] Although most Pentecostals thought of themselves as fundamentalists, the feeling was not reciprocated by the leaders of organized fundamentalism. By the time the fundamentalist movement hit its crest in the 1920's, it had already effectively barred the door to fellowship with the Pentecostals. In a 1928 convention of the "World's Christian Fundamentals Association," a group organized in 1919 to be the major voice of the movement, the Pentecostals were soundly condemned. The resolution that disfellowshipped the entire movement read:

> Whereas, the present wave of modern pentecostalism, often referred to as the "tongues movement," and the present wave of fanatical and unscriptural healing which is sweeping over the country today, has become a menace in many churches and a real injury to sane testimony of Fundamental Christians,
>
> Be it resolved, that this convention go on record as unreservedly opposed to Modern Pentecostalism, including the speaking in unknown tongues, and the fanatical healing known as general healing in the atonement, and the perpetuation of the miraculous sign-healing of Jesus and His apostles, wherein they claim the only reason the church cannot perform these miracles is because of unbelief.[50]

There were several reasons for this rejection by the fundamentalists. One was the probable failure to discriminate between the moderate, mainline Pentecostals and those that bordered on the cultic. There were, of course, the snake-handlers and the cults of Father Divine and Daddy Grace, which had been repudiated by most Pentecostals them-

---

evidence suggests that most Pentecostals were either unaware of or uninterested in the controversy. There is certainly no literature extant to show a deep Pentecostal involvement, and the fundamentalists generally disparaged Pentecostals along with Darwinists and Catholics. See Robertson, *Old-Time Religion*, pp. 88-96; L. L. Pickett, *God or the Guessers, Some Scriptures on Present Day Infidelity* (Louisville, 1926), pp. 7-83, with its "holiness" view of evolution. See also Smith's *Called Unto Holiness*, pp. 315-21. Smith suggests that fundamentalism's Calvinist underpinnings repelled Pentecostal and holiness thinkers, who were by and large Arminian.

49. Mead, *Handbook of Denominations*, p. 167.
50. *The Pentecostal Evangel*, Aug. 18, 1928, p. 7.

selves. The bizarre fringe groups had no doubt frightened them. The fundamentalists had also been swayed by a relatively new biblical hermeneutic known as "Scofieldian dispensationalism," which viewed the Pentecostalist practices of glossolalia and divine healing as signs heralding the "dispensation of Grace," destined to cease with the apostles of the New Testament. This "cessationist" theology was most fully developed by Benjamin Warfield. In his 1918 volume, *Counterfeit Miracles,* Warfield asserted that not a single miracle had occurred since the death of the last apostle.[51] The Pentecostals were therefore in grave error and beyond the pale of orthodox fundamentalism.[52]

As a result of this rejection, Pentecostals remained isolated from the rest of American Christianity as well as from each other until after World War II. It was, strangely enough, another rejection by fundamentalists that brought the Pentecostals into the mainstream of evangelical Protestantism and into closer fellowship with themselves. During World War II, there was a move to unite evangelical Christians into a nationwide fellowship outside the aegis of the more liberal National Council of Churches. First in the field was the American Council of Christian Churches headed by Carl McIntire, which began in 1941. This group, however, represented the old militant, belligerent spirit of rancor and disruption that had characterized the fundamentalist versus modernist wars of the 1920's and 1930's. Furthermore, the ACCC continued the fundamentalist rejection of the Pentecostals.[53]

Pentecostals and Evangelicals

In order to create an evangelical alliance without the unfortunate overtones of the now discredited fundamentalists, a new organization called the National Association of Evangelicals was formed in 1943. Several attempts were soon made to merge the ACCC with the younger NAE, but negotiations always broke down because of the fact that several

51. Benjamin Warfield, *Counterfeit Miracles* (Carlisle, PA, 1918), p. 21.

52. William W. Menzies, "The Assemblies of God, 1941-1967: The Consolidation of a Revival Movement" (unpublished Ph.D. dissertation, University of Iowa, 1968), pp. 51-54.

53. Menzies, *Anointed to Serve,* pp. 183-214; Conn, *Like a Mighty Army,* p. 258.

Pentecostal bodies had been founding members of the NAE. In his *Christian Beacon,* McIntire bitterly assailed the Pentecostals and the NAE by saying:

> "Tongues" is one of the great signs of the apostasy. As true Protestant denominations turn from the faith and it gets darker, the Devil comes more into the open, and people who are not fed in the old line denominations go out to the "tongues" movement, for they feel that they have some life.
>
> The dominance of the "tongues" groups in the NAE "denominations" and their compromise in regard to the Federal Council will not, we believe, commend this organization to those who desire to see a standard lifted in behalf of the historic Christian faith. . . .[54]

Following this volley, the NAE was forced to choose between the Pentecostal groups already within the fellowship and the ACCC of Carl McIntire. In the end, they chose the Pentecostals, the split between the NAE and the ACCC continuing to this day. For the Pentecostals, these moves meant that the future course of the movement would be a moderate position between the left-leaning National Council of Churches and the right-leaning American Council of Christian Churches. Without strong ideological fetters from either the right or left, the Pentecostals were thus in a fortunate position for greater theological and intellectual acceptance in the years to come.[55]

A historic by-product of the Pentecostal participation in the NAE was the formation of a nationwide fellowship between the larger Pentecostal denominations in the late 1940's. From the beginning of the movement in 1906 until World War II, the Pentecostals had remained isolated from each other and somewhat aloof, particularly because of doctrinal differences such as the problem of sanctification. The meetings of the NAE provided the first opportunities for the various Pentecostal leaders to meet together. It was in the lobbies between sessions of the NAE meetings that the idea of a national organization of Pentecostals was born. Many old antagonisms were forgotten, and a feeling of kinship began to replace the older suspicions. Another stimulus toward unity was the suggestion made in 1947 by the first World Pentecostal Fellow-

---

54. Carl McIntire, in the *Christian Beacon,* Apr. 27, 1944, p. 8.
55. Menzies, *Anointed to Serve,* p. 183; *The Church of God Evangel,* May 21, 1949, pp. 12-15; *The Pentecostal Evangel,* June 19, 1943, p. 8.

ship, meeting in Zurich, Switzerland, that North American Pentecostals form a closer fellowship. Among Pentecostals in the mid-twentieth century, the climate of togetherness seemed truly global.[56]

The Pentecostal Fellowship of North America

The first step toward uniting American Pentecostals came at the close of the May 1948 meeting of the NAE in Chicago. Here "exploratory" plans were laid for the inauguration of a fellowship that would encompass all of North America. A second exploratory conference was held in Chicago on August 3 and 4, 1948, which included representatives of twelve Pentecostal denominations. A name was proposed, the "Pentecostal Fellowship of North America," and a common statement of faith and aims was suggested. The conference closed by calling for a constitutional convention to be held in Des Moines, Iowa, at the headquarters of the Open Bible Standard Church in 1948.

The Des Moines Convention, which met from October 26 to 28, 1948, was composed of two hundred delegates from a dozen bodies. In short order a constitution was adopted and the PFNA became the voice of about one million Pentecostals in North America representing over 10,000 local churches. Founding members of the fellowship included the Assemblies of God, The Church of God, the Pentecostal Holiness Church, the International Church of the Foursquare Gospel, and the Open Bible Standard Church. By the time of the second meeting in 1949, membership had grown to include fourteen groups, including the Pentecostal Assemblies of Canada. Notable for their absence were the African-American Pentecostal bodies, the oneness Pentecostals, the Tomlinson branches of the Church of God, and churches such as the Pentecostal Church of God whose divorce and remarriage views were considered too liberal for the founding bodies. In essence, the PFNA represented the mainstream of respectable, white, orthodox Pentecostalism in North America.[57]

56. Menzies, *Anointed to Serve,* pp. 215-19; Gee, *The Pentecostal Movement,* p. 122; Nichols, *Pentecostalism,* pp. 211-16.

57. *The Church of God Evangel,* Apr. 15, 1944, p. 3; Sept. 28, 1948, pp. 4-5; *The Pentecostal Evangel,* Nov. 20, 1948, p. 13; *The Pentecostal Holiness Advocate,* May 27, 1948, pp. 2-6; Nov. 11, 1948, pp. 3-11. When the PFNA was disbanded and replaced by

The "Latter Rain Movement"

The growing success of the Pentecostal churches and the notoriety of such evangelists as Aimee Semple McPherson, masked an internal trend that concerned many Pentecostals in the 1940's, that is, the apparent gradual decline in the frequency of charismatic manifestations in the churches. The desire for respectability and fellowship with mainline churches often led to a muting of such Pentecostal distinctives as speaking in tongues, prophesying, and praying for the sick. Along with this came a sense of dryness and aridity in many Pentecostal congregations. Although few would recognize it, by the end of World War II the American Pentecostal movement needed a renewal.

The year 1948 was a crucial year for Pentecostals and evangelicals in the United States. The creation of the State of Israel in May opened the way for an explosion of Last Day prophetic preaching among churches influenced by dispensationalism. Added to this was the publicity surrounding the national debuts of such important evangelists as Billy Graham and Oral Roberts, both of whom hit the headlines in 1948.

A little noticed revival in a remote area of Saskatchewan, however, was to loom large for Pentecostals in the next few years. Beginning among students in the Sharon Orphanage and Schools in North Battleford in February, 1948, a movement known as the "latter rain" began to spread to the U.S. and elsewhere around the world. The leaders of the movement were brothers, Ern and George Hawtin, who spread their teachings through a periodical called the *Sharon Star.* The major teachings and phenomena of the movement were little different from what had been experienced at Topeka in 1901 and at Azusa Street in 1906. Tongues, prophecies, holy laughter, and healings were common, in prayer meetings that lasted into the night. What was different was the practice of imparting specific gifts of the Holy Spirit by the "laying on of hands," frequent cases of mass singing in tongues, and detailed personal prophecies directing individuals to make life-changing decisions. There also developed an expectation that the offices of apostle and prophet would be restored to the modern church. Also prominent was the older Pente-

the "Pentecostal and Charismatic Churches of North America" (PCCNA) in 1994, the Church of God of Prophecy and the Pentecostal Church of God joined as charter members, while Bishop Ithiel Clemmons of the Church of God in Christ was unanimously elected to head the new interracial organization.

costal teaching of an end-times "latter rain" that would herald the imminent rapture of the church.[58]

In time the leaders created a "New Order of the Latter Rain" which challenged the Pentecostal churches to a renewal and revival that would bring them back to their spiritual roots. Among Pentecostal leaders who accepted the "latter rain" revival were Mrs. Myrtle Beall of Detroit, Ivan Spencer of the Elim Bible Institute in New York, Thomas Wyatt of Portland, Oregon, Fred Poole of Philadelphia, and Stanley Frodsham, longtime editor of the Assemblies of God paper, the *Pentecostal Evangel.*[59]

In a short time, the mainline Pentecostal denominations rejected what they perceived to be errors and excesses in the movement, particularly the bestowal of specific charismatic gifts by the laying on of hands. A major turning point came in 1949 when the General Council of the Assemblies of God issued a paper roundly disapproving the movement. Among the specific practices and teachings they rejected were "present-day apostles and prophets," "bestowing or confirming gifts by the laying on of hands and prophecy," and "distortions of scripture interpretations which are in opposition to teachings and practices generally accepted among us."[60] Following the lead of the Assemblies of God, other major Pentecostal denominations adopted similar positions. By 1950, the "New Order of the Latter Rain" became a movement confined to independent churches and popular healing evangelists such as Thomas Wyatt and William Branham.[61]

It was no coincidence that the post–World War II healing explosion occurred simultaneously with the latter rain movement. In spite of official rejection by the Pentecostal churches, hundreds of congregations were revitalized and energized by the movement. Also, in the long term, the latter rain movement made major contributions to the neo-Pentecostal and charismatic movements which developed after 1960.

---

58. Richard Riss, *The Latter Rain Movement of 1948* (Mississauga, Ontario, 1987).

59. See also Richard Riss, "The Latter Rain Movement of 1948," *Pneuma* 4 (Spring 1982): 32-45.

60. William Menzies, *Anointed to Serve*, pp. 321-25.

61. For an evaluation of latter rain end times teaching see William D. Faupel, "The Everlasting Gospel: The Significance of Eschatology in the Development of Pentecostal Thought" (unpublished Ph.D. dissertation, University of Birmingham, U.K., 1989).

Pentecostals and Higher Education

The growth of Pentecostalism into a large worldwide family of churches also resulted in a new generation of Bible schools and colleges to serve the movement. Beginning with Holmes Bible College at Greenville, South Carolina, in 1898, the Pentecostal movement saw the founding of a score of colleges between that year and 1950. The first denominationally owned college was Lee College, founded in 1918 by the Church of God in Cleveland, Tennessee. The following year the Pentecostal Holiness Church founded Emmanuel College in Franklin Springs, Georgia. The Assemblies of God founded their first denominational school, called Central Bible Institute, in Springfield, Missouri, in 1922. It was not until 1955, however, that the denomination opened its first liberal arts college, Evangel College, also located in Springfield.[62]

In the early days, many Pentecostals feared liberal arts education as a possible Trojan horse that might eventually cool the fires of revival ardor that had produced the movement. But by the fifties and sixties, no efforts were being spared in the upgrading of denominational schools and having them gain regional accreditation. One event that seemed to promise much for the future of Pentecostalism was the creation of a school billed as the first distinctly Pentecostal university in the nation — Oral Roberts University in Tulsa, Oklahoma. Founded by two Pentecostal Holiness preachers, Oral Roberts and R. O. Corvin, the institution began classes in 1965 with plans for a hundred-million-dollar campus that would house a first-rate university, offering, in time, doctoral programs in several fields. One of its first schools was the Graduate School of Theology, headed by Corvin, which was accepted as the first Pentecostal seminary to offer postgraduate degrees. Symbolic of increasing acceptance by the traditional churches of the Pentecostals was the fact that Billy Graham assisted in the act of dedication in April of 1967.[63]

Soon after the dedication of the new university, however, Roberts

62. See Thomas, *Holmes Theological Seminary;* Mauldin Ray, "A Study of the History of Lee College, Cleveland, Tennessee" (unpublished Ph.D. dissertation, University of Houston, 1964); Vinson Synan, *Emmanuel College — The First Fifty Years;* and Brumback, *Suddenly from Heaven,* pp. 326-30.

63. *Abundant Life,* June 1967, pp. 1-32, gives the story of the founding and dedication of the school. See also the *Oral Roberts University Bulletin, 1966-1967* (Tulsa, OK, 1967); and *Oral Roberts University Outreach,* Winter 1967, pp. 1-24.

shocked the religious world by joining the Methodist Church in March 1968. He also transferred his ordination vows as an ordained minister. The world's best-known Pentecostal since Aimee Semple McPherson, Roberts had since 1947 built a tremendous faith-healing empire from his headquarters in Tulsa. The overwhelming source of his support during his earlier years had been the Pentecostals. But by the 1960's a larger share of his income had been from people in the more traditional churches. These people, most of whom had experienced speaking with other tongues, were dubbed "neo-Pentecostals" by old-line members of the Pentecostal movement. Roberts's defection from the church in which his parents had been pioneer ministers, and from the Pentecostal movement which had brought him to prominence, puzzled many. At any rate, the dream of Roberts's university becoming an intellectual center for the Pentecostal world seemed shattered by this event.[64]

Pentecostals and Charismatics

The fact that Roberts was accepted by the Methodist Church, even though he vowed never to change his Pentecostal doctrines, was indicative of the new acceptance of Pentecostalism in American society by the middle of the twentieth century. Perhaps one reason for this new acceptance was the fact that the Pentecostals were by then the fastest-growing segment of evangelical Christianity around the world. Their growth rates in the United States were also far above those of the more traditional denominations. As a result, a great deal of interest was increasingly being shown towards Pentecostals by the more liberal elements of both Protestantism and Catholicism. These new Pentecostals called their move-

64. Oral Roberts, *My Twenty Years of a Miracle Ministry* (Tulsa, OK, 1967), pp. 61-84; *Abundant Life*, Feb. 1970, pp. 5-8. For reaction to Roberts's conversion see *Christianity Today*, Apr. 12, 1968, p. 34; and *The Pentecostal Holiness Advocate*, Apr. 27, 1968, p. 13. More recent studies, both favorable and unfavorable, of Roberts's life and ministry include Jerry Shole's exposé, entitled *Give Me that Prime Time Religion: An Insider's Report on the Oral Roberts Evangelistic Association* (New York, 1979); and David Edwin Harrell's highly acclaimed *Oral Roberts: An American Life* (Bloomington, IN, 1985). Roberts's latest autobiography, *Expect a Miracle* (Nashville, 1995), details his career as both a Pentecostal and a Methodist and his eventual separation from the Methodists in 1988. By 1995, Oral Roberts University was billing itself as the world's only "Pentecostal/Charismatic University."

ment the "Charismatic Movement" to distinguish themselves from the older mainline Pentecostals. By the end of the 1960's, this movement was growing to such proportions that several denominations were forced to take official cognizance of the phenomenon. Reactions ranged from the denunciation of Pentecostals in the Episcopal Diocese of California by Bishop James Pike, to the acceptance of glossolalia by the Presbyterian Church, U.S.A., as an approved practice within the church.[65]

An even more arresting instance of the Pentecostal penetration into other church bodies was the outbreak of glossolalia among many Roman Catholics in the United States. Beginning with a startling outbreak at Duquesne University in 1966, the movement rapidly spread to Notre Dame University, where a major occurrence of tongues was in evidence among both students and faculty members by 1967. Although there were those who questioned the propriety of the meetings where the Pentecostal phenomenon occurred, most observers were in agreement that the movement was beneficial and caused the participants to be more loyal to the Catholic Church. Some saw in the movement hope for a spiritual renewal which would "stir up afresh the grace of baptism and confirmation." Far from condemning the phenomenon, Catholic theologians and ecclesiastical authorities called for an investigation of the possible value of glossolalia to the church. Of interest to those who studied the movement was the fact that the preponderance of Catholic Pentecostals were from the intellectual groups "such as university and college teachers and their wives." The chief apologist for this new Pentecostal wave among the Catholics was Kevin Ranaghan, a theology professor at Notre Dame University. In his book, *Catholic Pentecostals*, published in 1969, Ranaghan observed that the movement lacked the emotionalism of traditional Pentecostal meetings, but was resulting in deepened loyalty to the church and reverence for the rosary and the mass. By 1970 it was reported that the movement was "spreading like wildfire" among Catholics and that over 30,000 had experienced other

---

65. Frank Farrell, "Outburst of Tongues: The New Penetration," *Christianity Today,* Sept. 13, 1963, pp. 3-7. See also Russell Chandler, "Fanning the Charismatic Flame," Nov. 24, 1967, pp. 39-40. A survey of the new penetration of Pentecostalism into the traditional churches is given in Morton T. Kelsey's *Tongue Speaking* (New York, 1964), and McCandlish Phillips, "And There Appeared Unto Them Tongues of Fire," *Saturday Evening Post,* May 16, 1964, pp. 30-40. See also *Christianity Today,* June 19, 1970, p. 31.

tongues within the last two years. Taking cognizance of the new move, the U.S. Catholic hierarchy declared in November 1969 that the movement "should at this point not be inhibited but allowed to develop."[66]

A sign of the penetration of Pentecostal practice into traditional Protestant churches was the conversion of the widely read interdenominational monthly periodical, *Christian Life*, to the Pentecostal view. Reported on its pages were many stories of Baptists, Methodists, Presbyterians, and others who had received the Pentecostal experience. Among them were reports of some Methodist pastors and congregations that had experienced revivals of the phenomenon. To Wesleyan-oriented Pentecostals, this was taken as a sign that the Pentecostal movement was making the full cycle and finding a place in the church that had mothered the holiness-Pentecostal movement in the first place.[67]

Among the holiness denominations that had bitterly rejected Pentecostalism after 1906, there was a perceptible change of attitude by the late 1960's as a result of the neo-Pentecostal movement in the other churches. The older view, that "pentecostalism is the holiness movement gone to seed," was rapidly being changed. By 1965, the best minds of the National Holiness Association were declaring that "the pentecostal movement is one of the unpaid debts of the holiness movement." To be sure, the older, negative attitude persisted among many, but a new strand of tolerance was being seen among younger leaders of the movement. Illustrative of the new openness was the fact that the National Holiness Association, by the end of its first century of existence in 1967, was admitting to its membership bodies that practiced speaking in tongues. An example of this practice was the membership of the Bethany Fellowship of Minneapolis. Dr. Frank Bateman Stanger, President of Asbury Theological Seminary, supported the contention that "there is a new climate of understanding emerging between holiness and pentecostal people" and that this has been engendered in large measure by common participation in such evangelical agencies and enterprises as the National

66. Kevin and Dorothy Ranaghan, *Catholic Pentecostals* (New York, 1969), pp. 6-57; Edward O'Conner, "A Catholic Pentecostal Movement," *Ave Maria*, June 3, 1967, pp. 7-30; "Catholic Pentecostalism," *Jubilee*, June 1968, pp. 13-17; *Christianity Today*, Jan. 2, 1970, pp. 41-42; Kilian McDonnell, *Catholic Pentecostalism: Problems in Evaluation* (Pecos, NM, 1970); J. Massingberd Ford, *The Pentecostal Experience: A New Direction for American Catholics* (New York, 1970).

67. Marvin Buck, "When the Holy Spirit Came to a Methodist Church," *Christian Life*, Jan. 1962, pp. 34-36.

Association of Evangelicals. By 1988 Asbury Seminary hosted the annual meeting of the Society for Pentecostal Studies, an event that would have been impossible a generation earlier.[68]

A further probable reason for this new interest is the fact that the Pentecostal movement has far outgrown the older holiness movement around the world. Indeed, by the middle of the twentieth century, the Pentecostals were burgeoning into what some called "the third force in Christendom." Surveys of worldwide Christianity were revealing that three-fourths of all Protestants in Latin America were Pentecostals, that two-thirds of all non-Catholics in Italy were Pentecostals, and that the majority of all Christians in South Africa were Pentecostals. Furthermore, the largest free churches in Russia, Scandinavia, and France were Pentecostal and the growth rates indicated vastly greater growth for the future. These startling facts led some experts on church growth, such as Walter Hollenweger, Secretary of Evangelism of the World Council of Churches, to predict that the Christians of Africa and Latin America would outnumber Christians on the other three continents by the year 2000. Of this vast body of new Christians, "the majority or at least a very considerable part of this Christianity will belong to the spontaneous non-literary pentecostal type." Because of this explosive growth, the World Council of Churches has taken increased interest in the movement.[69]

By 1970 it was impossible to give precise figures of the size of the Pentecostal movement in the United States and the world. Part of this uncertainty was due to the aversion of Pentecostals to keeping accurate statistics, but it was also due to the sheer number of independent groups. A definitive count was simply not possible. The best-informed guesses were that by 1970 there were about four million Pentecostals in the United States. About half of these were in the mainline organized denominations and the other half in the thousands of independent storefront churches and missions across the nation. In addition there were uncounted thousands of "neo-Pentecostals" in the traditional denomi-

68. John Peters, *Christian Perfection and American Methodism,* p. 195; Kenneth E. Geiger et al., *The Word and the Doctrine: Studies in Contemporary Wesleyan-Arminian Theology* (Kansas City, 1965), pp. 317-51. Melvin Dieter, *The Holiness Revival of the Nineteenth Century* (Metuchen, NJ, 1980).

69. Henry P. Van Dusen, "The Third Force in Christendom," *Life,* June 9, 1958, pp. 122-24; Walter Hollenweger, "Pentecostalism and the Third World," *Pulse, Evangelical Committee on Latin America* 4, no. 6 (Dec. 1969): 11-13.

nations who were Pentecostal in experience and belief and generally designated themselves "the Charismatic movement."[70]

Globally, the numbers were even more difficult to estimate than in the United States. Using various standards of defining exactly what constituted a "Pentecostal" and educated guesses about statistics, estimates of the movement's world constituency in 1970 ranged from 12 to 35 million. The Pentecostals themselves accepted a figure in the range of 12 to 15 million, while officials of the World Council of Churches tended toward the 35 million figure. Whatever the actual number was, it was evident that the movement had experienced tremendous growth since its first faltering days at the beginning of the century.[71]

By the mid 1990's the movement had caught the attention of Harvey Cox, the Harvard professor who a generation earlier had written about the loss of faith in *The Secular City*. In the early 1990's, noting the vitality of black and Hispanic Pentecostal churches in the nation's inner cities, he began to offer a course on Pentecostalism at Harvard that soon attracted capacity registrations. As a result of intensive studies, he published a major book in 1994 entitled *Fire From Heaven: The Rise of Pentecostal Spirituality and the Reshaping of Religion in the Twenty-first Century*. For Cox, at least, religion seemed to be coming back to life again, mainly in the form of fast-growing Pentecostal and charismatic movements around the world.[72]

Regardless of its eventual size or influence, Pentecostalism is one of the few religious movements to originate in America and subsequently become a major force in other parts of the world. Whether it deserves to be ranked alongside Catholicism and traditional Protestantism as a "third force" in Christian history remains to be seen, but the statement by the Presbyterian writer Charles S. Sydnor, Jr., that Pentecostalism "is an authentic reformation-revival movement of historic significance, equal with those of other great movements of centuries past," seems to be well founded.[73]

70. Kelsey, *Tongue Speaking*, pp. 242-43; Atter, *The Third Force*, p. 227; Kendrick, *The Promise Fulfilled*, p. 4.

71. Hollenweger, "Pentecostalism and the Third World," p. 12; Atter, *The Third Force*, pp. 226-29.

72. Harvey Cox, *Fire from Heaven* (New York, 1994).

73. Charles S. Sydnor, Jr., "The Pentecostals," *The Presbyterian Survey*, June 1964, p. 37.

CHAPTER ELEVEN

The Neo-Pentecostal Movement

---

*Some 2,000 Episcopalians are said to be speaking in
tongues in Southern California (these Episcopal developments calculated to give fits to Vance Packard's status
seekers). Speaking in tongues are upwards of 600 folk
at First Presbyterian Church in Hollywood, the world's
largest Presbyterian church.*

Frank Farrell, in *Christianity Today*, 1963

The advent of neo-Pentecostalism in the traditional churches around
1960 began to shatter almost all the stereotypes, myths, and shib-
boleths that had plagued the movement for over half a century. Yet,
several years before the first Episcopalian spoke in tongues, significant
developments had already taken place which indicated a growing tolerance and acceptance of the Pentecostals on the part of mainstream
evangelical Christianity.[1]

The historic invitation to join the National Association of Evangelicals extended to several American Pentecostal denominations in 1943

---

1. Vinson Synan, *In the Latter Days: The Outpouring of the Holy Spirit in the
Twentieth Century* (Ann Arbor, MI, 1984).

marked a turning point in ecclesiastical history. It has been suggested that the admission of the Pentecostal churches into the N.A.E. was the first time in church history that a charismatic movement was accepted into the Church mainstream.[2] Pentecostalism was thus well on its way to social and ecclesiastical respectability before the first stirrings of charismatic developments in the mainline churches. The great change came after World War II, when Christianity at large began to make a major re-evaluation of the movement, a shift of thinking that continues to this day. At least five reasons can be cited for this new interest.

The Growth of the Pentecostal Churches

After the war, the old Depression-era stereotypes began to break down. The general postwar prosperity brought many Pentecostals out of the lower socioeconomic classes. According to the deprivation theories popular at the time, Pentecostal churches should have begun a decline in the face of this new prosperity. Yet, the evidence showed that the Pentecostal churches were growing by leaps and bounds. This was especially true of the churches outside the United States. Church specialists suddenly realized that Pentecostals formed the majority of evangelicals in Latin America, Italy, Spain, and Scandinavia. As Pentecostal growth rates accelerated, the growth rates of the major "mainline" denominations leveled off and eventually began to decline. Hurried re-assessments of the movement sparked a new and sympathetic interest among traditional church people.

The Ascent of the Pentecostals into the Middle Class

A second reason was the obvious ascent of many American Pentecostals into the middle class. In the postwar economic boom, the Pentecostals acquired unprecedented financial resources which soon showed up in large and often expensive church buildings. The edifices bore impressive and compelling witness to the fact that this form of Christianity could appeal to the "up and coming" as well as the "down and out."

Pentecostals were increasingly seen in leadership positions in in-

2. Menzies, *Anointed to Serve*, pp. 182-227.

dustry, business, finance, and education. A number of them were becoming millionaires. They began to show up in places where they had not been seen before. There were even Pentecostals in the professions; for the first time, there were Pentecostal lawyers, medical doctors, and university professors.

A most striking example of this phenomenon was the case of the Tatham family of eastern Oklahoma. Immortalized by John Steinbeck in his classic depression-era novel *The Grapes of Wrath,* the Tatham family was used as the model for the Okies and Arkies who fled the dust bowl of the 1930's to California. The Tathams were a Pentecostal Holiness family from Salisaw, Oklahoma who went to California in the 1930's to begin life anew in the new American promised land. Led by Oca Tatham, a Pentecostal Church of God preacher, the family prospered and eventually became wealthy. Tatham's son, Bill, became rich by building a chain of hospitals and nursing homes across California from his home in Fresno. He also became well known as the owner of the Tulsa professional football team, the "Tulsa Outlaws"[3]

The story of the Tathams was the story of innumerable Pentecostal families who rose from bitter poverty to become successful leaders of the middle class. Pentecostals became prime examples of Donald McGavran's theory of "redemption and lift," which holds that religious sects tend to rise from below *en masse* as they practice honesty, thrift, and hard work.

The Divine Healing Movement and Oral Roberts

A third reason for this new interest was the tremendous success and influence of William Branham, Jack Coe, and Oral Roberts. About 1948, a nation-wide interest in divine healing swept over America and thousands packed the tents of these Pentecostal crusaders.

By the mid 1950's, Oral Roberts, an unknown evangelist from the

3. The Joads, the fictional family in the *Grapes of Wrath*, were actually based on the Tathams, a family studied by Steinbeck as he wrote the novel. In the story, the grandmother spoke in tongues. See Steinbeck, *Grapes of Wrath* (Chicago, 1939). The story of the Tatham family is given in Dan Morgan's *Rising in the West: The True Story of an "Okie" Family from the Great Depression through the Reagan Years* (New York, 1992).

Pentecostal Holiness Church in Oklahoma, burst upon the consciousness of the nation through his pioneering ministry in the budding television industry. By the early 1960's millions of Americans were introduced to Pentecostalism in their living rooms by way of Roberts's ministry.[4]

Suddenly, the bishops of the Roman Catholic Church became concerned by Roberts's widespread appeal to Catholics across America. Leaders of other denominations also became aware of the large sums that flowed to the ministry of the Pentecostal evangelist. By 1967, computer studies showed that Roberts's largest financial support was no longer from Pentecostals but from Methodists. Roberts claimed that the crowds packing his tent to its 20,000 capacity were composed of "all faiths."[5] In his book *All Things Are Possible,* and in his biography of Roberts, Professor David Harrell of the University of Arkansas credits Roberts with being the most important religious figure of the twentieth century. With his university inaugurated in 1965, and his "City of Faith" hospital in 1980, Roberts was one of the leading symbolic figures in the emerging charismatic movement after 1960. His joining the Methodist church in 1969 further solidified his identification with the charismatic movement in the mainline denominations.[6]

The Full Gospel Business Men

A fourth influence was the Full Gospel Business Men's Fellowship International, begun by Demos Shakarian in 1952. An Armenian Pentecostal businessman who had prospered in the California dairy industry during the 1940's, Shakarian formed his group, with the help of Oral Roberts, to serve as a vanguard to spread the Pentecostal experience to those who might never have been interested in attending a Pentecostal church.[7]

This group, which admitted no women or preachers to its regular membership, became the propagator of a new gospel of wealth, health,

4. Oral Roberts, *My Story* (Tulsa, OK, privately printed, 1961), passim. For Roberts's relationships with the Pentecostals and the Methodists see his *Expect a Miracle,* pp. 52-86, 315-30.

5. Vinson Synan, *The Old-Time Power,* pp. 220-74.

6. David Harrell, *All Things Are Possible: The Healing and Charismatic Revivals in Modern America* (Bloomington, IN, 1975), pp. 225-38.

7. Demos Shakarian, *The Happiest People on Earth* (Old Tappan, NJ, 1975).

and glossolalia. Walter Hollenweger, in his monumental work, *The Pentecostals,* stated that this organization had made a "decisive contribution towards spreading the Pentecostal ideas over the world" despite the "incomprehensible" (to Europeans like himself) teaching that: ". . . the person who is filled with the Holy Spirit will prove more successful in business, make better tractors and automobiles than his competitors, live in a finer house and, if a footballer, score more goals than the person who is not converted or is not baptized with the Spirit.[8] These *nouveau riche* Pentecostal capitalists were creating a prosperous image for tongues-speakers.

The Full Gospel Business Men, dubbed "God's Ballroom Saints" by Oral Roberts, eventually grew to include over 3,000 chapters in 117 different nations. Despite their unabashedly Pentecostal *statement of faith,* hundreds of thousands of mainline Protestant and Catholic charismatics joined the group, and some became major speakers and leaders within the organization.[9]

Despite its exclusion of women, and its American capitalistic ethos, the Full Gospel Business Men played a major role in winning thousands of traditional churchgoers to the Pentecostal experience. As such, the organization served as an important catalyst in the rise of Pentecostalism in the older denominations. Its major technique was to serve as a platform for newly Spirit-baptized persons — whether businessmen, ministers, or priests — to give their testimonies on the "banquet circuit" as an encouragement to business leaders.[10]

David du Plessis

The one person, above all the others, who served as catalyst and spokesman for the new Pentecostals was David J. du Plessis, a South African descendant of exiled French Huguenots who was converted in a South African Pentecostal church known as the Apostolic Faith Mission. According to du Plessis' testimony, the inspiration for the ecumenical work he was destined to perform came to him in the form of a prophecy given

---

8. Hollenweger, *The Pentecostals,* pp. 6-7.

9. See Vinson Synan, *Under His Banner: History of the Full Gospel Business Men's Fellowship International* (Costa Mesa, CA, 1992), pp. 11-16.

10. Durasoff, *Bright Wind,* pp. 145-65.

in 1936 by the evangelist Smith Wigglesworth. One morning about 7:00 o'clock Wigglesworth burst into du Plessis' office and:

> laying his hands on his shoulders he pushed him against the wall and began to prophesy: "you have been 'Jerusalem' long enough.... I will send you to the uttermost parts of the earth.... You will bring the message Pentecost to all churches.... you will travel more than evangelists do.... God is going to revive the churches in last days and through them turn the world upside down even the Pentecostal movement will become a mere joke compared with the revival which God will bring through the churches."[11]

This vision remained unfulfilled for ten years, until the end of World War II made it possible for du Plessis to travel extensively. In 1947, he took a leading role in convening the first Pentecostal World Conference in Zurich, Switzerland, and in 1949 served a short term as General Secretary of the World Conference. His zeal for ecumenism, however, soon cost him his job.[12]

Although stung by the rejection of the Pentecostal leaders, du Plessis was still consumed by Wigglesworth's prophetic vision. In 1951, while pastoring an Assemblies of God congregation in Connecticut, he felt inspired to make contact with the World Council of Churches in nearby New York City. Although he had sternly opposed the Council in its formative stages, he now saw the mainline churches as an evangelistic opportunity. During a trip to the headquarters of the National Council of Churches (NCC), he was astounded by the "warm reception" accorded him. A later meeting with President John MacKay of Princeton Theological Seminary convinced him that the mainline churches were greatly interested in making contact with the Pentecostal churches. After joining the NCC as an individual member in 1954, du Plessis was seated as an unofficial representative of the Pentecostal churches at the second plenary session of the World Council of Churches that met in Evanston, Illinois. This action, and the fact that he attended Vatican II as the only Pentecostal observer, brought down upon his head the ire of his denom-

---

11. Michael Harper, *As at the Beginning: The Twentieth-Century Pentecostal Revival* (London, 1965), p. 51.

12. David du Plessis, *The Spirit Bade Me Go: The Astounding Move of God in the Denominational Churches* (Oakland, CA, 1961), pp. 9-29.

inational officials. He was excommunicated in 1962 by the Assemblies of God, whose leaders viewed him as a maverick without portfolio.[13]

In a short time, du Plessis became the leading figure in spearheading the charismatic movement in the traditional churches. His work as chairman of the Roman Catholic-Pentecostal Dialogue team and as a leading speaker at hundreds of Pentecostal-charismatic meetings around the world eventually earned him the unofficial title of "Mr. Pentecost.[14] In 1974 a group of reporters named du Plessis as one of the eleven "foremost theologians of the twentieth century." Also, for his work in the dialogue and other contributions to the Catholic charismatic movement, he was given, in 1983, the golden "Good Merit" medal by Pope John Paul II for excellent "service to all Christianity." He was the first non-Catholic in history to receive this honor. Though his work has often been controversial, du Plessis' place is secure as one of the most important Pentecostal figures in history. His influence was pivotal in shaping the charismatic movement in the historic churches.[15]

The Neo-Pentecostal Movement

For over fifty years, there were untold hundreds of ministers and thousands of lay persons in the traditional churches who received the Pentecostal experience and spoke in tongues. During this time these new Pentecostals had only two options: keep quiet about their experience, or be expelled from their churches. For example, under the ministry of Aimee Semple McPherson in the 1920's and 1930's, hundreds of Methodist, Baptist, and Presbyterian ministers were baptized in the Spirit and forced to leave their churches. Most of them joined a Pentecostal denomination since they were now unwelcome in their own churches. Some suffered actual persecution.

A case in point was the experience of the Mennonite pastor Gerald Derstine, pastor of the Strawberry Lake Mennonite congregation in Ogema, Minnesota. Late in 1954, a full-fledged Pentecostal revival broke

---

13. R. P. Spittler, "David Johannes du Plessis," in Burgess et al., *Dictionary of Pentecostal and Charismatic Movements,* pp. 250-54.

14. David du Plessis, *A Man Called Mr. Pentecost: David du Plessis as Told to Bob Slosser* (Plainfield, NJ, 1977).

15. David du Plessis, "Newsletter," Feb.-Mar. 1984, p. 2.

out in his church with many manifestations of the Holy Spirit. Rather than oppose the revival, Derstine himself received the baptism in the Holy Spirit and began to speak in tongues.[16]

Soon afterwards, the members of the church experienced many conversions, visions, healings, and prophecies, not only in the church sanctuary but also in home prayer meetings. Services often went on into the wee hours of the morning with many people manifesting charismatic gifts. Before long, Mennonite church authorities arrived on the scene and put an end to the meetings.

In the subsequent trial by the Mennonite elders, Derstine was given the choice of being removed as pastor of the church or of recanting his Pentecostal experience. Officials told him that if he would only admit that there had been demonic activity in the meetings, he would be exonerated. Derstine refused. He was then "silenced" and removed from his pastorate. He afterwards began an independent charismatic ministry in Florida.[17]

The first pastor of record in a mainline church who experienced and promoted the Pentecostal experience in his parish and was allowed to remain in his church was Father Richard Winkler of Wheaton, Illinois. In 1956, Winkler was rector of Wheaton's Trinity Episcopal Church when he came into contact with a Methodist layman who led him into the baptism in the Holy Spirit.

Winkler's church soon began to experience charismatic phenomena such as glossolalia and prayer for divine healing. In a short time, Winkler was featured on the cover of *Life Magazine* in an article featuring his ministry of exorcism. As a result of the activities at Trinity Church, an Episcopal commission officially studied the movement in Wheaton. The resulting report recognized that speaking in tongues could be "unquestionably genuine," but warned of "delusion" and "diabolical deception." It concluded by recommending moderation since, the report asserted, "reason is supremely the voice of the Holy Ghost." These warnings given, Winkler was allowed to continue as rector of the church, a privilege not given to any of his predecessors in America.[18]

The next Episcopal clergyman to receive the experience, Dennis Bennett, was not as fortunate as Winkler, but became a national celebrity

16. Gerald Derstine, *Following the Fire* (Plainfield, NJ, 1980), pp. 83-165.
17. Derstine, *Following the Fire.* See also J. A. Hewett, "Gerald Derstine," in Burgess et al., *Dictionary of Pentecostal and Charismatic Movements,* p. 239.
18. Kilian McDonnell, *Presence, Power, and Praise,* vol. 1 (New York, 1980), p. 20.

and a precursor of the neo-Pentecostal movement in America. In the late 1950's Father Bennett was rector of the fashionable St. Mark's Episcopal parish in Van Nuys, California. A graduate of the University of Chicago and the Chicago School of Divinity, he was the epitome of the sophisticated, respectable, slightly worldly clergy of his church. By 1959, his parish had grown to include some 2,600 members and a staff of four ministers, when he heard about the baptism in the Holy Spirit from a fellow Episcopal clergyman.[19]

After seeing some laypersons in his church who exhibited a high degree of commitment and spirituality, Bennett began to seek answers about their Pentecostal experiences. After a thorough investigation, he became convinced of the reality of the baptism in the Holy Spirit although he tended to view speaking in tongues as a "red herring" and quite unnecessary. Yet he hungered for a deeper reality in his Christian experience. As he studied the subject, he was surprised to see so many references to the Holy Spirit in the New Testament, the *Book of Common Prayer*, the early church fathers, the theology textbooks, church history books, "and even the hymn books."[20]

Early in 1959, Bennett finally began to seek the "baptism" with the aid of a fellow Episcopal priest and a young couple in the church who had already received the experience. In an early morning home prayer meeting, hands were laid on Father Bennett as his friends prayed over him. His "nine o'clock in the morning" experience could be considered typical of the thousands that have occurred among the clergy in recent years:

> I suppose I must have prayed out loud for about twenty minutes — at least it seemed to be a long time — and was about to give up when a very strange thing happened. My tongue tripped, just as it might when you are trying to say a tongue twister, and I began to speak in a new language!
>
> Right away I recognized several things: first, it wasn't some kind of psychological trick or compulsion. There was nothing compulsive about it. . . . It was a new language, not some kind of "baby talk." It had grammar and syntax; it had inflection and expression — and it was rather beautiful.[21]

19. Dennis Bennett, *Nine O'clock in the Morning* (Plainfield, NJ, 1970); see also Sherrill, *They Speak with Other Tongues,* pp. 61-63.
20. Bennett, *Nine O'clock,* p. 15.
21. Bennett, *Nine O'clock,* pp. 20-21.

In a short time, several members of St. Mark's parish received the same experience. In their joy and exhilaration they began to use such typical Pentecostal expressions as "praise the Lord" and "hallelujah" in the church office and parish house. As word spread among the church members about the pastor's strange new experience, some members of the vestry began to accuse him of fanaticism.

In order to quell false rumors and to answer questions circulating in the congregation, Bennett soon felt it necessary to tell his church about his experience of speaking with other tongues. Thus, on April 3, 1960, he shared his testimony in the three morning services of his church.

The reaction in the early morning service was "open and tender," according to Bennett, but in the second service the "lid blew off." In outrage, Bennett's curate "snatched off his vestments, threw them on the altar, and stalked out of church crying: 'I can no longer work with this man.'"

After the service concluded, outside on the patio, those who had set themselves to get rid of the movement of the Holy Spirit began to harangue the arriving and departing parishioners. One man stood on a chair shouting, "Throw out the damn tongue speakers."[22] After some members complained that "we're Episcopalians, not a bunch of wild-eyed hillbillies," the treasurer of the vestry called on Bennett to resign. Rather than cause disharmony in the congregation, the mild-mannered rector promptly resigned his parish, partly because he lacked enough understanding of the Pentecostal experience to defend himself. Thereupon the bishop sent a temporary priest to St. Mark's armed with a firm letter to the parish officers forbidding any further tongues-speaking under church auspices.[23]

The turmoil at St. Mark's caused a sensation in the nation's press as the story was picked up by the major wire services. *Time* magazine reported that "now glossolalia seems to be on its way back in U.S. churches — not only in the uninhibited Pentecostal sects, but even among Episcopalians, who have been called "God's frozen people."[24] *Newsweek* reported that to conservative Episcopalians in St Mark's "there was puzzlement, anger, even a wisp of envy" although some felt that it "was all a kind of shameful voodoo." Yet Bennett and about seventy of

22. Bennett, *Nine O'clock*, p. 61.
23. Bennett, *Nine O'clock*, pp. 61-72.
24. Bennett, *Nine O'clock*, pp. 52-55.

his parishioners were willing to pay a high price for their new Pentecostal experience — that of being ostracized from their own church.[25]

Bennett was then invited to assume the pastorate of St. Luke's Episcopal Church, a small inner-city parish in Seattle, Washington. Since the church was on the verge of closing anyhow, his friendly new bishop offered to support him, even in his Pentecostal practices. Free now to promote his experience without official hindrances, Bennett soon converted the church into a center of neo-Pentecostalism in the Pacific Northwest. Instead of closing the church, the bishop saw St. Luke's grow to be the largest parish in the region. Within a short time, Bennett was ministering to some 2,000 persons a week. Many of these new Pentecostals came from Catholic, Methodist, Presbyterian, Baptist, and Lutheran backgrounds. For over twenty years, an average of twenty persons were baptized in the Spirit each week at the church.[26]

The case of Dennis Bennett was only the most visible part of a process that had been quietly developing for years. In fact, by 1960, practically every denomination already had many "closet Pentecostals," who had received the experience but had remained quiet for fear of displeasing church officials. The Van Nuys incident brought the situation out into the open. Several months after Bennett resigned at St. Mark's, the *Living Church*, an Episcopal journal, carried the following editorial concerning glossolalia in the church:

> Speaking in tongues is no longer a phenomenon of some odd sect across the street. It is in our midst, and is practiced by clergy and laity who have stature and reputation in the church. Its widespread introduction would jar against our esthetic sense and some of our most sternly entrenched preconceptions. But we know that we are members of a church that definitely needs jarring — if God had chosen this time to dynamite what Bishop Sterling of Montana has called "Episcopalian respectabilianism," I know of no more terrifyingly effective explosion.[27]

25. *Newsweek*, July 4, 1960, p. 77.

26. Dennis Bennett, personal interview with the author (Kansas City, July 1977). See also Larry Christenson's "Dennis Joseph and Rita Bennett," in Burgess et al., *Dictionary of Pentecostal and Charismatic Movements*, pp. 53-54.

27. Sherrill, *They Speak with Other Tongues*, p. 6 (quoting *Living Church*, July 17, 1960.)

During the balance of the 1960's, Pentecostalism began to appear at the most unexpected places and among the most unexpected people. An outbreak of glossolalia at Yale University in 1963 was prophetic of what would occur on campuses nationwide by the end of the decade. The so-called "glossoyalies" were far removed from the "holy roller" stereotypes of years past. Among the twenty Yale students who caused a mild sensation on campus were five Phi Beta Kappas, who also happened to be Episcopalians, Lutherans, Presbyterians, and Methodists. The speaker who led these students into speaking in tongues was not even a Pentecostal preacher, but a Reformed pastor from Mt. Vernon, New York, Harald Bredesen. *Time* magazine carried the following report on the Yale Pentecostals: "They do not fall into any mystical seizures or trance; instead, onlookers report, they seem fully in control as they mutter or chant sentences that sometimes sound like Hebrew, sometimes like unkempt Swedish.[28]

Opinion on the Yale campus was mixed concerning the glossolalia phenomenon. The university chaplain, Sloane Coffin, Jr., stated that this was a "genuine religious experience" which gave the students a natural way to gain "emotional release from the tensions of college life." Others called it a "gentlemanly fad" and "similar to a ouija board."[29]

Later in 1963, a major article appeared in *Christianity Today* concerning a "new penetration" of Pentecostalism which the author, Frank Farrell, characterized as an "outburst of tongues." Episcopalians and Lutherans were "especially affected" although nearly all the major denominations had experienced the phenomenon:

> Some 2,000 Episcopalians are said to be speaking in tongues in Southern California (these Episcopal developments calculated to give fits to Vance Packard's status seekers); also speaking in tongues are upwards of 600 folk at First Presbyterian Church in Hollywood, the world's largest Presbyterian church; James A. Pike, Episcopal bishop of California, confronts the practice in the Bay area to the accompaniment of front-page headlines in San Francisco newspapers; a journal relates that in the entire state of Montana only one American Lutheran pastor has not received the experience of speaking in tongues.[30]

28. *Time*, Mar. 29, 1963, p. 52.
29. *Time*, Mar. 29, 1963, p. 52.
30. Frank Farrell, "Outburst of Tongues: The New Penetration," *Christianity Today*, Sept. 13, 1963, pp. 3-7.

These "Neo-Pentecostals," as they were soon dubbed, were somewhat different from the older, classical Pentecostals. An early leader, Jean Stone, editor of *Trinity* magazine, reported that the new Pentecostals exhibited:

> . . . less emotion in receiving the gift of tongues after which they are spoken at will—their private use more important than public, more oriented to clergy and professional classes, more Bible-centered as against experience, not separatist, more orderly meetings with strict adherence to Pauline directives, less emphasis on tongues.[31]

The response of most church leaders to this "new penetration" was a general mood of caution and forbearance. Few people desired to force the new wave of Pentecostals from the churches as had been done a half-century before. The one churchman who objected the loudest to these developments was James A. Pike, Episcopal bishop of California. In 1963, this prelate issued a 2,500 word letter to all 125 of his parishes which forbade speaking in tongues in the churches and which described glossolalia as "heresy in embryo." He also stated that "this particular phenomenon has reached a point where it is dangerous to the peace and unity of the church and a threat to sound doctrine and policy." Yet occasionally while making the rounds of his churches, Pike would be confronted by a congregation and its priest who would break into spontaneous singing in other tongues.[32] Joining with Pike in opposition to the movement was California's Methodist bishop, Gerald Kennedy, who dismissed the movement by saying, "in the past there have been movements of this sort, but they never did the church any good."[33]

Despite these warnings, there were thousands of men and women, both clergy and lay, who felt that the Pentecostal movement was the best hope of the church. One Baptist leader went so far as to say that for the world "the choice is Pentecost or holocaust." Throughout the decade the movement continued to grow rapidly, with leading pastors of many denominations following Bennett's lead in openly espousing Pentecostalism. Such early leaders as Howard Ervin (American Baptist), Harald Bredesen (Dutch Reformed), Howard Conatser (Southern Baptist), Ross Whetstone (United Methodist), Nelson Litwiler (Mennonite), Warren

31. Farrell, "Outburst of Tongues," pp. 3-7.
32. *Time,* May 17, 1963, p. 84.
33. *Time,* Aug. 15, 1960, p. 55.

Black (Nazarene), and Larry Christenson (American Lutheran Church) gave impetus to the movement. In a historic tour of Germany in 1964, Christenson sparked a neo-Pentecostal revival that actually saw much of the German laiety, both Catholic and Protestant, swept into the movement.[34]

By the end of the 1960's, Pentecostalism, roundly rejected a half-century before by the mainline churches, began a triumphal entry into the heart of those very churches. The cycle was complete. The movement was returning with a new fire and vigor to find a place of acceptance among its former critics and enemies. The "new wine" of the Spirit was now pouring into the "old bottles" of traditional churches. The problem to be faced was whether the new wine would burst the old bottles or if it could be successfully contained. Only time could answer that question. Within a decade of Bennett's experience, it was estimated that 10 percent of the clergy and a million lay members of the mainline churches had received the baptism and had remained in their churches. Many of the older Pentecostals were bewildered by these developments. Why, they wondered, were their neo-Pentecostal brethren escaping the suffering and persecution that had fallen on the early Pentecostal pioneers? Yet in general there was a feeling of joy and thanksgiving that others were finally enjoying the reality of the Spirit's fullness.

34. Larry Christenson, *The Charismatic Renewal among Lutherans* (Minneapolis, 1976), pp. 1-31. Also Larry Christenson, personal interview with author (Rome, Italy, 1975). For short histories of the major charismatic renewal movements in the churches, see Vinson Synan, *In the Latter Days* and *The Twentieth Century Pentecostal Explosion.*

CHAPTER TWELVE

The Catholic Charismatic Renewal

> *How then could this "spiritual renewal" not be a*
> *"chance" for the church and for the world? . . . It will*
> *be very fortuitous for our times, for our brothers, that*
> *there should be a generation of young people, who shout*
> *out to the world the greatness of the God of Pentecost. . . .*

Pope Paul VI

Perhaps the greatest surprise in the whole Pentecostal tradition was the sudden appearance of Catholic Pentecostalism in 1967. Though Catholics had shown a growing interest in the Holy Spirit during the nineteenth century, the struggles over the gifts of the Spirit, speaking in tongues, and the doctrine of "initial evidence" had been mainly a Protestant problem with little concern for Catholics. Most Protestants assumed that Catholics were not even Christians, much less candidates for the baptism in the Holy Spirit. On their part, Catholics before Vatican II tended to view Protestants as either heretics or sub-normal Christians without authentic clergy or valid sacraments.

For most of the century, ecumenical relations were also a Protestant preoccupation. The Federal and World Councils Churches were entirely made up of Protestant and Orthodox Christians, with no Catholic participation and seemingly little or no interest. On the Protestant side, the ecumenical movement was entirely an enterprise of the "liberal" churches, although the original ecumenical impulses were generated by evangelicals in the nineteenth century.

One reason for the Catholic Church's lack of interest in American ecumenism was the great growth of the church in the last half of the nineteenth century. In the 1880's millions of Catholic immigrants flooded into America from southern and eastern Europe. By 1900, the Roman Catholic Church was by far the largest denomination in the United States. The first half of the twentieth century continued to be a period of unbroken growth in both numbers and influence for the American Catholic church. After World War II, and especially after the election of John F. Kennedy to the presidency in 1960, Catholics began to speak of the "post-Protestant era" and of the day when an absolute majority of Americans would belong to the Roman church.[1]

This dream was to be rudely shaken by the end of the 1960's as the Catholic church in America experienced changes so dramatic that one could hardly recognize it as the same church. Between 1960 and 1970, the church's long history of steady growth came to an end. Catholic families became smaller as a result of the widespread practice of artificial birth control, in open disregard for the church's teachings. The few conversions to the faith came mainly as the result of marriages with non-Catholics.

Then came the disasters that began to stagger the church. Thousands of priests, monks, and nuns began to forsake their vocations and return to the secular world. The system of Roman Catholic parochial schools, once the crowning gem of the American church, began closing their doors; at one point an average of one school closed every week. Seminary enrollments saw similar declines. Protestants and Catholics together now began to speak of a "post-Christian America," as the mainline Protestant denominations also began to shrink.

At the beginning of the 1960's, Pope John XXIII sent a tremor through the religious world by calling together the first council in nearly a century. The new council, called Vatican II, met from 1962 to 1965. According to Pope John, the council was for the purpose of "opening the windows so that the church could get a breath of fresh air." As they gathered in Rome, the 2,500 bishops from all parts of the world spoke

1. Vinson Synan, *In the Latter Days,* pp. 97-118.

openly of a "new Reformation" within the church — even to the point of the "reformulation of doctrines." This was the first time such language had been used in the church since Martin Luther's day.[2]

Pope John had also spoken of the council prophetically as a "new Pentecost" and directed every Catholic in the world to pray daily during the three year's duration of the conclave: "Lord renew your wonders in this our day as by a new Pentecost." Could he know that this very prayer would be fulfilled within a year of the closing of the Council? In fact, one of the four presidents of Vatican II, Leon Joseph Cardinal Suenens of Belgium, would play a leading part in the charismatic renewal that soon broke out in the church.

What happened in Roman Catholicism after 1962 was more than a "reformation" — it was, in the words of David F. Wells, a *Revolution in Rome*. For the first time since the Council of Trent in the sixteenth century, the Catholic church abandoned its monolithic "fortress theology" designed to halt the progress of the Protestant reformation, and opened the door for many competing theologies to exist and contend for influence within the church.[3]

The Second Vatican Council ended in 1965 with a revolutionary program that took years to be fully implemented in Catholic churches around the world. The most striking change required the Mass to be said in the languages of the people rather than in Latin. The priests were required to face the congregation during the service. Hymns were to be sung by the congregations, instead of being chanted by the priests and choirs. The scriptures were read by the laity as well as the clergy. Although intercommunion was still forbidden, Catholics were encouraged to pray with other Christians. The informal "folk Mass" (or guitar Mass) was allowed. Nuns were permitted to abandon their traditional habits for conventional dress.

Because of these changes, which indeed seemed too revolutionary to Catholic traditionalists, the church became much less "strange" to Protestants, especially when Catholics began to sing the "theme song of the Reformation," Martin Luther's "A Mighty Fortress Is Our God." For

2. See David F. Wells, *Revolution in Rome* (Downers Grove, IL, 1972). David du Plessis was the only Pentecostal "observer" to Vatican II.

3. Kilian McDonnell and Arnold Bittlinger, *The Baptism in the Holy Spirit as an Ecumenical Problem* (South Bend, IN, 1972), pp. 29-30. See McDonnell's *Catholic Pentecostalism: Problems in Evaluation.*

the first time, Catholic priests began to share in Protestant services and Protestants were invited to speak in Catholic services. A new ecumenical age began in 1960 with the establishment of the Secretariat for the Promotion of Christian Unity in Rome, which immediately initiated dialogues with the Protestant churches. The fact that John XXIII spoke of Protestants as "separated brethren" opened the way for a mutual respect and appreciation that made ecumenical dialogue possible.

It was in the aftermath of these amazing changes that the Pentecostal movement suddenly appeared in the American church. In some ways the phenomenon of Catholic Pentecostalism was an unexpected and miraculous event, but a closer study shows that there were many developments over a long period of time that prepared the ground for Pentecostalism in the Roman church. In *Aspects of Pentecostal Charismatic Origins,* Father Edward O' Connor listed the following "hidden roots" of the charismatic renewal movement in the Catholic church.[4]

Pope Leo XIII and Elena Guerra

In 1897, Pope Leo XIII called for every Catholic in the world to say a novena annually to the Holy Spirit between the feasts of Ascension and Pentecost, at the suggestion of Elena Guerra, a nun from Lucca, Italy who led a group of sisters dedicated to the Christian education of young girls. As a novice, she had taken a lifelong devotion to the Holy Spirit and often observed a novena (nine-day cycle of prayer) to the Holy Spirit as part of her spiritual devotions. But she soon became distressed at the lack of attention and devotion paid by Catholics to the Holy Spirit. In 1897, against the advice of friends, Guerra wrote a letter to Pope Leo XIII suggesting that he proclaim a universal novena to the Holy Spirit between the feasts of Ascension and Pentecost to commemorate the days that the Apostles had waited in the upper room for the outpouring of the Holy Spirit.

To the astonishment of her friends, the Pope not only read her letter, but later in 1897 issued an encyclical entitled *On the Holy Spirit,* where he not only proclaimed the annual novena to the Holy Spirit, but also called the church to a new appreciation of the Holy Spirit and the gifts of the Spirit. In response, millions of Catholics, from theologians

4. O'Connor, "The Hidden Roots," pp. 169-92. Much of this section is taken from Synan, *In the Latter Days,* pp. 97-105.

to the humble faithful turned their attention to the Holy Spirit in a way that had not been seen in the church for centuries. Guerra also suggested that the Pope dedicate the new twentieth century to the Holy Spirit by singing "Come Holy Spirit" on the first day of the century. This was done on January 1, 1901.[5]

The Theology of Charisms

The positive response of Pope Leo to the letter of Elena Guerra was probably the result of a developing "theology of charisms" which had its beginnings in Germany in the 1820's through two German Catholic theologians, Johann Adam Moehler and Matthias Scheeben. Moehler's major work was *Unity in the Church,* published in 1825, which depicted the church as a charismatic body constituted and enlivened by the Holy Spirit. The later work of Scheeben (during the 1870's and 80's) laid stress on the unique action of the Holy Spirit in the formation of the Christian life. The effect of Moehler's and Scheeben's work was to bring into focus a "theology of the charismata" which resulted in a "revalorization" of the gifts of the Spirit, which had suffered a decline among both Catholics and Protestants during the bitter debates of the reformation era.[6]

Moehler and Scheeben opened a whole new school of interpretation of the ministries of the church. Their emphasis on the importance of the charisms in the church in modern times began to break down the generally accepted view of the cessation of the charismata. Both of these theologians broke new ground in relation to the Holy Spirit that was destined to bear much fruit in Vatican II and in the charismatic movement that followed.

5. O'Connor, "The Hidden Roots," pp. 171-72. An authoritative source for the background and text of the *Encyclical* is *Divinum Illud Munus, Acta Sanctae Sedis,* 29, pp. 896-97, 644-58. The English translation is *On the Holy Ghost* (New York, 1944). See also Val Gaudet, "A Woman and the Pope," *New Covenant* 3, no. 4 (Oct. 1973): 4-6. Her full correspondence with the Pope is recorded in L. Cristiana, *Apotre du Saint-Esprit* (Paris: Apostolat des editions, 1963).

6. O'Connor, "Hidden Roots," pp. 172-74.

The Liturgical Movement

A development of extreme importance was the liturgical reform effort, which drastically changed the forms of Catholic worship. The liturgical movement also had its roots in the nineteenth-century and came to fruition in the twentieth. Essentially, the movement was concerned with helping Christians understand and participate in the words and forms of public worship in order to make the church more meaningful to modern humanity. Implicit in the movement was an underlying need for the reform of corporate worship.

Although the sources of liturgical reform could be traced to the romantic movement of the early 1800's, its actual effects were first felt in the monasteries later in the century. In general, those promoting the reform wished the church to be seen less as a juridical body and more as a worshipping organism. By the twentieth century, their influence had gone beyond the monasteries and into the mainstream of the church.

After World War II, Pope Pius XII gave impetus to the movement in his encyclical on liturgy entitled, "Mediator Dei," in which he authorized changes in the rites for Holy Week and called for more lay participation in the Mass. Liturgical reform did not enter the full lifestream of the church, however, until the Second Vatican Council. New texts on the liturgy reflected the great advances in biblical studies made by the church in the previous decades. Also such innovations as guitars, hand-clapping, and a more biblically oriented sermon added many of the elements that were instantly adopted by charismatics after Vatican II. The liturgical movement also had an effect on Protestants, leading them to more frequent celebrations of the Eucharist, a new respect for the traditional "Catholic" roots of Christian worship, and an updating of archaic expressions of worship. On both Protestant and Catholic sides, there was a deeper appreciation of the liturgy as a proclamation of the gospel.

The Lay Movement

One of the bitter controversies of the Reformation concerned the place of laymen in the church. Martin Luther's teaching on the "priesthood of all believers" seemed to Catholics to be an attack on the unique ministry of the priesthood. The resulting positions adopted at the Council of Trent were primarily in reaction to the challenge of the Reformers who seemed to be granting all the privileges of the clergy to unordained laymen. For centuries, the Catholic laity, for all practical purposes, had no part to play in the liturgies or the leadership of the church.

The dignity and authentic ministry of the Catholic laity has come about due to the efforts of many important lay persons who in the past three centuries became effective spokesmen for the church. Also contributing to the rise of the laity was Pope Pius X (1903-14) who proclaimed that lay people were not only "crisis ministers" in the absence of priests, but were to:

> . . . share in his priestly function of offering spiritual worship for the glory of God and the salvation of men. For this reason, the laity, dedicated to Christ and anointed by the Holy Spirit, are marvelously called and equipped to produce in themselves ever more abundant fruits of the Holy Spirit.[7]

It is important to note that the first Catholic charismatic leaders were lay persons deeply involved in the liturgical reform movement before their baptism in the Holy Spirit in 1967. The Pentecostal movement in the Catholic church would be unimaginable without the thousands of talented lay leaders who gave it their imprint.

The Biblical Movement

Another major theme of the Protestant Reformation was the emphasis on scripture as the norm for faith and practice among Christians. In contrast to Protestantism, Catholics continued to stress the importance of tradition as well as scripture as a source of authority in the church. The divisions brought on by the Reformation caused a fear among Catholics of untrained Bible-reading and the attendant possibility of heresy and schism.

Although Catholics honored and reverenced the Bible as the word of God, they seldom read it simply for devotional purposes. Meanwhile, scholarly study of the scriptures suffered greatly among Catholics. While Protestants engaged in profound biblical research from Luther's day

---

7. O'Connor, "Hidden Roots," p. 177.

onward, Catholic biblical studies lagged behind. By the nineteenth and twentieth centuries, the major biblical research and scholarship was being done by Protestants. For Catholics, the scriptures were read in the Mass but not read by the masses.

After World War II, there occurred a resurgence of scholarship among Catholics around the world. A great effort was made on the part of Catholic scholars to catch up with their Protestant brothers in the academic understanding of the word of God. It was the charismatic renewal, however, that brought to the fore a hunger to read the Bible as a daily spiritual resource for the average church member. An intense taste for reading, enjoying, and applying the scriptures to everyday life was one of the most striking aspects of the renewal after 1967. But the roots of this resurgence in biblical studies had already taken place in the church long before.

The Ecumenical Movement

Like the biblical movement, the ecumenical movement had its origins in nineteenth-century Protestantism, flowered in the middle of the twentieth century, and only then sent its roots into the Roman Catholic Church.

Ecumenism has a long and varied history in the life of the church. The Great Schism of 1054 between the Roman Catholic Church and Eastern Orthodoxy has not been healed to this day, despite many attempts at reconciliation. The schisms of the Reformation period also continue after 500 years. The present religious settlement came as a political result of the Peace of Westphalia in 1648, when the European powers accepted pluralism and denominationalism. The "toleration of separation" which became the order of the day in the seventeenth century has persisted till now.

The road from pluralism back to ecumenism began with the creation of the London Sunday School Union in 1803, which marked the first joint effort of separate denominations since the Reformation. Other examples of nineteenth-century cooperation included the American Bible Society (1816), the YMCA (1851), and the Christian Endeavor (1881).

Twentieth-century ecumenism began with the Edinburgh conference of 1910, which sought to coordinate the world missions efforts of several evangelical denominations. The new idea then gaining currency was that competing missions programs gave a poor impression of Christian unity in pagan nations. Other twentieth-century developments included: the World Conference on Faith and Order (1927), the National Association of Evangelicals (1943), and the World Council of Churches (1948).

For Roman Catholics after the Council of Trent (1545-63), the road to unity meant only one thing, a return to Rome on the part of the Protestants. In 1928, Pope Pius XI reaffirmed the traditional Catholic position in his encyclical, *Mortalium Animos,* stating that the only avenue of unity was conversion to the Roman Catholic church and submission to the papacy and the canonical structures of the church. Perhaps because of the challenges of Fascism and Communism, coupled with the world Depression, the Catholic view of ecumenism began to change in the late 1930's. The dislocations and persecutions suffered by Catholics, Protestants, and especially the Jews of Europe caused a new openness after World War II that had not been seen in 400 years. The apostle of the most recent view of unity in the church was Yves Congar, a French Dominican, who in 1937 publish *Chretiens Desunis,* the textbook of modern Catholic ecumenism. In this epochal work, Congar pointed out the possibility that some authentic Catholic elements may have been richly developed in some non-Roman communions. Future unity would not obscure these differences in a "lowest common denominator" fashion, but would be a "sharing of treasures" across denominational lines.[8]

The man who began to put Congar's ideas into effect was Augustin Cardinal Bea, who was responsible for the creation of the Secretariat for the Promotion of Christian Unity in 1960. This body began to conduct "dialogues" with other Christian bodies after 1960 that continue to this day. In Vatican II, the vision of Congar became the official position of the Roman Catholic Church. By official decree of the council, the church of Jesus Christ "subsists" (rather than "consists") in the Roman Catholic Church. Other Christians are "separated brethren." The ecumenical task is, therefore, to discover the authentic elements in churches not in communion with the Church of Rome. Other Christian churches are "sister churches" which also "subsist" as part of the universal church, although the liturgies and theologies of these churches might not be as fully and richly developed as in the Roman communion.

If the charismatic renewal had begun in the Roman Catholic

8. Yves Congar, *Chrétiens Désunis* (1937).

Church before Vatican II, it would probably have been viewed as a "Protestant" phenomenon and therefore forbidden to Catholics. But by 1967, when glossolalia first appeared publicly in Catholic circles, Pentecostalism was seen as one of the "treasures" of the church to be freely shared by Catholics.

The Cursillo Movement

The Cursillo movement began in Spain in 1949 as an attempt to renew the personal faith of Catholics by means of a three-day retreat called *cursillo* (i.e., "short course"). Originally called the *Cursillo de Cristianidad,* it was first used by Bishop Juan Hervas of Ciudad Real, Spain. The movement spread to Latin America in the 1950's and eventually to the United States by way of the Hispanics of the southwest.

Cursillo consists of five "meditations" and five lessons on Christian doctrine given by priests and lay persons to church members who wish to deepen their faith. Discussion sessions show how to make practical applications of the ten talks. With the number of participants usually about forty persons, sessions are convivial in spirit and often enlivened by songs and skits.

The effect of the cursillo was to evangelize Catholics who had been "sacramentalized" but who lacked a deep understanding of what it meant to be a Christian. Many of the first Pentecostal Catholics not only had attended cursillos, but were leaders in the movement.

Vatican II, Pope John XXIII, and Cardinal Suenens

Pope John XXIII convened Vatican II in 1962 while many of these reform movements were reaching their peak of influence. Never was a council better timed to catch the "winds of the Spirit" that were blowing in the church. As Catholics followed Pope John in praying for a renewal of signs and wonders "in this our day as by a new Pentecost," steps were taken in the council to assure that such a Pentecost would be accepted when it did occur.

Pope John had called the council as a "sudden inspiration" of the Holy Spirit directed towards advancing Christian unity. In the last message he gave to the bishops, John predicted that when all the reforms and decrees of the Council had been put into effect, "then will dawn the new Pentecost which is the object of our yearning."[9]

One of the four "presidents" of the council was the Primate of Belgium, Leon Joseph Cardinal Suenens, who was one of the "liberal" prelates calling for change and renewal in the church. The only classical Pentecostal leader present was David du Plessis, who came as an official "observer." Suenens and du Plessis were destined to play major roles in the Catholic charismatic renewal that unfolded shortly after the completion of the Council.

As Vatican II progressed, many documents reflected an emphasis on the Holy Spirit and the charismatic nature of the church. Leading this focus on the person and work of the Holy Spirit were the bishops from Chile. As mentioned earlier, Chile had been experiencing a mighty surge of Pentecostalism since 1909, and the Chilean prelates had probably noted its effects. Altogether, the conciliar documents made reference to the Holy Spirit a total of 258 times.

When the old question of the cessation of the charismata surfaced, the council came down squarely on the side of the present-day manifestation of all the gifts of the Spirit. The issue was joined after the first reading of the Constitution on the Church, which stated that the Lord allotted his gifts "to everyone according as He will (I Cor. 12:11), and he tributes special graces among the faithful of every rank." It further stated that these charismatic gifts were "widely diffused" and are "to be received with thanksgiving and consolation for they are exceedingly suitable and useful for the needs of the church."

During the discussions that followed this reading, Cardinal Ruffini of Palermo, Italy, offered the following protest:

> It plainly implies that in our age many of the faithful are endowed with many charismatic gifts, but this is plainly contradicted by history and by daily experience. For the charisms . . . were abundant at the beginning of the church; but after that they gradually decreased and have almost completely ceased. . . . Contrary to the opinion of many of our separated brethren, who speak freely of the ministry of charismatics in the church, they are extremely rare and quite exceptional.[10]

9. O'Connor, "Hidden Roots," pp. 183-88.
10. O'Connor, "Hidden Roots," pp. 185-86.

Many of the bishops immediately disagreed with this statement of the traditional views of the church. On behalf of these bishops, Cardinal Suenens gave the classic reply which later became a "Magna Carta" for Catholic charismatics:

> This document says very little about the charisms of the faithful; this can suggest the impression that we are dealing here with a phenomenon that is merely peripheral and accidental to the life of the Church. But it is now time to bring out more explicitly and thoroughly the vital importance of these charisms for the building up of the Mystical Body. We must at all costs avoid giving the impression that the hierarchical structure of the Church is an administrative apparatus with no intimate connection with the charismatic gifts of the Holy Spirit which are diffused throughout the Church.
>
> To St. Paul, the Church of Christ does not appear as some administrative organization, but as a living, organic ensemble of gifts, charisms, and services. The Holy Spirit is given to all Christians, and to each one in particular; and He in turn gives to each and every one gifts and charisms "which differ according to the grace bestowed upon us." (Rom. 12:6)[11]

Suenens's plea won out over the traditionalist view and the groundwork was laid for the approval of the charismatic renewal only three years later. Usually the Spirit moves "wherever he wills," and the theologians attempt to explain things after the fact. This time, the theologians explained and approved charismatic renewal before it began. This is one of those unique times in history when the theologians were ahead of the prophets.

A "Surprise of the Holy Spirit"

With all of this preparation, it was nearly inevitable that Pentecostalism would break out in the Roman church. The only question was where it would happen, and when it would begin. These questions were soon answered in what Cardinal Suenens called a "surprise of the Holy Spirit."

11. O'Connor, "Hidden Roots," pp. 185-86. See also Francis Sullivan, *Charisms and Charismatic Renewal* (Ann Arbor, MI, 1982), pp. 9-15; Kilian McDonnell, *Charismatic Renewal and the Churches;* and Kilian McDonnell and George T. Montague, *Christian Initiation and Baptism in the Spirit.*

The Catholic Pentecostal movement began in Pittsburgh, Pennsylvania, at Duquesne University, a school run appropriately enough by the Holy Ghost Fathers. In 1966, two Duquesne University lay theology professors, Ralph Kiefer and Bill Storey, began a spiritual search which led them to a couple of recently published books: David Wilkerson's *The Cross and the Switchblade,* and John Sherrill's *They Speak with Other Tongues.* After reading these books, the two men began a search of the Pittsburgh area for someone who had received the baptism in the Holy Ghost with the accompaniment of tongues. In time, with the help of an Episcopal priest in a Presbyterian-led prayer group, Kiefer and Storey were baptized in the Holy Spirit and spoke languages they had never learned.[12]

These two Spirit-filled professors then made plans for a weekend retreat for several friends to seek an outpouring of the Holy Spirit in the Catholic Church. About twenty professors, graduate students, and their wives gathered in Pittsburgh over the weekend of February 17-19, 1967, for the first Catholic Pentecostal prayer meeting on record. The participants were asked to read the first four chapters of the Acts of the Apostles and *The Cross and the Switchblade.* The meetings were held in a large retreat house known as the Ark and the Dove, while the gathering was sponsored by a campus group called Chi Rho. In time, this gathering was dubbed "the Duquesne weekend."

> The Holy Spirit hovered over the Ark and the Dove during that fantastic weekend. After an intensive study of the book of Acts, and a day devoted to prayer and study, many of the participants were anxious to seek for the baptism in the Holy Spirit. But a birthday party for one of the priests had been planned for Saturday night. As the party began, a sense of conviction and expectancy pervaded the atmosphere. Soon, one student after another slipped out of the party and went upstairs to the chapel to pray.[13]

Strange things began to happen to these young people as they began to seek the Lord for Pentecostal fullness. A student by the name of David Mangan entered the room and was suddenly "slain in the Spirit," falling prostrate on the floor. He reported the following experiences:

12. Kevin and Dorothy Ranaghan, *The Catholic Pentecostal Movement,* pp. 6-16; see O' Connor, *The Pentecostal Movement in the Catholic Church,* pp. 39-43; see also *New Covenant,* Feb. 1973, pp. 1-17.

13. Synan, *In the Latter Days,* p. 110.

I cried harder than I ever cried in my life, but I did not shed one tear. All of a sudden Jesus Christ was so real and so present that I could feel Him all around. I was overcome with such a feeling of love that I cannot begin to describe it.

Later the entire group left the party downstairs and gathered in the chapel for the first totally Catholic Pentecostal prayer meeting. Patricia Gallagher described the meeting in this new "upper room":

That night the Lord brought the whole group into the chapel. I found my prayers pouring forth that the others might come to know him, too. My former shyness about praying aloud was completely gone as the Holy Spirit spoke through me. The professors then laid hands on some of the students but most of us received the "Baptism in the Spirit" while kneeling before the blessed sacrament in prayer. Some of us started speaking in tongues, others received gifts of discernment, prophecy, and wisdom. But the most important gift was the fruit of love which bound the whole community together. In the Lord's spirit we found a unity we had long tried to achieve on our own."[14]

As these Catholic seekers prayed through to Pentecost, many things familiar to classical Pentecostals began to take place. Some laughed uncontrollably "in the Spirit", while one young man rolled across the floor in ecstasy. Shouting praises to the Lord, weeping, and speaking in tongues characterized this beginning of the movement in the Catholic Church. Small wonder they were called "Catholic Pentecostals" by the public and the press when news spread about the strange events in Pittsburgh.[15]

The fire kindled at Duquesne University soon spread to Notre Dame University in South Bend, Indiana. This outbreak came after a letter from Ralph Kiefer sparked the interest of several student and faculty leaders who were also seeking a spiritual renewal of the church. After some investigation and initial skepticism, a group of some nine students gathered in the apartment of Bert Ghezzi, where they were

14. Ranaghan, *The Catholic Pentecostal Movement*, pp. 26, 35. The background of the Duquesne weekend as well as many eyewitness accounts is given in Patti Gallagher Mansfield's *As by a New Pentecost: The Dramatic Beginning of the Catholic Charismatic Renewal* (Steubenville, OH, 1992).

15. O' Connor, *Pentecostal Movement in the Catholic Church*, pp. 31-35. See also Paul Gray, *New Covenant*, Feb. 1973, p. 8.

baptized in the Holy Spirit, though without manifesting overt spiritual gifts. For further help, they made contact with Ray Bullard, a member of the Assemblies of God and president of the South Bend chapter of the Full Gospel Businessmen. Bert Ghezzi describes how this group of Catholic intellectuals received the gift of tongues:

> We went to Ray's house the following week and met in a basement room with eleven Pentecostal ministers and their wives from all over Indiana. They spent the evening attempting to persuade us that if you were baptized in the Spirit you had to be speaking in tongues. We let them know we were open to praying in tongues, but we held fast to conviction that we were already baptized in the Spirit because we could see it in our lives. The issue got resolved because we were willing to speak in tongues if it were not seen as a theological necessity to being baptized in the Holy Spirit. At a certain point, we said we were willing to give it a try, and a man explained to us what was involved. Very late that evening, sometime after midnight, down in that basement room, the brothers lined us up on one side of the room and the ministers on the other side of the room, and they began to pray in tongues and to walk toward us with outstretched hands. Before they reached us, many of us began to pray and sing in tongues.

After a time of praying in tongues, Ghezzi says, the students' Pentecostal friends asked them when they would be leaving the Catholic church and joining a Pentecostal one:

> The question actually left us a little shocked. Our response was that we wouldn't be leaving the Catholic Church, that being baptized in the Holy Spirit was completely compatible with our belief in the Catholic Church. We assured our friends that we had a great respect for them and that we would have fellowship with them, but we would be remaining in the Catholic Church.
>
> I think there's something significant about the fact that those of us who were baptized in the Holy Spirit then would never have thought about abandoning the Roman Catholic Church.
>
> Our Pentecostal friends had seen Catholics join Pentecostal churches when they were baptized in the Spirit. Because we did not do that, the Catholic charismatic renewal became possible.[16]

---

16. Personal interview with Bert Ghezzi.

The events at Duquesne were now repeated at Notre Dame — the intellectual capital of American Catholicism. The following passage describes a typical Catholic prayer meeting on campus. After much singing, praying, and Bible reading:

> . . . The leader announced that it was time for anyone who desired to be prayed over to receive the gifts of the Spirit. About half a dozen requested this, among them the two priests. After a few practical instructions about how to recognize the gift of tongues when it comes, five or six of those who had already received the baptism in the Spirit gathered in a semicircle around the first person to be prayed over. They laid their hands on his head, and started to pray, at first in English. After a few moments one of them began to speak something that sounded very much like Arabic. A moment later, another also went into another tongue, which sounded entirely different. Before long, all those who were praying over the "candidate" were praying in tongues."[17]

Campus newspapers soon began to report the news. The *National Catholic Reporter* picked up the story of the Notre Dame Pentecost and gave the following evaluation:

> There have been attempts to explain the Pentecostal movement at Notre Dame as a return to the devotional aspects of the Church. Some say that the movement attracts people with emotional problems. Still others say it creates a false community that needs constant reinforcement. And, of course, there are those who explain the whole phenomenon in terms such as "fanatic," "cracked," "off the deep end," or "nut." But the situation is not that simple.
>
> It would be so convenient to say that these Catholic Pentecostals were underfed, high-strung, groping intellectual misfits in a wholesome atmosphere of all-American football-hood. It would be quite convenient, but it would also be quite untrue. There seems to be no one level of conformity in this group except a common experience.[18]

In fact, the new Pentecostals at Notre Dame included several respected professors on the theology faculty, including Edward O'Connor, J. Massingberd Ford, and Kevin Ranaghan, a teacher at nearby St.

17. Ranaghan, *The Catholic Pentecostal Movement*, pp. 38-57.
18. Ranaghan, *The Catholic Pentecostal Movement*, p. 38.

Mary's College. Others baptized in the Holy Spirit at Notre Dame who became leaders in the movement were Steve Clark and Ralph Martin, staff members in the national secretariat of the Cursillo movement; George Martin, a worker in adult education for the Diocese of Lansing; Paul DeCelles, a professor of Physics at Notre Dame; and a group of students including Bert Ghezzi, Jim Cavnar, Gerry Rauch, Dorothy Ranaghan, Phil O'Mara, and Kerry Koller.[19]

From this group of capable and dedicated young people came the major leadership of the Catholic charismatic renewal movement. Most of them were in their twenties. Under their talented and inspired guidance Pentecostalism began to spread like wildfire among Catholics in the United States and ultimately around the world.

The early growth of the movement was astounding. New prayer groups sprang up daily around the nation. A communications network revealed a stunning acceptance of the movement among clergy and laity alike. In a short time, Pentecostalism was recognized as the fastest growing movement in the Catholic Church. This growth was dramatized by the international conferences convened annually in South Bend after 1967. Attendance at these conferences tended to triple every year for several years. The early attendance figures were as follows:[20]

1967	85	1971	4,000
1968	150	1972	12,000
1969	450	1973	22,000
1970	1,279	1974	30,000

By 1974, the movement had abandoned the term "Pentecostal" in favor of the more neutral "charismatic" in order not to be confused with the older Pentecostals. That same year there were estimated to be 1,800 prayer groups in America and 2,400 around the world, with the number of worldwide participants estimated at 350,000. Among these were about 2,000 priests.

Catholic Pentecostalism grew not only in size but in influence during the 1970's. By 1973, at least one Cardinal, Suenens of Belgium, had not only joined the movement, but was appointed by Pope Paul VI as advisor on charismatic developments. Additionally, several American

---

19. Ralph Martin, *Hungry for God* (London, 1976), pp. 10-20.
20. O'Connor, *The Pentecostal Movement in the Catholic Church*, pp. 99-102.

and Canadian bishops publicly identified with the charismatics. The leading American bishop was Joseph McKinney, auxiliary bishop of Grand Rapids, Michigan, who became the liaison between the Catholic Charismatic Renewal Service Committee and the American bishops.

A key to the rapid development of Pentecostalism within the Catholic Church was the careful theological attention devoted to it almost from the beginning. The earliest theological reflections were those of the Benedictine monk and scholar, Kilian McDonnell, who in 1970 published a ground-breaking study entitled *Catholic Pentecostalism: Problems in Evaluation,* which attempted to place the Pentecostal experience within the context of Catholic tradition.

Other early works that helped forge a Catholic charismatic theology were Edward O'Connor's *The Pentecostal Movement in the Catholic Church* (1971); Kevin and Dorothy Ranaghan's *Catholic Pentecostals* (1969); J. Massingberd Ford's *The Pentecostal Experience: A New Direction for Catholics* (1970); and Donald Gelpi's *Pentecostalism: a Theological Viewpoint* (1971). Because of these studies, Pentecostalism was received by Catholics as a phenomenon in full accord with their traditions and not as a Protestant import.

Another key to the early progress of the movement was the positive but cautious attitude of the bishops. In their 1969 "Report of the Committee on Doctrine" the bishops concluded that "theologically the movement has legitimate reasons for existence. It has a strong Biblical basis." They also observed that participants "experienced progress in their spiritual life," were "attracted to the reading of Scripture," and developed "a deeper understanding of their faith." At the end of the report, the bishops stated, "it is the conclusion of the Committee on Doctrine that the movement should at this point not be inhibited but allowed to develop."[21]

And develop it did! By 1975, the Catholic Pentecostal movement had reached Rome itself. In an international conference held in a tent over the ancient catacombs, over 10,000 Catholic charismatics gathered to bring their witness to the very seat of the papacy. At the feast of Pentecost, 1975, these Spirit-filled faithful joined a capacity crowd of 25,000 at St. Peter's to hear Pope Paul VI. Near the end of the service, when the Pentecostals began to "sing in the Spirit," the organist and choir joined them in an extemporaneous voicing of the "eightfold Alleluia," the international anthem of the movement.

21. McDonnell, *Presence, Power, Praise,* vol. 1, pp. 207-10.

On Pentecost Monday, Cardinal Suenens conducted the first specifically charismatic Mass ever held at St. Peter's. Young American charismatic leaders from Ann Arbor, Michigan delivered prophecies from the high altar of the basilica. Joyful and anointed singing filled the church. In his message to the charismatics at the end of the Mass, Pope Paul said prophetically:

> How then could this "spiritual renewal" not be a "chance" for the church and for the world? And how, in this case, could one not take all the means to ensure that it remains so? . . . It ought to rejuvenate the world, give it back a spirituality, a soul, a religious thought, it ought to reopen its closed lips to prayer and open its mouth to song, to joy, to hymns, and to witnessing. It will be very fortuitous for our times, for our brothers, that there should be a generation of young people, who shout out to the world the greatness of the God of Pentecost. . . .[22]

22. McDonnell, *Presence, Power, Praise,* vol. 3, pp. 70-76; *New Covenant,* July 1975, pp. 23-25.

CHAPTER THIRTEEN

The Charismatic Explosion

Come before me, with broken hearts and contrite spirit
For the body of my Son is broken. . . .

Prophecy given by Ralph Martin to the
Kansas City Conference, July 1977

The sudden and unexpected appearance of Catholic Pentecostalism, soon known as the "Catholic charismatic renewal," was a significant turning point in Pentecostal history. While presenting formidable theological problems, the very idea that the Roman Catholic Church could tolerate and even encourage Pentecostalism gave the movement a sudden respectability that raised eyebrows in the other mainline churches. The burgeoning crowds that attended the various Catholic charismatic conferences during the 1970's sent many churchmen back to the theological drawing boards to make new assessments of their own understanding.

It became clear during this decade that the mainline charismatics had developed a new view of the "baptism in the Holy Spirit" that allowed Pentecostalism to flourish in the historic churches without the "cultural baggage" and rigid exclusivism espoused by many of the Pentecostal churches. The Wesleyan teaching of an instantaneous second experience of sanctification was not adopted by these new charismatic groups, although much stress was laid on holiness as the goal of a Spirit-filled Christian lifestyle. Older Pentecostals were occasionally scandalized to hear of charismatics who used tobacco, drank wine, and also spoke in tongues. Hundreds of Pentecostal pulpits shook with indignation at the very thought.[1]

Even more incomprehensible to the older Pentecostals were claims by Catholics that their experiences of the rosary, the confessional, and devotion to Mary were deepened after receiving the baptism in the Holy Spirit. Because of such radical departures from the traditional understanding of Pentecostalism, some pastors and denominational leaders denounced the entire charismatic movement as a Satanic plot designed to replace the genuine latter rain with a diabolical counterfeit.[2]

A Charismatic Theology

Because the classical Pentecostals were either unwilling or unable to contribute to the developing mainline charismatic theology, charismatic scholars soon developed their own new position on the "baptism in the Holy Spirit" which became known as the "organic view" of the experience. Prime movers in this development were Kilian McDonnell (Roman Catholic), Arnold Bittlinger (Lutheran), and Larry Christenson (Lutheran). This theology was presented in developed form in Larry Christenson's 1976 book, *The Charismatic Renewal Among Lutherans.*

Essentially, the "organic view" saw the Pentecostal experience as an essential part of the "rites of initiation," i.e., baptism, confirmation, and the Eucharist. Being "baptized in the Holy Spirit" was thus identical with water baptism, while the later experiences of tongues and other gifts of the Spirit constituted a "release" or "actualization" of the grace given and received at baptism.

This view was contrasted with the classical Pentecostal view of a separate "baptism in the Holy Ghost" subsequent to conversion and water baptism, with the necessary "initial evidence" of speaking in tongues. Though most of the new charismatics rejected the classical

1. See Synan, *In The Latter Days,* pp. 119-35.
2. For a negative view, see Ray Hughes's "A Traditional Pentecostal Looks at the New Pentecostals," *Christianity Today,* June 7, 1974, pp. 6-10; see also Russell Spittler, *Perspectives on the New Pentecostalism* (Grand Rapids, MI, 1976).

Pentecostal position on the necessity of tongues, they nevertheless emphasized this "initial evidence." Most stated, as Christenson did, that "those who pray for the filling of the Spirit, in the context of charismatic renewal, usually speak in tongues, either at once or somewhat afterwards."[3]

To avoid the idea of "two baptisms" and to adhere to the principle of "one Lord, one faith, one baptism," a person could be baptized in the Holy Spirit at water baptism (as an infant) while the gifts of the Spirit could appear in one's later Christian experience. This view also, it was claimed, would avoid the pitfall of dividing the churches into two groups, one "spirit-filled," and the other "second-class" members who had received "the baptism."

It became common, therefore, for some charismatics to accept a "baptism in the Spirit" by faith without the accompanying manifestations while later seeking to "yield to tongues," not as "initial evidence" but as one of the authenticating gifts of the Spirit. In other words, most charismatics felt that their experience was somehow incomplete if they failed to speak in tongues. Most of the early charismatics did in fact speak with tongues and considered glossolalia integral to their Pentecostal experience.

Armed with a new theological respectability and without the trappings of sectarian warfare, the charismatic movement entered the mainline churches in the 1970's more as a cloudburst than a gentle shower. Thousands of ministers, priests, and pastors received the Pentecostal experience in hope of renewing their own spiritual lives as well as that of their parishes and even their denominations. At the grass-roots level, several million lay members received "the baptism" and chose to stay in their churches in an attempt to spread the good news among their own people.

The Jesus People

This new charismatic wave of the 1970's was also dramatically highlighted by the "Jesus People" revolution, a youth revival that began

3. Christenson, *Charismatic Renewal among Lutherans,* p. 48. See also Quebedeaux, *The New Charismatics,* vol. 2, pp. 127-92. For a wide-ranging examination of the history of tongues in the Pentecostal/charismatic tradition, see Vinson Synan, "The Role of Tongues as Initial Evidence," pp. 67-82.

in California and spread rapidly across the nation. One of the leaders in this movement was the Reverend Chuck Smith, pastor of the tiny Calvary Chapel Foursquare Church in Costa Mesa, California. The Jesus people first came to his church in the form of a dozen "hippies" who were converted and accepted into the church, to the horror of old-line saints who failed to understand what was happening. In two frantic years, Smith was deluged with thousands of converts from the drug-oriented southern California hippie culture who crowded into his church to find salvation and deliverance from drugs. In a few months, Smith baptized some 15,000 converts in the waters of the Pacific Ocean and was forced to move his young congregation into a temporary tent seating 3,000 persons. By the end of the decade, Calvary Chapel built a church sanctuary seating 4,000 and counted over 25,000 in attendance at their regular Sunday services.[4]

The revival in the youth drug culture was presaged by the story of David Wilkerson, the founder of a national youth ministry known as "Teen Challenge." This Assemblies of God preacher left a comfortable middle-class pastorate in Philipsburg, Pennsylvania, in 1958 to minister to the young drug addicts of New York City. His ministry of deliverance to thousands of addicts won the admiration of Christians everywhere. He claimed that his "thirty second cure" for addiction, the baptism of the Holy Spirit, far surpassed the cure rates of federal programs for hard-drug addiction. In time his best-selling 1963 book, *The Cross and the Switchblade,* became a major influence in spreading the renewal to mainline churches.[5]

Similar stories of mass conversions from the hippie culture spread across America during the early 1970's. Coffeehouse ministries sprang up in major cities to minister to the thousands of street people. "Christian commune" ministries were formed in various rural areas to care for those who fled the institutional world of traditional churches. In most cases, Pentecostalism was the common denominator for these refugees from the drug culture. It seemed to be the only religious force powerful enough

4. Quebedeaux, *The New Charismatics,* vol. 2, pp. 130, 230-31. See also Ed Plowman, *The Jesus Movement in America* (Elgin, IL, 1971); Pat King, *The Jesus People Are Coming* (Plainfield, NJ, 1971); *Time,* Aug. 3, 1970, pp. 31-32.

5. Wilkerson's autobiographical *The Cross and the Switchblade* (New York, 1963) was one of fifteen books written by Wilkerson. See also F. M. Reynolds's "David Ray Wilkerson," in Burgess et al., *Dictionary of Pentecostal and Charismatic Movements,* pp. 884-85.

to break the drug habit. Wherever it developed, the charismatic movement attracted masses of young people, who combined the energy of contemporary "Gospel Rock" with the expressive freedom of praise and worship characteristic of the classical Pentecostals.

The mainline churches, confronted with this spiritual explosion, decided to try conserving the Pentecostal "new wine" in the "old bottles" of their respective institutions. Gone were the old denunciations and criticisms of "holy rollerism." Faced with huge membership losses, mainline church leaders seemed unwilling to write off the hippie converts who were gravitating to Pentecostal churches or to independent charismatic churches that catered to the counterculture. Great efforts were made to accommodate these charismatics into the life of the traditional churches.

The Churches Discern the Renewal

The vigor and force of the charismatic and Jesus movement forced the churches into a major reassessment. Around the world, diverse denominations appointed study commissions to report on the charismatic movement, which now seemed to have entered into every congregation in Christendom. In 1970, the United Presbyterian church became the first major denomination to issue a comprehensive report on the movement. This became a model for the other denominational reports that followed. In producing their report, the Presbyterians appointed a subcommittee made up of both theologians and specialists in the behavioral sciences. Unlike similar studies made earlier in the century, the commission concluded that there was "no evidence of pathology in the movement." As far as tongues were concerned, the report stated that "the practice of glossolalia should neither be despised nor forbidden; on the other hand, it should not be emphasized nor made the norm for Christian experience."[6]

Other major studies by the Episcopal church (1971), the American Lutheran church (1973), and the Lutheran Church in America (1974) were similar to the Presbyterian study of 1970. These documents also voiced concerns about possible abuses, but firmly stated that tongues-

6. For a copy of the report see McDonnell, *Presence, Power, Praise,* vol. 1, pp. 207-10, 221-81.

speakers could remain members in good standing of their respective churches.[7]

Although the early roots of the renewal lay historically in the Methodist tradition, the United Methodist Church produced its first major evaluation of the movement rather belatedly, in 1976. While noting that Pentecostalism had emerged from the Wesleyan tradition, the report stated that it "has little to do with Wesley's theology." Nevertheless, tongues-speakers were welcomed in Methodist churches; the most dramatic example was Oral Roberts's reception, in 1969, by the Boston Avenue Methodist Church in Tulsa, Oklahoma. Roberts was also admitted as a local preacher in the Oklahoma Conference of the Methodist Church by Bishop Angie Smith after promising that he would change neither his Pentecostal theology nor his divine healing methods. The Graduate School of Theology of Oral Roberts University, headed by Methodist theologian Dr. Jimmy Buskirk, was approved by the United Methodist Church in 1982 as a seminary for Methodist ministry. Beyond Methodism, ORU became the epicenter for training charismatic leaders for all churches.[8]

The response of the American Roman Catholic hierarchy continued to be positive and supportive during the 1970's. Influenced by the 1969 bishops' report, which stated that the movement "should not be inhibited but allowed to develop," a report from the American bishops in 1975 saw "positive and desirable directions" in the charismatic movement. The report also stated:

> Where the movement is making solid progress there is a strongly grounded faith in Jesus Christ as Lord. This in turn leads to a renewed interest in prayer, both private and group prayer. Many of those who belong to the movement experience a new sense of spiritual values, a heightened consciousness of the action of the Holy Spirit, the praise of God and a deepening personal commitment to Christ. Many, too, have grown in devotion to the Eucharist and partake more fruitfully in the sacramental life of the church. Reverence for the mother of the Lord takes on fresh meaning and many feel a deeper sense of attachment to the Church.[9]

7. McDonnell, *Presence, Power, Praise,* vol. 1, pp. 369-73, 547-66.

8. McDonnell, *Presence, Power, Praise,* vol. 2, pp. 270-90. For the ORU story see Roberts's *Expect a Miracle,* pp. 155-200.

9. McDonnell, *Presence, Power, Praise,* vol. 2, pp. 104-13; see p. 108.

International Roman Catholic reaction to the renewal was most fully expressed in three publications known as the *Documents,* issued under the authority of Leon Joseph Cardinal Suenens. These documents dealt with various aspects of renewal, as reflected in their titles: *Theological and Pastoral Orientations I* (1974), *Ecumenism II* (1978), and *Social Action* (1979). All these documents accept the validity of the renewal, reject the idea of the cessation of the charismata, and offer pastoral guidelines on how to integrate the renewal into the ongoing life of the church. In Suenens's famous phrase, renewal was a "stream of grace" which would succeed ultimately when it had disappeared into the lifestream of the church, bringing renewal to the Body of Christ through the world.[10]

The most negative assessments of the renewal came from the older holiness and fundamentalist churches that had rejected Pentecostalism earlier in the century. The Christian and Missionary Alliance, for example, confirmed in 1963 the "seek not-forbid not" dictum that had first been taught by A. B. Simpson in 1907. Southern Baptists and Nazarenes rejected the renewal out of hand, not on scriptural or theological grounds, but because Pentecostalism did not accord with their doctrines and traditions. The Lutheran Church–Missouri Synod in a 1972 report suggested that the charismatic movement was incompatible with Lutheran theology and practice.[11]

The World Council of Churches was late in issuing its position on the renewal, despite the incessant labors of David du Plessis to bring a Pentecostal witness to the organization. Its report on the Pentecostal/charismatic renewal appeared in 1980. A long and detailed document that relied largely on work done in previous mainline Protestant reports, the WCC report viewed the vigorous grass-roots ecumenicity of the renewal as "a sign of hope." This was especially true for the "tired ecumenists" of the World Council, who had never been able to gather large masses of people from different churches on the scale that the charismatics had done. Although doubtful of the commitment of charismatics to socio-political action, the report on the whole was positive and supportive of the spiritual and community-building aspects of the movement.[12]

10. McDonnell, *Presence, Power, Praise,* vol. 3, pp. 13-69, 82-174, 291-357.

11. McDonnell, *Presence, Power, Praise,* vol. 1, pp. 63-69, 219-20; vol. 2, pp. 114-15.

12. McDonnell, *Presence, Power, Praise,* vol. 3, pp. 358-72.

While cautious and pastoral in tone, most of these reports accepted the major premise of Pentecostalism, i.e., that the miraculous gifts of the Spirit did not cease after the apostolic age, but are even now demonstrated in the church by Spirit-filled believers. The major problems encountered by mainline churches were related not to the authenticity of the charismata, but to how these gifts could best be integrated into the life of contemporary churches.

The Kansas City Conference of 1977

Armed with the accumulated discernment of the churches, the charismatics turned their attention to planning several massive public gatherings during the mid-1970's to impress their message on the soul of the church and the mind of the nation. As the result of a vision shared by several leaders at the 1975 "Glencoe Retreat," a call was issued in 1976 for a "general conference" of all charismatics and Pentecostals to gather in Kansas City, Missouri in 1977 for an international conference that would assemble all the sectors of the renewal for the first time. The purpose of the conference was to demonstrate the movement's unity and to make a "common witness" to the church and the world of the conference theme "Jesus Is Lord."[13]

For eighteen months an ecumenical team planned a "conference of conferences" under the leadership of Kevin Ranaghan, chairman of the Catholic Charismatic Renewal Service Committee. Under the "three streams" concept (classical Pentecostal, Protestant neo-Pentecostal, and Catholic charismatic) Larry Christenson (Lutheran) and Vinson Synan (Pentecostal) served on the "executive committee" with Ranaghan. Others serving on the committee indicated the broad ecumenical base of the event. They included: Brick Bradford (Presbyterian), Ithiel Clemmons (Church of God in Christ), Howard Courtney (International Church of the Foursquare Gospel), Robert Frost (Independent), Robert Hawn (Episcopal), Roy Lamberth (Southern Baptist), Nelson Litwiller

---

13. The "Glencoe Retreat" was an informal annual ecumenical gathering of about fifty national leaders of the various movements who constituted themselves informally as a "Charismatic Concerns Committee" whose purpose was to settle differences within the growing charismatic movement. In the early years it was led by Larry Christenson and Kevin Ranaghan. See David Moore, "The Shepherding Movement," pp. 53-79.

(Mennonite), Bob Mumford (Independent), Ken Pagard (American Baptist), Carlton Spencer (Elim Fellowship), Ross Whetstone (Methodist), and David Stern (Messianic Jewish).

The Kansas City charismatic conference served as the climactic ecumenical event in the history of the movement and as the largest ecumenical gathering in the history of the nation. For the first time, all the important groups in the entire tradition met together. In the mornings, the different denominational groups met in separate arenas and auditoriums throughout the city. Included were morning sessions for Catholics, Lutherans, Presbyterians, Episcopalians, denominational Pentecostals, independent Pentecostals, Methodists, and Messianic Jews. Afternoon workshops were offered by all the groups and were open to all. In the evening, sessions for everyone from all the conferences gathered in Arrowhead Stadium for the ecumenical worship and praise services. Chairman Ranaghan proclaimed that the conference was probably the most ecumenical large gathering of Christians in 800 years.[14]

Main speakers included Kevin Ranaghan, Bob Mumford, Larry Christenson and Jim Forbes. Other speakers included Terry Fullam, Michael Scanlan, Francis McNutt, Ruth Carter Stapleton, Maria Von Trapp, and Cardinal Suenens. These speakers constituted a veritable hall of fame for the charismatic movement. The most powerful word to the conference came in a prophetic call to unity that brought the huge assembly to its knees in tears of repentance:

Come before me, with broken hearts and contrite spirit
For the body of my Son is broken.

Come before me, with tears and mourning,
For the body of my Son is broken.

The light is dim, my people are scattered,
The body of my Son is broken.

I gave all I had in the body and blood of my Son,
It spilled on the earth.
The body of my Son is broken.

14. David Manual's *Like a Mighty River: A Personal Account of the Charismatic Conference of 1977* (Orleans, MA, 1977) gives a documented and pictorial account of the conference.

261

Turn from the sins of your fathers,
And walk in the ways of my Son.
Return to the plan of your Father.
Return to the purpose of your God.
The body of my Son is broken.

The Lord says to you: stand in unity with one another,
And let nothing tear you apart.
And, by no means separate from one another,
Through your jealousies and bitternesses,
And your personal preferences,
But hold fast to one another.
Because I am about to let you undergo
A time of severe trial and testing,
And you'll need to be in unity with one another.
But I tell you this also,
I am Jesus, the Victor King.
And I have promised you victory.[15]

Symbolic of the unity called for in this prophecy was a platform shared by leaders from widely divergent Christian traditions. In one memorable service, Cardinal Suenens (Roman Catholic), Thomas Zimmerman (Assemblies of God), J. O. Patterson (Church of God in Christ), and Archbishop Bill Burnett (Anglican) stood together before the vast multitude in an unprecedented demonstration of unity.[16]

Great rejoicing and celebration filled the stands as the ecumenical multitude sang in tongues and danced before the Lord. In reporting the conference, *Time Magazine* noted somewhat irreverently that "a charismatic time was had by all." The press estimated that the Kansas City crowds represented nine million Americans, 4 million of them classical Pentecostals and 5 million more charismatics in the mainline churches.[17]

To say the least, the Kansas City Conference made a tremendous impression on American churches. One observer, Jeremy Rifkin, described it as the "superbowl of the burgeoning new charismatic movement." His description of the event in *The Changing Order* gave some of its ecumenical flavor:

15. Manual, *Like a Mighty River,* p. 195; *New Covenant,* Feb. 1978, p. 6.
16. Manual, *Like a Mighty River,* pp. 137-47.
17. *Time,* Aug. 8, 1977, p. 43.

The Kansas City football stadium had never sported an event quite so unusual. Tens of thousands of Bible-carrying, hymn-singing Christians of all shades of denominations squeezed into the stands, the bleachers, and overflowed the playing field on July 21, 1977, for what turned out to be the first annual superbowl of the burgeoning new charismatic movement. They were Catholic, Baptist, Presbyterian, Episcopalian and Methodist, all praising the Lord and embracing each other in brotherly love. Even for an observer of Christian religious history, such a moment of ecumenical bliss certainly gave the impression that a miracle had, indeed, taken place.[18]

The most unforgettable moment of the conference came as Bob Mumford moved to the climax of his sermon of the evening sessions in the stadium. Lifting his Bible in the air, Mumford exclaimed, "If you sneak a peek at the back of the book, Jesus wins!" The crowd of some 50,000 roared their approval with 15 minutes of ecstatic and thunderous praise.[19]

Although many saw only the excitement and fervor of the meetings, others saw deeper currents of meaning. To some, Kansas City meant resistance to the secular, materialistic culture of the times and a return to spiritual values. According to David Stump, the Kansas City charismatics were "clearly seeing the years ahead as a time of struggle to determine if the future would be formed in a Christian image or in the image of secular materialism."[20]

Kansas City in 1977 represented a cresting of the movement in America. It was the greatest and most visible sign of unity in the entire history of the Pentecostal/charismatic movement. After Kansas City, the various denominational charismatic groups returned to their separate annual conferences. Many groups, such as the Roman Catholics, began to conduct large regional conferences which further reduced the visibility of the movement in the eyes of the media. Diversification and regionalization became the order of the day. Even so, the 15,000 Lutheran charismatics that gathered annually in Minneapolis remained the largest annual meeting of Lutherans in the country, while the 10,000 Catholics

18. Jeremy Rifkin with Ted Howard, *The Emerging Order — God in the Scarcity* (New York, 1979), pp. 177-78.

19. Rifkin and Howard, *The Emerging Order*, p. 166.

20. David X. Stump, "Charismatic Renewal: Up to Date in Kansas City," *America*, Sept. 24, 1977, p. 166.

who continued to meet each year at Notre Dame remained one of the most important annual gatherings of Catholics in the United States.

The Shepherding Controversy

The public unity displayed in the Kansas City conference masked a simmering dispute over the "shepherding-discipleship" movement, a division that Michael Harper described as "far and away the most disturbing controversy to hit the charismatic renewal." In fact, in Kansas City, the "non-denominational" delegations were divided into two separate "tracks" in order to separate the two factions that refused to meet together in the same hall.[21]

The roots of the controversy centered on the teachings of four independent ministers from Fort Lauderdale, Florida: Derek Prince, Bob Mumford, Charles Simpson, and Don Basham. Later joined by Ern Baxter, these men, sometimes known as "the Fort Lauderdale five," had conducted a joint teaching ministry since 1970 when they took over a failed magazine named *New Wine* founded by Eldon Purvis, the head of a charismatic ministry known as the "Holy Spirit Teaching Mission." This group of teachers enjoyed a mushrooming ministry throughout the 1970's that became the talk of the charismatic movement. According to Mumford, the Fort Lauderdale teachers were in demand because of the "highly subjective" and "experience oriented" tendencies among the multitudes of charismatics from the mainline churches who flocked to hear anyone who used the word "charismatic" in their advertisements.[22]

Borrowing from the Catholic tradition of "Spiritual Directors," and the teachings of the Argentine Pentecostal evangelist Juan Carlos Ortiz, the Florida teachers constructed a system of pastoral care known variously as "shepherding" or "discipleship." In order to care for the many roving and rootless charismatics, they constructed a system emphasizing committed "covenant relationships" between a male "covering" or "shepherd" (authority) who would direct the spiritual lives of his "disciples," many of whom would live under "submission" in "covenant communities" formed for the protection and nurturing of the group. Government in these communities would be based on the "five-

21. Michael Harper, *Three Sisters* (Wheaton, IL, 1979), p. 30.
22. Moore, "The Shepherding Movement," pp. 22-30.

fold pattern" of apostles, prophets, evangelists, and pastor-teachers. Such relationships could be trans-local and exist separately from the members' denominational connections.[23]

These teachings became popular with thousands of charismatics in need of pastoral care and teaching, and there was a huge demand for the Fort Lauderdale teachers to speak at the burgeoning charismatic conferences across the nation. Their books and tapes were in extremely high demand. Records show that from 1979 to 1984, the Fort Lauderdale teachers distributed 4,500,000 magazines, 1,000,000 newsletters, 600,000 cassette tapes, and 250,000 books. To consolidate the movement they organized three "Shepherds' Conferences" from 1973 to 1975, which were attended by thousands of followers. Needless to say, many other charismatic leaders were greatly concerned by these developments, as they apparently threatened to engulf the entire charismatic movement.[24]

An intense struggle surfaced in 1975, when several influential leaders openly attacked the Fort Lauderdale teachers, not only over their teachings but out of fear that they would start a massive new denomination. Critics feared a sinister pyramid scheme of sheep and shepherds where "down through the pyramid of disciples, a chain of command, came the orders, and up the same pyramid to the top (Fort Lauderdale) went the tithes...." [25] Others charged that the shepherds controlled the most intimate personal decisions of the sheep, including where to live and whom to marry.

In the spring of 1975, The Full Gospel Business Men suddenly issued a directive forbidding its leaders to invite any of the Fort Lauderdale teachers to speak in any chapter or convention meetings. Added to this was Pat Robertson's decision to forbid appearances of the teachers on "the 700 Club," his widely-watched television program. Kathryn Kuhlman added to the sense of crisis when she pointedly refused to appear on the same program in Jerusalem with Bob Mumford, saying "if Bob Mumford goes to Israel, I shall not go ... the man is a heretic." The crisis came to a head in June when Robertson issued a stinging letter that "blew the lid off the controversy." In it he accused the teachers of "heresy" and of "controlling the lives of their followers with the overuse of spiritual authority." These

23. Moore, "The Shepherding Movement," pp. 18-21. See also Harold Hunter's "Shepherding Movement," in Burgess et al., *Dictionary of Pentecostal and Charismatic Movements*, pp. 783-84.

24. Moore, "The Shepherding Movement," pp. 6, 39-43.

25. McDonnell, *Presence, Power, and Praise*, vol. 2, pp. 116-17.

charges led to a "shootout at the Curtis Hotel" in Minneapolis in August 1975 where such leaders as Larry Christenson, Jamie Buckingham, Dennis Bennett, and Pat Robertson met with the Fort Lauderdale teachers in an effort to defuse the controversy. Neither this meeting nor subsequent meetings of a newly-formed "Charismatic Concerns Committee" in Oklahoma City in 1976 was able to resolve the issue.[26]

After the Kansas City Conference of 1977, where the 12,000 registrants to the shepherding conference marked the high point of the movement, the controversy continued to occupy the attention of charismatic leaders — although interest began to wane among the rank and file. By 1983 Derek Prince broke ranks with the other teachers, followed by the closing of *New Wine* magazine in 1986 and the break-up of the remaining team members in the same year. It was only in 1989 that Bob Mumford issued an apology for his former associations and recanted most of his former shepherding teachings. The remnants of the movement continued, however, in Charles Simpson's "Covenant Church of Mobile" in Alabama.[27]

Pentecost Celebrations

The diversification that followed Kansas City included the beginning of a worldwide observance of Pentecost Sunday as ecumenical demonstration of the unity of the churches. Jointly suggested by Cardinal Suenens and Vinson Synan, these celebrations spread to many of the major cities of the world. In 1979, over 250,000 people attended celebrations in the United States. The largest such celebration was in New York in 1979, where 35,000 people met in Giant Stadium to celebrate the birthday of the church. Huge Pentecost celebrations were held also in cities as far removed as London and Bombay. In many cities such as Dallas and Oklahoma City, these annual ecumenical meetings became a regular part of the local church calendar.[28]

A preview of political developments occurred at the Kansas City

26. Edward E. Plowman, "The Deepening Rift in the Charismatic Movement," *Christianity Today*, Oct. 10, 1975, pp. 52-54. See also Vinson Synan, "Reconciling Charismatics," *Christianity Today*, Apr. 9, 1976, p. 46.

27. Jamie Buckingham, "The End of the Discipleship Era," *Ministries Today*, Jan./Feb. 1990, pp. 46-51; Moore, "The Shepherding Movement," pp. 2-95.

28. Leon Joseph Cardinal Suenens, *Ecumenism and Charismatic Renewal: Theological and Pastoral Orientations, Malines Document II* (Ann Arbor, MI, 1978), pp. 86-87. See also McDonnell, *Presence, Power, Praise*, vol. 3, pp. 170-71.

conference when Ruth Carter Stapleton, the charismatic Baptist healing evangelist, helped the charismatics to side with the "born-again" politics of her brother, President Jimmy Carter. The president's letter, which was read to the Kansas City conference, not only brought the crowd to its feet but brought presidential politics into the evangelical religious arena. This lesson was well learned by Carter's successor, Ronald Reagan, who openly courted evangelicals and charismatics in his quest for the White House.

Washington for Jesus 1980

By 1980, the movement's political potential was effectively displayed in the "Washington for Jesus" demonstration, which brought over 500,000 Christians to the mall in Washington for one of the largest gatherings in the history of the capital. A then-unknown Pentecostal preacher, John Gimenez, pastor of the Rock Church in Virginia Beach, Virginia, issued the call for this multitude to preach and pray from sunup to sunset on July 4, 1980.

The speakers did not support any candidate or political party in the 1980 election; but they loudly and unanimously spoke against drug abuse, homosexuality, and abortion, and in support of prayer in public schools. The candidate in 1980 whose platform most closely matched the temper of the charismatics was Ronald Reagan, although Carter's public Christian testimony was much closer to that of the latter-rain people. Of even more significance than the rally's political overtones were its history-making ecumenical aspects. Evangelicals and charismatics stood together in demonstration of their unity on vital matters of public policy.[29]

World Evangelization:
New Orleans, Indianapolis, and Bern

During the last half of the 1980's a dramatic change of emphasis engulfed the Pentecostal-charismatic movement in North America. This was es-

29. David Manual, *The Gathering: The Story Behind Washington for Jesus* (Orleans, MA, 1980); David Manual, "But Who Is John Gimenez?" in *Charisma Magazine*, July/Aug. 1981, pp. 22-27. See also Corwin E. Smidt et al., "Spirit Filled Movements and American Politics," in John C. Green et al., *Religion and the Culture Wars* (New York, 1996), pp. 219-39.

sentially an addition to the previous goals of the Kansas City Conference (renewal of the churches), and the Washington for Jesus Rally (national moral renewal). The new orientation was now directed towards world evangelization, an area previously lacking among charismatic renewalists.

The first impetus for this historic move came as a result of a meeting in Nairobi, Kenya in 1983, as three renewal leaders discussed the future over a cup of tea. These men, Tom Forrest, Larry Christenson, and Michael Harper, began to consider the year A.D. 2000 and to ask what the Spirit was saying to the churches with regard to the new millennium. It was here that the vision for a "decade of world evangelization" was born. It was Tom Forrest, the Catholic Redemptorist priest, who first suggested a goal of winning a majority of the world's population to Christ by the year A.D. 2000.

The idea of a decade of world evangelization during the 1990's soon spread around the world. To carry the vision forward, two "Charismatic Consultations" were convened in Singapore in 1987 and 1988 under the leadership of Larry Christenson. In these meetings about 60 world leaders planned a series of major conferences which would prepare the way for the decade. The first was a "Pentecost Vigil," which brought together over 100 renewal leaders in Jerusalem in 1989. A second meeting of about 4,000 leaders met in 1991 in Brighton, England under the leadership of Anglican Michael Harper. To carry out these projects, a global ecumenical organization was formed in 1989 known as "International Consultation on World Evangelization (ICOWE)," with Harper as chairman.

In the meantime, North American and European leaders were planning major world evangelization conferences. In North America, a major congress was already being planned as a successor to the Kansas City conference of 1977. Hearing the vision of a decade of world evangelization, North American leaders immediately adopted this goal, and planned a series of congresses in the United States leading up to 1990. To accomplish this, a new organization was formed in 1985 known as the "North American Renewal Service Committee" (NARSC).[30]

During the late 1980's the North Americans, under the leadership of NARSC, planned and presented three ecumenical meetings, each with

---

30. For more information on NARSC see Vinson Synan and Ralph Rath, *Launching the Decade of Evangelization* (South Bend, IN, 1990).

the name "Congress on the Spirit and World Evangelization." The first, a leaders' congress, attracted about 7,500 pastors, priests, and prayer leaders to the Superdome in New Orleans in 1986. The second, billed as a "general congress," drew some 40,000 to the Superdome in 1987. Other major gatherings in this series were the Indianapolis Congress of 1990, which drew almost 25,000 persons (clergy and lay) to the Hoosier-dome, and the Orlando Congress of 1995, which drew 10,000 leaders to plan further evangelistic efforts for the remaining years of the century.

Europeans also became involved by calling for a conference in Bern, Switzerland, in 1990, where about 4,000 leaders challenged the European church to become more evangelistic. To the surprise of the conference planners, about half the delegates came from Eastern Europe, where the fall of Communism in 1989 had opened the door for 2,000 leaders to attend.

In all these conferences, evangelicals were invited to participate. The evangelical response was dramatically highlighted when Billy Graham addressed the 1987 New Orleans Congress by means of video, congratulating Pentecostals and charismatics for their record of world evangelization. The coming together of evangelicals and charismatics in the 1980's presaged other changes in American church life. Although little had been said by mainline church mission boards, Pentecostalism had long since swept into their mission fields. Southern Baptists whispered the rumor that an estimated 75 percent of their third-world missionaries had spoken in tongues in the various "renovation" and charismatic movements during the 1970's. Large numbers of Methodist, Presbyterian, Anglican, and Lutheran missionaries had become practicing Pentecostals in the field — a fact they did not broadcast back home.

Pentecostalism was also making advances in the major independent seminaries of the nation as well as in many of the denominational schools, leading to a fever of research and doctoral dissertations on all things Pentecostal. Literally hundreds of theses were churned out in universities and seminaries around the world after 1970. As a result, the "Society for Pentecostal Studies" was formed in 1970 to promote and coordinate this research explosion. The SPS soon became one of the most active and vigorous theological societies in the United States.[31]

A sign of the times in the academic world was the development of the most popular course ever offered at Fuller Theological Seminary.

31. Quebedeaux, *New Charismatics,* vol. 2, pp. 82, 188, 208.

Taught by professors John Wimber and Peter Wagner, "Signs, Wonders, and Church Growth," in its first year the course attracted over 100 students to study the use of the gifts of the Spirit in the churches. Wimber's classes often ended with tongues, prophecies, and prayers for the sick. Wimber put his theories into practice in his "Vineyard Christian Fellowship" congregation in Yorba Linda, California, where 4,000 persons attended Sunday worship services in a church that by 1982 was only five years old.[32]

As large numbers of young converts from the "Jesus movement" felt the call to preach, they increasingly entered seminaries and schools of theology. By 1983, about one-third of the student bodies of Fuller and Gordon-Conwell seminaries were comprised of charismatics. Many of these graduates were called to serve traditional mainline congregations as pastors, musicians, or ministers of Christian education. By the 1980's most of them were being welcomed with open arms and few questions asked about their charismatic experiences.

The great army of young "Jesus people" accepted into the ministry of mainline churches constituted a bridgehead of Spirit-filled ministers and priests destined to bring on the next phase of the movement. Since most of these young enthusiasts were not raised in classical Pentecostal homes, they felt few ties to the older Pentecostal denominations, although they spoke in tongues and espoused Pentecostal practices.

Some of them founded new congregations and even denominations that were charismatic in practice, but not labelled as such; their articles of faith could often not be distinguished from other mainline evangelical bodies. The Maranatha campus ministries of Bob Weiner, for example, were Pentecostal in worship and experience, although nothing in the official doctrinal statements would distinguish them from the average evangelical denomination.

Untold numbers of similar young ministers entered the ministries of Baptist, Lutheran, Methodist, and Presbyterian churches. The same was true of Roman Catholic and Eastern Orthodox churches. Great numbers of young people with a charismatic spiritual formation entered the seminaries of these churches without specific labels to distinguish them from other seminarians. These young people would become the vanguard for the next chapter in the story of the latter rain people.

32. David Allen Hubbard, "Hazarding the Risks," *Christian Life*, Oct. 1982, pp. 18-26.

A Third Wave?

By 1983, some leaders were talking about a "third wave" of Pentecostalism which would enter the mainline churches with little struggle or notoriety. This "third wave" would be a successor to the first two, i.e., the classical Pentecostals and the charismatics. The new wave would be made up of evangelicals in the major traditional churches who would receive and exercise the gifts of the Spirit without accepting the labels. Peter Wagner, the professor at Fuller Theological Seminary who coined the phrase, is such a man. Although he speaks in tongues, he refuses to call himself a Pentecostal or a charismatic. In explaining the "third wave," Wagner stated:

> I see in the 80's an opening of the straightline evangelicals and other Christians to the supernatural work of the Holy Spirit that the Pentecostals and charismatics have experienced, but without becoming either charismatic or Pentecostal.[33]

Using his own experience as an example, Wagner further elaborated on the future of the "third wave" people:

> I see myself as neither a charismatic nor a Pentecostal. I belong to the Lake Avenue Congregational Church. I'm a Congregationalist. My church is not a charismatic church, although some of our members are charismatic. There is a charismatic prayer group that meets on Monday nights in a home.
>
> However, our church is more and more open to the same way that the Holy Spirit does work among charismatics. For example, our pastor gives an invitation after every service (we have three services on Sunday morning) for people who need physical healing and inner healing to come to the prayer room and be anointed and prayed for, and we have teams of people who know how to pray for the sick.
>
> We like to think that we are doing it in a congregational way; we're not doing it in a charismatic way. But getting the same results. I myself have several theological differences with Pentecostals and charismatics, which don't mar any kind of mutual ministry, but keep me from saying I'm a charismatic.[34]

33. Peter Wagner, "A Third Wave?" *Pastoral Renewal* 8, no. 1 (July-Aug. 1983): 1-5.
34. Wagner, "A Third Wave?" pp. 3-4.

In addition to the lack of labels proclaimed by Wagner, the "Third Wave" people denied that there was even a subsequent crisis experience known as a "baptism in the Spirit" — the touchstone of both the Pentecostal and charismatic movements. Indeed tongues, far from being the "initial evidence" of such a baptism, was only one of the many gifts a Spirit-filled believer might or might not experience. Wagner explained,

> Doctrinally the third wave takes the position that the baptism in the Holy Spirit occurs at conversion and is not to be sought as a separate work of grace in the believer's life subsequent to the new birth. Furthermore the third wave does not consider speaking with other tongues as a validation of the believer's having reached some higher spiritual plane.[35]

While Wagner's "Third Wave" idea described the experience of thousands of churches and pastors, it did not point to an organized movement as such. It did, however, open the door for thousands of mainline evangelicals to practice Pentecostal worship and exercise spiritual gifts, even if they felt uncomfortable with classical Pentecostalism.

Although the third wave never caught on as a major category of Christians, it inspired a backlash from several "neo-Pentecostals," including Dennis Bennett, one of the pioneers of Pentecostalism in the mainline churches. Upon hearing of Wagner's third wave, Bennett published several heated articles in his paper *Morning Watch,* warning of the dangers inherent in the third wave. In what was called Bennett's "last battle" he said:

> What I hear is: 'If you good people would just stop insisting there is a baptism in the Holy Spirit following salvation, and that it's important to speak in tongues, we will get along fine. In other words, 'if you will drop the idea that we need the same enduement of supernatural power today that the first Christians did, with the same signs and evidences, all will be peace. . . . Peace among Christians is a precious thing but not at the price of losing the Power, lest we fulfill that prophecy about having a form of Godliness but denying the power thereof.[36]

---

35. C. P. Wagner, "Power of the Spirit: The Third Wave," *AD 2000 Together* (1988): 6-7.

36. Dennis Bennett, "The Old Paths," *Morning Watch,* Spring 1989, p. 1.

Notwithstanding Bennett's warnings, by the mid-1980's there was evidence that the "third wave" was indeed entering the mainline churches without the confusion of labels that had caused such great problems in the past. A symbol of the new attitudes developing among evangelicals were the striking views of Harold Lindsell, well-known theologian and former editor of *Christianity Today*. In his 1983 book, *The Holy Spirit in the Latter Days*, Lindsell said:

> We have been talking about the glorious work of the Holy Spirit in the lives of God's people. It should be apparent to all that I accept as a fact that some of God's people are filled or baptized with the Holy Spirit, and that nomenclature is purely a secondary matter that should not keep us from appropriating what lies behind differing terms for the experience. It is also a fact that God, through His Spirit, does perform miracles and healings. Speaking in tongues does happen and is a bona fide gift of the Spirit. There are a few people of God here and there who receive healing or miracles. These gifts have not ceased. They are still there even though they occur with less frequency than some people suppose.[37]

Lindsell's credentials as an evangelical leader are impeccable. If his thinking is typical of a large proportion of mainline evangelicals, there would seem to be nothing to stop a spiritual tidal wave in the traditional churches.

A major reason for the appearance of Pentecostal/charismatic movements and the new "third wave" movement in the mainline churches may have been an emotional hunger for a more expressive worship, a need not being satisfied by the traditional liturgies. In a major study of Minnesota's mainline churches in 1983, church members demonstrated what Martin Marty called a "pick and choose" attitude toward their faith.[38] About 90 percent of the respondents, most of them Lutheran and Roman Catholic, desired a "free form" type of communication with a God who "intervenes in their lives and directs them in their vocations," rather than the stylized forms of their traditional worship.[39] Where the churches were not meeting

---

37. Harold Lindsell, "My Search for the Truth about the Holy Spirit," *Christian Life*, Sept. 1983, p. 29.

38. Kenneth L. Woodward, "Pick and Choose Christianity," *Newsweek*, Sept. 19, 1983, pp. 82-83.

39. Martin Marty and Joan Chittister, *Faith and Ferment* (Minneapolis, 1983).

this need, people were voting with their feet. By 1983, many charismatic leaders in Catholic and mainline Protestant churches were growing concerned over the increasing numbers of charismatic laypersons leaving these churches and joining Pentecostal or independent charismatic churches.

The "third wave" may have represented the reaction of the churches to this felt need. As more churches opened up to freer and more "charismatic" worship, fewer church members were likely to desert their local churches. In time, as the Pentecostal churches moderated some of their more extreme practices, and the mainline churches opened up to more freedom in exercising the gifts of the Spirit, the differences between them were likely to diminish.

In 1983, an updated edition of Richard Quebedeaux's book *The New Charismatics* bore a subtitle that aptly described the outcome of the recent charismatic renewal: "how a Christian renewal movement became part of the American religious mainstream." Quebedeaux believed that by the end of the 1970's, Pentecostalism had achieved its primary goal — "that of making the once-despised Pentecostal experience acceptable within mainline Protestantism and Catholicism." Thereafter "there was no longer any need for its continued existence as a *Movement*." It could then merge into the mainstream church without a particular separate identity. According to Quebedeaux, by the late 1970's the charismatic movement "had run out of steam but not out of abiding significance."[40]

Throughout the history of Pentecostalism, similar pronouncements had been made during periods of relative quiet and subdued fervor. Invariably, an even stronger wave had followed. By the 1990's, the rising ministries of newer American Pentecostal evangelists, including Bennie Hinn, Kenneth Copeland, and T. D. Jakes, indicated that the sawdust trail was far from dead. Also, the rising star of Reinhard Bonnke in South Africa, with massive crusades that at times reached 500,000 in one service, showed that the Pentecostal message still resonated powerfully with the struggling masses of the Third World. Thousands of unknown classical Pentecostal evangelists continued to spread the word to the humble and forgotten peoples of world.

This book was published simultaneously by Augsburg Press (Lutheran) and the Liturgical Press (Roman Catholic).

40. Quebedeaux, *The New Charismatics*, vol. 2, p. 239.

The "Toronto Blessing"

A key factor in the expansion of Pentecostalism throughout the century was the appearance of unexpected waves of renewal that constituted sources of both tension and growth. In the middle of the 1990's a new and different type of awakening hit the churches in the form of a "laughing revival" sparked by the ministry of Rodney Howard-Browne of South Africa. Coming to America in 1987, Browne was soon known for the uproarous laughter that often broke out in his services. His ministry made national news in 1992 during a meeting in Lakeland, Florida where crowds of 10,000 people crowded the Carpenter's Home Assemblies of God church to hear the South African preacher and to experience the laughing phenomenon. At the end of a month of services, a swimming pool was installed in the church where 1,500 converts were baptized in water. Soon "holy laughter" broke out in churches around the nation and spread rapidly to other countries. In short order, however, the most important center for the new movement emerged in Toronto, Ontario, where a laughter-inspired revival in a local Vineyard congregation soon caught the attention of the world.[41]

The Toronto revival had been sparked by a meeting in 1993 at the Airport Vineyard church led by Randy Clark, pastor of a St. Louis Vineyard who had attended a Rodney Howard-Brown meeting. The Toronto services were first known for the "holy laughter" that was common in the early meetings. But soon other manifestations began to occur that raised concerns among the Vineyard leaders in California, including the founder John Wimber. The Toronto meetings included occasional instances of roaring like lions, barking like dogs, and crowing like chickens. These "animal sounds" were often accompanied by prophecies speaking of a final worldwide revival just before the end of the age. Pastor John Arnott and his staff did their best to direct the services with a modicum of decency and order, but the manifestations attracted more and more attention as thousands came to investigate the Toronto meetings.

As the sensational services continued in Toronto, the manifestations spread around the world, sparking intense local revivals in many cities. The movement gained impetus when the same motor phenomena broke out in Holy Trinity Anglican church in Brompton, a suburb of

41. See Vinson Synan, "Revival Phenomenon Spreads Around the World," *Timelines,* Spring/Summer 1994, pp. 3-4.

London. The English newspapers were the first to dub the manifestations "the Toronto Blessing." Thousands of pastors and laypersons from all denominations soon began to flock to Toronto to participate in what was seen as possibly one of the great revivals in history. Historian Richard Riss spread news to the world through regular accounts on the Internet.[42]

By the end of 1995 the numbers of visitors to the Toronto church reached astronomical proportions, with 600,000 first-time visitors from almost every nation. As the 400-seat church soon was unable to handle the crowds, the congregation in 1995 moved into a new building with seating for 3000 persons. Although the "manifestations" attracted thousands, there were many testimonies of inner and physical healing, of marriages and families restored, and ministries rescued. Most importantly, explained Pastor Arnott, over 9,000 first-time conversions were recorded in the services.[43]

In the first stages of the revival, most church leaders were supportive of the Toronto awakening. Peter Wagner of Fuller Theological Seminary, himself overtaken by the laughter, said that the Toronto manifestations might be "part of the things the Lord is doing to prepare us for a coming revival." At first John Wimber and the national Vineyard staff were also supportive of the Toronto movement with various Vineyard researchers going so far as to produce historical studies comparing the Toronto awakening to previous revivals centering on Jonathan Edwards, John Wesley, Charles Whitefield, and the Azusa Street Revival. But as time went on, attention was more and more drawn to what John Wimber called "exotic and non-Biblical manifestations" such as those involving animal noises. Soon several critics weighed in with articles and broadcasts condemning the Toronto manifestations as "self-induced hysteria." Others, like Tony Payne of Australia, in his diatribe *No Laughing Matter* dismissed the movement as "simply another pentecostal incarnation."[44]

---

42. This awakening was the first to be reported on the Internet. For many months, Richard Riss sent out updated reports from around the world on his website chronicling the Toronto revival, entitled "A History of the Worldwide Awakening of 1992-1995" (http://www.grmi.org/renewal/Richard_Riss/history.html). Documents telling the official Vineyard story were reported on http:/www./groke.beckman.uiuc.edu/AVC/avc.html, while the Toronto version was told on http:www.tacf.org.

43. "What is the Toronto Blessing? Facts and Figures," Internet http://www.tacf.org/facts.htm (Jan./Feb. 1995). See also Margaret Paloma's *By Their Fruits: A Sociological Assessment of the "Toronto Blessing"* (Akron, OH, 1996.)

44. Guy Chevreau's *Catch the Fire* (Toronto, 1994) is a firsthand account of the early days of the Toronto renewal. Dave Roberts's *The 'Toronto Blessing'* (East-

276

Over a period of several months Wimber was overwhelmed with inquiries about the Toronto movement, causing the Vineyard leadership to produce a "Board Report" in October 1994 with "guidelines" for the pastoral care of the movement. The crux of the report was that leaders were not to forbid such manifestations, but that they should not be promoted or displayed. Furthermore, Toronto leaders should focus on the "main/plain issues of Scripture," with "no doctrine . . . based on a prophetic interpretation of a particular manifestation." In a separate document titled, "John Wimber Responds to Phenomena," he called for the Toronto leaders to "channel these people into work" that would "express that refreshing in a solid Biblical context."[45]

Despite this counsel, reports continued to arrive at Vineyard offices that Arnott and the Toronto staff were ignoring the guidelines by continuing to defend and feature the "exotic" manifestations. The final straw seems to have been the publication in December of John Arnott's new book *The Father's Blessing.*[46] In December, Wimber flew to Toronto where he announced that the "Association of Vineyard Churches was formally withdrawing its endorsement of Airport Toronto Vineyard." Explaining this action, Wimber said, ". . . we cannot at any time endorse, encourage, offer theological justification or biblical proof-texting for any exotic practices that are extra-biblical — whether in Toronto or elsewhere. Neither can these practices be presented as criteria for true spirituality or as a mark of true renewal. . . ."[47]

During the height of the Toronto awakening, another massive revival broke out in the Brownsville Assemblies of God Church in Pensacola, Florida, that soon outstripped the Toronto meetings in size

---

bourne, U.K., 1994), pp. 11-59, gives an excellent account of the Holy Trinity meetings. The September 1995 issue of *Christianity Today* featured several articles both favorable and critical of the meetings under the heading "The Surprising Works of God: Toronto's Mixed Blessing" by Richard Lovelace, pp. 23-32. For a Wesleyan defense of the awakening see Steve Beard's *Thunderstruck: John Wesley and the Toronto Blessing* (Wilmore, KY, 1996). A compendium of anti-Toronto tracts can be found in Derek Morphew's *Renewal Apologetics* (Claremont, CA, 1995). See also Tony Payne, *No Laughing Matter* (Sydney, 1995), pp. 9-21.

45. Association of Vineyard Churches, "Board Report," Sept./Oct. 1994, pp. 1-4; and "John Wimber Responds to Phenomena," a letter to Vineyard pastors, 1995.

46. John Arnott, *The Father's Blessing* (Orlando, FL, 1996). Arnott pointedly titled his book the "Father's Blessing" rather than the "Toronto Blessing."

47. Association of Vineyard Churches, "Board Report," pp. 1-4. See also "Toronto Churches Ousted from Vineyard," *Charisma*, Feb. 1996, p. 12.

and numbers of converts. The revival began on Fathers' Day in June of 1995, when Brownsville pastor John Kilpatrick invited evangelist Steve Hill to preach in the Sunday services. Hill, who had previously visited the Toronto Vineyard and Holy Trinity, Brompton, soon saw the church filled with teenagers and others who responded to his fiery sermons on sin and repentance. Although there were many who experienced such "Toronto blessing" manifestations as shaking and falling, the central atmosphere of the meetings was that of repentance for sinners and "backsliders" alike.[48]

As the revival continued, some 5,000 persons per night jammed every available space in the church as well as in makeshift tents put up on the grounds for viewing on close-circuit television. Unlike Toronto, the Brownsville revival gained the approval of the Assemblies of God leadership, both in Florida and in the national headquarters. By the spring of 1997, the cumulative numbers of attendees had surpassed 1,600,000 persons, with over 100,000 converts who had responded to the altar calls. To feed the bodies as well as the souls of the worshipers, as many as eight food trucks came each day to serve the thousands who lined up before dawn in order to make it into the evening services.[49]

As the 1990's drew to a close, reports of other astonishing revivals similar to the ones in Toronto and Pensacola continued to pour in from all over the world, filling the pages of religious periodicals and Internet websites in the United States and abroad. These reports suggested that the long dark night of the televangelist scandals had given way to a new wave of revival that would likely continue through the end of the millennium. In retrospect, the Toronto and Brownsville revivals indicated that, after nearly a century, the spirit of Azusa Street was very much alive among Pentecostals and charismatics and that such classical Pentecostal denominations as the Assemblies of God had not yet lost their revival zeal and fire.

48. Jim DeWitt and J. Lee Grady, "Pensacola Outpouring Continues to Draw Huge Crowds," *Charisma*, Nov. 1996, pp. 15-18; Steve Rabey, "Pensacola Outpouring Keeps Gushing," *Christianity Today*, March 3, 1997, pp. 54-57. For first-hand accounts of the revival see John Kilpatrick, *When the Heavens Are Brass: Keys to Genuine Revival* (Shippensburg, PA, 1997); and Steve Hill, *White Cane Religion and Other Messages from the Brownsville Revival* (Shippensburg, PA, 1997).

49. Michael L. Brown, personal interview with the author, April, 9, 1997. Much of the information came from the Brownsville Internet website: http://www.Brownsville-revival.org.

CHAPTER FOURTEEN

Centennial Reflections

With pentecostals/charismatics now active in 80% of the world's 3,300 large metropolises, all in process of actively implementing networking and cooperation with Great Commission Christians of all confessions, a new era in world mission would clearly appear to have got under way.

David Barrett, 1988

The Christian world was mildly shocked in 1995 with the appearance of Harvey Cox's new history of Pentecostalism titled *Fire From Heaven* with the meaningful subtitle, *The Rise of Pentecostal Spirituality and the Reshaping of Religion in the Twenty-first Century.* The shock value came from the fact that Cox had become famous in the 1960's for publishing *The Secular City,* a book that proclaimed the end of religion as part of the modern world. His works were toasted by such "God is dead" theologians as Thomas J. Altizer, Paul Van Buren, and William Hamilton. Yet three decades later, Cox was celebrating the resurrection of Christianity through the exploding Pentecostal and charismatic movements around the world.[1]

---

1. Harvey Cox, *Fire from Heaven: The Rise of Pentecostal Spirituality and the*

279

Cox explained his metamorphosis as stemming from a class on Pentecostalism that he offered at Harvard University in the early 1990's, a course so popular that he was forced to limit the size of the classes. Serving with him as team teacher was a local Hispanic Pentecostal pastor, Eldin Villafane, whose congregation flourished in a lower-class neighborhood of Cambridge, Massachusetts. Indeed, as Cox studied the local situation, he saw that the mainline churches had long ago abandoned the cities. All that remained, it seemed, were storefront Pentecostal churches — most of them Hispanic, Black, or Haitian — which seemed to thrive while all the others had failed.

Cox visited many of these congregations to learn the reasons for their success. In short order, he became a regular participant in the Society for Pentecostal Studies and began to research and write his book *Fire From Heaven*. With the appearance of this book, a new wave of interest in Pentecostalism awakened in the media. Major series on Pentecostalism appeared in such papers as the *Boston Globe*, and sympathetic stories were aired on the major news networks. It was as if the media were saying, "if Cox thinks this is important, then perhaps we should take a look at it." In fact, Cox feels that the future of Christianity will be shaped by the fast-rising Pentecostal and charismatic movements of the world.

Cox was by no means the first one to make this "Pentecostal" discovery. In 1955 Henry Van Dusen had also surprised the religious world by proclaiming a new "Third Force in Christendom" in a major article in *Life Magazine*. Bishop Leslie Newbigin had made much the same point in his 1954 book, *The Household of God* where he prophetically saw Christianity moving towards a convergence of three streams — the Sacramental, the Evangelical, and the Pentecostal. By the 1960's, such World Council of Churches researchers as Walter Hollenweger predicted that somewhere around the turn of the century, over half of the Christians of the world would be "non-white, pentecostal, and from the third world."

The statistical case for Hollenweger's prophecy came in 1982 with the publication of David Barrett's *World Christian Encyclopedia*. His research showed that by 1980, Pentecostals had become the largest family

---

Reshaping of Religion in the Twenty-First Century (New York, 1994). See also his article "The Warring Visions of the Religious Right," in *Atlantic Monthly*, Nov. 1995, pp. 59-69.

of Protestants in the world, just barely ahead of the Anglicans. By 1990, Barrett's continuing research showed the Pentecostals/charismatics growing at about 19,000,000 per year; with 372,000,000 adherents, they had become the second largest family of Christians in the world, exceeded only by the Roman Catholic Church, with 900,000,000 members. Indeed, by this time the movement accounted for 21% of all Christians. They worshiped in some 1,000,000 churches led by 1,000,000 full time ministers and workers. By 1995, Pentecostals had come to the point where they appeared to number more than all the reformation Protestant churches combined.[2]

The growth patterns for the movement were remarkable to say the least. Beginning in 1901 with only about 40 students in Charles Parham's Bethel Bible School in Topeka, Kansas, and gaining world-wide prominence through William Seymour's Azusa Street Mission after 1906, the growth has been exponential. According to Peter Wagner, "In all of human history, no other non-political, non-militaristic, voluntary human movement has grown as rapidly as the Pentecostal-charismatic movement in the last 25 years."[3] The following table from the research of David Barrett and Peter Wagner illustrates the phenomenon of growth from the first Pentecostal prayer meeting on the first day of the twentieth century to the projected membership of all Pentecostal and charismatic groups at the end of the century:

Global Pentecostal/Charismatic Membership

1901	40 members	1985	247,000,000
1945	16,000,000	1990	372,000,000
1955	27,000,000	1995	460,000,000
1965	50,000,000	2000	550,000,000 members[4]
1975	96,000,000		

2. See Synan, *The Spirit Said "Grow."* Earlier sources on Pentecostalism from a worldwide perspective include Walter Hollenweger's *The Pentecostals: The Charismatic Movement in the Churches* (Minneapolis, 1972); John Nichol's *Pentecostalism* (New York, 1966); and Nils Bloch-Hoell's *The Pentecostal Movement* (Oslo, Norway, 1964).

3. Synan, *The Spirit Said "Grow,"* p. ii.

4. David Barrett, *World Christian Encyclopedia* (New York, 1982). Some of these estimates are taken from interviews with Barrett by the author on June 14, 1995, based on research and projections made in 1995.

Types of Pentecostal and Charismatic movements

Just who are these millions of people and how do they differ from Christians in other traditions? David Barrett, in his 1988 *Survey of the Twentieth Century Pentecostal/Charismatic Renewal in the Holy Spirit With its Goal of World Evangelization,* emphasized the term "Renewal in the Holy Spirit" in reference to the many and various strands within the movement. This is a fortunate neutral term that all Christians could use. A more theological definition, by leading Catholic theologian and sociologist Fr. Kilian McDonnell, reads as follows:

> Those Christians who stress the power and presence of the Holy Spirit and the gifts of the Spirit directed toward the proclamation that Jesus Christ is Lord to the glory of God the Father.[5]

In his *Survey,* Barrett also introduced new words not yet in common usage, such as "pre-Pentecostals," "quasi-Pentecostals," "Third Wavers," "Crypto-Charismatics," and "post-Charismatics." Definitions would perhaps be in order:[6]

Pre-Pentecostals

These include many pre-twentieth-century persons and movements who could be considered antecedents of the modern Pentecostal movements. They would include:

a. Monks, priests, and nuns; brothers and sisters in Catholic, Orthodox, or Anglican churches who exercised spiritual gifts over the centuries.

b. Quakers, Shakers, Mormons, and other similar sects outside the mainline churches.

c. Nineteenth-century Holiness, Higher Life, and social reform

5. Kilian McDonnell and Arnold Bittlinger, *The Baptism in the Holy Spirit as an Ecumenical Problem.*

6. All of the following definitions may be found in David Barrett's survey titled "The 20th Century Pentecostal/Charismatic Renewal in the Holy Spirit, with Its Goal of World Evangelization," *International Bulletin of Missionary Research* (1988). This also appeared in Burgess et al., *Dictionary of Pentecostal and Charismatic Movements,* pp. 810-29.

movements such as the "sanctified Methodists;" the Holiness churches springing from Methodism, and the "Higher Life" movements with roots in the Keswick conferences.[7]

Classical Pentecostals

These were the original Pentecostals in the United States. About 1970 they were given the title "Classical Pentecostals" to distinguish them from the "Neo-Pentecostals," as they were then called, in the Mainline Protestant and Catholic churches. They include three identifiable streams: the Holiness or Methodistic Pentecostals, the Baptistic Pentecostals, and the "Oneness" or unitarian Pentecostals.[8]

Non-white Indigenous Quasi-Pentecostals

These are "quasi" ("apparently-seemingly-largely") Pentecostal movements indigenous to Christians in non-white races across the world who are phenomenologically Pentecostal (i.e., experiencing of dreams, visions, filling with the Spirit, tongues, prophecies, healing through prayer, expressive worship and praise, etc.). These were begun without Western mission board support. Barrett places their beginnings in 1741 in the Caribbean region.

7. For those movements that preceded modern Pentecostalism, one should consult Ernest Sandeen, *The Roots of Fundamentalism: British and American Millenarianism, 1830-1930* (Chicago, 1970); Timothy Smith, *Revivalism and Social Reform in Mid-Nineteenth-Century America*; Donald Dayton, *Theological Roots of Pentecostalism*; William Faupel, *The Everlasting Gospel: The Significance of Eschatology in the Development of Pentecostal Thought* (Sheffield, UK, 1996); Charles E. Jones, *Perfectionist Persuasion*; and Edith Blumhofer, "The Overcoming Life: A Study in the Reformed Evangelical Origins of Pentecostalism" (unpublished Ph.D. dissertation, Harvard University, 1977), 225 pp.

8. Histories of American Pentecostal denominations include Edith Blumhofer, *The Assemblies of God: A Chapter in the Story of American Pentecostalism*, 2 vols.; Klaude Kendrick, *The Promise Fulfilled*; Charles W. Conn, *Like a Mighty Army Moves the Church of God*; Vinson Synan, *Old Time Power: A History of the Pentecostal Holiness Church*; William Menzies, *Anointed to Serve: The Story of the Assemblies of God*; J. O. Patterson et al., *History and Formative Years of the Church of God in Christ with Excerpts from the Life and Writings of C. H. Mason*.

Black and Other Non-white Indigenous Pentecostals

These groups are related to the classical Pentecostals, but are not supported or controlled by western (white) churches. This category would include the 5,500,000 members of the American Church of God in Christ, or the 6,000,000 members of the South African Zionist Church, which annually convenes the largest gathering of Christians in the world (2 million) in their Easter conferences in Pietermaritzburg, South Africa.

Protestant Charismatics

Known first as "neo-Pentecostals," this stream began about 1960 with the ministry of Episcopal priest Dennis Bennett in Van Nuys, California. Although Bennett and many of the first neo-Pentecostals accepted the "initial evidence" theory, many others saw tongues as only one of many gifts that come with the baptism of the Holy Spirit. Bennett's groundbreaking success in remaining in his denomination opened the way for thousands of other ministers and lay people to begin charismatic "renewal" movements within their own churches.[9]

Catholic Charismatics

Beginning at Duquesne University in 1967 and spreading rapidly around the world, this movement finally proved the universality of Pentecostalism and opened the door for massive Catholic charismatic renewal movements in over 100 nations. Catholics, along with most Protestant charismatics, spoke of the Pentecostal experience as a "release" of the Holy

9. The literature of these groups is surveyed in Charles Jones's *Guide to the Holiness Movement.* See also Vinson Synan's *Holiness-Pentecostal Movement in the United States,* pp. 95-116; and *In the Latter Days: The Outpouring of the Holy Spirit in the Twentieth Century,* pp. 25-69. The best popular source on the charismatic movement in the mainline churches is Richard Quebedeaux, *The New Charismatics,* vol. 2. See also Synan, *In the Latter Days* and *The Twentieth Century Pentecostal Explosion.* The official statements of the churches of the world are found in Kilian McDonnell's three-volume work, *Presence, Power, Praise: Documents on the Charismatic Renewal.* A survey of the literature of the movement is Charles Jones's *The Charismatic Movement* (Metuchen, NJ, 1995).

Spirit, bringing with it tongues as the usual consequence and also releasing other gifts of the Spirit.[10]

Third Wavers

Beginning about 1980, these are mainline evangelicals who exercise spiritual gifts and emphasize signs and wonders, but who do not identify with either the Pentecostal or charismatic movements. This tendency may have started in California, in John Wimber's classes at Fuller Seminary. Third Wavers do not teach a crisis experience of baptism in the Holy Spirit subsequent to conversion, and they see tongues as only one of the many gifts of the Spirit.[11]

Crypto-Charismatics

This category refers to individuals who exercise spiritual gifts but who, because of persecution or peril to their ecclesiastic standing, keep their experience a secret. They also include Spirit-filled Christians in non-Christian nations where the practice of Christianity is forbidden.

Pentecostals and Church Growth

The Church Growth movement has been greatly affected by the phenomenal growth record of the Pentecostal movement, especially in Third World countries. Much of the research and resultant theory of the

10. Early histories of the Catholic Pentecostal movement include Kevin and Dorothy Ranaghan's *Catholic Pentecostals;* and Edward D. O'Connor's *The Pentecostal Movement in the Catholic Church.* For a fine scholarly treatment see James Connolly's "Neo-Pentecostalism: The Charismatic Revival in the Mainline Protestant and Roman Catholic Churches of the United States." See also Quebedeaux, *New Charismatics,* vol. 2, pp. 72-80; and Synan, *In the Latter Days,* pp. 97-117. The most important recent Catholic historical and theological work is Kilian McDonnell and George Montague, *Christian Initiation and Baptism in the Holy Spirit: Evidence from the First Eight Centuries* (Collegeville, MN, 1991).

11. For information on the Third Wave, see Peter Wagner's "A Third Wave?" pp. 1-5. See also his *The Third Wave of the Holy Spirit: Encountering the Power of Signs and Wonders Today* (Ann Arbor, MI, 1988).

Estimated Numbers of Adherents of World Religions

World Population in 1995   5,795,000,000

Population of Major World Religions in 1995
Christian	1,939,000,000
Muslim	1,058,000,000
Hindu	777,000,000
Buddhist	341,000,000
Jewish	13,000,000

Christians
Roman Catholic	1,052,116,000
Pentecostal/Charismatic	463,741,000
Evangelicals	350,000,000
Eastern Orthodox	189,000,000

Protestants
Denominational Pentecostals	217,000,000
Anglicans	57,401,000
Baptists	56,000,000
Lutherans	52,000,000
Presbyterians	46,000,000
Methodists	32,000,000
Holiness (Non-Pentecostals)	6,000,000

Pentecostals/Charismatics
Denominational Pentecostals	217,000,000
Protestant Charismatics	51,300,000
Active	9,300,000
Post-charismatic	42,000,000
Catholic Charismatics	90,000,000
Active	17,000,000
Post-charismatic	73,000,000
Chinese Pentecostals	59,000,000

Mainline Third Wavers   75,000,000

Total Pentecostal/Charismatic Christians
in 1995   463,741,000

Percentage of World Christians   23.9%

movement has been based on the observation of Pentecostal growth patterns, in contrast to those of mainline churches. The cultural and theological adaptability of Pentecostalism has caused immense church growth, and has given classical Pentecostals the distinction of constituting the largest family of Protestants in the world.[12]

Church growth researchers are especially impressed with the record of Pentecostals in church planting and in the development of super churches. Statistics from David Barrett's *World Christian Encyclopedia* indicate the importance of Pentecostalism in the area of church growth. According to Barrett, the Pentecostals had by 1980 surpassed in size all Protestant families of churches. In addition to these Pentecostal churches, the charismatic movement had entered all the traditional churches. In his 1995 projections Barrett estimated the figures in the table on page 286 for World Christianity.[13]

In addition to these worldwide projections, the Pentecostals have excelled in producing the world's largest "mega churches." Many of these are in Korea and include the world's largest congregation, the Yoido Full Gospel Church in Seoul, pastored by David Paul Yonggi Cho.

The following is a list of the five largest congregations in the world according to Peter Wagner based on membership figures:

Largest churches in the world by membership

Church	City	Members
Yoido Full Gospel Church	Seoul, Korea	700,000
Jotabeche Methodist Pentecostal	Santiago, Chile	350,000
Vision Del Futuro	Buenos Aires, Argentina	145,000
Deeper Life Bible Church	Lagos, Nigeria	110,000
Brazil Para Cristo	Sao Paulo, Brazil	85,000

And on page 288 is a list of the largest churches based on Sunday worship attendance.

It was only in the 1980's that surveys began to show the incredible growth of the movement in the United States. Based on a 1979 poll,

---

12. Important church growth texts include Donald McGavran's *How Churches Grow* (London, 1957) and *Understanding Church Growth* (Grand Rapids, MI, 1970). See also Peter Wagner's *Your Church Can Grow* (Glendale, CA, 1976) and *Leading Your Church to Growth* (Ventura, CA, 1984).

13. David Barrett, *World Christian Encyclopedia* (New York, 1982), pp. 815-48.

Largest churches by Sunday Worship Attendance[14]

Worship Attendance	Church	Pastor
240,000	Yoido Full Gospel	David Yonggi Cho
80,000	Vision del Futuro Buenos Aires, Argentina	Omar Cabrera
70,000	Waves of Joy and Peace Buenos Aires, Argentina	Hector Jimenez
65,000	Deeper Christian Life Lagos, Nigeria	William Kumuyi
50,000	Jotabeche Pentecostal Santiago, Chile	Javier Vasquez
50,000	Kum Ran Methodist Seoul, Korea	Hong Do Kim
47,000	Nambu Full Gospel Seoul, Korea	Yong Mok Cho
40,000	Soon Eui Methodist Inchon, Korea	Ho Moon Lee
35,000	Jesus is Lord Fellowship Manila, Philippines	Eddie Villanueva
30,000	Maduriera Assembly of God Rio de Janeiro, Brazil[15]	Francesco Fonte

George Gallup estimated that by 1980 no less than 19% of the American population identified in some way with the movement. These figures showed that some 29,000,000 Americans over the age of eighteen thought of themselves as "pentecostal or charismatic Christians." Also striking was the finding that about 20 percent of all mainline Catholic and Protestant church members identified themselves as "charismatic" despite the fact that less than 5 percent had ever spoken in tongues.[16]

14. See Elmer Towns, "The World's Ten Largest Churches," *Christian Life*, Jan. 1983, pp. 60-66; see also John Vaughn, *The Large Church* (Grand Rapids, MI, 1985); and *The World's 20 Largest Churches* (Grand Rapids, MI, 1984).

15. These figures were published by John Vaughn in the 1990 edition of *The World Christian Almanac* (Wheaton, IL, 1990)

16. George Gallup, "The Christianity Today-Gallup Poll: An Overview," *Christianity Today*, Dec. 21, 1979, pp. 12-27; Kenneth Kantzer, "The Charismatics Among Us," *Christianity Today*, Feb. 22, 1980, pp. 25-29. See also the series titled "America's Pentecostals: Who Are They?" *Christianity Today*, Oct. 16, 1987, pp. 16-29.

The Televangelists

While the bare statistics may have aroused some academic interest, ordinary people were probably more influenced by the burgeoning television ministries of Oral Roberts, Pat Robertson, Jim Bakker, and Jimmy Swaggart — Pentecostal preachers whose sheer visibility added the word "televangelist" to the modern vocabulary. By the end of the decade, Pentecostal voters even had a Republican presidential candidate in the figure of Pat Robertson. Although he lost his bid for the nomination in 1988, Robertson continued to be a major force in American politics through a new conservative pressure group known as the "Christian Coalition."[17]

In the late 1980's, the Pentecostal/charismatic televangelists proved also to be a bane and embarrassment to the movement. Beginning in 1987 a series of scandals rocked the Christian world and seriously discredited the whole genre of television evangelism, seriously crippling some and destroying others. By that year, the three leading televangelists were Oral Roberts in Tulsa, Oklahoma; Jim Bakker in Charlotte, North Carolina; and Jimmy Swaggart in Baton Rouge, Louisiana. Each ministry took in millions of dollars annually from their viewing audiences.

By the end of the decade, however, Bakker and his popular "PTL" program was off the air, his Christian retreat center in Fort Mill, South Carolina was bankrupt, and he was in jail after a sensational sex scandal that rocked the nation.[18] At the same time, Oral Roberts was severely criticized for his fund-raising tactics on behalf of his medical school in Tulsa. Within a few months, Jimmy Swaggart's empire also began to fall apart after another sex scandal erupted into national headlines. Although Roberts survived the ordeal with his University intact, his evangelistic association never rebounded to the pre-1987 income levels that made him at one time the nation's leading television preacher.[19]

The one televangelist who escaped largely unscathed in this period was Pat Robertson and his Christian Broadcast Network, based in

17. On Robertson's run for president see Maynard Good, "CBN's Pat Robertson: White House Next?" *Saturday Evening Post,* Mar. 1985, pp. 50-57; and Steven Strang and Bert Ghezzi, "Pat Robertson — What Would He Do if He Were President?" *Charisma,* May 1986, pp. 31-35.

18. Martin Marty, "Religion, Television, and Money," *Encyclopedia Britannica Book of the Year* (1988), pp. 294-95.

19. See Frank Razelle, *Religious Television: Controversies and Conclusions* (Norwood, NJ, 1990).

Virginia Beach, Virginia. Both his flagship program, the "700 Club," and his newly founded Regent University continued to flourish through the entire dark period of the television scandals. Indeed, by 1996 some observers contended that Robertson had become one of the "major religious figures of the twentieth century." According to Tim Stafford of *Christianity Today*:

> Robertson has shaped three major religious developments: the charismatic renewal, Christian TV, and evangelical politics. The charismatic renewal, of which Robertson is a founding member, modernized and broadened Pentecostalism, giving evangelicalism a renewed vitality. Robertson played a leading role in developing religious television, which has deeply (some would say insidiously) affected the church. Most recently, Robertson has led evangelical Christians into political re-engagement. Together, these developments helped transform evangelicals from a small, defended backwater to the leading force in American Christianity.[20]

In the end, the scandals were only a temporary setback for the broad Pentecostal and charismatic movements, which continued to grow impressively around the world throughout the 1990's. The scandals demonstrated not only the immense television appeal of the Pentecostal style of preaching, teaching, and worship, but also the frailty of the messengers.

In the wake of the sensational events surrounding the televangelists was a gradual shift to what Peter Wagner termed a "post denominational" era for the churches. For several years Wagner had observed the growth of large evangelical and charismatic congregations that seemed to function outside the historic denominational frameworks. In 1996, he called together a conference of leaders for a symposium to examine the phenomenon. Because of criticism from pastors of several large denominational churches, he changed the name of the movement to the churches of "the New Apostolic Reformation." Although most of the megachurches involved were either Pentecostal or charismatic in orientation, a significant number were "third wave" or straightline evangelical churches.[21]

---

20. Tim Stafford, "When Evangelicals Look in the Mirror, Do We See the Host of the 700 Club Staring Back?" *Christianity Today*, Aug. 12, 1996, pp. 26-33.

21. See Peter Wagner, "Those Amazing Postdenominational Churches," in *Ministries Today*, July/Aug. 1994, p. 50; and "The New Paradigms of Today's Emerging Churches," in *Ministries Today*, Mar./Apr. 1996, p. 52.

Only time would tell whether this conference marked the beginning of a new "post-denominational" period in church history, or whether the large networks of "new apostolic reformation" churches would themselves become new denominations.

Three Streams — One River

For decades, church leaders have recognized that Pentecostalism had become one of the three major divisions of Christianity. The idea was first mentioned by Leslie Newbigin of south India in his 1953 book entitled, *The Household of God*. In this pioneering work, Bishop Newbigin saw three major types of Christianity in the world, each with an authentic contribution to make to the Body of Christ. According to Newbigin, the first was the Catholic tradition, which emphasized continuity, orthodoxy, and the importance of the sacraments to the life of the church. The Protestant tradition, on the other hand, emphasized the centrality of the scriptures and the importance of the proclaimed word of God. The Pentecostals added to these first two historic expressions of the faith an emphasis on the present action of the Spirit in the church through the gifts of the Holy Spirit. According to Newbigin, the church needed all three emphases in order to be a powerful force in the modern world.[22]

The same point was made also by Ralph Martin, a leader from the earliest days in the Catholic charismatic renewal. In his 1976 book, *Fire on the Earth*, Martin saw the charismatic renewal as the vehicle for bringing these "three streams" together. In Martin's view, the charismatic movement was the only force that could weld these forces together for a unified Christian witness.[23]

As exemplified in an individual's life, this concept was given powerful testimony in Michael Harper's autobiographical book *Three Sisters*, published in 1979. An early leader in the Anglican charismatic movement in England, Harper stated that:

> One sister (evangelical) taught me that the basis of Christian life is a personal relationship with Jesus Christ. A second (Pentecostal) helped

22. Lesslie Newbigin, *The Household of God* (New York, 1954); Van Dusen, "The Third Force," *Life*, pp. 113-24.
23. Ralph Martin, *Fire on the Earth* (Ann Arbor, MI, 1975), pp. 30-42.

me experience the spiritual dynamic of the Holy Spirit. Yet another (Catholic) ushered me into a whole new world where I began to see the implications of Christian community.[24]

By 1984, Episcopal charismatic renewal leaders could refer to their church as follows: "Episcopal Church: Catholic evangelical-charismatic." According to Bruce Rose:

> What we are is a church which has attempted to preserve in its teaching and worship the best of Catholic tradition, while remaining open to learning from others. In the sixteenth century this meant learning a renewed reverence for and love of the Word of God from the Evangelical Protestant reformers. In the twentieth it has meant learning of the empowerment of the Holy Spirit available today as in the days of the Apostles, from the "Pentecostal" churches such as the Assemblies of God. Yes, we have changed, and hopefully we will go on changing as we continue to learn and grow in the ways of our Lord Jesus Christ until that day when we shall all truly be one in Him.[25]

Indeed, by 1984, there were signs that the Episcopal Church was finally ending its long period of declining numbers and entering a period of growth. This growth, many believed, was being led by the army of young charismatic rectors. Of 7,200 Episcopal parishes in the United States, about 400 were experiencing charismatic renewal. Many were openly experiencing the gifts of the Spirit in their regular services. In addition, by 1984 no less than 47 percent of all the world's Anglican bishops were baptized in the Spirit and openly espousing the charismatic renewal.

Making news were parishes in Houston, and Dallas, Texas; Darien, Connecticut; and Fairfax, Virginia. Others, such as Philips Cathedral in Atlanta (the largest Episcopal parish in the United States), conducted regular charismatic "prayer/praise rallies," separate from the regular services, that attracted hundreds of enthusiastic worshipers. Of special note were three northern Virginia parishes that experienced phenomenal growth after choosing "to go the charismatic route."

One of these, The Church of the Apostles in Fairfax — described as an "exuberant charismatic parish" — grew from 200 to over 2,000 mem-

---

24. Michael Harper, *Three Sisters* (Wheaton, IL, 1979), pp. 9-15.
25. Bruce L. Rose, "Episcopal Church: Catholic-Evangelical-Charismatic," *Acts 29*, Feb. 1984, pp. 1-6.

bers in about seven years. At Truro, thirty-six shepherding groups meet weekly under lay leadership for Bible study and spiritual growth. The three pastors speak of their experience as: "three streams, one river — Protestant (Bible-based), Catholic (liturgical and sacramental), and Pentecostal (Spirit-filled) . . . all three indispensable to a thriving church."[26]

The story of these Episcopal churches is an example of a trend affecting churches in most denominations around the world. At one and the same time, churches from many varied backgrounds seem to be combining these three elements to form a new type of church that just may be the shape of the future for Christendom. Because of the extensive ecumenical contacts brought about by charismatic renewal, there is a growing appreciation for the strengths of the three streams and a spirit of sharing the treasures that have been given to each tradition by the Lord.

In the case of the Episcopal Church, the growth of the renewal movement was not fast enough for a number of ambitious charismatics who became more and more impatient with the slow pace of change and with the increasing control of the church by more liberal bishops. In 1992 a group of Pentecostal ministers formed the first American denomination to use the word "charismatic" in its name. The "Charismatic Episcopal Church" was founded by Bishop Randy Adler, a former Pentecostal minister, who wanted to combine "charismatic Christianity with high church style." By 1996, the Charismatic Episcopal Church had grown to 180 congregations, several of which transferred from the mainline Episcopal Church.[27]

Also making news was the occasional case of a Pentecostal congregation joining the Episcopal Church *en masse*. The most celebrated case was the 500 member Evangel Assembly of God Church in Valdosta, Georgia which in 1990 followed its pastor, Stan White, into the Episcopal Church. White, whose father and grandfather were Assemblies of God ministers, said that "pentecostalism, despite its insistence upon the gifts of the Spirit from the Acts of the Apostles, had not fully appropriated the richness of worship in the early church."[28]

26. Beth Spring, "Spiritual Renewal Brings Booming Growth to Episcopal Churches in Northern Virginia," *Christianity Today*, Jan. 13, 1984, pp. 38-39.

27. J. Lee Grady, "Denomination Blends Charismatic Spirituality with High Church Style," *Charisma*, Sept. 1996, pp. 25-27.

28. See Randall Balmer, "Why the Bishops Went to Valdosta," *Christianity Today*, Sept. 24, 1990, pp. 19-24; and Robert Libby, "Newest Episcopalians Are a Spirited Group," *Episcopal Life*, June 1990, p. 6.

The examples of the Charismatic Episcopal Church and the Valdosta congregation pointed to a growing phenomenon in the 1990's involving Pentecostal churches and individuals returning to the historic mainline churches in search of deeper Christian "roots" and a sense of ritual and decorum felt to be lacking in the free-flowing worship of their former churches. By 1990, like minded pastors were banding together in what they called a "convergence movement" designed to bring the three streams together in a new and powerful spiritual configuration.

Even more striking were the cases of charismatic ministers, priests, and congregations joining the ranks of Orthodoxy. In 1993, pastor Charles Bell led his San Jose, California Vineyard Christian Fellowship into the Antiochian Evangelical Orthodox Mission. As an Orthodox church, the congregation changed its name to St. Stephen Orthodox Church while its pastor changed his name to "Father Seraphim Bell." Soon "rock music, public prophesying, and speaking in tongues gave way to liturgical readings, lit candles, and kissed paintings of the Virgin Mary." Bell had been influenced by Franky Schaeffer and Peter Gillquist who earlier had pioneered a movement of evangelicals and charismatics towards orthodoxy.[29] Meanwhile in England, Michael Harper, the noted Anglican Charismatic pioneer, joined the Antiochian Greek Orthodox Church in 1995, taking with him no less than nine fellow Anglican priests on a "journey to Orthodoxy." Harper's action was triggered by the Anglican vote to ordain women priests in 1992. This was done despite the fact that the Archbishop of Canterbury, George Carey, was an acknowledged charismatic who had earlier been influenced by Harper's ministry.[30]

Of Pilgrims, Settlers, and the Landed Aristocracy

Someone has said that the first generation of a religious movement is made up of the "pilgrims" who leave their secure and comfortable homes

29. Calmetta Coleman, "A Charismatic Church Deals With a Preacher Who Finds New Faith," *The Wall Street Journal,* June 14, 1996, pp. 1-7. For his side of the story see Charles Bell, *Discovering the Rich Heritage of Orthodoxy* (Minneapolis, 1994), pp. 1-7, 86-90. See also Peter Gillquist, *Becoming Orthodox: A Journey to the Ancient Christian Faith* (Ben Lamond, CA, 1992).

30. See Michael Harper, *Equal but Different* (London, 1993), pp. 131, 171, 213. Letter from Michael Harper to Vinson Synan, Mar. 17, 1995.

to carve out a new home in a harsh and forbidding land. They are the revolutionaries who abandon everything to follow a new ideal. The second generation becomes the settlers who domesticate the land, build fences, and bring the basic elements of law and order to the society. The third generation, however, evolves into the landed aristocracy. These become the social arbiters — the economic barons and vested interests who, above all, wish to prevent any more new pilgrims or settlers from entering the land.

By the mid 1980's, it could be said that the three streams fit into the foregoing categories, at least chronologically. Classical Pentecostals were well into the third generation, and in some quarters had become the "landed aristocracy" of the tradition. The Protestant neo-Pentecostals were entering the second generation and were becoming "settlers" in the evangelical world. The Catholic charismatics, however, were still "pilgrims" carving out a home in the world of the Roman Catholic Church.

The major problem facing all of these streams was to maintain the revolutionary fervor of the latter rain until it could be said that the churches had truly been renewed. But even the more optimistic leaders of the 1960's and 1970's had learned that renewal was a long and arduous task and would not be accomplished overnight.

Beyond the renewal of the churches is an aspect of the movement that few Charismatics have confronted — that of transforming society. By the end of the 1970's, no group in America had a greater opportunity to challenge the existing order. With its vast armies of committed followers from denominations, with its overwhelming faith and ardor, with its able leadership, the charismatic movement was in a position to change America's lifestyle.

In 1979, Jeremy Rifkin stated that "today's Charismatics are providing the most significant challenge to the truths of the expansionary era yet mounted. Faith healing, speaking in tongues, and prophesying are, indeed, weapons of rebellion against the authority of the modern age.[31] Seeing the Charismatics as "a new liberating force," Rifkin put much faith in them as agents of positive change. As to the possibilities of future change, he stated:

> While it is too early to tell which way the charismatic movement will eventually lean, a great deal will depend on their understanding of

31. Rifkin and Howard, *The Emerging Order,* p. 231.

the nature of our secular-materialist culture. If they see the problem simply as one of saving fallen individuals from an evil world, leaving the institutional basis of materialism untouched, then it is likely the existing order will change them, rather than they it. If, however, the evangelical participants in the new awakening are able to introduce a Biblical notion of fallen "powers and principalities" as a dual concern along with individual renewal, then this new awakening may, indeed, combine liberation with covenant and change the course of history.[32]

The Future of the Pentecostal Tradition

In light of many studies made in the past, a possible future may be glimpsed. According to projections made by the World Council of Churches in the early 1970's, by the year 2000 over 50 percent of all the Christians in the world will be: (1) non-white; (2) from the Southern Hemisphere; and (3) of the Pentecostal or charismatic variety. Events and church growth patterns of the past several years seem to confirm these trends.

If these projections hold, it is not unreasonable to predict that by the end of the century Christendom could approximate the following configuration:

Twenty-five percent will be classical Pentecostals, coming predominantly from the burgeoning Pentecostal movements in the Third World. These Christians will continue to have a minimum of liturgy and ritual and will emphasize the gifts of the Holy Spirit in their regular services. They will continue to be the fastest growing churches in the world. Many "superchurches" will emerge in third-world nations as well as in the United States.

Twenty-five percent will be charismatic, but in mainline Protestant and Catholic churches — mainly in the "developed" nations of Europe and North America. Their services will be the mildly charismatic affairs typical of the "third wave," and may or may not carry the label "Pentecostal" or "charismatic." They will gradually surpass the older "liberal" churches in size and influence. In a sense, they will become the "mainline" churches of the twenty-first century.

Twenty-five percent will be non-charismatic Christians from the

---

32. Rifkin and Howard, *The Emerging Order*, p. 231.

mainline Protestant and Catholic churches. These will include two groups; the "liberal" churches, which will continue to decline in numbers, and the non-charismatic evangelical churches, which will continue to grow while becoming a smaller proportion of the total number of Christians. The "liberals" will have less power in the denominational structures but will continue to dominate the ecumenical movement. The "evangelicals" will be about equally divided between those who are more open to charismatic worship and those who will more and more be drawn into a defensive fundamentalist shell.

Twenty-five percent will be nominal Christians from all churches, people who do not practice their faith and are Christians only in a cultural sense. Most of these will be in a progressive condition of apostasy, and Christian only in a faintly historical way. They will constitute a large number of Western (mostly white) church members who find the church increasingly irrelevant, and will, as apostates, leave their names on the church rolls while seldom if ever attending services, or else they will leave the church entirely.

One of the first observers to note these trends was John Alexander Mackay, President of Princeton Theological Seminary, who once called the American Pentecostals "the fly in the ointment of Protestantism." By 1967, however, he was calling the charismatic renewal "the most influential and significant movement of our time." Mackay also saw the possibility of "a more cordial rapprochement between Catholics and Pentecostals than between the adherents of the mainline denominations." After reviewing the decline of the mainline Protestant churches and the growth of the Pentecostal churches, Mackay offered the following prophecy: "The Christian future may lie with a reformed Catholicism and a matured Pentecostalism."[33]

If Mackay's vision proves to be correct, it is altogether possible that the future of Christianity will be molded by the developing Pentecostal churches of the Third World interacting with the vigorous charismatic elements in the traditional churches. The recent history of church growth

33. For Mackay's views see his *Christian Reality and Appearance* (Richmond, 1969), pp. 88-89. Also see Chandler, "Fanning the Charismatic Flame," *Christianity Today*, Nov. 24, 1967, p. 40; and David du Plessis, *A Man Called Mr. Pentecost*, pp. 172-80. For Mackay's relationship to the charismatic renewal, see Robert R. Curlee and Mary Ruth Isaac-Curlee, "Bridging the Gap: John A. Mackay, Presbyterians, and the Charismatic Movement," *American Presbyterians* 72, 3 (Fall 1994): 142-56.

in Africa and Latin America indicates that Christian affairs of the twenty-first century may be largely in the hands of surging Pentecostal churches in the Third World and a Roman Catholicism inspired and revivified by the charismatic renewal.

Bibliography

Collections

Archives of Asbury Seminary. Located in Wilmore, Kentucky, this houses the most extensive collection of holiness materials in the United States.

Archives of the Church of God. This collection is housed in the headquarters of the denomination in Cleveland, Tennessee. This is the best source for documents pertaining to the family of churches known as The Church of God.

Archives of the Church of the Nazarene. Located in Kansas City, Missouri, this constitutes an extensive source for manuscripts, periodicals, and general accounts relating to the National Holiness Movement and the holiness denominations which issued from it.

Archives of the Pentecostal Holiness Church. Located in Franklin Springs, Georgia, this collection is the best source for materials on the Pentecostal Holiness Church and the groups in the southeast associated with that church.

Oral Roberts University Pentecostal Collection. This collection, in Tulsa, Oklahoma, is the most complete grouping of materials relating to the Pentecostal movement in the world. An excellent file of manuscripts and periodicals as well as rare publications pertaining to the modern Pentecostal denominations can also be found here.

The Pentecostal File of the Assemblies of God. This collection, relating to the history of the Assemblies of God group and others derived from this church, is located in the national headquarters in Springfield, Missouri.

Sources for the holiness movement in the Southern Methodist Church can be found in the libraries and archives of Emory University in Atlanta, Georgia; Duke University in Durham, North Carolina; Drew University in Madison, New Jersey; and Perkins School of Theology at Southern Methodist University in Dallas, Texas.

Primary Sources

Arnott, John. *The Father's Blessing.* Orlando, FL: Creation House, 1996.

Asbury, Francis. *The Journal of the Rev. Francis Asbury.* 3 vols. New York: Bangs and Mason, 1821.

Bailey, S. Clyde. *Pioneer Marvels of Faith.* Morristown, TN, n.d.

Barratt, Thomas Ball. *In the Days of the Latter Rain.* Oslo, Norway, 1909. Reprinted by the Garland Publishing Company in the Higher Life Series, New York, 1985.

————. *When the Fire Fell: An Outline of My Life.* Oslo, Norway: Alfons, Housen & Soner, 1927. Reprinted by the Garland Publishing Company in the Higher Life Series, New York, 1985.

Bartleman, Frank. *How Pentecost Came to Los Angeles.* Los Angeles, 1925.

Bell, Charles. *Discovering the Rich Heritage of Orthodoxy.* Minneapolis: Light and Life Publishing Co., 1994.

Bennett, Dennis. *Nine O'Clock in the Morning.* Plainfield, NJ: Bridge Publishing Co., 1970.

Berg, Daniel. *Enviado Por Deus: Memorias de Daniel Berg.* Sao Paulo, Brazil, 1959.

Bernard, David. *The Oneness of God.* St. Louis: Word Aflame Press, 1983.

————. *The Oneness of Jesus Christ.* St. Louis: Word Aflame Press, 1994.

Bilheimer, Paul. *Destined for the Throne.* Fort Washington, PA: Christian Literature Crusade, 1975.

Brasher, John. *The Sanctified South: John Lakin Brasher and the Holiness Movement.* Urbana, IL, 1994.

Britton, F. M. *Pentecostal Truth, or Sermons on Regeneration, Sanctification, the Baptism of the Holy Spirit, Divine Healing, the Second Coming of Jesus, etc.* Royston, GA: Publishing House of the Pentecostal Holiness Church, 1919.

Brumback, Carl. *God in Three Persons.* Cleveland, TN: Pathway Press, 1959.

Buckalew, J. W. *Incidents in the Life of J. W. Buckalew.* Cleveland, TN: Church of God Publishing House, 1920.

Carey, Thurman A. *Memoirs of Thurman A. Carey.* Columbia, SC: A. E. Robinson, 1907.

Cho, Yonggi. *The Fourth Dimension.* Plainfield, NJ: Bridge Publishing Co., 1979.

Clemmons, Ithiel. *Bishop C. H. Mason and the Roots of the Church of God in Christ.* Bakersfield, CA, 1996.

Congar, Yves. *Chrétiens Désunis: Principes d'un "oecumenisme" Catholique.* Paris: Editions du Cerf, 1964 (1937 reprint).

Cox, B. L. *My Life Story.* Greenwood, SC: Congregational Holiness Publishing House, 1959.

Curnock, Nehemiah, ed. *The Journal of the Rev. John Wesley, A.M.* 8 vols. London: Robert Culley, 1910.

Derstine, Gerald. *Following the Fire.* Plainfield, NJ: Bridge Publishing Co., 1980.

Duffield, Guy, and Nathaniel Van Cleave. *Foundations of Pentecostal Theology.* Los Angeles: L.I.F.E. Bible College, 1983.

du Plessis, David (as told to Bob Slosser). *A Man Called Mr. Pentecost.* Plainfield, NJ: Logos International, 1977.

Etter, Mrs. M. B. Woodworth. *Marvels and Miracles; Signs and Wonders.* Indianapolis, 1922.

—————. *Signs and Wonders God Wrought in the Ministry for Forty Years.* Indianapolis, 1916.

Ewart, Frank J. *The Phenomenon of Pentecost: A History of the Latter Rain.* St. Louis: Pentecostal Publishing House, 1947.

—————. *The Revelation of Jesus Christ.* St. Louis: Pentecostal Publishing House, n.d.

Finney, C. G. *Memoirs of Reverend Charles G. Finney.* New York: Fleming H. Revell Company, 1876.

Fletcher, John. *The Works of the Reverend John Fletcher.* 4 vols. New York: Lane and Scott, 1851.

Ford, J. Massingberd. *The Pentecostal Experience: A New Direction for Catholics.* New York: Paulist Press, 1970.

Francescon, Luigi. *Resumo de uma Ramificacao da Obra de Deus . . . .* 3rd ed. Chicago, 1958.

Gillquist, Peter. *Becoming Orthodox: A Journey to the Ancient Christian Faith.* Ben Lamond, CA: Conciliar Press, 1992.

Godbey, W. B. *Commentary on the New Testament.* 7 vols. Cincinnati: M. W. Knapp, 1896.

Goff, Florence. *Tests and Triumphs.* Falcon, NC, 1924.

Goss, Ethel A. *Winds of God.* New York: Comet Press Books, 1958.

Harper, Michael. *Equal but Different: Male and Female in Church and Family.* London: Hodder & Stoughton, 1993.

Haygood, Atticus G. *Growth in Grace: A Sermon by Atticus G. Haygood, D.D., LL.D., Preached Before the District Conference of the Oxford District, North Georgia Conference, M.E. Church, South, Held at Covington, Ga., July 18th, 1885, and Published by Formal Request of the Conference.* Macon, GA, 1885.

Haynes, B. F. *Tempest-Tossed on Methodist Seas.* Kansas City: Nazarene Publishing House, 1914.

Hill, Steve. *White Cane Religion and Other Messages from the Brownsville Revival.* Shippensburg, PA: Destiny Image, 1997.

Holmes, N. J. *Life Sketches and Sermons.* Franklin Springs, GA: Publishing House of the Pentecostal Holiness Church, 1920.

Horton, Stanley, ed. *Systematic Theology: A Pentecostal Perspective.* Springfield, MO: Gospel Publishing House, 1994.

————. *What the Bible Says about the Holy Spirit.* Springfield, MO: Gospel Publishing House, 1976.

Hughes, George. *Days of Power in the Forest Temple.* Boston, 1874.

Ironside, H. A. *Holiness, the False and the True.* Neptune, NJ: Loizeaux Brothers, 1912.

Irving, Edward. *The Day of Pentecost or the Baptism With the Holy Ghost.* Edinburgh: John Lindsay, 1831.

Jackson, Thomas, ed. *The Works of John Wesley.* 14 vols. Grand Rapids, MI: Zondervan Publishing House, 1959.

Juillerat, L. Howard, ed. *Book of Minutes, General Assemblies, Churches of God.* Cleveland, TN: Church of God Publishing House, 1922.

Keen, S. A. *Pentecostal Papers or the Gift of the Holy Ghost.* Cincinnati: M. W. Knapp, 1896.

Kiergan, A. M. *Historical Sketches of the Revival of True Holiness and Church Polity from 1865-1916.* Fort Scott, KS: Church Advocate Board, 1971.

Kilpatrick, John. *When the Heavens Are Brass: Keys to Genuine Revival.* Shippensburg, PA: Destiny Image, 1997.

King, Joseph H. *From Passover to Pentecost.* Memphis, TN: H. W. Dixon Printing Company, 1914.

————, and Blanche L. King. *Yet Speaketh, Memoirs of the Late Bishop Joseph H. King.* Franklin Springs, GA: Publishing House of the Pentecostal Holiness Church, 1949.

La Berge, Agnes N. O. *What God Hath Wrought — Life and Work of Mrs. Agnes N. O. La Berge, Nee Miss Agnes N. Ozman.* Chicago: Herald Publishing Company, 1921.

Lake, John G. *The Astounding Diary of Dr. John G. Lake.* Dallas: CFNI Press, 1987.

Lee, R. H., and G. H. Montgomery, eds. *Edward D. Reeves, His Life and Message.* Franklin Springs, GA: Publishing House of the Pentecostal Holiness Church, 1940.

Lindsay, Gordon. *John G. Lake: Apostle to Africa.* Dallas: CFNI Press, 1981.

Mackay, John Alexander. *Christian Reality and Appearance.* Richmond: John Knox Press, 1969.

Mansfield, Patti Gallagher. *As by a New Pentecost: The Dramatic Beginning of the Catholic Charismatic Renewal.* Steubenville, OH: Steubenville University Press, 1992.

McDonnell, Kilian. *Presence, Power, and Praise.* 3 vols. New York: Paulist Press, 1980.

McDonnell, Kilian, and Arnold Bittlinger. *The Baptism in the Holy Spirit as an Ecumenical Problem.* South Bend, IN: Charismatic Renewal Services, 1972.

McDonnell, Kilian, and George Montague. *Christian Initiation and Baptism in the Holy Spirit: Evidence from the First Eight Centuries.* Collegeville, MN: Liturgical Press, 1991.

McLean, A., and Joel W. Eaton, eds. *Penuel, or Face to Face with God.* New York, 1869.

McPherson, Aimee Semple. *The Foursquare Gospel.* Los Angeles: Robertson Printing Company, 1946.

————. *In the Service of the King.* New York: Boni and Liveright, 1927.

————. *The Story of My Life.* Los Angeles: Echo Park Evangelistic Association, 1951.

————. *This Is That: Personal Experiences, Sermons and Writings of Aimee Semple McPherson.* Los Angeles: Echo Park Evangelistic Association, 1923.

Officer, Sam E. *The Jesus Church.* Cleveland, TN: private printing, n.d.

Parham, Charles Fox. *Kol Kare Bomidbar: A Voice Crying in the Wilderness.* Joplin, MO: Joplin Printing Company, 1944 (1902 reprint).

Parham, Sarah E. *The Life of Charles F. Parham, Founder of the Apostolic Faith Movement.* Joplin, MO: Tri-State Printing Company, 1930.

Pickett, L. L. *God or the Guessers: Some Scriptures on Present Day Infidelity.* Louisville, KY: Pentecostal Publishing Company, 1926.

————. *The Pickett-Smith Debate on Entire Sanctification, A Second Blessing.* Terrell, TX: private printing, 1896.

Pierce, Lovick. *A Miscellaneous Essay on Entire Sanctification, How It Was Lost to the Church, and How It May and Must Be Regained.* Atlanta: private printing, 1897.

Pruitt, Raymond M. *Fundamentals of the Faith.* Cleveland, TN: White Wing Publishing House, 1981.

Riggs, Ralph M. *The Spirit Himself.* Springfield, MO: Gospel Publishing House, 1949.

Roberts, Oral. *Expect a Miracle: My Life and Ministry — Oral Roberts, an Autobiography.* Nashville: Thomas Nelson, 1995.

Robinson, A. E. *A Layman and The Book.* Franklin Springs, GA: Publishing House of the Pentecostal Holiness Church, 1936.

Sauls, Ned. *Pentecostal Doctrines: A Wesleyan Approach.* Dunn, NC: Heritage Bible College, 1979.

Shaw, S. B. *Echoes of the General Holiness Assembly.* Chicago: S. B. Shaw Publisher, 1901.

————. *The Great Revival in Wales.* Toronto: A. Sims, Publisher, 1905.

Simpson, A. B. *Emblems of the Holy Spirit.* Nyack, NY: Christian Alliance Publishing Company, 1901.

Smith, Amanda. *An Autobiography.* New York: Oxford University Press, 1988 (originally published in 1893).

Smith, Joseph. *History of the Church of Jesus Christ of Latter-Day Saints.* Salt Lake City: Desert News, 1902.

Sorrow, Watson. *Some of My Experiences.* Franklin Springs, GA: Publishing House of the Pentecostal Holiness Church, 1954.

Steinbeck, John. *Grapes of Wrath.* Chicago: J. G. Ferguson, 1939.

Stolee, Haakon J. *Speaking in Tongues.* Rev. ed. Minneapolis: Augsburg Press, 1963.

Stone, Barton. *The Biography of Eld. Barton Stone: Written by Himself with Additions and Reflections.* Cincinnati, 1847.

Suenens, Leon Joseph Cardinal. *Ecumenism and Charismatic Renewal: Theological and Pastoral Orientations, Malines Document II.* Ann Arbor, MI: Word of Life, 1978.

Sugden, E. A., ed. *Wesley's Standard Sermons.* 2 vols. Nashville: Lamar and Barton, 1920.

Synan, J. A. *Christian Life in Depth.* Franklin Springs, GA: Advocate Press, 1964.

Taylor, G. F. *The Spirit and the Bride.* Dunn, NC: private printing, 1907.

Taylor, William. *Story of My Life.* New York: Eaton & Mains, 1896.

Telford, John, ed. *The Letters of the Rev. John Wesley.* 8 vols. London: Epworth Press, 1931.

Tomlinson, A. J. *Answering the Call of God.* Cleveland, TN: White Wing Publishing House, n.d.

—————. *God's Twentieth Century Pioneer.* Vol. 1. Cleveland, TN: White Wing Publishing House, 1962.

—————. "Journal of Happenings." Manuscript diary of A. J. Tomlinson, in the Archives of the Church of God. Cleveland, TN, 1901-23.

—————. *The Last Great Conflict.* Cleveland, TN: Walter E. Rodgers Press, 1913.

Tomlinson, Homer A., ed. *Diary of A. J. Tomlinson.* 3 vols. New York: The Church of God, World Headquarters, 1949-55.

—————. *The Shout of a King.* New York: The Church of God, World Headquarters, 1965.

Tomlinson, M. A. *Basic Bible Beliefs.* Cleveland, TN: White Wing Publishing House, 1961.

Warfield, Benjamin. *Counterfeit Miracles.* Carlisle, PA: The Banner of Truth Trust, 1918.

Wells, David F. *Revolution in Rome.* Downers Grove, IL: Intervarsity Press, 1972.

White, Alma. *Demons and Tongues.* 4th ed. Zeraphath, NJ: The Pillar of Fire, 1949.

Wilkerson, David. *The Cross and the Switchblade.* New York: Random House, 1963.

Williams, Rodman. *Renewal Theology,* 3 vols. Vol. 1: *God, the World and Redemption;* vol. 2: *Salvation, The Holy Spirit;* vol. 3: *Christian Living: The Church, the Kingdom, and Last Things.* Grand Rapids, MI: Zondervan, 1988, 1990, 1992.

Wilson, George W. *Methodist Theology vs. Methodist Theologians.* Cincinnati: Jennings and Pye, 1904.

Wimber, John. *Power Evangelism.* San Francisco: Harper & Row, 1986.

Wood, J. A. *Auto-Biography of Rev. J. A. Wood.* Chicago: The Christian Witness Company, 1904.

Minutes, Yearbooks, and Dictionaries

Annual Revision of the Compilation of the Local Churches. The Pentecostal Church of God of America. Joplin, MO: Messenger Publishing House, 1966.

Ashworth, C. A. *Yearbook of the Church of God in Christ.* Memphis, 1961.

Barrett, David. *World Christian Encyclopedia.* New York: Oxford University Press, 1982.

Bedell, Kenneth B., ed. *Yearbook of American Churches, 1995.* New York: National Council of Churches (Abingdon Press), 1995.

Burgess, Stanley; Gary B. McGee; and Patrick Alexander. *Dictionary of Pentecostal and Charismatic Movements.* Grand Rapids, MI: Zondervan Publishing House, 1988.

Clark, Elmer T. *The Small Sects in America.* Rev. ed. Nashville: Abingdon Press, 1959.

Constitution and General Rules of the Fire-Baptized Holiness Church. Royston, GA: Live Coals Press, 1905, 1910.

Crayne, Richard. *Pentecostal Handbook.* Morristown, TN: private printing, 1963.

Directory, The Assemblies of God. Springfield, MO: The Gospel Publishing House, 1962.

Discipline of the Evangelical United Brethren Church. Harrisburg, PA: The Evangelical Press, 1951.

Discipline of the Fire-Baptized Holiness Church. Pembroke, NC, 1916.

Discipline of the Fire-Baptized Holiness Church of God of the Americas. Atlanta, 1962.

Discipline of the Pentecostal Free-Will Baptist Church, Inc. Dunn, NC, n.d.

Doctrines and Discipline of the Methodist Episcopal Church, South. Nashville: Southern Methodist Publishing House, 1866, 1878.

DuPree, Sherry. *Biographical Dictionary of African-American Holiness Pentecostals, 1880-1990.* Washington, DC: Middle Atlantic Regional Press, 1989.

Holy Convocation, Church of God in Christ, Souvenir Book and Official Program (59th). Memphis, 1966.

Jones, Charles E. *Black Holiness: A Guide to the Study of Black Participation in Wesleyan Perfectionist and Glossolalic Pentecostal Movements.* Metuchen, NJ: Scarecrow Press, 1987.

———. *The Charismatic Movement: A Guide to the Study of Neo-Pentecostalism with an Emphasis on Anglo-American Sources.* Metuchen, NJ: Scarecrow Press, 1995.

———. *A Guide to the Study of the Holiness Movement.* Metuchen, NJ: Scarecrow Press, 1974.

———. *A Guide to the Study of the Pentecostal Movement.* 2 vols. Metuchen, NJ: Scarecrow Press, 1983.

Journal, General Conference of the Methodist Episcopal Church, South. Nashville: Southern Methodist Publishing House, 1866, 1870, 1878.

Landis, Benson Y., and Constant H. Jacquet, Jr. *Yearbook of American Churches.* New York: National Council of Churches, 1964-70.

Mayer, F. E. *The Religious Bodies of America.* St. Louis: Concordia Publishing House, 1961.

McDonnell, Kilian. *Presence, Power, Praise.* 3 vols. Collegeville, MN: Liturgical Press, 1980.

Mead, Frank S. *Handbook of Denominations in the United States.* 4th ed. New York: Abingdon Press, 1965.

Melton, Gordon. *Encyclopedia of American Religions.* 2nd ed. Detroit: Gale Research Company, 1987.

Minutes of the Beulah Pentecostal Holiness Church. Franklin Springs, GA, 1896-1956.

Minutes, Church of God of the Mountain Assembly, Inc. Jellico, TN, 1965.

Minutes and Discipline of the Emmanuel Holiness Church Annual State Assemblies of Alabama, Florida, Georgia, North Carolina, and South Carolina. Franklin Springs, GA, 1959, 1965.

Minutes of the General Assemblies of the Church of God (Cleveland, Tennessee). Cleveland: The Pathway Press, 1906-66.

Minutes of the General Conferences of the Pentecostal Holiness Church. Franklin Springs, GA, 1910-93.

Minutes of the Holiness Church of North Carolina. Kingston, NC, 1908, 1909, 1910.

Minutes of the 1963 Sessions of the Conferences of the Congregational Holiness Church. Greenwood, SC: Publishing House of the Congregational Holiness Church, 1963.

Minutes of the 60th Annual Assembly of the Church of God of Prophecy. Cleveland, TN: White Wing Publishing House, 1965.

Murphy, Larry; J. Gordon Melton; and Gary Ward, eds. *Encyclopedia of African American Religions.* New York: Garland Reference Library of Social Science, 1993.

Tomlinson, M. A., ed. *Cyclopedic Index of Assembly Minutes (1906-1940) of the Church of God Over Which A. J. Tomlinson Was General Overseer and M. A. Tomlinson Is Now General Overseer* (Church of God of Prophecy). Cleveland, TN: White Wing Publishing House, 1950.

Twentieth Anniversary of the Garr Auditorium. Charlotte, NC, 1950.

U.S. Bureau of the Census. *Historical Statistics of the United States, Colonial Times to 1957.* Washington, DC: Government Printing Office, 1961.

————. *Religious Bodies: 1926.* 2 vols. Washington, DC: Government Printing Office, 1929.

———. *Religious Bodies: 1936.* 2 vols. Washington, DC: Government Printing Office, 1941.

The World Christian Almanac. Wheaton, IL: Tyndale House Books, 1990.

Yearbook of the Church of God in Christ. Memphis, 1960-61.

Periodicals

Abundant Life (Tulsa, OK), 1967.

Altamont Witness (Greenville, SC), 1911-15.

Apostolic Evangel (Falcon, NC), 1908-26.

Apostolic Faith (Baxter Springs, KS), 1900-1927.

Apostolic Faith (Los Angeles), 1906-9.

Beulah Christian (Providence, RI), 1895-1900.

Bridal Call, Foursquare (Los Angeles), 1921-24.

Bridegroom's Messenger (Atlanta), 1908-24.

Bridegroom's Messenger (Dunn, NC), 1907.

Charisma Magazine (Orlando, FL), 1975-96.

Christian Evangel, The. 1914-19.

Church of God, The (Queen's Village, NY), 1966.

Church of God Evangel (Cleveland, TN), 1910-95.

Evangelist Speaks, The (Chester, PA), 1966.

International Outlook (Los Angeles), 1963, 1964.

Life Magazine (New York), 1944, 1958.

Live Coals of Fire (Royston, GA), 1900-1907.

Living Words (Pittsburgh), 1903.

Los Angeles Times, 1906, 1907.

Pentecostal Evangel (Springfield, MO), 1919-95.

Pentecostal Herald (St. Louis), 1967.

Pentecostal Holiness Advocate (Franklin Springs, GA), 1917-95.

Presbyterian Survey (Atlanta), 1964.

Saturday Evening Post (Philadelphia), 1964.

Sent of God (Tabor, IA), 1896-1920.

Timelines (Oklahoma City), 1991-96.

Voice of Holmes (Greenville, SC), 1948-96.

Way of Faith (Columbia, SC), 1901-8.

White Wing Messenger (Cleveland, TN), 1910-24.

Williamsburg Gazette (Williamsburg, VA), 1739-72.

Word and Witness (Malvern, AR), 1913-16.

Articles

Aikman, Duncan. "The Holy Rollers." *American Mercury* 15 (Oct. 1928): 180-91.

Aker, Ben. "Initial Evidence: A Biblical Perspective," in Burgess et al., *Dictionary of Pentecostal and Charismatic Movements,* pp. 455-60.

Balmer, Randall. "Why the Bishops Went to Valdosta." *Christianity Today,* Sept. 24, 1990, pp. 19-24.

Barrett, David. "The Twentieth-Century Pentecostal/Charismatic Renewal in the Holy Spirit, with Its Goal of World Evangelization." *International Bulletin of Missionary Research,* July 1988.

Blumhofer, Edith. "Alexander Boddy and the Rise of Pentecostalism in Britain." *Pneuma* 8 (1986): 31-40.

———. "The Finished Work of Calvary." *A/G Heritage,* Fall 1983, pp. 9-11.

———. "John Alexander Dowie," in Burgess et al., *Dictionary of Pentecostal and Charismatic Movements,* pp. 248-49.

Boisen, A. T. "Religion and Hard Times." *Social Action* 5 (Mar. 1939): 8-35.

Boland, J. M. "A Psychological View of Sin and Holiness." *Quarterly Review of the M.E. Church, South* 12 (July 1892): 342-54.

Buck, Marvin. "When the Holy Spirit Came to a Methodist Church." *Christian Life,* Jan. 1962, pp. 34-36.

Bundy, David. "The Keswick Higher Life Movement," in Burgess et al., *Dictionary of Pentecostal and Charismatic Movements.*

———. "Spiritual Advice to a Seeker . . ." *Pnuema,* Fall 1992, pp. 167-68.

Carter, Herbert, and Ruth K. Moore. "History of the Pentecostal Free Will Baptist Church." *The Bridegroom's Messenger,* Oct. 1966, pp. 4-16.

Chandler, Russell. "Fanning the Charismatic Flame." *Christianity Today,* Nov. 24, 1967, pp. 39-40.

Christenson, Larry. "Dennis Joseph and Rita Bennett," in Burgess et al., *Dictionary of Pentecostal and Charismatic Movements,* pp. 53-54.

Clemmons, Ithiel. "Racial and Spiritual Unity in the Body of Christ." *Advance,* Fall 1995, pp. 66-68.

Coleman, Calmetta. "A Charismatic Church Deals With a Preacher Who Finds New Faith." *The Wall Street Journal,* June 14, 1996, pp. 1-7.

Corvin, R. O. "The Pentecostal Fellowship of North America," *Pentecost,* Dec. 1949, pp. 2.

Curlee, Robert R., and Mary Ruth Isaac-Curlee, "Bridging the Gap: John A. Mackay, Presbyterians, and the Charismatic Movement." *American Presbyterians* 72, 3 (Fall 1994): 142-56.

Daniels, David. "Pentecostalism," in Larry Murphy, J. Gordon Melton, and Gary Ward, eds., *Encyclopedia of African American Religions,* pp. 585-95. New York: Garland Reference Library of Social Science, 1993.

Dorries, David. "Edward Irving and the 'Standing Sign,'" in *Initial Evidence: Historical and Biblical Perspectives on the Pentecostal Doctrine of Spirit Baptism.* Edited by Gary B. McGee. Peabody, MA: Hendrickson Publishers, 1991.

Durham, William. "Personal Testimony of Pastor Durham." *Pentecostal Testimony* 2, no. 3 (1912): 1-16.

Farrell, Frank. "Outburst of Tongues: The New Penetration." *Christianity Today,* Sept. 13, 1963, pp. 3-7.

Fidler, R. L. "Historical Review of the Pentecostal Outpouring in Los Angeles at the Azusa Street Mission in 1906." *The International Outlook,* Jan.-Mar. 1963, pp. 3-14.

Flower, J. R. "Birth of the Pentecostal Movement." *Pentecostal Evangel* 38 (Nov. 26, 1950): 3.

Gaudet, Val. "A Woman and the Pope." *New Covenant* 3, no. 4 (Oct. 1973): 4-6.

Galli, Mark. "Revival at Cane Ridge." *Christian History* issue 45, vol. 14, no. 1, pp. 9-15.

Gill, Deborah M. "The Contemporary State of Women in Ministry in the Assemblies of God." *Pneuma,* Spring 1995, pp. 33-36.

Griffis, Guion. "Camp Meetings in Ante-Bellum, North Carolina." *North Carolina Historical Review,* Apr. 1933.

Hollenweger, Walter. "Pentecostalism and the Third World." *Pulse, Evangelical Committee on Latin America* 4, no. 6 (Dec. 1969): 11-13.

Holt, John B. "Holiness Religion: Cultural Shock and Social Reorganization." *American Sociological Review* 5 (1940): 740-47.

Hubbard, David Allen. "Hazarding the Risks." *Christian Life,* Oct. 1982, pp. 18-26.

Kendrick, Klaud. "Initial Evidence: A Historical Perspective," in Burgess et al., *Dictionary of Pentecostal and Charismatic Movements,* pp. 459-60.

King, J. H. "History of the Fire-Baptized Holiness Church." *The Pentecostal Holiness Advocate,* Mar.-Apr. 1921, a series of four articles.

Lapsley, James N., and John H. Simpson. "Speaking in Tongues." *The Princeton Seminary Bulletin* 58 (Feb. 1965): 6-7.

Lee, Young Hoon. "The Holy Spirit Movement in Korea." *Journal of Soon Shin University* 4 (Dec. 1993): 151-73.

Lewis, Jesse Penn. "The Revival: Revival in Wales Progresses." *The Christian Patriot,* Oct. 7, 1905, pp. 6-7.

Lindsell, Harold. "My Search for the Truth about the Holy Spirit." *Christian Life,* Sept. 1983, p. 29.

Lovett, Leonard. "Black Origins of the Pentecostal Movement," in Vinson Synan, *Aspects of Pentecostal-Charismatic Origins,* pp. 123-42. Plainfield, NJ: Logos International, 1975.

Manual, David. "But Who Is John Gimenez?" *Charisma,* July/Aug. 1981, pp. 22-27.

Mattke, Robert A. "The Baptism of the Holy Spirit as Related to the Work of Entire Sanctification." *Wesleyan Theological Journal,* Spring 1970, pp. 22-32.

Maxwell, Joe. "Building the Church (of God in Christ)." *Christianity Today,* Apr. 8, 1996, pp. 22-28.

McIntire, Carl. *Christian Beacon* 9 (Apr. 27, 1944): 1-8.

Montgomery, G. H. "Christianity, the South, and Race Agitation." *The Pentecostal Holiness Advocate,* Sept. 6, 1946, p. 3.

Murray, J. S. "What We Can Learn from Pentecostal Churches." *Christianity Today* 11 (June 9, 1967): 10-12.

O'Connor, Edward. "A Catholic Pentecostal Movement." *Ave Maria,* June 3, 1967, pp. 7-30.

————. "The Hidden Roots of the Charismatic Renewal in the Catholic Church," in Synan, ed., *Aspects of Pentecostal-Charismatic Origins.* Plainfield, NJ: Logos International, 1975.

Ostling, Richard. "Strains on the Heart," *Time Magazine,* Nov. 19, 1990, pp. 88-90.

Parham, Charles F. "A Critical Analysis of the Tongues Question." *The Apostolic Faith,* June 1925, pp. 2-6.

————. "Sermon by Charles F. Parham." *The Apostolic Faith,* Apr. 1925, pp. 9-14.

"Pentecostals Experience a 'Miracle in Memphis.'" *Memphis Commercial Appeal,* Oct. 20, 1994, A1–p. 10.

Phillips, McCandlish. "And There Appeared Unto Them Tongues of Fire." *Saturday Evening Post,* May 16, 1964, pp. 30-40.

Pinson, M. M. "The Finished Work of Calvary." *Pentecostal Evangel,* Apr. 5, 1964, pp. 7, 26-27.

Plowman, Edward E. "The Deepening Rift in the Charismatic Movement." *Christianity Today,* Oct. 10, 1975, pp. 52-54.

Ralston, Thomas N. "Holiness and Sin — New Theory Noticed." *Quarterly Review of the M.E. Church, South* 14 (July 1881): 441-51.

Reed, David. "Aspects of the Origins of Oneness Pentecostalism," in Synan, ed., *Aspects of Pentecostal-Charismatic Origins,* pp. 143-68. Plainfield, NJ: Logos International, 1975.

Reynolds, F. M. "David Ray Wilkerson," in Burgess et al., *Dictionary of Pentecostal and Charismatic Movements,* pp. 884-85.

Riggs, Ralph M. "Those Store-Front Churches." *United Evangelical Action* 4 (Aug. 1, 1945): 4-5.

Robeck, Cecil M., Jr. "The International Significance of Azusa Street." *Pneuma,* Spring 1986.

Roberts, Oral. "The Firstfruits of Our Labors." *Oral Roberts University Outreach,* Winter 1967, pp. 1-24.

Roebuck, David. "Perfect Liberty to Preach the Gospel: Women Ministers in the Church of God." *Pneuma,* Spring 1995, pp. 25-32.

Spittler, R. P. "David Johannes du Plessis," in Burgess et al., *Dictionary of Pentecostal and Charismatic Movements,* pp. 250-54.

Spring, Beth. "Spiritual Renewal Brings Booming Growth to Episcopal Churches in Northern Virginia." *Christianity Today,* Jan. 13, 1984, pp. 38-39.

Stafford, Tim. "When Evangelicals Look in the Mirror, Do We See the Host of the 700 Club Staring Back?" *Christianity Today,* Aug. 12, 1996, pp. 26-33.

Stevenson, Janet. "A Family Divided." *American Heritage* 18 (Apr. 1967): 4-24.

Stump, David X. "Charismatic Renewal: Up to Date in Kansas City." *America,* Sept. 24, 1977, p. 166.

Sumner, Allene M. "The Holy Rollers on Shin Bone Ridge." *The Nation* 121 (July 29, 1925): 138.

Sydnor, Charles S., Jr. "The Pentecostals." *Presbyterian Survey,* May 1964, pp. 30-32; June 1964, pp. 36-39.

Synan, Vinson. "An Equal Opportunity Movement," in Harold Smith, ed., *Pentecostals from the Inside Out,* pp. 43-50. Wheaton, IL: Victor Books, 1990.

———. "Frank Bartleman and Azusa Street," in Frank Bartleman, *Azusa Street,* pp. ix-xxv. Plainfield, NJ: Bridge Publishing, Inc., 1980.

———. "Paul Morton Organizes Full Gospel Baptist Fellowship." *Timelines,* Spring 1993, pp. 1-4.

———. "Prophecy in the Pentecostal and Charismatic Movements." *Faith & Renewal,* July-Aug. 1991, pp. 8-13.

———. "The Role of Tongues as Initial Evidence," in Mark W. Wilson, ed., *Spirit and Renewal: Essays in Honor of J. Rodman Williams.* Sheffield, U.K.: Sheffield Academic Press, 1994.

———. "Who Are the Modern Day Apostles?" *Ministries Today,* Mar./Apr. 1992, pp. 42-47.

———. "Women in Ministry: A History of Women's Roles in the Pentecostal and Charismatic Movement." *Ministries Today,* Jan./Feb. 1993, pp. 44-50.

Taylor, G. F. "Our Church History." *The Pentecostal Holiness Advocate,* Jan. 20–Apr. 14, 1921, a series of twelve articles.

Tinney, James S. "A Wesleyan-Pentecostal Appraisal of the Charismatic Movement." *The Pentecostal Holiness Advocate,* Jan. 7, 1967, pp. 4-10.

Towns, Elmer. "The World's Ten Largest Churches." *Christian Life,* Jan. 1983, pp. 60-66.

Turner, William C. "Movements in the Spirit: A Review of African American Holiness/Pentecostal/Apostolics," in *Directory of African American Religious Bodies,* ed. Wardell Payne. Washington, DC: Howard University Press, 1991.

Van Dusen, Henry P. "The Third Force in Christendom." *Life,* June 9, 1958, pp. 113-24.

Wagner, Peter. "A Third Wave?" *Pastoral Renewal* 8, no. 1 (July-Aug. 1983): 1-5.

Ward, Horace. "The Anti-Pentecostal Argument," in Synan, ed., *Aspects of Pentecostal-Charismatic Origins,* pp. 99-122. Plainfield, NJ: Logos Publishing House, 1975.

Wolff, M. J. "We Are Not Unitarians." *The Pentecostal Herald,* Mar. 1967, p. 5.

Woodward, Kenneth L. "Pick and Choose Christianity." *Newsweek,* Sept. 19, 1983, pp. 82-83.

Unpublished Materials

Beacham, Paul F. "Historical Narrative: A Bible School." Unpublished manuscript in the Library of Holmes Theological Seminary, Greenville, SC. Written in March 1917.

Brown, Kenneth O. "Leadership in the National Holiness Association with Special Reference to Eschatology, 1867-1919." Unpublished Ph.D. thesis, Drew University, 1988.

Connolly, James. "Neo-Pentecostalism: The Charismatic Revival in the Mainline Protestant and Roman Catholic Churches of the United States." Unpublished Ph.D. dissertation, University of Chicago, 1977.

Corvin, R. O. "A History of Education in the Pentecostal Holiness Church."

Unpublished DRE dissertation, Southwestern Theological Seminary, Dallas, 1957.

Faupel, William D. "The Everlasting Gospel: The Significance of Eschatology in the Development of Pentecostal Thought." Unpublished Ph.D. dissertation, University of Birmingham, U.K., 1989.

Flower, J. Roswell. "History of the Assemblies of God" (n.p., n.d.), a short summary by one of the participants in a class at Central Bible College.

Gaddis, M. E. "Christian Perfectionism in America." Unpublished Ph.D. dissertation, University of Chicago, 1929.

Gilley, Billy Hawkins. "Social Trends as Reflected in American Fiction, 1870-1901." Unpublished Ph.D. dissertation, University of Georgia, 1966.

Goodrum, C. L. "Some Studies in the Life and Times of John Wesley." Unpublished Master's thesis, University of Georgia, 1939.

Hollenweger, Walter J. "Handbuch Der Pfingstbewegung, II. Hauptteil, Nordamerika." Unpublished Ph.D. dissertation, University of Zurich, 1965.

Hoover, Mario G. "Origin and Structural Development of the Assemblies of God." Unpublished Master's thesis, Southwest Missouri State College, 1968.

Hunter, Harold. "Beniah at the Apostolic Crossroads." Unpublished paper presented to the Society for Pentecostal Studies, Wycliffe College, Toronto, 1996.

Lee, Jae Bum. "Pentecostal Type Distinctives and Protestant Church Growth." Unpublished Ph.D. dissertation, Fuller Theological Seminary, 1986.

Menzies, William W. "The Assemblies of God, 1941-1967: The Consolidation of a Revival Movement." Unpublished Ph.D. dissertation, University of Iowa, 1968.

Moore, David. "The Shepherding Movement in Historical Perspective." Unpublished Master's thesis, Oral Roberts University, 1996.

Moore, Everett Leroy. "Handbook of Pentecostal Denominations in the United States." Unpublished Master's thesis, Pasadena College, Pasadena, CA, 1954.

Nelson, Douglas. "For Such a Time as This: The Story of Bishop William J. Seymour and the Azusa Street Revival." Unpublished Ph.D. dissertation, University of Birmingham, U.K., 1981.

Paloma, Margaret. "By Their Fruits: A Sociological Assessment of the Toronto Blessing." Unpublished research project, University of Akron, 1996.

Phillips, Wade. "Richard Spurling and the Baptist Roots of the Church of God." Unpublished paper presented to the Society for Pentecostal Studies, November 1993, Guadalajara, Mexico.

Ray, Mauldin A. "A Study of the History of Lee College, Cleveland, Tennessee." Unpublished Ph.D. dissertation, University of Houston, 1964.

Robeck, Cecil M. "The Past Historical Roots of Racial Unity and Division in American Pentecostalism." An unpublished paper presented at the founding convention of the Pentecostal and Charismatic Churches of North America, Memphis, Tennessee, October 1994.

Sala, Harold J. "An Investigation of the Baptizing and Filling Work of the Holy Spirit in the New Testament Related to the Pentecostal Doctrines of Initial Evidence." Unpublished Ph.D. dissertation, Bob Jones University, Greenville, SC, 1966.

Traettino, Giovanni. "Il Movimento Pentecostali in Italia (1908-1959)." Unpublished Ph.D. dissertation, University of Naples, 1971.

Turner, W. H. "The 'Tongues Movement': A Brief History." Unpublished Master's thesis, University of Georgia, 1948.

Vivier, Lincoln Morse. "Glossolalia." Unpublished Ph.D. dissertation, University of Witwatersrand, Johannesburg, South Africa, 1960.

Waldvogel, Edith (Blumhofer). "The Overcoming Life: A Study in the Reformed Evangelical Origins of Pentecostalism." Unpublished Ph.D. dissertation, Harvard University, 1977.

Personal Interviews with Author

The author interviewed the following people for this book: Dennis Bennett, Johnny Bartleman, Reinhard Bonnke, Pat Boone, Brick Bradford, Michael L. Brown, Larry Christenson, David Yonggi Cho, Ithiel Clemmons, Charles W. Conn, R. O. Corvin, Donald Dayton, Gerald Derstine, Melvin Dieter, David du Plessis, Steve Durasoff, Howard Ervin, J. Roswell Flower, Donald Gee, Bert Ghezzi, L. R. Graham, Michael Harper, David Harrell, Bennie Hinn, Walter Hollenweger, Mrs. Nina Holmes, Mario Hoover, Ray Hughes, Charles E. Jones, Klaud Kendrick, William Kumuyi, Bob Mumford, Lewi Pethrus, Ralph Martin, Kilian McDonnell, William W. Menzies, Efrain Rios Montt, Edward O'Connor, Richard Ostling, Pauline Parham, J. O. Patterson, Kevin Ranaghan, Oral Roberts, Ernest Sandeen, Demos Shakarian, Charles Simpson, Timothy Smith, H. T. Spence, Leon Cardinal Joseph Suenens, Jimmy Swaggart,

Joseph A. Synan, Milton Tomlinson, Nathaniel Urshan, Javier Vasquez, Peter Wagner, David Wilkerson, Peter Veronaev, and Thomas Zimmerman.

Secondary Sources

Anderson, Robert Mapes. *Vision of the Disinherited: The Making of American Pentecostalism.* New York: Oxford University Press, 1979.

Armstrong, Ben. *The Electric Church.* Nashville: Thomas Nelson, 1979.

Arthur, William. *The Tongue of Fire, or the True Power of Christianity.* Columbia, SC: L. L. Pickett, 1891.

Atter, Gordon. *The Third Force.* Peterborough, Ont.: The College Press, 1962.

Bach, Marcus. *They Have Found a Faith.* New York: Bobbs-Merrill Company, 1946.

Bates, Arlo. *The Philistines.* Boston: Ticknor & Company, 1888.

Beacham, Douglas. *A Brief History of the Pentecostal Holiness Church.* Franklin Springs, GA: Advocate Press, 1983.

Beard, Steve. *Thunderstruck: John Wesley and the Toronto Blessing.* Wilmore, KY: Thunderstruck Communications, 1996.

Bloch-Hoell, Nils. *The Pentecostal Movement: Its Origin, Development, and Distinctive Character.* Oslo, Norway: Universitetsforlaget, 1964.

Blomgren, David. *Song of the Lord.* Portland, OR: Bible Press, 1966.

Blumhofer, Edith. *Aimee Semple McPherson: Everybody's Sister.* Grand Rapids, MI: Wm. B. Eerdmans Publishing Co., 1993.

———. *The Assemblies of God: A Chapter in the Story of American Pentecostalism.* 2 vols. Springfield, MO: Gospel Publishing House, 1989.

Boland, J. M. *The Problem of Methodism: Being a Review of the Residue Theory of Sanctification and the Philosophy of Christian Perfection.* Nashville: Southern Methodist Publishing House, 1888.

Braden, Charles S. *Protestantism: A Symposium.* Nashville: Abingdon Press, 1944.

Brasher, John. *The Sanctified South: John Lakin Brasher and the Holiness Movement.* Urbana: University of Illinois Press, 1994.

Brengle, Colonel S. L. *When the Holy Ghost Is Come.* New York: The Salvation Army Printing and Publishing House, 1914.

Bresson, Bernard L. *Studies in Ecstasy.* New York: Vantage Press, 1978.

Brockett, Henry E. *The Riches of Holiness.* Kansas City: Beacon Hill Press, 1951.

Bucke, Emory Stevens, et al. *The History of American Methodism.* 3 vols. Nashville: Abingdon Press, 1964.

Burnett, C. C. *In the Last Days: A History of the Assemblies of God.* Springfield, MO: Gospel Publishing House, 1962.

Burr, Nelson R. *A Critical Bibliography of Religion in America.* Princeton, NJ: Princeton University Press, 1961.

Campbell, Joseph E. *The Pentecostal Holiness Church, 1898-1948.* Franklin Springs, GA: Publishing House of the Pentecostal Holiness Church, 1951.

Candler, Warren A. *Christus Auctor: A Manual of Christian Evidences.* Nashville: Publishing House of the Southern Methodist Church, 1900.

————. *On with the Revolution: By One of the Revolutionaries.* Atlanta: private printing, 1887.

————. *Theater-Going and Dancing Incompatible with Church Membership.* Nashville, 1904.

Carradine, Beverly. *The Better Way.* Cincinnati: God's Revivalist Office, 1896.

————. *A Box of Treasure.* Chicago, 1910.

————. *Golden Sheaves.* Boston: Joshua Gill, 1901.

Cash, W. J. *The Mind of the South.* New York: Alfred A. Knopf, 1941.

Chapman, J. F. *A History of the Church of the Nazarene.* Kansas City: Nazarene Publishing House, 1926.

Chevreau, Guy. *Catch the Fire: The Toronto Blessing, an Experience of Renewal and Revival.* Toronto: HarperCollins, 1994.

Christenson, Larry. *The Charismatic Renewal Among Lutherans.* Minneapolis: International Lutheran Renewal Center, 1976.

Clark, Elmer T. *The Psychology of Religious Awakening.* New York: Macmillan, 1929.

————. *The Small Sects in America.* Rev. ed. New York: Abingdon Press, 1949.

Clark, Stephen. *Building Christian Communities.* Notre Dame: Ave Maria Press, 1972.

Conkin, Paul. *Cane Ridge: America's Pentecost.* Madison: University of Wisconsin Press, 1989.

Conn, Charles W. *The Evangel Reader: Selections from the Church of God Evangel, 1910-1958.* Cleveland, TN: Pathway Press, 1958.

————. *Like a Mighty Army, Moves the Church of God.* Cleveland, TN: Church of God Publishing House, 1955.

Conwell, Russell. *Acres of Diamonds.* New York: Harper & Brothers, 1915.

Coulter, E. Merton. *College Life in the Old South.* New York: Macmillan, 1928.

Cox, B. L. *History and Doctrine of the Congregational Holiness Church.* Greenwood, SC: Publishing House of the Congregational Holiness Church, 1959.

Cox, Harvey. *Fire from Heaven: The Rise of Pentecostal Spirituality and the Reshaping of Religion in the Twenty-first Century.* New York: Addison-Wesley, 1994.

Crawford, R. R. *A Historical Account of the Apostolic Faith.* Portland, OR, 1965.

Crews, Mickey. *The Church of God: A Social History.* Knoxville: University of Tennessee Press, 1993.

Cross, Robert D., ed. *The Church and the City, 1865-1910.* New York: Bobbs-Merrill, 1967.

Cross, Whitney R. *The Burned-Over District: The Social and Intellectual History of Enthusiastic Religion in Western New York.* New York: Harper & Row, 1965.

Curti, Merle. *The Growth of American Thought.* 2nd ed. New York: Harper & Row, 1964.

Cutten, George Barton. *Speaking with Tongues.* New Haven: Yale University Press, 1927.

Damboriena, Prudencio. *Tongues as of Fire: Pentecostalism in Contemporary Christianity.* Washington: Corpus Books, 1969.

Davenport, Frederick Morgan. *Primitive Traits in Religious Revivals: A Study in Mental and Social Evolution.* New York: Macmillan, 1905.

Dayton, Donald. *Discovering an Evangelical Heritage.* New York: Harper & Row, 1976.

————. *Theological Roots of Pentecostalism.* Grand Rapids, MI: Francis Asbury Press, 1987.

De Forest, John W. *The Wetherel Affair.* New York: Sheldon and Company, 1873.

Degler, Carl N. *Out of Our Past: The Forces That Shaped Modern America.* New York: Harper & Row, 1959.

Demerath, N. J., III. *Social Class in American Protestantism.* Chicago: Rand McNally & Company, 1965.

Dieter, Melvin. *The Holiness Revival of the Nineteenth Century.* Metuchen, NJ: Scarecrow Press, 1980.

Dorries, David. "Edward Irving and the 'Standing Sign,'" in *Initial Evidence: Historical and Biblical Perspectives on the Pentecostal Doctrine of Spirit Baptism,* ed. by G. B. McGee. Peabody, MA: Hendrickson Publishers, 1991.

Duggar, Lillie. *A. J. Tomlinson, Former General Overseer of the Church of God.* Cleveland, TN: White Wing Publishing House, 1964.

Dunnavant, Anthony L., ed. *Perspectives on Barton W. Stone and the Revival.* Nashville: Disciples of Christ Historical Society, 1992.

Durasoff, Steve. *Bright Wind of the Spirit: Pentecostalism Today.* Englewood Cliffs, NJ: Prentice-Hall, 1972.

Eggleston, Edward. *The Circuit Rider: A Tale of the Heroic Age.* New York: Charles Scribner's Sons, 1909.

Ensley, Eddie. *Sounds of Wonder: A Popular History of Speaking in Tongues in the Catholic Tradition.* New York: Paulist Press, 1977.

Epstein, Daniel. *Sister Aimee: The Life of Aimee Semple McPherson.* New York: Harcourt Brace Jovanovich, 1993.

Evans, Avery D. *A. J. Tomlinson.* Cleveland, TN: White Wing Publishing House, 1943.

Farish, Hunter D. *The Circuit Rider Dismounts: A Social History of Southern Methodism, 1865-1900.* Richmond, VA, 1938.

Faupel, D. William. *The Everlasting Gospel: The Significance of Eschatology in the Development of Pentecostal Thought.* Sheffield, UK: Sheffield Academic Press, 1996.

Fisher, H. L. *History of the United Holy Church of America.* N.p., n.d.

Flew, Newton R. *The Idea of Perfection in Christian Theology.* London: Oxford University Press, 1934.

Foster, Fred J. *Think It Not Strange: A History of the Oneness Movement.* St. Louis: Pentecostal Publishing House, 1965.

Frederick, Harold. *The Damnation of Theron Ware.* Cambridge, MA: Belknap Press of Harvard University Press, 1960.

Frodsham, Stanley H. *With Signs Following: The Story of the Pentecostal Revival in the Twentieth Century.* Springfield, MO: Gospel Publishing House, 1946.

Gause, R. H. *Church of God Polity.* Cleveland, TN: Pathway Press, 1958.

Gee, Donald. *All with One Accord.* Springfield, MO: Gospel Publishing House, 1961.

Geiger, Kenneth, et al. *The Word and the Doctrine: Studies in Contemporary Wesleyan-Arminian Theology.* Kansas City: Beacon Hill Press, 1965.

Gewehr, Wesley M. *The Great Awakening in Virginia, 1740-1790.* Durham, NC: Duke University Press, 1930.

Gibson, Luther. *History of the Church of God, Mountain Assembly.* N.p., 1954.

Giese, Ernst. *Und Flicken Die Netze.* Marburg, Germany: Erschienen im Selbstverlag, 1976.

Girvin, E. A. *P. F. Bresee: A Prince in Israel.* Kansas City: Nazarene Publishing House, 1916.

Goff, Florence. *Life of Rev. J. A. Hodges.* Benson, NC: private printing, 1903.

Goff, James R. *Fields White Unto Harvest: Charles Fox Parham and the Missionary*

Origins of Pentecostalism. Fayetteville, AR: University of Arkansas Press, 1988.

Gregory, Chester W. *The History of the United Holy Church of America, Inc., 1886-1986.* Baltimore: Gateway Press, 1986.

Gresham, John Leroy. *Charles G. Finney's Doctrine of the Baptism of the Holy Spirit.* Peabody, MA: Hendrickson Publishers, 1987.

————. *The Pentecostal Movement.* London: Victory Press, 1949.

————. *Upon All Flesh: A Pentecostal World Tour.* Springfield, MO: Gospel Publishing House, 1947.

Gross, Alexander. *History of the Methodist Episcopal Church, South.* New York: Christian Literature Company, 1894.

Hardman, Keith. *Charles Grandison Finney 1792-1875: Revivalist and Reformer.* Syracuse, NY: Syracuse University Press, 1987, 1990.

Harper, Michael. *As at the Beginning: The Twentieth-Century Pentecostal Revival.* London: Hodder and Stoughton, 1965.

————. *Three Sisters.* Wheaton, IL: Tyndale Publishers, 1979.

Harrell, David. *All Things Are Possible: The Healing and Charismatic Revivals in Modern America.* Bloomington: Indiana University Press, 1975.

————. *Oral Roberts: An American Life.* Bloomington: University of Indiana Press, 1985.

Hazeltine, Rachel C. *Aimee Semple McPherson's Kidnapping.* New York: Carleton Press, 1965.

Hofstadter, Richard. *Social Darwinism in American Thought.* Philadelphia: University of Pennsylvania Press, 1945.

Hollenweger, Walter. *The Pentecostals: The Charismatic Movement in the Churches.* Minneapolis: Augsburg Press, 1972.

Horton, Wade H., ed. *The Glossolalia Phenomenon.* Cleveland, TN: Pathway Press, 1966.

Hudson, Hilary T. *The Methodist Armor, or a Popular Exposition of the Doctrines, Peculiar Usages, and Ecclesiastical Machinery of the Methodist Episcopal Church, South.* Nashville: Publishing House of the Southern Methodist Church, 1919.

Hurst, J. F. *The History of Methodism.* 7 vols. New York: Eaton & Mains, 1902.

Hyatt, Eddie L. *2000 Years of Charismatic Christianity.* Tulsa, OK: Hyatt Ministries, 1996.

Issacson, Alan. *Deeper Life: The Extraordinary Growth of the Deeper Life Bible Church.* London: Hodder and Stoughton, 1990.

Irving, Edward. *The Day of Pentecost or the Baptism with the Holy Ghost.* Edinburgh: John Lindsay, 1831.

James, William. *The Varieties of Religious Experience.* New York: Longman, Green & Company, 1902.

Johnson, Charles A. *The Frontier Camp Meeting: Religious Harvest Time.* Dallas: Southern Methodist University Press, 1955.

Johnson, Ruby F. *The Development of Negro Religion.* New York: Philosophical Library, 1954.

————. *The Religion of Negro Protestants.* New York: Philosophical Library, 1956.

Jones, Charles E. *Perfectionist Persuasion.* Metuchen, NJ: Scarecrow Press, 1974.

Jones, W. M. D. *The Doctrine of Entire Sanctification Scripturally and Psychologically Examined.* Philadelphia: International Holiness Publishing House, 1890.

Kendrick, Klaud. *The Promise Fulfilled: A History of the American Pentecostal Movement.* Springfield, MO: Gospel Publishing House, 1961.

Kimbrough, David L. *Taking up Serpents: Snake Handlers of Eastern Kentucky.* Chapel Hill: University of North Carolina Press, 1995.

King, Pat. *The Jesus People Are Coming.* Plainfield, NJ: Logos Press, 1971.

Klaw, Spencer. *Without Sin: The Life and Death of the Oneida Community.* New York: Penguin, 1994.

Knapp, Martin Wells. *Christ Crowned Within.* Cincinnati: God's Revivalist Office, 1886.

————. *Lightning Bolts from Pentecostal Skies, or Devices of the Devil Unmasked.* Cincinnati: Pentecostal Holiness Library, 1898.

Law, William. *A Serious Call to a Devout and Holy Life.* New York: E. P. Dutton & Company, 1955.

Lawrence, B. F. *The Apostolic Faith Restored.* Springfield, MO: Gospel Publishing House, 1916.

Lemons, Frank W. *Our Pentecostal Heritage.* Cleveland, TN: Pathway Press, 1963.

Lincoln, C. Eric, and Lawrence H. Mamiya. *The Black Church in the African American Experience.* Durham, NC: Duke University Press, 1990.

Lindblade, Frank. *The Spirit Which Is from God.* Duncan, OK: Christian Life Books, 1995.

Lindsay, Gordon. *The Life of John Alexander Dowie.* Dallas: The Voice of Healing Publishing Company, 1951.

Lindstrom, Harold. *Wesley and Sanctification.* Translated by H. S. Harvey. London: Epworth Press, 1946.

Mann, Harold W. *Atticus Greene Haygood.* Athens, GA: University of Georgia Press, 1965.

Manual, David. *The Gathering: The Story Behind Washington for Jesus.* Orleans, MA: Rock Harbor Press, 1980.

—. *Like a Mighty River: A Personal Account of the Charismatic Conference of 1977.* Orleans, MA: Rock Harbor Press, 1977.

Martin, David. *Tongues of Fire: The Explosion of Protestantism in Latin America.* London: Oxford University Press, 1990.

Martin, George. *Reading Scripture as the Word of God.* Ann Arbor, MI: Servant Books, 1975.

Martin, Ira J. *Glossolalia in the Apostolic Church.* Berea, KY: Berea College Press, 1960.

Martin, Larry. *In the Beginning: Readings on the Origins of the Twentieth-Century Pentecostal Revival and the Birth of the Pentecostal Church of God.* Duncan, OK: Christian Life Books, 1994.

Martin, Ralph. *Fire on the Earth.* Ann Arbor, MI: Servant Books, 1975.

—. *Hungry for God.* London: Collins, 1976.

Marty, Martin, and Joan Chittister. *Faith and Ferment.* Minneapolis: Augsburg Press, 1983.

Mason, Mary. *The History and Life Work of Bishop C. H. Mason, Chief Apostle, and His Co-Laborers.* Memphis: private printing, 1934.

Mavity, Nancy Barr. *Sister Aimee.* Garden City, NY: Doubleday, Doran, & Company, 1931.

May, Henry F. *Protestant Churches in Industrial America.* New York: Harper & Row, 1949.

McCrossan, T. J. *Speaking with Other Tongues: Sign or Gift, Which?* Seattle: Christian Publications, 1927.

McDonald, William. *The Life of Rev. John S. Inskip.* Salem, OH: Allegheny Publications, 1986.

McDonnell, Kilian. *Catholic Pentecostalism: Problems in Evaluation.* Pecos, NM: Dove Publications, 1970.

—. *Charismatic Renewal and the Churches.* New York: Seabury Press, 1976.

McGavran, Donald. *The Bridges of God: A Strategy of Missions.* New York: Friendship Press, 1955.

—. *How Churches Grow.* London: World Dominion, 1957.

—. *Understanding Church Growth.* Grand Rapids, MI: Wm. B. Eerdmans Publishing Co., 1970.

McGee, Gary, ed. *Initial Evidence: Historical and Biblical Perspectives on the Pentecostal Doctrine of Spirit Baptism.* Peabody, MA: Hendrickson Publishers, 1991.

McKenna, John. *A Future with a History: The Wesleyan Witness of the Free Methodist Church, 1860-1995.* Indianapolis: Light & Life Press, 1995.

McKitrick, Eric. *Slavery Defended: The View of the Old South.* Englewood Cliffs, NJ: Prentice-Hall, 1963.

McLeister, Ira Ford. *History of the Wesleyan Methodist Church of America.* Marion, IN: Wesley Press, 1959.

McLoughlin, William G. *Modern Revivalism.* New York: Ronald Press, 1959.

MacRobert, Lian. *The Black Roots and White Racism of Early Pentecostalism in the USA.* London: MacMillan, 1988.

McTyeire, Holland N. *A History of Methodism.* Nashville: Publishing House of the Southern Methodist Church, 1885.

Menzies, William. *Anointed to Serve: The Story of the Assemblies of God.* Springfield, MO: Gospel Publishing House, 1971.

Miller, Thomas William. *Canadian Pentecostals: A History of the Pentecostal Assemblies of Canada.* Mississauga, Ont.: Full Gospel Publishing House, 1994.

Moberg, David O. *The Church as a Social Institution.* Englewood Cliffs, NJ: Prentice-Hall, 1962.

Moody, William R. *The Life of Dwight L. Moody.* New York: Fleming H. Revell, 1900.

Morgan, Dan. *Rising in the West: The True Story of an "Okie" Family from the Great Depression through the Reagan Years.* New York: Alfred A. Knopf, 1992.

Morris, Eddie. *The Vine and the Branches, John 15:5: Historic Events in the Holiness and Pentecostal Movements.* Franklin Springs, GA: Advocate Press, 1981.

Morris, James. *The Preachers.* New York: St. Martin's Press, 1973.

Myland, David Wesley. *The Latter Rain Covenant and Pentecostal Power.* Chicago: Evangel Publishing House, 1910.

Newbigin, Lesslie. *The Household of God.* New York: Friendship Press, 1954.

Nichols, John Thomas. *Pentecostalism.* New York: Harper & Row, 1966.

Niebuhr, H. Richard. *The Social Sources of Denominationalism.* Hamden, CT: Shoestring Press, 1929.

Nienkirchen, Charles W. *A. B. Simpson and the Pentecostal Movement.* Peabody, MA: Hendrickson Publishers, 1992.

O'Connor, Edward. *The Pentecostal Movement in the Catholic Church.* Notre Dame, IN: Ave Maria Press, 1971.

Officer, Sam. *Wise Master Builders, and the Wheel of Fortune.* Cleveland, TN: The Jesus Church, n.d.

Outler, Albert, ed. *John Wesley.* New York: Oxford University Press, 1964.

Paul, Harold. *Dan T. Muse: From Printer's Devil to Bishop.* Franklin Springs, GA: Advocate Press, 1976.

323

Paulk, Earl P., Jr. *Your Pentecostal Neighbor.* Cleveland, TN: Pathway Press, 1958.

Payne, Tony. *No Laughing Matter: The Toronto Blessing and Real Christianity.* Sydney, Australia: St. Matthias Press, 1995.

Peters, John Leland. *Christian Perfection and American Methodism.* New York: Abingdon Press, 1956.

Pierce, Alfred M. *Giant Against the Sky.* New York: Abingdon Press, 1958.

Plowman, Edward. *The Jesus Movement in America.* Elgin, IL: Cook Publishers, 1971.

Pope, Liston. *Millhands and Preachers: A Study of Gastonia.* New Haven: Yale University Press, 1946.

Prince, Derek. *Purposes of Pentecost.* N.p., n.d.

Pulkingham, Graham. *Gathered for Power: Charisma, Commercialism, Christian Witness.* New York: Morehouse-Barlow, 1972.

Quebedeaux, Richard. *New Charismatics,* vol. 2. San Francisco: Harper & Row, 1983.

Ranaghan, Kevin and Dorothy. *Catholic Pentecostals.* New York: Paulist Press, 1969.

Raser, Harold E. *Phoebe Palmer: Her Life and Thought.* Lewiston, NY: Mellen Press, 1987.

Rauschenbusch, Walter. *Christianity and the Social Crisis.* New York: Macmillan, 1907.

Redford, M. E. *The Rise of the Church of the Nazarene.* Kansas City: Nazarene Publishing House, 1951.

Rifkin, Jeremy, with Ted Howard. *The Emerging Order — God in the Scarcity.* New York: G. P. Putnam's Sons, 1979.

Riss, Richard. *The Latter Rain Movement of 1948.* Mississauga, Ont.: Honeycomb Visual Productions, 1987.

———. *A Survey of Twentieth Century Revival Movements in North America.* Peabody, MA: Hendrickson Publishers, 1988.

Roberts, B. T. *Why Another Sect?* New York: Garland Publishing (1984 reprint).

Roberts, Dave. *The "Toronto Blessing."* Eastbourne, U.K.: Kingsway Publications, 1994.

Robertson, Archie. *That Old-Time Religion.* Boston: Houghton Mifflin Company, 1950.

Root, Jean Christie. *Edward Irving: Man, Preacher, Prophet.* Boston: Sherman, French, & Company, 1912.

Rose, Delbert R. *A Theology of Christian Experience.* Minneapolis: Bethany Fellowship, 1965.

Salisbury, W. S. *Religion in American Culture: A Sociological Interpretation.* Homewood, IL: Dorsey Press, 1964.

Sandeen, Ernest. *The Roots of Fundamentalism: British and American Millenarianism, 1830-1930.* Chicago: University of Chicago Press, 1970.

Sanders, Cheryl J. *Saints in Exile: The Holiness-Pentecostal Experience in American Religion and Culture.* New York: Oxford University Press, 1996.

Schaff, Philip. *History of the Christian Church.* New York: Charles Scribner's Sons, 1910.

Schroeder, W. Widick, and Victor Obenhaus. *Religion in American Culture.* London: Collier-Macmillan, 1964.

Seldes, Gilbert. *The Stammering Century.* New York: Harper & Row, 1965.

Sheldon, Charles M. *In His Steps.* New York: Thompson and Thomas, n.d.

Sheldon, H. C. *History of Christian Doctrine,* 2 vols. 2nd ed. New York: Harper & Brothers, 1895.

Sherrill, John L. *They Speak with Other Tongues.* New York: McGraw-Hill Book Company, 1964.

Shole, Jerry. *Give Me that Prime Time Religion: An Insider's Report on the Oral Roberts Evangelistic Association.* New York: Hawthorne Books, 1979.

Simkins, Francis Butler. *The South Old and New: A History, 1820-1947.* New York: Alfred A. Knopf, 1947.

Simmons, E. L. *History of the Church of God.* Cleveland, TN: Church of God Publishing House, 1938.

Smith, George G. *The History of Georgia Methodism from 1786 to 1866.* Atlanta, 1913.

Smith, Timothy L. *Called Unto Holiness.* Kansas City: Nazarene Publishing House, 1962.

———. *Revivalism and Social Reform in Mid-Nineteenth-Century America.* New York: Abingdon Press, 1957.

Smith, Warren. *John Wesley and Slavery.* Nashville: Abingdon Press, 1986.

Snyder, Howard. *The Divided Flame: Wesleyans & the Charismatic Renewal.* Grand Rapids, MI: Francis Asbury Press, 1986.

Southey, Robert. *The Life of John Wesley.* 2 vols. London: Longman Hurst and Company, 1820.

Spittler, Russell. *Perspectives on the New Pentecostalism.* Grand Rapids, MI: Baker Book House, 1976.

Steele, Daniel. *A Defense of Christian Perfection.* New York: Hunt and Eaton, 1896.

———. *Love Enthroned: Essays on Evangelical Perfection.* New York: Nelson and Phillips, 1877.

Steele, Ron. *Reinhard Bonnke's Vision: Plundering Hell to Populate Heaven.* Tulsa, OK: Albury Press, 1987.

Stevenson, Herbert F. *Keswick's Authentic Voice.* Grand Rapids, MI: Zondervan Publishing House, 1959.

Stewart, I. D. *History of the Freewill Baptists.* Dover, NH: The Freewill Baptist Printing Establishment, 1943.

Stoll, David. *Is Latin America Turning Protestant?* Los Angeles: University of California Press, 1990.

Strachan, Gordan. *The Pentecostal Theology of Edward Irving.* London: Dartman, Longman and Todd, 1973.

Sullivan, Francis. *Charisms and Charismatic Renewal.* Ann Arbor, MI: Charismatic Renewal Services, 1982.

Sweet, William Warren. *Methodism in American History.* New York: Abingdon Press, 1933.

————. *Religion in Colonial America.* New York: Cooper Square Publishers, 1965.

————. *Religion on the American Frontier. IV: The Methodists.* Chicago: University of Chicago Press, 1946.

————. *Revivalism in America.* New York: Charles Scribner's Sons, 1944.

————. *The Story of Religion in America.* New York: Harper & Brothers, 1950.

Synan, Vinson, *Charismatic Bridges.* Ann Arbor, MI: Word of Life, 1974.

————. *Emmanuel College — The First Fifty Years.* Washington, DC: North Washington Press, 1968.

————. *In the Latter Days: The Outpouring of the Holy Spirit in the Twentieth Century.* Ann Arbor, MI: Servant Books, 1984.

————. *The Old-Time Power: A History of the Pentecostal Holiness Church.* Franklin Springs, GA: Advocate Press, 1973.

————. *The Spirit Said "Grow": The Astounding Worldwide Expansion of Pentecostal and Charismatic Churches.* Monrovia, CA: MARC (World Vision), 1992.

————. *The Twentieth Century Pentecostal Explosion.* Lake Mary, FL: Creation House, 1987.

————. *Under His Banner: History of the Full Gospel Business Men's Fellowship International.* Costa Mesa, CA: Gift Publications, 1992.

————, ed. *Aspects of Pentecostal-Charismatic Origins.* Plainfield, NJ: Logos International, 1975.

————, and Ralph Rath. *Launching the Decade of Evangelization.* South Bend, IN: North American Renewal Service Committee, 1990.

Thomas, Burton G. *Serpent Handling Believers.* Knoxville: University of Tennessee Press, 1993.

Thomas, Iva. *History of Holmes Theological Seminary.* Franklin Springs, GA, n.d.

Thomas, Lately. *The Vanishing Evangelist.* New York: Viking Press, 1959.

Torrey, R. A. *The Holy Spirit.* New York: Fleming H. Revell, 1927.

Turner, George Allen. *The More Excellent Way: The Scriptural Basis of the Wesleyan Message.* Winona Lake, IN: Light and Life Press, 1951.

Turner, William. H. *The Difference Between Regeneration, Sanctification, and the Pentecostal Baptism.* Franklin Springs, GA: Publishing House of the Pentecostal Holiness Church, 1947.

———. *Pentecost and Tongues.* Shanghai: Shanghai Modern Publishing House, 1939.

Tuttle, Robert. *Mysticism in the Wesleyan Tradition.* Grand Rapids, MI: Francis Asbury Press, 1989.

Tyson, James L. *The Early Pentecostal Revival: History of the Twentieth Century Pentecostals and the Pentecostal Assemblies of the World.* Hazelwood, MO: Word Aflame Press, 1992.

Underwood, B. E. *Fiftieth Anniversary History of the Virginia Conference of the Pentecostal Holiness Church.* Dublin, VA, 1960.

Vaughn, John. *The Large Church.* Grand Rapids, MI: Baker Book House, 1985.

———. *The World's 20 Largest Churches.* Grand Rapids, MI: Baker Book House, 1984.

Vergara, Ignacio. *El Protestantismo en Chile.* Santiago: Editorial del Pacifico, 1962.

Vulliamy, C. E. *John Wesley.* New York: Charles Scribner's Sons, 1932.

Wagner, Peter. *Leading Your Church to Growth.* Ventura, CA: Regal Books, 1984

———. *Look Out, The Pentecostals Are Coming.* Carol Stream, IL: Creation House, 1973.

———. *The Third Wave of the Holy Spirit: Encountering the Power of Signs and Wonders Today.* Ann Arbor, MI: Vine Books, 1988.

———. *Your Church Can Grow.* Glendale, CA: Regal Books, 1976.

———. *Your Spiritual Gifts Can Make Your Church Grow.* Glendale, CA: Regal Books, 1979.

Warfield, Benjamin B. *Counterfeit Miracles.* Carlisle, PA, 1918.

———. *Perfectionism.* 2 vols. New York: Oxford University Press, 1931.

Washburn, Josephine M. *History and Reminiscences of the Holiness Church Work in Southern California and Arizona.* New York: Garland Publishing, 1985 (1912 reprint).

Waugh, Thomas. *The Power of Pentecost.* Chicago: Bible Institute Colportage Association, n.d.

Weatherford, W. D. *The American Churches and the Negro.* Boston: Christopher Publishing House, 1957.

Weisberger, Bernard. *They Gathered at the River.* New York: Little, Brown, 1958.

White, Charles Edward. *The Beauty of Holiness: Phoebe Palmer as Theologian, Revivalist, Feminist, and Humanitarian.* Grand Rapids, MI: Francis Asbury Press, 1986.

Wilson, Mark, ed. *Spirit and Renewal: Essays in Honor of J. Rodman Williams.* Sheffield, U.K.: Sheffield Academic Press, 1994.

Wimberly, C. F. *Are You a Christian?* Louisville, KY: Pentecostal Publishing Company, 1917.

Winchester, Charles Wesley. *The Wells of Salvation.* New York: Eaton & Mains Publishing Company, 1897.

Winehouse, Irwin. *The Assemblies of God: A Popular Survey.* New York: Vantage Press, 1959.

Wood, J. A. *Perfect Love, or Plain Things for Those Who Need Them.* Chicago: Christian Witness Company, 1880.

Wood, William W. *Culture and Personality Aspects of the Pentecostal Holiness Religion.* The Hague: Mouton Company, 1965.

Woodward, C. Vann. *Origins of the New South.* Baton Rouge: Louisiana State Press, 1951.

Yoo, Boo-Wong. *Korean Pentecostalism: Its History and Theology.* New York: Verlag Peter Lang, 1987.

Zenos, Andrew C. *The Elements of Higher Criticism.* New York: Funk & Wagnalls Company, 1895.

Index

Three-Godism, 159
Three Streams, 291-92
Tillett, Wilbur F., 37
Tipton, Joe, 56, 72
Tobacco, 87, 64, 192
Tomlinson, A. J., 74-77, 123-24, 128, 175, 197-99
Tomlinson Church of God, 197-98
Tomlinson, Homer, 80, 199
Tomlinson, Milton, 199
Tomlinson schism, 197-99
Tongue of Fire, The, 144
Tongues, speaking with other, 13, 52, 84, 87-91, 96, 98-99, 103, 105-6, 108-12, 120, 123, 146-47, 190
Tools and Men, 46
Toronto Airport Christian Fellowship, 278
Toronto Blessing, the, 275-76
Torrey, R. A., 146
Tozer, A. W., 147
Transcendentalism, 16
Trask, Thomas, 186
Trinitarians, 158-60, 163-64
Trinity Magazine, 232
Troeltsch, Ernst, 203
Tucker, W. J., 23
Tuesday Meetings for holiness, 17-18, 32

Union Meeting for the Promotion of Practical Holiness, 144
Unitarianism, 16
United Brethren Church, 110
United Holy Church, 65-67, 169, 185
United Methodist Church, 258
United Pentecostal Church, The, 160-62
United Presbyterian Church, 257

Vanderbilt University, 37
Vasquez, Javier, 288
Vatican II, 235, 243-45
Villanueva, Eddie, 288
Vineland, NJ, 24-26
Vineyard Christian Fellowship, 270
Vingren, Gunnar, 134
Violence, 191, 192-95

Vision del Futuro (Argentina), 287
Volunteers of America, 47
Von Trapp, Maria, 261
Voronaev, Ivan, 138-39

Wagner, Peter, 272-72, 276, 281, 290
Waldensians, 110
Wallace, Hardin, 36
Warfield, Benjamin, 209
Warner, Daniel S., 35, 48, 68
Washburn, Josephine, 94, 101
Washington, Booker T., 179
Watson, George D., 62, 127
Waves of Joy and Peace (Argentina), 288
Way of Faith, 53, 62, 87, 98, 99, 108, 113, 116, 118, 122
Webb, Captain Thomas, 7
Weiner, Bob, 270
Welch, John W., 159
Welsh Revival, 86, 88
Wesley, John, 1-11
Wesleyan Advocate (Georgia), 39
Wesleyan Methodist Church, 19, 66, 126, 204
Wetherel Affair, The, 45
Whedon, D. D., 35
Whetstone, Ross, 232, 261
White, Alma, 95, 101, 145
White, Stan, 293
Whitefield, George, 5, 7
Whitefield, George C., 28
White supremacy, 167
White Wing Messenger, 199
Widney, J. P., 41
Wigglesworth, Smith, 225
Wilkerson, David, 246, 256
Williams, Robert, 9
Wilson, George W., 38
Wimber, John, 170, 275, 276, 277, 285
Winebrenner Church of God, 48, 69
Winkler, Richard, 227
Winrod, Gerald, 207
With Signs Following, 149
Women preachers, 190-93
Wood, J. A., 24, 143

Called "a pioneer contribution" by *Church History* when it was first published in 1971 as *The Holiness-Pentecostal Movement in the United States,* this volume has now been revised and enlarged by Vinson Synan to account for the incredible changes that have occurred in the church world during the last quarter of the twentieth century.

Synan brings together the stories of the many movements usually labeled "holiness," "pentecostal," or "charismatic," and shows that there is an identifiable "second blessing" tradition in Christianity that began with the Catholic and Anglican mystics, that was crystallized in the teaching of John Wesley, and that was further perpetuated through the holiness and Keswick movements of the nineteenth and twentieth centuries to the appearance of modern Pentecostalism. Synan then chronicles the story of the spread of Pentecostalism around the world after the heady days of the Azusa Street awakening, with special attention given to the beginnings of the movement in those nations where Pentecostalism has become a major religious force. He also examines the rise of various mainline-church charismatic movements that have their roots in Pentecostalism.

Because of the explosive growth of the Pentecostal movement in the last half of the century, Pentecostals and Charismatics now constitute the second largest family of Christians in the world. "This could well be the major story of Christianity in the twentieth century," writes Synan. "Pentecostalism has grown beyond a mere passing 'movement' . . . and can now be seen as a major Christian 'tradition' alongside the Roman Catholic, Orthodox, and Reformation Protestant traditions."

The Holiness-Pentecostal Tradition will continue to be an important handbook for shaping our understanding of this phenomenon.

VINSON SYNAN is dean of the School of Divinity at Regent University in Virginia Beach, Virginia.

Cover photo: tent meeting (1925), courtesy of Assemblies of God Archives

Cover design: Lorraine White

WM. B. EERDMANS PUBLISHING CO.
Grand Rapids/Cambridge